Certainty and Ambiguity in Global Mystery Fiction

Certainty and Ambiguity in Global Mystery Fiction

Essays on the Moral Imagination

Edited by John J. Han, C. Clark Triplett, and Matthew Bardowell

BLOOMSBURY ACADEMIC
NEW YORK • LONDON • OXFORD • NEW DELHI • SYDNEY

BLOOMSBURY ACADEMIC
Bloomsbury Publishing Inc, 1359 Broadway, New York, NY 10018, USA
Bloomsbury Publishing Plc, 50 Bedford Square, London, WC1B 3DP, UK
Bloomsbury Publishing Ireland, 29 Earlsfort Terrace, Dublin 2, D02 AY28, Ireland

BLOOMSBURY, BLOOMSBURY ACADEMIC and the Diana logo are
trademarks of Bloomsbury Publishing Plc

First published in the United States of America 2024
Paperback edition published in 2025

Copyright © John J. Han, C. Clark Triplett, and Matthew Bardowell, 2024
Each chapter © of Contributors

For legal purposes the Acknowledgments on p. vii constitute an
extension of this copyright page.

Cover design: Eleanor Rose
Cover image: New York at Night by George Frank Dixon © RTRO / Alamy

All rights reserved. No part of this publication may be: i) reproduced or transmitted in any form, electronic or mechanical, including photocopying, recording or by means of any information storage or retrieval system without prior permission in writing from the publishers; or ii) used or reproduced in any way for the training, development or operation of artificial intelligence (AI) technologies, including generative AI technologies. The rights holders expressly reserve this publication from the text and data mining exception as per Article 4(3) of the Digital Single Market Directive (EU) 2019/790.

Bloomsbury Publishing Inc does not have any control over, or responsibility for, any third-party websites referred to or in this book. All internet addresses given in this book were correct at the time of going to press. The author and publisher regret any inconvenience caused if addresses have changed or sites have ceased to exist, but can accept no responsibility for any such changes.

Library of Congress Cataloging-in-Publication Data
Names: Han, John J., editor. | Triplett, C. Clark, editor. | Bardowell, Matthew R., editor.
Title: Certainty and ambiguity in global mystery fiction : essays on the moral imagination / edited by John J. Han, C. Clark Triplett, and Matthew Bardowell.
Description: New York : Bloomsbury Academic, 2024. | Includes bibliographical references and index. | Summary: "This essay collection explores mystery fiction as a genre that renders moral judgments not only about detectives and criminals but also concerning the cultural structures within which these mysteries unfold"– Provided by publisher.
Identifiers: LCCN 2023029762 (print) | LCCN 2023029763 (ebook) |
ISBN 9798765105795 (hardback) | ISBN 9798765105788 (paperback) |
ISBN 9798765105801 (epub) | ISBN 9798765105818 (pdf) | ISBN 9798765105825
Subjects: LCSH: Detective and mystery stories–History and criticism.|
Ethics in literature. | Ambiguity in literature. | LCGFT: Essays. | Literary criticism.
Classification: LCC PN3448.D4 C425 2024 (print) | LCC PN3448.D4 (ebook) |
DDC 809.3/872–dc23/eng/20230731
LC record available at https://lccn.loc.gov/2023029762
LC ebook record available at https://lccn.loc.gov/2023029763

ISBN:	HB:	979-8-7651-0579-5
	PB:	979-8-7651-0578-8
	ePDF:	979-8-7651-0581-8
	eBook:	979-8-7651-0580-1

Typeset by Integra Software Services Pvt. Ltd.

For product safety related questions contact productsafety@bloomsbury.com.

To find out more about our authors and books visit www.bloomsbury.com
and sign up for our newsletters.

CONTENTS

Acknowledgments vii

Introduction John J. Han, C. Clark Triplett, and Matthew Bardowell 1

Part I Narrative Structure and Moral Imagination

1 A Memoir Without Conscience: Agatha Christie's *The Murder of Roger Ackroyd* Timothy Ruppert 15

2 A Not-So-Certain Morality: Adaptations in *Murder on the Orient Express* Annette Wren 29

3 *The Colorado Kid*, *Joyland*, and *Later*: Genre Hybridity and the Moral Imagination in Stephen King's Hard Case Crime Novels Alissa Burger 45

4 "They've already killed him": Moral Ambiguity in *Chronicle of a Death Foretold* Andrea Tinnemeyer 67

5 "What's luck got to do with it?": Privilege, Morality, and the Victim in Tana French's *Wych Elm* Deirdre Flynn 83

6 Beyond "Puzzles and Bugaboos": A Family Systems Interpretation of Dorothy L. Sayers's "Monster," *Gaudy Night* Beth McFarland-Wilson 99

Part II World Literature and Moral Ambiguity

7 Opaque Feminine Ethics in Kirino's *Out* Aya Kubota and John J. Han 121

8 Moral Certainty or Ambiguity in Clerical Detective Novels: Discovering a Middle Way in F. H. Batacan's *Smaller and Smaller Circles* C. Clark Triplett 137

9 "Life's messy complexity": Moral Ambiguity, Compromise, and Vigilante Justice in Kishwar Desai's Simran Singh Trilogy *Nikita Gloria Pinto* 147

10 Mystery Pierced with Social Evil: Reading Caste and Class Issues in *The Quills of the Porcupine* *Debaditya Mukhopadhyay* 161

Part III Faith, Certainty, and Doubt in Mystery Fiction

11 Between Faith and Nihilism: Greene's Moral Imagination in *The Third Man* *John J. Han* 179

12 Brother Cadfael, Social Justice, and the Medieval Mystery Novels of Ellis Peters *Jane Beal* 195

13 A Vocation of Truth: The Pursuit of Moral Certainty in the Detective Fiction of Dorothy L. Sayers *Andrew J. Spencer* 211

14 "What if a war was what he was waiting for?": Graham Greene, Patrick Hamilton, and the Writing of Crime between the Wars *Michael Hallam* 227

15 The Restorative Vision of Justice in G. K. Chesterton's Father Brown *Matthew Bardowell* 253

About the Contributors 271
Index 275

ACKNOWLEDGMENTS

The co-editors appreciate all the contributors who submitted their respective chapters to this volume. Without their participation, cooperation, and patience, this book would not have seen the light of day. Thanks go to Bloomsbury's two blind peer reviewers who offered invaluable comments and suggestions for improving our manuscript. We are also thankful to four Missouri Baptist University students who assisted us in one way or another during our editing process: Sydney Carr, Aurora McCandless, Emma King, and Mia McIsaac. Finally, special appreciation goes to Mason Arledge and Mary Ellen Fuquay, who thoroughly copyedited the manuscript.

An earlier version of John J. Han's essay, "Between Faith and Nihilism: Greene's Moral Imagination in *The Third Man*," appeared on pages 17–26 of the Spring 2021 issue (vol. 21, no. 1) of *Intégrité: A Faith and Learning Journal*. Republished with permission.

Introduction

John J. Han, C. Clark Triplett, and Matthew Bardowell

The editors of this book have undertaken to collect chapters that speak to the moral vision of mystery fiction. We are, as one might expect, avid readers of the genre, and we are also intrigued by the complex methods by which these novels raise the question of morality. The central question of morality is this: what makes people good? Mystery fiction as a genre may be concerned with the good (indeed many of the chapters collected here will argue some version of this claim), but more often they are concerned with what is lawful. Yet the law, as it is framed within a liberal society, can only police the boundaries of what behavior is acceptable.[1] A pluralistic society refrains from writing into law things that pertain to an ultimate good because it must allow for differences among its citizens about what that good is. For this reason, the legal dimensions of mystery fiction determine what *cannot* be done but may not address what *ought* to be done.

Herein lies the rub: as readers of these stories, we are invested in the law being maintained, but we are also deeply invested in goodness. When the law is broken by a perpetrator in a mystery novel—the jewels are stolen, a person is murdered—we want the law to matter. We want there to be a fitting consequence when the law is broached, and it offends our latent sense of justice if there is not. Of course, mystery fiction writers know this and sometimes fulfill their readers' expectations or intentionally frustrate them. But what is often invisible to us as readers, what thrums away beneath the surface of these novels, is the implicit assumptions we have about what is good that give us this investment and that inform the author's awareness of what their audience expects. The challenge of assembling a collection like this one—a collection that aims at the moral vision undergirding this delightful genre of potboilers and whodunnits—is to lay bare those assumptions of goodness. If one ventures to write about morality in mystery fiction, one seeks to render visible that invisible sense of what makes us good and subject it to exploration and analysis.

In a world rife with injustice, the reader's expectation of justice has always been presumptuous. Such an inclination presumes that we have any right to expect justice at all. Where would we get such an outlandish idea that the universe operates within a system that would lead to restitution for the wronged and punishment for the wicked? Stephen Knight discusses this impulse toward moral certainty in the origins of modern crime fiction, which stretches back to the seventeenth and eighteenth centuries.[2] In its early phase, the genre looked to "divine providence" for justice, but soon enough this driving force of moral certainty was weighed and found wanting.[3] Moral ambiguity, then, leads to the advent of the detective—an agent of justice—and thus we expect the detective to pursue the fulfillment of our own moral demands. But, of course, these moral demands are not monolithic and may differ from reader to reader, author to author, imagined audience to imagined audience. As a result, mystery fiction must respond to demands for moral clarity while also allowing room for the moral ambiguity of contemporary life.

Scholars have considered mystery fiction as a particularly fecund site for exploring the moral calculations within the societies from which these stories emerge. In *Mystery Fiction and Modern Life*, R. Gordon Kelly argues that "works of fiction can be understood as forms of human action" which emphasize the author as being a "situated historical actor utilizing cultural resources—of language, narrative convention, and the like—to act within a complex of factors that simultaneously enable and constrain their activity."[4] In this study, Kelly focuses on the trappings of modern life and the way these features pose a unique set of problems for detectives. Within this framework, a detective is constantly weighing the intentions of strangers to fit his or her response to the demands of the plot.[5] In so doing, mystery fiction presents the reader with a pattern of action and consequence, "thereby embodying an implicit (and very often explicit) moral dimension."[6] Given this evaluative quality of mystery fiction, Kelly argues that the mystery genre functions as a vehicle for social commentary.[7] This approach to mystery fiction identifies the agent of justice within these stories as particularly important in these moral evaluations.

Kate Morrison's *Morality and the Law in British Detective and Spy Fiction, 1880–1920*, considers the way detectives sometimes take the law into their own hands. Morrison identifies three common approaches to morality within mystery fiction: "deontology, which emphasizes duties and rules; consequentialism, focusing on the consequences of actions, and virtue ethics that center on virtues or moral character."[8] Morrison finds that the detective is a disruptive moral figure—one who "questions the credibility of legal institutions by challenging their power and authority and the judgments they implement."[9] Thus, the tension between moral certainty and ambiguity in mystery fiction has been the subject of academic study for some time, yet questions regarding the tension between the lawful and the good remain.

Any moral theory we would use to shed light on mystery fiction's unique moral nature will need to account for both this certainty and ambiguity we have discussed above. Thus, we must consider what theories have explanatory power for the way authors construct their fictional moral world. Even cursory exposure to moral theories is sufficient to show that issues of right and wrong are not always clear-cut. It is not easy to determine why humans choose one behavior over another and whether they choose based on enduring principles (deontological), a set of circumstances (utilitarian), or personal habits (character). Jeffrey Stout argues that there are many "distinct moral languages, organized around different central concepts and at home in different social settings."[10] Every culture has its own mores, values, and conventions, and not everyone within that specific culture finds its values to be right and just. Such a claim does not preclude that there may be underlying moral principles shared across cultures, but these principles will often be worked out or translated into action in unique ways by each culture.

One way to accommodate these varying cultural interpretations of ethics is to consider a theory that admits a kind of moral reasoning that goes beyond acceptance of static precepts and requires imagination to determine what action is best suited to a given situation in the diverse world of social interactions. Mark Johnson, Chair of the Department of Philosophy at the University of Oregon, introduced the idea of *moral imagination* into ethical discourse. He argues that "our moral understanding depends in a large measure on various structures of imagination, such as images, image schemas, metaphors, narratives, and so forth."[11] Absent this imaginative element, Johnson claims that "moral principles ... [become] trivial, impossible to apply."[12] Yet, while imagination is essential to right moral judgment, static principles are also needed because "moral imagination without principles or some form of grounding, on the other hand, is arbitrary, irresponsible and harmful."[13] Johnson, then, argues that moral agents must be aware of the vast array of metaphors used to describe moral behaviors in different situations and across cultures. The metaphorical nature of the moral imagination may help us account for the shifting cultural constructs that leave readers of mystery fiction with the feeling of moral ambiguity.

Rachel Haliburton offers a recent iteration of this framework that proves instructive for the approach the essays in this volume take toward the question of moral certainty and ambiguity. In her book *The Ethical Detective: Moral Philosophy and Detective Fiction*, Haliburton argues that while at first blush murder mysteries and moral philosophy seem to have little to do with each other, closer investigation reveals that mystery fiction can be fruitfully analyzed to test and refine our moral reasoning.[14] Haliburton, herself a moral philosopher, argues that this literary genre has much to offer those concerned with virtue. According to Haliburton, all ethical theories share three traits in common. These theories aim to (1) help us resolve moral conflicts, (2) form the disposition necessary for acting morally, and (3) avoid social conflict.[15] The moral imagination is one such theory, and Haliburton views this theory as particularly useful in understanding the nature of the moral claims mystery fiction makes on its readers.

Haliburton takes the description of the moral imagination as formulated by Martha Nussbaum as the point of departure for her own articulation of the ethical theory. For Nussbaum, moral imagination is a radical act of perception. To illustrate this theory, Nussbaum analyzes characters from Henry James's novel *The Golden Bowl*, focusing specifically on a scene between a daughter and a father approaching a decision concerning her marriage which will inevitably separate the two. In this analysis, Nussbaum describes an important discussion on which so much of their relationship's health depends. The father must contemplate and understand his daughter's need for independence, and his daughter must approach him with tender but firm insistence on herself as separate from her father's life. The conversation is a triumph for both characters as moral agents because they achieve a moral knowledge of one another. As Nussbaum observes, for James this moral knowledge is founded not on propositions but on a keen and penetrating perception of the other. It is to know, as she phrases it, "without missing anything."[16] Whereas propositional knowledge leads to dogmatism, the moral imagination is more versatile in its ability to regard the other not as an idealized version of themselves but to contemplate the other, imperfect as they are, with attention to the need that arises from their flawed humanity. Nussbaum speaks of the pride one feels in the knowledge of the other but notes that "pride in, belief in the dignity of, another human being is not opposed to tenderness toward human limits."[17] The perception that gives rise to the moral imagination, therefore, entails both certainty and ambiguity.

Haliburton aims to extend Nussbaum's notion of the moral imagination so that it includes the ability to view the world through the ethical framework of another. For Haliburton, the moral imagination is "the capacity that not only helps us determine what we ought to do when faced with ethical conflicts ... but which, even more fundamentally, makes us *want* to do the right thing in the first place."[18] Here, Haliburton uses the concept of the moral imagination to refer to a rational capacity, that which "helps us determine what we ought to do when faced with ethical conflicts," but also an emotional capacity—that which causes us to desire to do an ethical act.[19] The mystery fiction the contributors to this volume explore centers on the novel and the short story, and the structural qualities of these genres will yield much that is fruitful for considering the desires, expressed and unexpressed, of the characters examined here. The depth of description, psychological development, and social implications of these novels and short stories all provide rich material for considering the unique act of perception that is moral imagination.

I. Narrative Structure and Moral Imagination

In this collection, we offer essays from fellow avid mystery fiction readers and scholars who bring their literary acumen to bear on how the genre engages questions of morality. The first section of this book aims to examine morality by reflecting on the narrative techniques writers use to reckon with tension between goodness and the law. Narratology is particularly helpful in uncovering the moral assumptions within a mystery novel. Tzvetan Todorov developed the term *narratology* to describe the methods and theories of a group of structuralists and post-structuralists led by Gérard Genette and others. Some of their methods were similar to those of Russian formalism and the work of Vladimir Propp in his *Morphology of the Folk Tale*. Although Genette went on to expand these constructs of formalism that would be applied to more complex narratives, the basic idea was adopted by many of these theorists. The theory focused on the contrast between the normal, historical events in a story and "the story-as-told." In Russian formalism there is a distinction between fable (*fabula*) and plot (*sjuzhet*). The fable is a chain of events tied together in time, and the plot is how the reader makes sense of that sequence of events. So, for the formalists and narrative theorists, there are always at least two parts to a narrative: a sequence of events (time or history) and how the content of that event is communicated (discourse or telling).[20] In his best-known work *Narrative Discourse*, Genette expands these concepts into more specific ones, including order, duration, frequency, voice, and mood, which change how the sequence of events is presented in telling the story.

This narrative structure is particularly important in detective stories:

> The plot of a detective story ... may entail holding back information about sequentially prior events until the dénouement near the end. It may entail flash-backs of events perceived through the eyes of different witnesses as these are reconstructed, in turn, in accordance with the purposes of the narrator and the movement of the plot. In *Great Expectations* Charles Dickens withholds from the reader until the end information about the identity of Pip's benefactor, and this is essential to the movement of the plot, not to "natural" time.[21]

This reconstruction of the plot is not only a way of organizing events, but also a way of bringing a particular meaning and directedness to the story. It could be organized in many different ways, but in this case, it is organized or re-figured in this particular way. Perhaps more importantly, this reconstruction becomes a way of impacting the moral world of the reader. It is, if you will, a re-making or creation of a possible reality through the story line or emplotment. More contemporary works of mystery fiction complicate simple resolutions because of conflicted characters and corrupt social structures. These messy stories tend to play havoc with the plot line and the moral of the story. In the Golden Age, the primary task of the protagonist was to set things in order according to accepted social structures and practices. As will be seen in many of the essays that follow, what may sometimes seem like the right pattern may very well be a false one because of the complicity of the social or ecclesiastical systems that are sometimes as corrupt or broken as the criminal world. When crime novels are viewed as narratives in search of a resolution, the real resolution may be too complex to be captured in a simple moral framework.

The chapters included in this section all address some aspect of how narrative structure can be used in mystery fiction to align with or resist moral conventions. Timothy Ruppert's "A Memoir without Conscience: Agatha Christie's *The Murder of Roger Ackroyd*" explores the choices of the narrator, Dr. James Sheppard, and the detective, Hercule Poirot, to consider the moral calculus each employs to make decisions. Ruppert discusses the objective as well as pragmatic concerns that drive each character's determination of what counts as justice. In another chapter on Christie, Annette Wren places greater emphasis on the question of moral certainty for Poirot in Christie's *Murder on the Orient Express*. Working with Mark Johnson's concept of the metaphorical basis for moral imagination and Kenneth Branagh's 2017 film adaptation, Wren argues that Poirot must employ elements of Johnson's moral imagination to determine whether justice has been done in accordance with an objective moral framework.

In her chapter, "*The Colorado Kid, Joyland*, and *Later*: Genre Hybridity and the Moral Imagination in Stephen King's Hard Case Crime Novels," Alissa Burger considers the narrative form of the coming-of-age genre in a study of Stephen King's Hard Case Crime novels. Burger argues the blend of genres—horror, mystery, and the coming-of-age story—provide a glimpse of the young protagonists' burgeoning understanding of the world's harsh realities. Burger goes on to consider the narrative techniques King uses in these novels to reveal the ambiguity inherent in the very act of storytelling. Similarly, Andrea Tinnemeyer's chapter utilizes the notion of "story-as-told" to expose places in Gabriel García Márquez's novel *Chronicle of a Death Foretold* where the author uses narrative to arouse the reader's moral judgment. Tinnemeyer argues that the moral clarity presented in the novel finds each townsperson guilty. According to Tinnemeyer, the *Chronicle* tests the structural conventions of the mystery genre to challenge those institutions typically associated with moral authority. Ultimately, Tinnemeyer finds that

García Márquez plays with narrative structure and moral ambiguity to reject the cultural practice of honor killing.

Thus, narrative structure can reinforce or destabilize moral certainty. With respect to the latter, Deirdre Flynn's chapter explores the destabilizing consequences narrative structure can have on moral certainty. In "'What's Luck Got to Do with It?': Privilege, Morality, and the Victim in Tana French's *Wych Elm*," Flynn examines the relationship between morality and privilege as they relate to French's protagonist, Toby Hennessy. Flynn argues that Toby's privileged social status plays a significant role in the moral consequences he experiences in the novel. Flynn's chapter demonstrates how characters and readers alike make moral compromises based on nearly invisible social constructs. Conversely, Beth McFarland-Wilson offers a sociological analysis of Sayers's novel. McFarland-Wilson brings the concepts of *transgenerational influence, triangulations, secrets,* and *morphogenesis* to bear on family relations within the novel, showing, ultimately, a positive vision of human morality and the role of women in effecting justice.

II. World Literature and Moral Ambiguity

The narrative structure of a mystery novel can reveal a writer's moral vision for their work, but what informs this vision? Certainly, a writer's private beliefs will form their moral expressions in the novel, but we must acknowledge the other forces that shape their concerns. Prominent among these is the culture out of which the novel emerges. This section of our book asks: how do the moral concerns of mystery fiction change in the context of a more global literary corpus? These chapters show how writers use the mystery genre to expose the moral ambiguity of cultural constructed values. The result is to reveal some of the invisible forces at work in forming moral certainty, thereby demanding stronger moral engagement from readers.

Aya Kubota and John J. Han's "Opaque Feminine Ethics in Kirino's *Out*" considers moral ambiguity along cultural lines by offering readers a glimpse of injustice as it appears in the novel's Japanese social milieu. Kubota and Han explore the uncertain moral landscape of Kirino's *Out* with special attention to the novel's commentary on gender inequality and social alienation. Kubota and Han argue that a feminist ethic pervades the novel, revealing the severe dysfunction of a culture that the novel's protagonist has no hope to reform but instead can only hope to escape. Similarly, C. Clark Triplett's chapter, "Moral Certainty or Ambiguity in Clerical Detective Novels: Discovering a Middle Way in F. H. Batacan's *Smaller and Smaller Circles*," centers on the social climate of the Philippines to explore Batacan's use of moral ambiguity. Triplett describes the ways the two Jesuit priests-turned-detectives operate parallel to a corrupt justice system to seek resolution for the victims of a serial killer in the Philippines. Triplett presents Batacan's novel as an incisive social commentary on social ills ranging from failed methods for addressing national poverty to police corruption and the Catholic sex-abuse scandal.

Nikita Gloria Pinto's chapter analyzes Kishwar Desai's crime fiction trilogy, which depicts cases taken from actual events in India. Pinto examines these novels with a particular focus on how political corruption and patriarchal beliefs complicate the protagonist's desire to see justice served. Pinto argues that Desai frustrates the reader's expectations to reveal the moral ambiguity in Desai's depiction of contemporary Indian culture. In sum, Pinto shows that this kind of ambiguity provokes the reader into recognizing the good even as it is rejected through a lack of concern for justice. Debaditya Mukhopadhyay's chapter also centers on Indian moral conventions as he considers Saradindu Bandyopadhyay's Bengali detective novel *The Quills of the Porcupine*. The moral ambiguity of this novel arises from the extreme violence perpetrated against victims based on class and caste differences. Mukhopadhyay argues that the novel explores the evils of class and caste bias by refusing to view the perpetrator of these crimes as evil but instead using flashbacks, narratorial comments, and characterization to criticize caste-class hierarchies.

III. Faith, Certainty, and Doubt in Mystery Fiction

One source of certainty amidst the changing tides of time and location leads us back to moral certainty. That source is religious faith. Faith can bind people together like the law, but it can also bind us together in our vision of what is good. Faith can confer a sense of certainty about morality, but religion can also become entangled in culturally constructed values and depart from or compromise its role in forming moral values. Religion can be wielded as a cudgel for the powerful against the weak and vulnerable. In these cases, the compulsion to adhere to a set of religious principles may produce doubt. Mystery fiction writers may employ this certainty or this doubt to grapple with the difficult questions the genre so often presents. For instance, what role does violence play in asserting or undermining the moral vision of a given novel? How do characters allow religious beliefs to inform their decisions? What happens when an authority figure—either legal or religious—fails to live up to their own ideals? When moral clarity does emerge within these novels, what role does faith play in achieving that certainty? The chapters collected in this section respond to these questions. Some discuss that special and interesting sort of law enforcement figure: the clerical detective. Others negotiate the complex relationship between certainty and ambiguity, either as it concerns the moral character of detectives or other figures within these texts.

John J. Han analyzes the moral imagination of Graham Greene's *The Third Man* by comparing the respective moral attitudes of Holly Martins and Harry Lime. Han views Martins as a representative of objective moral standards while Lime is decidedly nihilistic in his approach to morality. Han explores the tensions that exist even within those who view themselves as proponents of moral certainty. The result, Han shows, is a paradoxically clear moral vision on Greene's part, even as his characters struggle with certainty and doubt. Shifting from the *noir* detective to the clerical sleuth, Jane Beal's chapter centers on Brother Cadfael and discusses the critique of social injustice exemplified by the mistreatment of Lazarus in *The Leper of St. Giles*. Beal's analysis of this social injustice includes a biographical sketch of Edith Pargeter, the woman behind the Ellis Peters's pen name, as well as a comparative reading of the television adaptation of the novel.

Andrew J. Spencer's chapter offers an examination of the amateur sleuth's moral reasoning. This chapter juxtaposes the universal moral obligation to pursue truth with the particular calling to function as an agent of justice within a particular social structure. Given that the consequences of error can sometimes lead to the execution of the accused, Spencer reflects on the moral obligations of a citizen not authorized by any governing body to dispense justice. Furthering the influence of social structures on moral clarity, Michael Hallam offers a reading of Greene's and Hamilton's interwar novels that roots itself in the historical environment in which they were written. Here Hallam argues that these novels repurpose the typical genre conventions of interwar mystery fiction to address the moral concerns embedded within the genre itself. According to Hallam, Hamilton's *Rope* and *Hangover Square* and Greene's *Brighton Rock* render a self-conscious appraisal of violence and evil as well as the political and moral ambiguities that condition the reader's responses to these tropes. Finally, Matthew Bardowell reflects on the clearest case for moral certainty we see in mystery fiction: the clerical detective who represents not merely the law but God himself. Bardowell considers the rather unique approach that Chesterton's priest-detective brings to his policing. Justice for Father Brown, Bardowell argues, is not punitive but restorative. Father Brown aims for the highest aspiration of any agent of justice within the mystery genre: the repentance of the offender. In exploring this feature of Father Brown's vision of justice, Bardowell shows how such an aim stems from Chesterton's Thomistic ideas concerning the external world and the moral claims it makes on each one of its inhabitants. From Bardowell's exploration of Chesterton's Father Brown, we see how faith can re-establish certainty after doubt introduces confusion.

These chapters explore how mystery fiction engages a reader's desire for concrete morality while presenting readers with a complex moral world. Even within the morally ambiguous world of some mystery fiction, these stories are situated with perhaps the ideal genre for raising moral questions whether through formulaic plots and characters or through complex stories that leave the reader wondering about the resolution. Angelina Stanford makes a strong emotional argument for the moral intent of detective novels:

> In a modern world that increasingly denies that there is any order or any real virtues like truth and justice, the detective story creates a longing in us for the very things our culture rebels against. We hate this chaos created by the dead body and we desperately want to see the truth revealed and justice enacted. We want to see good guys rewarded and the bad guys punished. Our souls cry out for order to be restored. And if the book fails to deliver, readers rebel.[22]

Unfortunately, in the real world, the good guys are not always rewarded, and the bad guys are not always punished. Nevertheless, there is always a moral dilemma that the reader must grapple with. This grappling is precisely what makes analysis of the moral vision of mystery fiction a worthwhile and rewarding endeavor.

Notes

1. Joel James Shuman, "Ethics, Liberalism, and the Law: Toward a Christian Consideration of the Morality of Civil Law in Liberal Policies," *Journal of the Society of Christian Ethics* 23, no. 2 (2003): 38.
2. Stephen Knight, *Crime Fiction 1800–2000: Detection, Death, Diversity* (London: Palgrave MacMillan, 2004), 3–9.
3. Ibid., 9.
4. R. Gordon Kelly, *Mystery Fiction and Modern Life* (Jackson: University Press of Mississippi, 1998), xvi–xvii.
5. Ibid., xii.
6. Ibid., xix.
7. Ibid.
8. Kate Morrison, *Morality and the Law in British Detective and Spy Fiction, 1880–1920* (Jefferson: McFarland, 2020), 6.
9. Ibid., 7.
10. Jeffrey Stout, *Ethics after Babel: The Languages of Morals and Their Discontents* (Princeton: Princeton University Press, 2001), ix–x.
11. Mark Johnson, *Moral Imagination: Implications of Cognitive Science for Ethics* (Chicago: University of Chicago Press, 1994), ix.
12. Ibid., x.

13 Ibid.
14 Rachel Haliburton, *The Ethical Detective: Moral Philosophy and Detective Fiction* (Lanham: Lexington Books, 2018), ix.
15 Ibid., 141.
16 Martha Nussbaum, *Love's Knowledge: Essays on Philosophy and Literature* (Oxford: Oxford University Press, 1990), 152.
17 Ibid., 153.
18 Haliburton, *The Ethical Detective*, 141.
19 Ibid., 141.
20 Anthony C. Thistleton, *New Horizons in Hermeneutics: The Theory and Practice of Transforming Biblical Reading* (Grand Rapids: Zondervan, 1997), 354–5.
21 Ibid., 355.
22 Angelina Stanford, "The Moral Universe of the Detective Novel," *CiRCE Institute*, August 13, 2016, https://circeinstitute.org/blog/blog-moral-universe-detective-novel/, para. 8. Accessed October 29, 2021.

Bibliography

Haliburton, Rachel. *The Ethical Detective: Moral Philosophy and Detective Fiction*. Lanham: Lexington Books, 2018.

Johnson, Mark. *Moral Imagination: Implications of Cognitive Science for Ethics*. Chicago: University of Chicago Press, 1994.

Kelly, R. Gordon. *Mystery Fiction and Modern Life*. Jackson: University Press of Mississippi, 1998.

Knight, Stephen. *Crime Fiction 1800–2000: Detection, Death, Diversity*. London: Palgrave MacMillan, 2004.

Morrison, Kate. *Morality and the Law in British Detective and Spy Fiction, 1880–1920*. Jefferson: McFarland, 2020.

Nussbaum, Martha. *Love's Knowledge: Essays on Philosophy and Literature*. Oxford: Oxford University Press, 1990.

Shuman, Joel James. "Ethics, Liberalism, and the Law: Toward a Christian Consideration of the Morality of Civil Law in Liberal Policies." *Journal of the Society of Christian Ethics* 23, no. 2 (2003): 37–54.

Stanford, Angelina. "The Moral Universe of the Detective Novel." *CiRCE Institute*. August 13, 2016. https://circeinstitute.org/blog/blog-moral-universe-detective-novel/. Accessed November 2, 2021.

Stout, Jeffrey. *Ethics after Babel: The Languages of Morals and Their Discontents*. Princeton: Princeton University Press, 2001.

Thistleton, Anthony C. *New Horizons in Hermeneutics: The Theory and Practice of Transforming Biblical Reading*. Grand Rapids: Zondervan, 1997.

PART ONE

Narrative Structure and Moral Imagination

1

A Memoir Without Conscience: Agatha Christie's *The Murder of Roger Ackroyd*

Timothy Ruppert

A dozen years before the 1926 debut of Agatha Christie's *The Murder of Roger Ackroyd*, the immensely successful Mary Roberts Rinehart published *Locked Doors*, a novella in which nurse-investigator Hilda Adams asks, "[I]f the criminal uses every means against society, why not society against the criminal?"[1] Adams initially struggles with this question but soon comes to terms with its implications:

> At first I had used this as a flag of truce to my nurse's ethical training; now I flaunted it, a mental and moral banner. The criminal against society, and I against the criminal! And, more than that, against misery, healing pain by augmenting it sometimes, but working like a surgeon, for good.[2]

Adams predicates her new identity on a picture of the medical professional as altruistic, principled, and honorable. Despite the sincere alacrity of her resolve, what Adams here presents—an idealized image of the benevolent healer whose virtues create a pattern for administering justice—invites counterexamples from the fictional world and beyond. Consider a classic monster such as Dr. Edmund Bickleigh, the seemingly fainthearted village physician at the center of Francis Iles's 1931 novel *Malice Aforethought*, whose reading of Thomas de Quincey reassures him that "murder was a fine art for the superman" he eventually takes himself to be.[3] One finds similar demons today, such as in Marilyn Todd's 2020 story "Beyond the Tree

Line," in which a would-be sororicide takes heart after studying the crimes of William Palmer, Victorian England's infamous Prince of Poisoners, in her town's newspaper.[4]

Perhaps nowhere in the crime fiction corpus does this image of the ethically ambiguous medical practitioner emerge more compellingly than in Christie's *The Murder of Roger Ackroyd*. While she makes much of indecisive and unsettled ethics throughout her oeuvre, as works like *Murder on the Orient Express*, *The Witness for the Prosecution and Other Stories*, and *Curtain* show, Christie took a special interest in the type of killer who might have an address in Harley Street. Herbert Kinnell notes that "where the occupation of the murderer is known, doctors make up the largest group" of perpetrators in Christie's fiction, totaling eleven (excluding *And Then There Were None*'s Edward Armstrong, "who kills by operating while drunk").[5] Dr. James Sheppard, *Ackroyd*'s narrator and the best known of this sinister lot, exemplifies the sort of Christie physician for whom, in the face of exigency, the Hippocratic Oath proves a disposable ethics. And Sheppard reveals his eely sense of right and wrong through his storytelling as surely as through his crimes: his is a memoir without conscience.

While his narratorial cold-bloodedness puts him in the company of wolves such as Michael Rogers in *Endless Night* and Lawrence Wargrave in *And Then There Were None*, Sheppard merits particular scrutiny for doing harm as both a healer and a writer. His manuscript account of Ackroyd's death and Hercule Poirot's investigation, guided by situational and selective ethical judgments, not only recreates but co-creates his misdeeds. Christie's interweaving of crime and chronicle in *The Murder of Roger Ackroyd* thus reflects significant experimentation with metafictional techniques popular in postwar European literature—an idea neglected in the scholarship on the novel. What I want to accomplish in this piece, then, is to read the ethical ambivalence of *Ackroyd*'s narrator in relation to the book's seldom-noted avant-garde design. By doing so, I hope to spark interest in the novel as a distinctly unconventional achievement in the literature of crime and detection. Ideally, this revaluation will also encourage a better sense of Christie as a literary innovator whose *Ackroyd* places her with contemporaries like Ford Madox Ford, Luigi Pirandello, and André Gide, all of whom have received greater critical validation than has Christie.

Trends in Christie Criticism

In a recent panel advertisement for the Northeast Modern Language Association's 52nd Convention, Abby Bardi asks, "Is crime writing inherently disreputable?"—a question that invites us to reimagine our perspectives on "genre-writing" and its place in creative writing pedagogy.[6]

Bardi's concerns bear relevance as well to the scholarly reception of Agatha Christie's work. Alistair Rolls makes this point when he recalls how, after seeking unsuccessfully in the University of Newcastle's library for a copy of *Murder on the Orient Express*, he was told that "the library's clients did not have the time for 'leisure reading.'"[7] The university library, Rolls discovered, did not archive a single Christie volume, including of course *The Murder of Roger Ackroyd*.[8]

Long-standing biases against the literature of crime and detection have almost surely contributed to the marginalization of Christie and her work in literary studies. While much good criticism exists on the novel, few scholars treat *Ackroyd* as a step forward in literary experimentation beyond its remarkably successful use of unreliable narration. Theresa Heyd, for one, looks at Dr. Sheppard alongside Mr. Stevens of Kazuo Ishiguro's *The Remains of the Day* and the nameless narrator of Edgar Allan Poe's "The Tell-Tale Heart" to apply Paul Grice's cooperative principle to the study of narratorial untrustworthiness.[9] Heyd's effort to bring the ideas of Wayne Booth and Ansgar Nünning together in a Gricean framework[10] proves generative in its own right, but the attempt also indicates the topical boundaries of much *Ackroyd* scholarship. Victoria Stewart's 2019 essay on Christie and Virginia Woolf, a study in objects that in part focuses on *The Mysterious Affair at Styles* as well as on *Ackroyd*, gestures toward new ground by situating these novels in "an increasingly cluttered and confusing postwar world" to show the interest both authors take in our experience of material reality as "a constantly shifting, historically-inflected ebb and flow of significance."[11] Stewart's approach marks a change in direction for our study of *Ackroyd*, suggesting that the conventional emphasis on Sheppard as an unreliable storyteller may be fitted effectively into conversations about the novel's status as an experimental text.

If a reassessment of the novel's literary quality is in order, as Stewart's recent contribution suggests, then a closer look at the matter of ethics in *Ackroyd* seems an auspicious way to carry forward, especially given that such a focus helps to bridge traditional criticism to more recent perspectives. The book surely invites us to think about ethical choices in terms of both crime and punishment. After all, Hercule Poirot's questionable approach to meting out justice once the Belgian identifies Sheppard as Ackroyd's killer is to some degree a corollary of Sheppard's contingent morality. When Poirot sanctions Sheppard's death, as recounted by the narrator in his "Apologia" (in effect the suicide note with which *Ackroyd* closes), the investigator steps well beyond the law, as well as beyond his role as a restorer of order in the village of King's Abbot. Poirot appears to satisfy justice while saving Sheppard from the courts and his sister, Caroline, from penury and disgrace, yet the detective's unorthodox accommodations for the Sheppard family amplify the work's ambiguities rather than resolve them. Sheppard's acceptance of his friend's offer further muddies the water if, with Pierre

Bayard, we believe that the doctor gives his own life to protect his sister; in other words, his confession serves as a red herring, alibiing the actual culprit: Caroline.[12] If this is so, and if Poirot knows it (and surely, he would), then the great investigator and seeker after truth allows a murderer to go free.

While his performance in *Ackroyd* captures the elastic sense of legal rightness that Poirot often shows, as when he permits Jacqueline de Bellefort's suicide in *Death on the Nile*,[13] we should note that allowing his friend James to take his own life rather than to be hanged for murder reflects more than the fondness Poirot has for the Sheppards. Naturally, Poirot's clemency is in itself ethically vexed given that Sheppard, sworn to heal, has knowingly killed—a plain contravention of long-standing ethical codes. But Poirot's questionable idea of mercy has much to do with the novel's metafictional design as well. To better understand the uniqueness of Poirot's choices in *Ackroyd*, we must first consider how Sheppard's ethical disposition shapes a narrative in which *choice* is an infernal machine with its own dangerous inner mechanism.

Curiosity, Codification, and Deviance

Some two decades ago, the late bioethicist David C. Thomasma advised that "we should cultivate a healthy respect for the role of evil in the human heart and human affairs."[14] He offered this warning partly in response to the maxim, "Only a good person can be a good physician"—words written by the Nazi doctor Rudolph Ramm.[15] Of course, this sort of irony gets noted elsewhere. For example, Albert Camus records in one of his postwar notebooks that, after the Nuremberg Doctors' Trial, Heinrich Himmler's personal physician lamented "that there is still injustice in this world" just before being hanged for war crimes.[16] Such observations distress or even shock us because we so often accept the integrity of medical practitioners as a given. We think of such people as professionally *and* personally devoted to a benevolent humaneness; their commitment to Hippocratic values signals completeness of character and decency of perspective. We presume, too, that the vow to do no harm influences the practitioner's moral imagination beyond the surgery, and that the Fifth Commandment is more than a company policy posted beside the timeclock. We thus feel profoundly disturbed to encounter persons who put these beliefs into question, as Courtney S. Campbell suggests in discussing Edmund D. Pellegrino's condemnation of physician-assisted suicide. Acts such as facilitating suicides or engaging in euthanasia conflict with traditions of ethical propriety founded upon "a core vocational proscription against killing" without which medical professionals "would be morally indistinguishable from plumbers, electricians, or computer repair persons."[17] In this formulation, ministration becomes trade work, and the art of healing patients compassionately gives way to repairing objects expertly.[18]

What distinguishes the empathetic and human-centered practice of medicine from its depersonalized and disengaged alternative has occupied ethicists since the Classical Age, as Patricia Benner observes when she writes that, for Aristotle, "*techné* or procedural knowledge is insufficient for action" when crucial ethical choices are at stake.[19] While a comprehensive treatment of this question's history lies beyond the scope of the present discussion, I deem it valuable to consider how certain traditions of writing have fostered an objectifying impulse in some medical outlooks. Meegan Kennedy's work on Samuel Warren's early-Victorian novel *Passages from the Diary of a Late Physician* shows how new approaches to the case history, "the fundamental textual vehicle for medical information," supported the development of "professional identity"[20] for medical practitioners in nineteenth-century Britain. "Because the borders of professional medicine remained fuzzy" when Warren's sensationalized fiction first appeared, "the case history, as the public face of medicine, became a crucial site in which to construct an ideal of clinical medicine against the onslaught of sectarian methods."[21] According to Kennedy, the medical community's outrage over Warren's *Diary* involved an aversion to what she calls the "Gothic medicine" of the eighteenth century and to medical histories that elevated "the curious," the exotic, and the anomalous above more sober and expressly "realist" accounts.[22] While this strain of Gothicism in medical writing contributes much to works by such authors as Mary Shelley, Charles Reade, Robert Louis Stevenson, and Bram Stoker,[23] Victorian medical professionals such as Philip Henry Pye-Smith balked at "medicine's 'curious' past"[24] and advocated for a style of practice—and writing—in which impassive disengagement seemed companionate with sound and honest science.

The Victorians thus bequeathed a complex ethical legacy to the physicians of Edwardian and Georgian Britain, and this inheritance influences still the ways in which medical practitioners of the Great War era are portrayed in British detective literature. In Jacqueline Winspear's 2003 novel *Maisie Dobbs*, for example, a shared sense of responsibility, driven by selfless detachment, registers the immense courage and resolve that Maisie and Captain Simon Lynch show when they operate on a wounded soldier even as enemy shells descend on their hospital encampment—this not long after Lynch has asked Maisie to marry him.[25] Lynch's refusal to discontinue the surgery leads to Lynch sustaining catastrophic injuries that leave him permanently unable to speak or to move on his own, as we learn when, years afterward, Maisie at last visits Lynch at a military facility outside of London.[26] This moving episode presents an ideal enactment of the ethics of medical conduct so sharply drawn by the Victorians. But as some of my earlier illustrations suggest, the dispassionate clinician is not invariably a noble figure. The very ethical codes that empower Maisie and Lynch likewise enable James Sheppard to blackmail and to kill, as well as to chronicle his transgressions in a narrative that, its deceptiveness aside, essentially respects the precepts of conscientious medical authorship in the Victorian vein—a paradox at *Ackroyd*'s heart and a key to better appreciating the work's innovations.

The Castle Within

As an heir to a certain Victorian mindset, James Sheppard sets up definitive boundaries between his professional and personal lives. Like the lawyer's clerk John Wemmick in Charles Dickens's 1861 novel *Great Expectations*, Sheppard takes pains to separate the public and domestic realms. But Dickens's clerk has resources to ensure his privacy that Christie's doctor lacks: when young Pip visits Wemmick at Walworth, he discovers that Wemmick's home, the Castle, lies behind a moat only crossable by a seldom-lowered drawbridge.[27] Sheppard, though, receives patients in his home surgery after making his daily rounds.[28] What is more, Wemmick's housemate, his elderly father, scarcely resembles Sheppard's elder sister Caroline, who regularly harangues her brother for keeping confidential information from her and her gossipy circle. Because he cannot distance his private life from the outside world with any consistency, Sheppard in effect internalizes Wemmick's Castle, dividing the doctor from the man so successfully that the ethical identity of the former has little to do with the moral logic of the latter. His two selves coexist but seemingly never coalesce.

If this interpretation of him is valid, we may see Sheppard as someone whose sense of ethical duty has meaning solely within the parameters of his role as the general practitioner of King's Abbot; beyond that role, Sheppard's ethics become a matter of expedience. The moments before Sheppard murders Ackroyd prove telling in this regard. After having dined with Ackroyd and his guests at Fernly Park, Sheppard goes with his friend to the study on the pretext that the latter feels sick: "It struck me that he was anxious to convey the impression that our conference was a medical one. I played up accordingly."[29] When alone, Sheppard produces medicine that he knows Ackroyd does not need from a bag that plays a crucial part in the murder plan.[30] With the command to put "those damn tablets" away, Ackroyd frees Sheppard from his doctorly responsibilities by calling upon him as a confidant rather than as a physician.[31] Naturally, his trust in Sheppard's friendship is a grave misjudgment, and because of it Ackroyd unwittingly facilitates his own death. The subsequent exchange between the two men takes on an especially menacing cast given Sheppard's apparently honest record of it: as Ackroyd recounts his late fiancée's killing of Ashley Ferrars and suffering a blackmailer's manipulation, Sheppard presents what seems a disinterested narrative rendered by an uninvolved party. The narrative sustains this illusion even as a letter to Roger from Mrs. Ferrars arrives—a letter that includes the blackmailer's name.[32] Sheppard documents his exit in suitably precise yet equivocating prose:

> The letter had been brought in at twenty minutes to nine. It was just on ten minutes to nine when I left him, the letter still unread. I hesitated with my hand on the door handle, looking back and wondering if there was anything I had left undone. I could think of nothing. With a shake of the head I passed out and closed the door behind me.[33]

In his "Apologia," Sheppard takes a self-congratulatory moment to revisit this passage, asking "What could be neater" than its concealment of his guilt: "All true, you see. But suppose I had put a row of stars after the first sentence! Would someone then have wondered what exactly happened in that blank ten minutes?"[34] The chilling delight that Sheppard takes in his prose does more than simply gesture toward the ethical disengagement that allowed him to perpetrate atrocities despite the Hippocratic code and its centuries-old tradition. The manuscript that Sheppard creates belongs among the instruments of his crimes as surely as does the Tunisian dagger with which he stabs his friend. More than an instance of unreliable narration, the manuscript is a key to the success of Sheppard's bloody project. Other killers in the Poirot canon have written *to* the Belgian investigator; consider Jane Wilkinson, whose insouciant confession letter—in which she wishes that she could be hanged before an audience—eerily closes *Lord Edgware Dies*.[35] But Sheppard writes *for* Poirot, and *The Murder of Roger Ackroyd* itself represents a work in progress, fitted in its later chapters to the ways in which the detective reads and reacts to the earlier sections. True, Captain Arthur Hastings authors Poirot often in their first adventures together, and so performs for Poirot as Dr. John H. Watson does for Conan Doyle's Sherlock Holmes. Sheppard, though, is neither Hastings nor Watson, as clearly his writing serves less-noble ends. All the same, his disingenuousness creates a unique opportunity for Christie to take sophisticated risks with *Ackroyd*'s design and execution.

The Mysterious Affair of Metafictional Style

Not long after Sheppard first meets Poirot, who has recently moved into a neighboring house called The Larches, the investigator reminisces about his chronicler Hastings, "a friend who for many years never left my side. Occasionally of an imbecility to make one afraid, nevertheless he was very dear to me. Figure to yourself that I miss even his stupidity."[36] Poirot then distinguishes between Hastings and Sheppard: "But you are a man of middle age, a doctor, a man who knows the folly and the vanity of most things in this life of ours."[37] Poirot seems sanguine that his neighbor may become his intimate in place of Hastings, who now resides in South America.[38] Such a relationship would entail Sheppard serving as the recorder of any investigative activities that Poirot may undertake. Although at this point in the book Ackroyd still lives, Sheppard likely has his friend's death already in mind; "I suppose I must have meant to murder him all along," the doctor later concedes.[39] Sheppard may also even now see in Poirot an audience, and quite a special one at that: both actor and onlooker all at once, critic of a story in which he inevitably must appear.

When Ackroyd's killing involves Poirot as a consulting detective, Sheppard indeed becomes a stand-in for Hastings, assisting the investigator on a case as changeable from moment to moment as "a kaleidoscope."[40] And, inspired by Hastings's work, Sheppard too crafts a written treatment of events, as he discloses to Poirot: "I thought, why not try my hand at something of the same kind. Seemed a pity not to."[41] Poirot demands with alacrity to see the pages, and Sheppard acquiesces:

> Still somewhat doubtful, I rummaged in the drawers of my desk and produced an untidy pile of manuscript which I handed over to him. With an eye on possible publication in the future, I had divided the work into chapters, and the night before I had brought it up to date with an account of Miss Russell's visit. Poirot had therefore twenty chapters.[42]

While he substitutes ably for Poirot's former companion, his reasons for writing set Sheppard apart from Hastings, and Poirot as reader responds incisively to the narrative's self-conscious contrivance. "Not so did Hastings write," Poirot notes, commending Sheppard for his precision but taking his guardedness to task: "On every page, many, many times was the word 'I.' What *he* thought—what *he* did. But you—you have kept your personality in the background; only once or twice does it obtrude—in scenes of home life, shall we say?"[43] The manuscript comprises the opening twenty chapters of *The Murder of Roger Ackroyd*, and Poirot's critique of Sheppard's "reticence"[44] will significantly influence the seven as-yet-unwritten chapters with which the novel concludes. This engagement with the text in progress goes far past the Belgian's passion for mystery stories, a love that lasts late into his career—one thinks of Poirot's reverence for Conan Doyle, and for Christie's own Ariadne Oliver, in *The Clocks*[45] Poirot does not merely read *Ackroyd*; he *intervenes* in *Ackroyd*, a work that, as Sheppard authors it, serves not as a chronicle but as a device implemented to buoy his alibi, to amplify the illusion of Ralph Paton's guilt, and to taunt Poirot, as the doctor affirms in his "Apologia": "I meant [my manuscript] to be published some day as the history of one of Poirot's failures! Odd, how things pan out."⁴⁶ His keen eye for authorial legerdemain means that Poirot the reader has outthought Sheppard the writer, and the text that undoes the physician is not Mrs. Ferrars's letter but the manuscript intended to obscure, through its perfectly responsible *accuracy*, both the provenance and the fate of that letter.

By recognizing the fictionality of Sheppard's history of the case, Poirot achieves more than exposing a clever killer; his critique alters the novel's very identity, recasting what seems a niche piece as a meaningful contribution to the metafictional literature of the early twentieth century. Poirot's evaluation of Sheppard's manuscript, to borrow from Mark Currie, "places [*Ackroyd*] on the border between fiction and criticism" through a process of self-reference within a novel that takes apart its own claims to realism.⁴⁷ Given Poirot's assertion that "the truth, however ugly in itself, is always curious and beautiful to the seeker after it,"⁴⁸ we may consider Linda Hutcheon's words as fitting: "the most authentic and honest fiction might well be that which most freely acknowledges its fictionality."⁴⁹ With her *Ackroyd*, Christie brings metafictional techniques into play not for lightness or novelty but as a proper means to engage serious questions concerning medical, legal, and authorial ethics. Because Sheppard is a unique villain in whom Poirot has a special interest (perhaps owing more than anything to Poirot's sincere affection for Caroline), the metafictional approach, "deeply connected with the view of reality as inherently provisional,"⁵⁰ offers Poirot a chance to evaluate his insights into the Ackroyd affair against the "fictional illusion"⁵¹ that Sheppard's narrative renders. Beyond this, her literary experimentation allows Christie to look at faulty or anomalous ethical choices in relation to the act of storytelling, which, as Laura María Lojo Rodríguez argues, constitutes the *story* that in fact gets told.⁵² In this respect, Christie anticipates what the real-life doctor John Sassall makes plain in John Berger and Jean Mohr's *A Fortunate Man*, when, fearing that he has "simplified" both his patients and himself, he comes to believe that, "to remain honest," one must "judge from a second position."⁵³ As the metacognitive activity for which Sassall advocates exposes hypocrisy and indifference, so the metafictional method undertaken by Christie in *Ackroyd* challenges the verbal conventionalities upon which inauthentic ethics rely.

Published one year after Gide's *Les Faux-monnayeurs* and two years before Woolf's *Orlando: A Biography*, Christie's *The Murder of Roger Ackroyd* warrants inclusion in scholarly conversations on metafictional literature of the 1920s and, of course, beyond. A reassessment of the novel's experimentality seems timely and worthwhile in light of the ongoing use of metafictional tropes in narratives of mystery such as Jasper Fforde's *The Eyre Affair* (2001), Mark Haddon's *The Curious Incident of the Dog in the Night-time* (2003), and Simon Stephens's stage adaptation of *Curious Incident* (2012). Ideally, revaluing the piece will also sharpen our sense of *Ackroyd*'s deep engagement with problems in the practical stewardship of moral codes.

Whether the heir of nineteenth-century medical specialists who took "living flesh" for "scientific commodity"[54] or a devil of the first water, James Sheppard and his too-supple ethics continue to have much to teach us about medicine, storytelling, and conscience.[55]

Notes

1. Mary Roberts Rinehart, "Locked Doors" (1914), in *The Big Book of Female Detectives*, ed. Otto Penzler (New York: Vintage Crime/Black Lizard, 2018), 446.
2. Ibid.
3. Francis Iles, *Malice Aforethought: The Story of a Commonplace Crime* (1931; Mineola, NY: Dover, 2018), 179.
4. Marilyn Todd, "Beyond the Tree Line," *Ellery Queen Mystery Magazine* 155, nos. 5–6 (2020): 122–3.
5. Herbert Kinnell, "Agatha Christie's Doctors," *The BMJ: British Medical Journal* 341, no. 7786 (December 18–25, 2010): 1324.
6. Abby Bardi, "Pulp Fiction, with Real Pulp: Crime Writing as Creative Writing (Panel)," NeMLA Call for Papers. *NeMLA: Northeast Modern Language Association*. www.cfplist.com/nemla/Home/S/18640, para. 3. Accessed November 7, 2020.
7. Alistair Rolls, "Creative, Critical, Intertextual: Agatha Christie's The Murder of Roger Ackroyd." *TEXT: Journal of Writing and Writing Courses*, Special Issue 37 (October 2016): 2.
8. Ibid., 2.
9. Theresa Heyd, "Understanding and Handling Unreliable Narratives: A Pragmatic Model and Method." *Semiotica: Journal of the International Association for Semiotic Studies* 162, nos. 1–4 (2006): 217, 219. For a similar reading, see Emanuela Gutkowski, "An 'Investigation in Pragmatics': Agatha Christie's *The Murder of Roger Ackroyd*." *CLUES: A Journal of Detection* 29, no. 1 (2011): 51–60.
10. Ibid., 219.
11. Victoria Stewart, "Objects, Things and Clues in Early Twentieth-Century Fiction." *Modernist Cultures* 14, no. 2 (2019): 173, 190.
12. Alistair Rolls and Jesper Gulddal, "Pierre Bayard and the Ironies of Detective Criticism: From Text Back to Work." *Comparative Literature Studies* 53, no. 1 (2016): 151.
13. Agatha Christie, *Death on the Nile* (1938; New York: William Morrow, 2011), 332.
14. David C. Thomasma, "The Principle of Dominion," in *The Health Care Professional as Friend and Healer: Building on the Work of Edmund D.*

Pellegrino, ed. David C. Thomasma and Judith Lee Kissell (Georgetown: Georgetown University Press, 2000), 145.

15 Quoted in Thomasma, "The Principle of Dominion," 145.
16 Quoted in Albert Camus, *Notebooks 1942–1951* (1964; trans. Justin O'Brien. St. Paul, MN: Paragon House, 1991), 208. Camus records a similar irony earlier in the same book: "Radici, a member of the French militia who had volunteered for the Waffen SS, tried for having had twenty-eight prisoners in La Santé shot (he was present as the five groups were executed), belonged to the Humane Society for the Protection of Animals" (151).
17 Courtney S. Campbell, "Prophet to the Profession: Healing and Physician-Assisted Suicide," in *The Health Care Professional as Friend and Healer: Building on the Work of Edmund D. Pellegrino*, ed. David C. Thomasma and Judith Lee Kissell (Washington, DC: Georgetown University Press, 2000), 200.
18 Ibid., 200. For more on the distinction between *healing* and *fixing* in the medical field, particularly in dentistry, see Jos V. M. Welie, "The Dentist as Healer and Friend," in *The Health Care Professional as Friend and Healer: Building on the Work of Edmund D. Pellegrino*, ed. David C. Thomasma and Judith Lee Kissell (Washington, DC: Georgetown University Press, 2000), 35–7.
19 Patricia Benner, "Learning through Experience and Expression: Skillful Ethical Comportment in Nursing Practice," in *The Health Care Professional as Friend and Healer: Building on the Work of Edmund D. Pellegrino*, ed. David C. Thomasma and Judith Lee Kissell (Washington, DC: Georgetown University Press, 2000), 61.
20 Meegan Kennedy, "The Ghost in the Clinic: Gothic Medicine and Curious Fiction in Samuel Warren's *Diary of a Late Physician*," *Victorian Literature and Culture* 32, no. 2 (2004): 332.
21 Ibid., 332.
22 Ibid., 327.
23 Ibid., 345.
24 Ibid., 331.
25 Jacqueline Winspear, *Maisie Dobbs* (New York: Soho Press, 2003), 282.
26 Ibid., 287–91.
27 Charles Dickens, *Great Expectations* (1861; ed. Edgar Rosenberg. New York: Norton, 1999), 222.
28 Agatha Christie, *The Murder of Roger Ackroyd* (1926; New York: William Morrow, 2020), 13.
29 Ibid., 36.
30 Ibid., 37.
31 Ibid.
32 Ibid., 42–3.
33 Ibid., 43.

34 Ibid., 284.
35 Agatha Christie, *Lord Edgware Dies* (1933; New York: William Morrow, 2011), 269.
36 Christie, *Ackroyd*, 20.
37 Ibid., 21.
38 Ibid., 20.
39 Ibid., 284.
40 Ibid., 225.
41 Ibid., 253.
42 Ibid., 254.
43 Ibid., 255.
44 Ibid., 282.
45 Agatha Christie, *The Clocks* (1963; New York: Harper, 2011), 134–42.
46 Christie, *Ackroyd*, 283.
47 Quoted in Prema Arasu, "All the Disc's a Stage: Terry Pratchett's *Wyrd Sisters* as Metafiction," *Colloquy: Text, Theory, Critique* 38 (2019): 5.
48 Christie, *Ackroyd*, 145.
49 Quoted in Arasu, "All the Disc's a Stage," 6.
50 Laura María Lojo Rodríguez, "Parody and Metafiction: Virginia Woolf's '*An Unwritten Novel*'," *Links & Letters* 8 (2001): 73.
51 Ibid., 74.
52 Ibid., 74–5.
53 John Berger, *A Fortunate Man: The Story of a Country Doctor* (1967; photographs by Jean Mohr. New York: Vintage International, 1997. Kindle.), 55.
54 Megan Coyer, *Literature and Medicine in the Nineteenth-Century Periodical Press: Blackwood's Edinburgh Magazine, 1817–1858* (Edinburgh: Edinburgh University Press, 2017), 73.
55 I thank Danette DiMarco, Tom Sparrow, and Matthew Vickless for their input and advice on earlier versions of this piece.

Bibliography

Arasu, Prema. "All the Disc's a Stage: Terry Pratchett's *Wyrd Sisters* as Metafiction." *Colloquy: Text, Theory, Critique* 38 (2019): 3–19.
Bardi, Abby. "Pulp Fiction, with Real Pulp: Crime Writing as Creative Writing (Panel)." NeMLA Call for Papers. *NeMLA: Northeast Modern Language Association*. www.cfplist.com/nemla/Home/S/18640. Accessed November 7, 2020.

Benner, Patricia. "Learning through Experience and Expression: Skillful Ethical Comportment in Nursing Practice." In *The Health Care Professional as Friend and Healer: Building on the Work of Edmund D. Pellegrino*, edited by David C. Thomasma and Judith Lee Kissell, 49–64. Washington, DC: Georgetown University Press, 2000.

Berger, John. *A Fortunate Man: The Story of a Country Doctor*. 1967. Photographs by Jean Mohr. New York: Vintage International, 1997. Kindle.

Campbell, Courtney S. "Prophet to the Profession: Healing and Physician-Assisted Suicide." In *The Health Care Professional as Friend and Healer: Building on the Work of Edmund D. Pellegrino*, edited by David C. Thomasma and Judith Lee Kissell, 198–209. Washington, DC: Georgetown University Press, 2000.

Camus, Albert. *Notebooks 1942–1951*. 1964. Translated by Justin O'Brien. St. Paul, MN: Paragon House, 1991.

Christie, Agatha. *The Clocks*. 1963. New York: Harper, 2011.

Christie, Agatha. *Death on the Nile*. 1938. New York: William Morrow, 2011.

Christie, Agatha. *Lord Edgware Dies*. 1933. New York: William Morrow, 2011.

Christie, Agatha. *The Murder of Roger Ackroyd*. 1926. New York: William Morrow, 2020.

Coyer, Megan. *Literature and Medicine in the Nineteenth-Century Periodical Press: Blackwood's Edinburgh Magazine, 1817–58*. Edinburgh: Edinburgh University Press, 2017.

Dickens, Charles. *Great Expectations*. 1861. Edited by Edgar Rosenberg. New York: Norton, 1999.

Gutkowski, Emanuela. "An 'Investigation in Pragmatics': Agatha Christie's *The Murder of Roger Ackroyd*." *CLUES: A Journal of Detection* 29, no. 1 (2011): 51–60.

Heyd, Theresa. "Understanding and Handling Unreliable Narratives: A Pragmatic Model and Method." *Semiotica: Journal of the International Association for Semiotic Studies* 162, no. 1–4 (2006): 217–43.

Iles, Francis. *Malice Aforethought: The Story of a Commonplace Crime*. 1931. Mineola, NY: Dover, 2018.

Kennedy, Meegan. "The Ghost in the Clinic: Gothic Medicine and Curious Fiction in Samuel Warren's *Diary of a Late Physician*." *Victorian Literature and Culture* 32, no. 2 (2004): 327–51.

Kinnell, Herbert. "Agatha Christie's Doctors." *The BMJ: British Medical Journal* 341, no. 7786 (December 18–25, 2010): 1324–5.

Rinehart, Mary Roberts. "*Locked Doors*." 1914. In *The Big Book of Female Detectives*, edited by Otto Penzler, 444–69. New York: Vintage Crime/Black Lizard, 2018.

Rodríguez, Laura María Lojo. "Parody and Metafiction: Virginia Woolf's '*An Unwritten Novel*.'" *Links & Letters* 8 (2001): 71–81.

Rolls, Alistair. "Creative, Critical, Intertextual: Agatha Christie's *The Murder of Roger Ackroyd*." *TEXT: Journal of Writing and Writing Courses*, Special Issue 37 (October 2016): 1–11.

Rolls, Alistair, and Jesper Gulddal. "Pierre Bayard and the Ironies of Detective Criticism: From Text Back to Work." *Comparative Literature Studies* 53, no. 1 (2016): 150–69.

Stewart, Victoria. "Objects, Things and Clues in Early Twentieth-Century Fiction." *Modernist Cultures* 14, no. 2 (2019): 172–92.
Thomasma, David C. "The Principle of Dominion." In *The Health Care Professional as Friend and Healer: Building on the Work of Edmund D. Pellegrino*, edited by David C. Thomasma and Judith Lee Kissell, 133–47. Georgetown: Georgetown University Press, 2000.
Todd, Marilyn. "Beyond the Tree Line." *Ellery Queen Mystery Magazine* 155, nos. 5–6 (2020): 117–24.
Welie, Jos V. M. "The Dentist as Healer and Friend." In *The Health Care Professional as Friend and Healer: Building on the Work of Edmund D. Pellegrino*, edited by David C. Thomasma and Judith Lee Kissell, 35–48. Washington, DC: Georgetown University Press, 2000.
Winspear, Jacqueline. *Maisie Dobbs*. New York: Soho Press, 2003.

2

A Not-So-Certain Morality: Adaptations in *Murder on the Orient Express*

Annette Wren

> *"And then, Messieurs, I saw light. They were* all *in it. For so many people connected with the Armstrong case to be travelling by the same train by a coincidence was not only unlikely, it was impossible. It must be not chance, but design."*
> —HERCULE POIROT, MURDER ON THE ORIENT EXPRESS (1934)

Agatha Christie's popular *Murder on the Orient Express* is a novel that asks readers to follow Hercule Poirot as he searches for a murderer sans the help of forensics, his trusty sidekick Arthur Hastings, or even a local policeperson. As the only representative of the metaphorical idea of "law and order" aboard the Orient Express, Poirot is an agent of righteousness acting to "an objective moral standard"[1]—namely whether or not justice has been served in the murder of one Edward Ratchett. Over eighty years later, Kenneth Branagh directed and starred in a film adaptation of Christie's novel, which was released in November 2017. While this film respects the same plot, cast of characters, and conclusion as Christie's novel, the key difference lies in Poirot's moral imagination.

I posit that a shift occurs between Agatha Christie's original work and Kenneth Branagh's adaptation. In Christie's novel, the Belgian detective remains clinically removed from the emotional turmoil of Linda Arden and her cast of conspirators. His judgment that their actions are morally right is impartial; Ratchett was a notorious villain who killed an innocent baby girl and corrupted a trial by jury in the United States, so he must face a vengeful, vigilante jury on the Orient Express. However, such impartiality is not the case in Branagh's adaptation. In this adaptation, Poirot begins as an absolutist who cannot reconcile murder with justice. Over the course of the film, he develops a moral imagination that allows him to see past the murder of Ratchett itself and feel empathy with the avengers and their pain over Daisy Armstrong's loss. Both Christie's Poirot and Branagh's Poirot ultimately decide in favor of the vigilante avengers, but exploring this shift in moral imagination between novel and film emphasizes the absolute necessity of moral imagination to the pursuit of justice. Moreover, this shift both privileges the detective's influence as a moral agent and deemphasizes the exact identity of the detective himself/herself, per Margaret Urban Walker's theoretical-juridical model of morality and moral theory:

> In moral theorizing conducted within the expectations set out in this template, *who* the moral philosopher is that is doing the theorizing is unimportant. ... Instead, what is important is that the philosopher has the rational capacity to identify the set of moral laws that ought to guide all rational moral agents. In this picture of morality, then, the moral philosopher does not see herself to be a part of the moral world that she is thinking about, but understands herself, instead, as standing outside or above it, adopting the perspective of the unencumbered rational agent.[2]

Branagh's Poirot is not successful until he releases himself from his absolutist principles and becomes an unencumbered agent who can step into Linda Arden and the other avengers' metaphorical shoes to see their pain and empathize with their loss.

In exploring this shift, what both novel and film emphasize is that human beings are imaginative animals: "Every one of us is continually about the vital business of weaving together the threads of our lives. In order for us to have coherent experiences ... we must organize and reorganize our experiences from moment to moment."[3] The shift in moral imagination from novel to film exemplifies this reorganization as both reader and viewer follow Poirot's decisions as to how to best reconcile morality and justice. As such, in this chapter, I approach moral imagination as a form of narrative and a "cognitive aptitude that contributes to the ability of agents to act well according to an objective moral standard."[4] As an international detective not bound to any government or higher authority, Poirot utilizes his imagination to find that objective moral standard. The result is that an "objective moral standard" is prone to subjectivity and empathy.

Moreover, detective fiction is one of the most apt genres for just such an exploration. As Rachel Haliburton states in her text on the ethical detective,

"Readers of detective fiction must pay active attention to the story they are reading; they must play a game with the author which requires them to notice clues, to distinguish genuine clues from the red herrings that also confront them, to construct multiple possible narratives that make sense of the evidence with which they have been presented," and, at the end, "discover who the villain is before the author chooses to reveal all."[5] Such active engagement ensures that the reader participates in Poirot's cognitive investigations and the construction of a narrative that ultimately leads to justice. In what follows, I expand upon the significance of moral imagination to mystery fiction. Next, I examine how Agatha Christie's Poirot utilizes his moral imagination to come to the objective conclusion that Linda Arden has ensured justice is served. The third section of this chapter turns to Branagh's adaptation and how the moral imagination takes on a new form, but with the same outcome. Finally, I reflect on the mystery genre and the detective himself/herself as a moral, imaginative agent.

Moral Imagination in Mystery Fiction

As stated in my introduction, this chapter approaches moral imagination as the ability to act according to an objective moral standard and to exemplify that standard through the act of narration. The question, then, remains how that definition translates into the mystery novel and the detective figure. If a detective's purpose is to seek the truth,[6] a ploy that often involves an element of critical reflection on society, then this figure represents an objective moral standard not necessarily beholden to any specific nation, society, or culture. In Christie's *Murder on the Orient Express*, Poirot identifies himself as an "international detective," one who "belong[s] to the world."[7] This independence implies that the private detective, in short, cannot deal in moral absolutes, a position supported by Mark Johnson in his influential work *Moral Imagination* (1993).[8] Instead, the detective seeks to test the available options to decide on the most correct objective moral path. Thus, "moral imagination" is "the capacity that not only helps us determine what we ought to do when faced with ethical conflicts ... but which, even more fundamentally, makes us *want* to do the right thing in the first place."[9] Indeed, that is Poirot's ultimate purpose after Ratchett's body is discovered in both novel and film. As he assures M. Bouc after examining the body, "You place the matter in my hands."[10] Poirot is the only person on the train qualified to investigate the murder, and therefore he wants to do the "right thing" by his friend and fellow passengers.

We find precedent for Poirot's actions in another influential and well-recognized private detective. Sherlock Holmes, Sir Arthur Conan Doyle's famous pseudo-scientist operating out of 221B Baker Street in London, is perhaps still the most well-recognized embodiment of this quest for moral justice. In his chapter on Sherlock Holmes and the moral imagination, Christopher Clausen emphasizes that, in solving cases, Holmes "does more than simply satisfy his clients or uphold the abstractions of the law. He singlehandedly defends an entire social order."[11] In other words, Holmes "reserves to his own judgment the complicated questions of what constitutes justice in a given set of circumstances and how far it involves people who have committed crimes to the notice of those institutions."[12] For example, in "The Boscombe Valley Mystery" (1891), Holmes does not hand an elderly murderer by the name of John Turner over to Scotland Yard as the man is on his deathbed and will soon "answer for [his] deeds in a higher court than the Assizes."[13] Holmes himself has obtained justice by confronting Turner and obtaining his confession; Holmes further perceives that a court trial and sentence is pointless in Turner's current position and that justice has been served. Therefore, Holmes has fulfilled his duty as an investigator. Holmes's ability to act independently of the official governing laws of England exemplifies Clausen's point that perpetuating "the social order is not the same thing as making human sacrifices to it, still less abandoning one's own private judgment."[14]

Such actions from detectives (both private and government-sanctioned) are revealed through the act of narration. This act is central to the detective's significance to moral imagination because it bridges the divide between moral philosophy and the detective figure. According to Johnson, there is "abundant empirical evidence that narrative is a fundamental mode of understanding, by means of which we make sense of all forms of human action."[15] When we read a detective narrative, we are presented with a practical example of moral imagination that is otherwise abstract or technical in the works of moral philosophers.[16] Specifically, this genre "requires its readers to draw on many of the same skills that philosophy requires of its practitioners: analytic methods, deductive reasoning, the ability to distinguish what is important in the analysis of the problem from what is peripheral or even irrelevant."[17] Therefore, a detective's narrative is crucial to understanding and assessing moral obligations. In what follows, I examine both Christie's textual narrative and Branagh's visual narrative to determine how their respective Hercule Poirot characters engage with moral imagination. In performing this analysis, I emphasize not the detective in and of himself, but his actions and the need for empathy with others.

Hercule Poirot's Little Gray Cells

In *Murder on the Orient Express*, Hercule Poirot faces an ethical dilemma that can only be resolved through moral imagination: does he turn the blind eye to the murder of Edward Ratchett (also known as Cassetti) or hold Linda Arden and the other passengers on the Orient Express under his authority until the Yugoslavian police can reach them? Poirot's ability to not only deduce the perpetrators but also justify their roles in Ratchett's murder underscores Mark Johnson's central claim that "human moral understanding is fundamentally imaginative."[18] Poirot's skills allow him not only to uncover the identity of the murderer but also to decide on the greater meaning of "justice" in the context of Daisy Armstrong's death.

Imagination itself "has often been identified as the capacity for taking someone else's point of view or stepping into his/her shoes."[19] When such an imagination is present in a detective, s/he steps into the shoes of the murderer to discern not only method but motive. As the reader follows Poirot's investigations onboard the Orient Express, Poirot not only puts himself in the murderer's shoes but also uncovers the damage Ratchett inflicted on the Armstrong family. So, when Poirot reveals the results of his investigation and provides M. Bouc with the opportunity to decide the case, the Belgian detective is implicitly deciding in favor of Linda Arden and the other passengers. By the time readers arrive at this pivotal scene in the novel, they cannot help but agree with Poirot and M. Bouc: justice has been served.

To step into the murderer's shoes, Poirot must first unveil Ratchett's true identity and the motive behind his murder. In the process, Poirot establishes one important fact: Edward Ratchett was a force of evil. Christie gives the reader the first clue to this characterization when Ratchett crosses Poirot's path on the Orient Express. Poirot's observations of the American help the reader begin to draw distinct connections between good and evil:

He was a man of between sixty and seventy. From a slight distance he had the bland aspect of a philanthropist. His slightly bald head, his domed forehead, the smiling mouth that displayed a very white set of false teeth, all seemed to speak of a benevolent personality. Only the eyes belied this assumption. They were small, deep set and crafty. Not only that. As the man, making some remark to his young companion, glanced around the room, his gaze stopped on Poirot for a moment, and just for that second there was a strange malevolence, and unnatural tensity in the gaze.[20]

Poirot's instincts tell him not to accept Ratchett's offer as a traveling companion.[21] In making this pivotal decision, Poirot again engages in a significant characteristic of moral imagination: while motivation and moral character are important, "the nature of relationships between the protagonists" is of equal importance.[22] Poirot refuses Ratchett because the Belgian detective does not like the other man's face, a euphemism for his instinctual distrust of the dangerous man. In contrast, Poirot's treatment of and interviews with the other Orient Express passengers reveal a group of individuals sympathetic to the Armstrong family and righteous in their anger toward the dead gangster.

Before interviewing the passengers on the train, Poirot establishes the second pivotal point for the reader: Daisy Armstrong's death is tragic, horrifying, and still unresolved. As Poirot tells M. Bouc, "the child's dead body was discovered. ... And there was worse to follow. Mrs. Armstrong was expecting another child. Following the shock of the discovery, she gave birth to a dead child prematurely, and herself died. Her broken-hearted husband shot himself."[23] Both Poirot and M. Bouc comment that they "cannot regret that [Ratchett] is dead" in light of this revelation.[24] In fact, not one passenger regrets Ratchett's death, as Poirot and Dr. Constantine learn as they interview the Orient Express passengers.

For example, Hector MacQueen feels no empathy for his dead employer and does not hide his feelings from Poirot: "I'll tell you the truth, Mr. Poirot. I disliked and distrusted him. He was, I am sure, a cruel and dangerous man."[25] Greta Ohlsson's "yellow bun of hair quiver[s]" with emotion as she tells Poirot, "That there are in the world such evil men! It tries one's faith. The poor mother. My heart aches for her."[26] These reactions, however, lack the ferocity of those from Princess Dragomiroff, the only passenger willing to admit her connection to the Armstrong family from the outset. In her conversations with Poirot, the noblewoman comments, "In my view ... this murder is an entirely admirable happening! You will pardon my slightly biased point of view."[27] A more sympathetic character is Countess Andrenyi, better known as Helen Goldberg, Daisy Armstrong's aunt and Linda Arden's last living daughter: "This man who was killed is the man who murdered my baby niece, who killed my sister, who broke my brother-in-law's heart. Three of the people I loved best and who made up my home—my world!"[28] As Poirot interviews the passengers and hears their reactions to Ratchett's identity as both a gangster and Daisy Armstrong's killer, readers become less sympathetic toward Ratchett while Poirot, unbeknownst to the reader until the end, begins to unravel the case through these interviews.

What Poirot ultimately establishes are two key attributes to Ratchett's person: first, that the man was a violent criminal; and second, that his murderers have quite possibly prevented the further kidnap and murder of other children. As Linda Arden tells Poirot, "There had been other children before Daisy—there might be others in the future."[29] Given such a context, Colonel Arbuthnot's comments are both heartily felt and ironic: "Then in my opinion the swine deserved what he got. Though I would have preferred to have seen him properly hanged—or electrocuted, I suppose, over there."[30] In fact, however, just such a trial has occurred on the train, as Poirot reveals at the close of the novel:

> And then, Messieurs, I saw the light. They were *all* in it. For so many people connected with the Armstrong case to be travelling by the same

train by a coincidence was not only unlikely, it was *impossible*. It must be not chance, but *design*. I remembered a remark of Colonel Arbuthnot's about trial by jury. A jury is composed of twelve people—there were twelve passengers—Ratchett was stabbed twelve times.[31]

The literal court of justice failed Daisy Armstrong; Linda Arden's makeshift court has ensured that such a miscarriage of justice will never happen again.

Thus, the last chapter of Christie's novel is the most significant. In "Poirot Propounds Two Solutions," the Belgian detective gathers the passengers of the Orient Express together for a final explanation of the murder and confrontation with the perpetrators. Before announcing the solution to Ratchett's murder, Poirot makes an important request to M. Bouc and Dr. Constantine: "There are two possible solutions of the crime. I shall put them both before you, and I shall ask M. Bouc and Dr. Constantine here to judge which solution is the right one."[32] In offering this final decision to these two men, Poirot is implicitly telling the passengers that either solution is morally right. As M. Bouc exclaims, the first solution is absurd: a stranger boarded the coach, murdered Ratchett, and snuck back out again, despite the snowstorm. However, M. Bouc quickly walks back that comment after Poirot reveals the second and true solution: excepting himself, his conductor friend, and Dr. Constantine, the other passengers onboard the Orient Express and including the Wagon Lit conductor are all connected to the Armstrong family and trapped Ratchett on the train to murder him. Poirot's skills earn the admiration of the two most commanding players in the scheme, both Princess Dragomiroff ("You have thought of everything, Monsieur. I—I admire you"[33]) and Linda Arden, alias Mrs. Hubbard ("You're a wonderful man"[34]). After this revelation from Poirot, Linda Arden admits to the scheme and employs a plea for her co-conspirators: "Society had condemned him; we were only carrying out the sentence. But it's unnecessary to bring all these others into it. All these good and faithful souls—and poor Michel—and Mary and Colonel Arbuthnot—they love each other. ..."[35] However, such a plea is unnecessary because Poirot has already decided that no matter which scenario M. Bouc and Dr. Constantine elect as the true solution, justice has been served. So, when the decision is in favor of the strangers on the train, Poirot's final words seal the innocence of the Orient Express passengers: "Then ... having placed my solution before you, I have the honour to retire from the case ...."[36]

Poirot's choice of the word *honour* is particularly important and embodies his role as a detective in relation to moral imagination. Johnson's characterization of a moral agent perfectly answers to Christie's Belgian detective: "Moral agents are rationally transparent individuals who possess desires they understand completely. They have complete knowledge of their ends, which are regarded as completely determinate, fixed, and given in advance of their moral deliberations about means to these ends."[37] Poirot is entirely transparent in his purpose after Ratchett's untimely death: to solve the case. Moreover, Poirot is a master at his investigative craft, as M. Bouc is quick to point out after Ratchett's body is discovered: "I know your reputation. I know something of your methods. This is the ideal case for you."[38] In performing his investigative role, Poirot not only reveals the murderer's motives but fulfills his mission to solve Ratchett's murder.

To exemplify Poirot's investigative skills and provide the reader with a sense of justice, Christie structures this novel in three discrete parts, and each part builds to create a sympathetic view of the twelve jurors and their grief. By the time Poirot forces Linda Arden into a confession, the reader cannot help but sympathize with the grieving woman. These parts work together to create a facsimile court case, one that will be successful in persecuting Daisy Armstrong's killer. In "Part One: The Facts," Christie has Poirot and the reader board the Orient Express and discover the murder of Edward Ratchett; in "Part Two: The Evidence," Poirot and his allies interview the passengers on the train, seemingly with iron-clad alibis and without obvious motives. Finally, in "Part Three: Hercule Poirot Sits Back and Thinks," Poirot makes the correct deduction that, aside from himself, M. Bouc, and Dr. Constantine, the passengers on the Orient Express all had a hand in Ratchett's murder, with Linda Arden as lead conspirator. This narrative provides the reader with a sense of security; in creating a pseudo-court case, Poirot acts as both detective and judge as he examines the crime, studies the potential suspects, and arrives at a conclusion. Thus, the narrative construction of the novel itself lends not only to Poirot's final judgment but to the reader's moral conclusion as well. Both Poirot and the reader return to Haliburton's key point that a moral imagination enables an individual to determine the "right" course of action in any given situation.[39] What we see, too, is that, regarding questions of justice, "rights may win out over perfectionist ends."[40] Linda Arden's method of justice is neither desired nor legal; it was, however, the "right" course of action.

Imagination in Adaptation

In his adaptation of Christie's novel, Branagh examines the definition of moral imagination with Johnson's comments in mind regarding absolutism:

> Absolutism is motivated by a quest for certainty. It draws its appeal from the universal human need for security, control, and order. Moral absolutism thus seeks principles valid for all people, at all times, and in all historical contexts. It assumes that moral laws come out of an allegedly

essential structure of rationality. It seeks a single unified criterion (or set of hierarchically ranked criteria) for the moral evaluation of all actions.[41]

Moral absolutism and moral imagination are ultimately not compatible. Branagh's Poirot embodies this moral absolutism until he makes his final decision regarding the passengers on board the Orient Express. The decision that Linda Arden is justified in her actions is only possible after Poirot considers the concept of "justice" from her perspective.

Poirot's absolutism is first revealed in the beginning of the film when he uncovers that the Chief of Police is behind the theft of an invaluable relic in Jerusalem. As he tells his British military escort, "I can only see the world as it should be. And when it is not, the imperfection stands out like the nose in the middle of the face. It makes life most unbearable. But it is useful in the detection of crime".[42] While this absolutism works well for Poirot at Jerusalem and in his profession in the past (as he tells his fellow Orient Express passengers, "My name is Hercule Poirot and I am probably one of the greatest detectives in the world"),[43] Ratchett's murder will expose how such "absolutist orientation denies ... the existence of genuine irresolvable moral conflict—conflict among competing conceptions of good, justice, and reason."[44] In other words, ideals such as good, justice, and reason are not absolute entities. Thus, the narrative focus shifts between novel and film—no longer is the reader concerned with feeling satisfied that a great injustice has been righted; instead, the focus is on challenging the detective's absolute sense of right and wrong.

When Ratchett's body is first discovered on the Orient Express, Poirot is hesitant to investigate and Bouc is forced to plead to his friend's sense of justice. While Bouc appeals to Poirot as an impartial and unprejudiced detective (according to Bouc, "If we leave this to the police, they will choose a culprit right or wrong. ... Most probably Mr. Marquez for no other reason than his name is Marquez. Or Dr. Arbuthnot for the color of his skin"),[45] Poirot accepts based on his inability to let a murderer escape. As he tells Bouc, "Evidence, order and method, until one culprit emerges. I do not approve of murder, my friend. Every day, we meet people the world could do better without yet we do not kill them. We must be better than beasts. So let us find this killer."[46] This statement from Poirot establishes two key facets of his identity as a detective: first, that murder under any circumstance is unacceptable; and second, that murder is a vulgar action not in keeping with humanity's sophistication. His discoveries on the Orient Express will force Poirot to be flexible in these philosophies.

Like Christie's novel, Branagh's adaptation does emphasize Ratchett's villainy and infamous career. When Ratchett first introduces himself to Poirot, he names the detective as "the avenger of the innocent" and requests assistance with unknown enemies. Poirot takes Ratchett's comment and turns it around on the criminal-turned-antique dealer: "I detect criminals. I do not protect them. ... I say 'no' to you, Mr. Ratchett. ... I do not like your face."⁴⁷ Moreover, Branagh directs this film to also emphasize the horror of Daisy Armstrong's death and the absolute havoc it wrought on her family. Branagh's Poirot recounts a similar story as Christie's Poirot, commenting that Daisy's death "shocked the world."⁴⁸ Princess Dragomiroff further carries this point saying, "They endured an unspeakable tragedy."⁴⁹ And Linda Arden, disguised as Mrs. Hubbard, triumphantly tells Poirot that she "knew [Ratchett] was a rotten one" when Poirot reveals the criminal's true identity to her. Mary Debenham uses stronger words, combatively saying to Poirot, "Cassetti was a pig. He deserved to die."⁵⁰ However, Poirot is not only *not* swayed by these revelations but exhibits rage towards the conspirators when he confronts them. While he admits that "this crime is the murdering of a murderer" and that the benefit of such an act is "an ease of suffering,"⁵¹ he cannot reconcile their actions with his belief that murder is absolutely wrong.

Thus, like Christie's novel, the true test for Poirot comes in the final scenes of Branagh's film. When Poirot presents his two solutions to the case before the vigilante jurors and Bouc, he does not leave the final decision to others. Instead, Poirot presents the Orient Express passengers with an entirely new challenge. If they want to escape, they must commit one more murder:

> Poirot: And so it is done. For the death of the innocent. A life for a life. Revenge.
> Arden: No one should hang for this but me. It was my plan! Tell the police it was me, alone. There's no life left in me anymore. They have a chance now. ... They can go live, find some joy somewhere. Let it end with me. They're not killers. They're good people. They can be good again.
> Poirot: There was right, there was wrong. Now there is you. I cannot judge this. You must decide. You wish to go free without punishment for your crime, then you must only commit one more. I will not stop you.
> Bouc: You can't let them kill you.
> Poirot: You give my body to the lake, and you walk away innocent at the station. You must silence me. Bouc can lie. I cannot. Do it! One of you!
> Arden: I already died with Daisy.⁵²

However, Linda Arden does not shoot Poirot, and the detective leaves Bouc and the passengers to struggle more over his decisions. The final voice of persuasion comes not from Linda Arden, but from Pilar Estravados, Daisy's nurse, who approaches Poirot after he has returned to the train:

> Estravados: You said your role was to find justice.
> Poirot: What is justice here?

Estravados: Sometimes, the law of man is not enough.
Poirot: Where does conscience lie?
Estravados: Buried with Daisy.[53]

With those final words, she leaves Poirot. As the train engine starts again, the viewer hears Poirot's voice as he narrates a reply to Colonel Armstrong's letter before his death.[54] Scenes of the various passengers on board the Orient Express flash across the screen:

> My dear Colonel Armstrong. Finally, I can answer your letter, at least with the thoughts in my head and the feeling in my heart that somewhere, you can hear me. I have now discovered the truth of the case, and it is profoundly disturbing. I have seen the fracture of the human soul. So many broken lives, so much pain and anger giving way to the poison of deep grief until one crime became many. I have always wanted to believe that man is rational and civilized. My very existence depends upon this hope upon order and method and the little gray cells. But now, perhaps, I am asked to listen, instead, to my heart.[55]

Poirot has reached his decision: he will not turn over the passengers to the Yugoslav authorities. In this case, Poirot has learned to not only be flexible in his understanding of morality and justice, but he has been forced to acknowledge what Christie's Poirot already knew: a perfect version of justice is not always possible.

And Poirot admits this imperfection to the avengers before he disembarks from the Orient Express, telling them all, "I have understood in this case that the scales of justice cannot always be evenly weighed. And I must learn, for once, to live with the imbalance. There are no killers here. Only people who deserve a chance to heal. ... You are all free to go."[56] Poirot's newfound ability to listen to his heart is a metaphor for a greater moral imagination that emphasizes that tradition or formal principal is not reason in and of itself;[57] Poirot's principle that murder is always a base act is not in itself always correct. Instead, he must practice moral imagination to understand the most ethical outcome, however imperfect such an outcome or decision might be compared to formal laws of any given society or government. As Haliburton emphasizes, "the detective ... is often committed to a vision of justice that is only imperfectly realized in the fictional world ... but which is nonetheless worth fighting for."[58] Poirot has enabled Daisy Armstrong's beloved friends and family the chance for justice and peace, something not possible in the formal sense of law and order. He must be satisfied with that imperfection and learn from it.

The Importance of the Detective

In his article on moral imagination and moral judgment, Michael J. Pardales asserts that "literature is one of the best cultivators of the moral imagination."[59] Pardales's comments are echoed by Rachel Haliburton and her assertion that the detective is a key fictional figure in this conversation of literature and moral imagination; this genre "explores the nature of good and evil, virtue and vice, and, as such, it can easily provide virtue ethicists with a useful education and motivational tool."[60] Haliburton's and Pardales's comments are linked through narrative. "Narratives can embody our moral ideas and can give us the means for exploring possible actions within concrete day-to-day situations that make up the moral fabric of our lives";[61] while we, as readers of narratives, might not consider murder as a day-to-day situation, the detective's role as societal critic challenges the reader's preconceived or traditionally unchallenged notions of what is ethically and morally right.

The difference between Christie's Poirot and Branagh's Poirot emphasizes the pitfalls of absolutism to justice and morality. Christie's Poirot, while not infallible, acknowledges "the tension between the homogenizing forces of institutions, laws, and moral codes on the one hand and, on the other, humanity's resurgent, unsuppressed individuality."[62] This Poirot understands that the case of Edward Ratchett is unique and therefore requires empathy and flexibility from the detective. Branagh's Poirot, by contrast, must learn to embrace the fact that humans are "imaginative beings" who "can go beyond the givenness of … past experience" and "develop novel organizations."[63] And, in the end, Branagh's Poirot does go beyond his past experiences of absolutism to develop a new empathy and understanding that underscore that a vigilante's quest for justice is, in the rare instance, morally right.

Thus, we find that one of Haliburton's more controversial claims that "murder mysteries can actually do a better job of educating and motivating their readers than many great literary novels" should not be provocative.[64] What I have shown in this chapter is that the narrative and the detective's moral imagination, rather than the detective's identity, are significant in the quest for justice. Those imaginings "have the power to generate emotions and appeal to desires,"[65] and it is through emotions that we find justice.

Notes

1 Mavis Biss, "Moral Imagination, Perception, and Judgment," *The Southern Journal of Philosophy* 52, no. 1 (March 2014): 2.

2 Margaret Urban Walker, *Moral Understandings: A Feminist Study in Ethics* (New York: Oxford University Press, 2007), quoted in Rachel Haliburton,

The Ethical Detective: Moral Philosophy and Detective Fiction (Lanham: Lexington Books, 2018), 9.

3 Mark Johnson, *Moral Imagination: Implications of Cognitive Science for Ethics* (Chicago: University of Chicago Press, 1993), 152.
4 Biss, "Moral Imagination," 2.
5 Haliburton, *The Ethical Detective*, 13.
6 Ibid., 83.
7 Agatha Christie, *Murder on the Orient Express* (1934. New York: William Morrow, 2017), 124.
8 Johnson, *Moral Imagination*, 108.
9 Haliburton, *The Ethical Detective*, 141.
10 Christie, *Murder*, 47.
11 Christopher Clausen, "Sherlock Holmes, Order, and the Late-Victorian Mind," in *The Moral Imagination: Essays on Literature and Ethics* (Iowa City: University of Iowa Press, 1986), 60.
12 Ibid., 75.
13 Arthur Conan Doyle, "The Boscombe Valley Mystery" (1891), in *The Complete Sherlock Holmes*, ed. Christopher Roden and Barbara Roden (New York: Barnes & Noble, 2009), 199.
14 Clausen, "Sherlock Holmes," 70.
15 Johnson, *Moral Imagination*, 11.
16 Haliburton, *The Ethical Detective*, 93.
17 Ibid., 14.
18 Johnson, *Moral Imagination*, 33.
19 Philipp Dorstewitz, "Imagination in Action," *Metaphilosophy* 47, no. 3 (July 2016): 400.
20 Christie, *Murder*, 16.
21 Ibid., 30.
22 Haliburton, *The Ethical Detective*, 17.
23 Christie, *Murder*, 70.
24 Ibid., 71.
25 Ibid., 54.
26 Ibid., 108.
27 Ibid., 117.
28 Ibid., 221.
29 Ibid., 264.
30 Ibid., 131.
31 Ibid., 257–8.
32 Ibid., 250.

33 Ibid., 253.
34 Ibid., 262.
35 Ibid., 264.
36 Ibid., 265.
37 Johnson, *Moral Imagination*, 123.
38 Christie, *Murder*, 46.
39 Haliburton, *The Ethical Detective*, 141.
40 Michael J. Pardales, "'So, How Did You Arrive at that Decision?': Connecting Moral Imagination and Moral Judgement," *Journal of Moral Education* 31, no. 4 (2002): 425.
41 Johnson, *Moral Imagination*, 124.
42 Kenneth Branagh, dir., *Murder on the Orient Express*. Los Angeles: 20th Century Fox, 2017. Movie.
43 Ibid.
44 Johnson, *Moral Imagination*, 124.
45 Branagh makes a few character changes in his film. First, Antonio Foscarelli's name is changed to Biniamino Marquez (his profession of chauffeur remains the same). Colonel Arbuthnot is changed to Dr. Arbuthnot. Leslie Odom Jr. plays this Dr. Arbuthnot, and Bouc is implying that Arbuthnot's race will be a source of prejudice.
46 Kenneth Branagh, dir., *Murder*.
47 Ibid.
48 Ibid.
49 Ibid.
50 Ibid.
51 Ibid.
52 Ibid.
53 Ibid.
54 Poirot reveals to Bouc after telling the story of Daisy Armstrong that he had received a letter from Colonel Armstrong begging the detective's help with his daughter's case, but that the note arrived too late for Poirot to reply.
55 Kenneth Branagh, dir., *Murder*.
56 Ibid.
57 Johnson, *Moral Imagination*, 111.
58 Haliburton, *The Ethical Detective*, 132.
59 Pardales, "'So, How Did You Arrive,'" 431–2.
60 Haliburton, *The Ethical Detective*, 115.
61 Johnson, *Moral Imagination*,171.
62 Maurizio Ascari, "After Sherlock: The Age of Fallible Detectives," *Clues* 35, no. 1 (Spring 2017): 8.

63 Johnson, *Moral Imagination*, 161.
64 Haliburton, *The Ethical Detective*, 114.
65 Dorstewitz, "Imagination in Action," 394.

Bibliography

Ascari, Maurizio. "After Sherlock: The Age of Fallible Detectives." *Clues* 35, no. 1 (Spring 2017): 8–18.
Biss, Mavis. "Moral Imagination, Perception, and Judgment." *The Southern Journal of Philosophy* 52, no. 1 (March 2014): 1–21.
Branagh, Kenneth, dir. *Murder on the Orient Express*. Los Angeles: 20th Century Fox, 2017. Movie.
Christie, Agatha. *Murder on the Orient Express*. 1934. New York: William Morrow, 2017.
Clausen, Christopher. "Sherlock Holmes, Order, and the Late-Victorian Mind." *The Moral Imagination*: Essays on Literature and Ethics, 51–85. Iowa City: University of Iowa Press, 1986.
Dorstewitz, Philipp. "Imagination in Action." *Metaphilosophy* 47, no. 3 (July 2016): 385–405.
Doyle, Arthur Conan. "The Boscombe Valley Mystery." 1891. *The Complete Sherlock Holmes*, edited by Christopher Roden and Barbara Roden, 184–99. New York: Barnes & Noble, 2009.
Haliburton, Rachel. *The Ethical Detective: Moral Philosophy and Detective Fiction*. Lanham: Lexington Books, 2018.
Johnson, Mark. *Moral Imagination: Implications of Cognitive Science for Ethics*. Chicago: University of Chicago Press, 1993.
Pardales, Michael J. "'So, How Did You Arrive at that Decision?': Connecting Moral Imagination and Moral Judgement." *Journal of Moral Education* 31, no. 4 (2002): 423–37.
Walker, Margaret Urban. *Moral Understandings: A Feminist Study in Ethics*. New York: Oxford University Press, 2007. Quoted in Haliburton. *The Ethical Detective: Moral Philosophy and Detective Fiction*. Lanham: Lexington Books, 2018.

3

The Colorado Kid, *Joyland*, and *Later*: Genre Hybridity and the Moral Imagination in Stephen King's Hard Case Crime Novels

Alissa Burger

Stephen King is a best-selling horror author, but his work often transcends traditional genre boundaries, running the gamut from fairy tales and fantasy to melodrama and the Western. One genre with which King has engaged, particularly over the last twenty years, is mystery, with novels including *The Colorado Kid* (2005), *Joyland* (2013), *Later* (2021), and the *Bill Hodges* trilogy of *Mr. Mercedes* (2014), *Finders Keepers* (2015), and *End of Watch* (2016).

King is an atypical mystery writer, and this genre designation has at times proven contentious, resulting in the resistance from some authors and critics when the Mystery Writers of America named King a Grandmaster in 2007.[1] King's mysteries often surpass the traditional boundaries of the genre, delving into horror and the uncanny as he "introduce[s] elements of the supernatural and the irrational that cannot be resolved by the deductive method employed in a classic of detective and mystery fiction."[2] For example, while Ben Mears and his friends are tracking a killer in *'Salem's Lot* (1975), following a trail of clues to deduce his identity and hiding place, the villain is a vampire rather than a flesh-and-blood murderer, while in *The Dark Half* (1989), Sheriff Alan Pangborn believes he is close to solving a series of grisly murders before realizing that the real killer is Thad Beaumont's fictional pseudonym George Stark, who has been impossibly brought to life.

While Sir Arthur Conan Doyle's Sherlock Holmes has noted, "When you have eliminated the impossible, whatever remains, *however improbable*, must be the truth,"[3] these supernatural explanations push the boundaries of the mystery genre too far for uncomplicated categorization. However, as Nick Kolakowski argues in "The Uneasy Noirs of Stephen King," this genre hybridity has an established tradition, and while "a hardcore noir or mystery fan might regard supernatural interferences as a cop-out of sorts … lots of other genres—from science fiction to history—have blended exceptionally well with mystery and hardboiled tropes: Just look at all the classics of cyberpunk noir, from 'Johnny Mnemonic' to 'Blade Runner.'"[4] King embraces this approach of genre hybridity, effectively combining elements of mystery, horror, and the supernatural.

While King's twenty-first-century mysteries have been more traditional than those featured in *'Salem's Lot* or *The Dark Half*, elements of the supernatural continue to complicate the understanding of what is possible, what can be known, and which questions must remain unanswered. The eponymous protagonist of King's *Bill Hodges* trilogy, for example, is a largely traditional detective, following clues and trusting in the value of deductive reasoning and the power of observation as he works to identify the man responsible for the mayhem-style violence at the center of *Mr. Mercedes*. However, Brady Hartsfield's development of inexplicable powers in the series' third novel, *End of Watch*, requires readers to contend with both the horrific violence of which people are capable and supernatural terrors beyond the realm of the everyday.[5] While King's mysteries often draw readers off the beaten path and beyond the traditional boundaries of the genre, J. Madison Davis argues that horror and the mystery are not so far afield from one another:

> A fear of the power of darkness underlies most effective mystery writing. Both genres exploit our feelings that what we see and hear isn't nearly all there is. In the case of the mystery, there is a rational and worldly explanation behind the incredible; in the case of horror, there is not. Nevertheless, we all want an explanation when bad things happen. Why does a good person suffer? Why does someone of promise die young? Why are human monsters inadequately punished?[6]

Mystery and horror plumb the same questions, though the answers they offer are often very different, providing readers with divergent understandings of the world as either one in which questions can be solved and conclusions pronounced or, conversely, one in which the mysteries abide.

Three particularly notable King mysteries that follow this genre-blurring pattern are *The Colorado Kid*, *Joyland*, and *Later*, all of which King published with Hard Case Crime, an imprint committed to providing readers with "the best in hardboiled crime fiction, ranging from lost noir masterpieces to new novels by today's most powerful writers."[7] Hard Case Crime embraces both the narrative and visual styles of vintage crime novels, with riveting mysteries and striking pulp-style cover art.[8] With *The Colorado Kid*, *Joyland*, and *Later*, King simultaneously embraces and subverts this hard-boiled tradition, providing readers with mysteries that also draw on elements of horror and the supernatural. These novels have several characteristics of a traditional mystery, with each including at least one mysterious death, a series of clues, and an inquiring protagonist set on finding the truth, though in these novels the "detectives" are non-professionals, curious regular Joes (and Janes) rather than expert deducers like Holmes, Miss Marple, or Hercule Poirot. *The Colorado Kid*, *Joyland*, and *Later* also each follow the central moral imperative of detective fiction, in which the reader's "emotional involvement in crime novels typically comes from our identification with the hero's or heroine's indignation with crime, and passion for justice," a need to see order righteously restored.[9] Finally, much as the traditional detective reveals his reasoning and unveils the solution to conclude the mystery, the act of storytelling and narrative construction is central to *The Colorado Kid*, *Joyland*, and *Later*, both in the tellers' account of the mystery itself and in their consideration of the moral imagination engaged by each.

Joyland

Of the three novels considered here, *Joyland* is the most traditional of King's Hard Case Crime mysteries. Devin Jones is spending his summer break from college working at a mid-size amusement park called Joyland when he hears the story of Linda Gray, a murdered young woman whose ghost haunts the park's House of Horrors.

Devin is an Everyman detective, his curiosity and earnestness inviting easy reader self-identification. Like so many ghost story aficionados, Devin longs to have his own supernatural encounter, to see the ghost and experience the inexplicable, but even more than that, he wants to find out who killed Linda Gray. In *The Ethical Detective: Moral Philosophy and Detective Fiction*, Rachel Haliburton writes, "The detective, as G.K. Chesterton puts it, is a poetic and heroic figure, an 'agent of social justice' who protects the weak and vulnerable from the actions of the vicious through 'a successful knight errantry.'"[10] Despite Devin's amateur detective status, he lives up to this expectation. In the months he spends at Joyland, Devin saves the lives of two people: first performing the Heimlich maneuver on a young girl who is choking and later, after the park has closed for the season, administering CPR to a curmudgeonly fellow employee, Eddie Parks, when the older man has a heart attack. Haliburton argues that the traditional detective's goodness is also inextricably connected to his or her power and agency, and "since the detective chooses to act honestly because she values truth and must act with courage and for the sake of justice, these attributes become an essential part of the way in which she expresses not only her virtue, but her autonomy as well."[11] The detective is not inherently good—some ethereal and righteous hero—but rather a flawed and complex individual who chooses to do the right thing time and time again. Devin also falls into this expectation of making the moral choice, despite temptation. For example, when the father of the girl whose life he saved offers Devin $500, Devin turns this reward down because, as he says, "I didn't think he could afford to be giving money away" despite the semester of leisure the cash would have provided for Devin.[12] Devin also develops a close and protective relationship with Mike Ross, a terminally ill young boy who lives with his mother just down the beach from Joyland. While Mike's mother, Annie, is initially cold and standoffish with Devin, his selfless dedication to Mike—which includes a well-orchestrated private excursion to the otherwise closed amusement park—eventually wins her over. While Devin may not fit the traditional detective mold, it is this morality, kindness, and connection with others that ensure his survival in his final confrontation with Linda Gray's murderer, suggesting that the detective's moral compass—at least in this specific case—may be even more important than his actual powers of deduction.

Another element of the traditional detective story that is significant in *Joyland* is the role of women in the mystery-solving process, in this case through the curiosity and research skills of Devin's friend Erin Cook. While *femme fatales* are staples of noir detective fiction, Keli Masten argues that the "dependable woman," or *femme fiable*, is just as essential. Masten argues that in contrast to the *femme fatale* who leads the detective astray and into danger, the *femme fiable* is a figure of "power and trustworthiness ... [and] the steadfast persona of the *femme fiable* becomes a major contributor to [the detective's] success."[13] The *femme fiable* also introduces a uniquely feminist ethics to the mystery, particularly through an ethics of care that foregrounds the ways in which "moral agents ... focus on the needs of those one cares for in relational contexts rather than on abstract, universal principles."[14] In addition to prioritizing individuals over the intellectual solving of the mystery itself, feminist ethics explicitly note the shortfalls of traditional philosophical exploration, arguing that "top-down, juridicial, principalist theorizing has largely neglected the centrality of physical, social, and psychological situatedness, [and] power differentials."[15] Through this privileging of feminist ethics, the detectives in question not only tackle the mysteries as human problems rather than abstract puzzles, but also acknowledge the complexity and inequality inherent in some of those positions and experiences. Devin's *femme fatale*, his college girlfriend Wendy Keegan, is disposed of fairly early in the novel when she breaks up with him long-distance, leaving him for another man, with Devin nursing his broken heart over the months he spends at Joyland. Erin, however, proves to be far more steadfast, both in her friendship and in her dedication to assisting Devin in solving the murder of Linda Gray, plumbing the resources of her campus library when she returns to college in the fall and providing him with essential information, including the fact that Linda Gray is one of many murdered young women matching the same pattern, a victim of a serial killer rather than an isolated tragedy. Erin also fulfills another traditional expectation of the *femme fiable*, in the "trait of 'mixed femininity.'"[16] Erin works at Joyland as one of the feminine "Hollywood Girls" who wear beautiful costumes and walk the park snapping commemorative pictures of visitors. However, she has a default of being "all business" with a professional and no-nonsense manner, capable of holding her own with any of the men who challenge her.[17] Another *femme fiable* in *Joyland* is Annie Ross, the mother of young Mike. Annie is a beautiful and sexually desirable woman, but she is also formidable, an award-winning rifle-shooter, and an abrasive and fearless defender of her son, demonstrating a maternal and feminist ethics of care that privileges maternal strength and ferocity. While these two women may not be chasing the same mystery to which Devin has devoted himself—or at least not with the same intensity, in Erin's case—like their "detective" friend, they are both driven by a moral imperative to do the right thing and help the people they love.

Annie plays another significant role as well, with her presence and skill highlighting the ways Devin fails to fulfill the expectations of the traditional detective. Through the research Erin has provided, Devin solves the mystery and identifies the murderer, but is unable to bring him to justice. Instead, Devin is lured into a trap by his moral instinct to protect Mike and Annie, as he is led to the deserted Joyland park and his almost certain death. In this sense, Devin takes on a position similar to that of the slasher film's "Final Girl," a term coined by Carol J. Clover to designate the virtuous survivor who perseveres in the face of the killer's violent rampage, usually surviving through a combination of quick thinking and moral goodness.[18] The subversion of Devin's expected role also engages with feminist ethicists' interrogation of "the binary view of gender,"[19] highlighting the complexity of his personal identity and experience. Rebecca Frost uses a framework similar to that of Clover's "Final Girl" to consider the "final victim[s]"[20] in some of King's twenty-first-century serial killer fiction, including the novellas *The Gingerbread Girl* (included in the 2008 collection *Just after Sunset*)[21] and *Big Driver* (included in the 2010 collection *Full Dark, No Stars*). Though Devin is a virtuous and intelligent young man—fulfilling some of the key requirements of an effective detective—he is unable to orchestrate an escape and is bantering to buy time, unfolding his solving of the mystery to his captor, and contemplating the seeming inevitability of his own impending death when Annie comes to his rescue. When Annie shouts at Devin to duck, he recalls, "I didn't think about it, I just did it. There was a whipcrack report, an almost liquid sound against the blowing night."[22] Devin is rescued, and Annie, one of his two *femme fiables*, is the hero, a formidable figure "standing on the ramp with a rifle in her hands,"[23] in a vision that like Devin's representation challenges and transcends expectations of the traditional gender binary. While Devin embodies many of the traits of the traditional detective, including an unwavering moral compass, there is a good chance he would not have solved the mystery without Erin's dedication to research or survived this final confrontation without Annie's intercession.

In another deviation from the traditional mystery genre narrative pattern that signals *Joyland*'s genre hybridity, in this case with horror, Devin also likely would not have survived his ordeal without supernatural intervention. There are two significant ghosts in *Joyland*, and, though Devin desperately wants to see Linda Gray with his own eyes and plays a significant role in the stories of both spirits, he ends up seeing neither of them. Devin's friend Tom Kennedy sees Linda Gray when he, Devin, and Erin ride through the funhouse together, and afterward Tom refuses to go near the funhouse or talk about what he saw. Mike Ross also sees Linda Gray, hearing her warning and watching as her spirit at last crosses over.[24] Just as with his desire to solve the mystery of her murder, Devin's longing to see Linda Gray has philosophical and moral implications, as he works to understand justice, life, death, and what lies beyond. Faced with their own deaths, Tom and Mike interpret their memories of Linda Gray differently: while Tom's voice is "filled with horror"[25] and uncertainty, Mike sees her at peace and is comforted by this encounter. Linda Gray means different things to Tom and Mike, symbolizing the inexplicable and terrifying for the former but offering comfort and peace to the latter. Devin similarly does not see the ghost of Eddie Parks, who appears to Mike to warn the boy of Devin's impending murder and prompts Annie's rescue. While Linda Gray's motivations seem fairly straightforward, Eddie Parks's are more of a mystery, and as Devin wonders, "Did Eddie appear to Mike because I had saved the bad-tempered old geezer's life? ... I doubt it."[26] In the end, Devin comes to the tentative conclusion that Eddie Parks warned Mike because "I'd made the effort. In the end, so had he. For whatever reason."[27] This explanation is far from conclusive, and Eddie Parks's motivations ultimately remain a mystery, but in the end, Devin's goodness seems to once again be his saving grace.

While Devin's morality sees him heroically through his endeavors and the mystery of Linda Gray's murder is solved, *Joyland* does not end happily ever after, and Devin and the reader are drawn back to the questions raised by Davis: those ruminations on evil, the unfairness of the world, and the "never-ending fear embedded in these deeply disturbing fundamental conundrums."[28] Just as solving her murder cannot bring Linda Gray back, nothing can be done to save Mike, who dies not long after their shared adventures at Joyland. Similarly, nothing can stop the aggressive brain tumor

Tom is diagnosed with twenty years later, despite Devin's rumination that "[y]ou want to ask how a thing like that can be fair. Weren't there supposed to be a few more good things for Tom, like a couple of grandchildren and maybe that long-dreamed-of vacation in Maui?"[29] The bottom line, the foundation which underlies both mystery and horror, is that life is not fair. Answers and justice are both few and far between. Telling his story decades later, Devin remembers the young man he was, the mystery he solved, and the questions that still haunt him, even after the ghosts themselves have been laid to rest.

The Colorado Kid

In *Joyland*, Devin tells his own story, but in *The Colorado Kid*, the mystery is pieced together from evidence alone, the narrative constructed through deduction and speculation rather than experience and memory. The bulk of *The Colorado Kid* consists of one long storytelling session, as two aging newsmen, Vince Teague and Dave Bowie, relate the mystery of the eponymous Kid to their intern, Stephanie McCann. The first inkling of the Kid's story, however, is doubly couched in mystery. Vince and Dave have just been talking to a reporter from Boston who has stopped at Moose-Lookit Island, Maine, on a New England tour looking for local legends and mysteries, and while they have trotted out several old tales, the Colorado Kid's was not one of them. This is a story they keep to themselves, making it an untold story as well as an unsolved mystery.

The story of the Colorado Kid begins in a traditional mystery fashion. Angelina Stanford notes that within the genre, "Each story begins in chaos, a dead body, and the entire story moves toward justice and the restoration of order."[30] On a spring morning in 1980, this is just what happens: a mysterious body appears on the beach, an unknown dead man with no identification. While *Joyland*'s Devin is an Everyman detective, Vince and Dave are investigators of a different kind: reporters who are hunting leads and finding stories. In the end, however, this amateur detection is once again what yields the most rewarding evidence. The official detectives sent out to investigate consider the case open and shut with no interest in collecting evidence or digging further once the medical examiner informs them that the man choked on a piece of meat. However, who the man is, where he came from, and what he is doing there remain a mystery, and it is the two newsmen, the medical examiner, and a college student job-shadowing the detectives who continue asking questions and eventually find some answers. Stephanie serves as the reader's proxy throughout *The Colorado Kid*, asking the questions the reader would ask, positing a number of theories, and following along with the mystery in the hope of resolution. Like *Joyland*'s

Erin Cook, Stephanie occupies the inquisitive and resourceful role of the *femme fiable*. Stephanie also highlights the intersection of feminist ethics and narrative ethics, in which "narrative ethicists take the practices of storytelling, listening, and bearing empathetic, careful witness to these stories to be central to understanding and evaluating not just the unique circumstances of particular lives, but the wider moral contexts within which we all exist."[31] Stephanie hears and honors the story of the Colorado Kid, though in doing so, she is also developing and demarcating her understanding of morality, truth, and a duty of care in the wider world, which carries over to the reader's understanding of the story Vince and Dave share. In this position, Michael Perry explains:

> Stephanie becomes, at once, the protagonist of one storyline and the audience for the other, thus inviting an immersive experience for King's actual readers as they at once find themselves identifying with Stephanie as the focus of the apprenticeship, as well as becoming Stephanie as they sit down for a conversation with the two old newsmen.[32]

The answers Vince, Dave, and the others find are hard-won, coming over a span of years and through loose, largely coincidental connections rather than in a direct or contained narrative progression. There is no method to the madness, and even years later, telling the Kid's tale is a challenge and can be only imperfectly achieved. As Vince tells Stephanie, readers go looking for "a *story*—but then you discover there just *isn't* [one]. That it's only a bunch of unconnected facts surrounding a *true* unexplained mystery. And that, dear, is what folks don't want."[33] While the prospect of a mystery is tantalizing, audiences tend to have little patience with one that has no resolution. There is a genre expectation that all questions will be answered, all riddles will be solved, and when that is not the case, it may make for a compelling mystery, but not a very good mystery *story*.

In the end, the verifiable facts are these: the Kid is James Cogan, an adman from Colorado. He had been at work in Denver until late morning on the day of his disappearance when he walked out the door of his office building for a cup of coffee and was never seen again. He ate fish and chips in Maine early that same evening, though he had no connections to Maine and it was impossible for him to get there that quickly without taking an expensive private plane, for which there was no flight record or financial proof. He had his wallet when he paid for his dinner, but not when he was found on the beach. He had lost his own overcoat and suit jacket but acquired a green coat somewhere along the way. He had a Russian coin in his pocket and a pack of Colorado-stamped cigarettes, but he did not smoke. With resolution seeming increasingly unlikely, Vince and Dave consider the mystery from another angle and reframe their engagement with it. When they are unable to achieve moral equilibrium through restoring order and solving the mystery of the Kid's death, they instead turn their attention to doing right by the dead man himself, finding out who he is and letting his family know what happened to him, even though they have no explanations to offer of why or how. They find Cogan's wife, and while there are no additional clues or answers to be had, the fact that she gains some closure and can begin to grieve—as well as put her long-running dispute with the insurance company to rest—is a moral victory in and of itself. They keep tracking the mystery, through the years and more than halfway across the country, not because they expect resolution, but because it is the right thing to do.

There is a similar moral imperative at work in when, how, and to whom Vince and Dave tell the Kid's story. They do not tell it to the reporter from the Boston *Globe*, but they do tell it to Stephanie, and in doing so, they tell it well, maintaining each facet of the mystery and every unanswered question, emphasizing the process of unfolding the narrative rather than the narrative itself. In considering the nature of the genre, Stanford argues that the crime that precipitates a mystery story disrupts the community, and "[w]hen the mystery is unraveled and the bad guy is caught, order is restored. ... But more importantly, with the removal of the criminal and the threat to the community, the *community* is restored."[34] The exact opposite is true for Moose-Lookit Island and the Colorado Kid. Here it is not the resolution but the mystery itself that belongs to the community. When Stephanie asks Vince and Dave why they kept the story from the *Globe* reporter, Vince tells her, "We didn't tell him about the Colorado Kid because he would have taken a true unexplained mystery and made it into just another feature story,"[35] imposing a narrative structure where there is not one, selectively highlighting or eliminating elements of the mystery to package it as a consumable, containable story. These newsmen follow a moral imperative to protect their mystery and the man at its center, who has posthumously become a part of their community and the island's story. Sharing this story with Stephanie serves a distinct purpose and one that—like the traditional solving of the mystery—highlights identification of and inclusion within a community. Stephanie has come to the island for an internship but has fallen in love with Moose-Lookit and has decided to stay if they will have her. While Vince and Dave have drawn clear demarcations between islanders and outsiders, in telling the Kid's story, they are identifying and welcoming Stephanie as one of them, passing the mystery on to her to carry forward and protect. Through this storytelling process, King subverts traditional genre expectations, as how the mystery is told and who gets to hear it are much more significant than its solution, while also underscoring King's genre hybridity in the combination of mystery and the coming-of-age narrative, as Stephanie works to find her place in the world and a way to tell her own stories.

The Colorado Kid is not a traditional mystery, and it refuses the narrative closure that the genre almost invariably offers. Instead, it is a mystery about the nature of mystery itself. Much like the series of events its characters recount, *The Colorado Kid* is a story that is not quite a story, one that refutes the expectation of narrative form and function. As Grady Hendrix notes, "Fiction requires motives, drama, resolutions, and compelling endings, all tendencies that real life resists."[36] Given this reality, the unanswered questions and the unsolved mystery are likely more plausible and authentic than the tidy resolution of the traditional mystery, in which the detective lays out their series of deductions, answers all questions, and achieves complete and satisfying narrative closure. King reflects on this expectation and readers' anticipated dissatisfaction in his afterword to *The Colorado Kid*, writing, "Mystery is my subject here, and I am aware that many readers will feel cheated, even angry, by my failure to provide a solution to the one posed."[37] However, the truth arguably lies within the mystery itself. As King continues:

> I ask you to consider the fact that we live in a *web* of mystery, and have simply gotten so used to the fact that we have crossed out the word and replaced it with one we like better, that one being *reality*. Where do we come from? Where were we before we were here? Don't know. Where are we going? Don't know. …
>
> [W]hat I found out writing *The Colorado Kid* was that maybe—I just say *maybe*—it's the beauty of the mystery that allows us to live sane as we pilot our fragile bodies through this demolition-derby world.[38]

But the fact that the abiding mystery is more realistic or existentially authentic than a neatly resolved narrative does not mean that mystery readers will be satisfied with such an ending. Stanford notes that "writers and publishers of detective fiction know how important this resolution is. They know that audiences require it … the pattern is written on our hearts and we need it to be played out."[39] This traditional resolution restores order and reinforces the expectations of the moral imagination: good will triumphs, the bad guys will be held accountable, and all questions will be answered.

There is no such resolution in *The Colorado Kid*, and there is not even any real certainty that a "bad guy" exists, whether the Kid traveled to Maine of his own free will (and inexplicable impulse) or was brought there by someone else, whether he traveled through some untraceable means of private transportation or simply slipped through a fissure in the fabric of the universe, like one of the "thinnys" that punctuate King's larger body of fiction from *The Talisman* (1984, coauthored with Peter Straub) to the *Dark Tower* series[40] and beyond. In addition to the permeable passage between worlds that the Dark Tower universe paradigm offers, the complicated negotiation of mystery and questions better left unanswered are essential in that series' conclusion as well, where in the final pages, before King reveals Roland's purgatorial fate, he offers a neatly resolved conclusion, writing "my dear Constant Reader, I tell you this: You can stop here. … And pretty close to happily ever after, too."⁴¹ But just as readers clamored for a solution to the Colorado Kid's abiding mystery, King knows his readers want to know what Roland sees, where he goes, and what he finds in the Dark Tower. King tries once more, saying, "Should you go on, you will surely be disappointed, perhaps even heartbroken. ... There is no such thing as a happy ending. I never met a single one equal to 'Once upon a time.'"⁴² Readers will not be satisfied by what Roland finds within the Dark Tower, by the narrative and the quest that fold back on themselves, beginning again with no end in sight. However, the desire to know how it all ends, to at last achieve narrative resolution, is too tempting, and the reader must read on, only to be plunged once more into mystery and a distinct denial of closure, just as Vince and Dave are compelled to trace the Colorado Kid's story as far as they can. In the end, however, questions vastly outnumber the answers, and like Roland's eventual fate, the mystery of the Colorado Kid will likely never be solved.

Later

While *Joyland* and *The Colorado Kid* both have elements of horror and supernatural, with their ghosts and unsolvable mysteries, genre hybridity is particularly pronounced in *Later*, with horror and mystery evenly balanced. As the protagonist Jamie Conklin reminds readers several times throughout the novel, "this is a horror story."⁴³ Jamie sees dead people and while most of them are relatively benign, lingering around for just a few days and posing little threat to Jamie, others are more distressing, carrying the marks of the physical violence they have endured or, very occasionally, aggressively interacting with him.

Devin and Stephanie are unconventional detectives, drawn in by the mysteries they encounter and the stories they find, but Jamie has no interest in being a detective at all. However, he sees things that other people cannot see and, as a result, is able to find information and answer questions that would otherwise remain mysteries. For example, when six-year-old Jamie's neighbor Mona Burkett dies unexpectedly, her husband is unable to find her engagement and wedding rings, though when Jamie asks her, she freely tells him that the rings are on the "[t]op shelf of the hall closet. ... Way in the back, behind the scrapbooks."⁴⁴ Jamie does not want to be a detective, but as the only person who is able to ask the question and get the answer, he feels a moral responsibility to find a way to share this information and put Martin Burkett's mind at ease. In another instance, Jamie sees a young dead boy crying because he cannot find his way home and walks him to his apartment so that the boy can be back where he belongs in his final moments before drifting away, free of the disorientation and fear of being lost.⁴⁵ While in these cases, Jamie acts as the reluctant detective out of sympathy for his neighbor and the murdered young boy, others' realization of Jamie's ability leads to his exploitation, forcing him into situations that are opportunistic, unsettling, and even dangerous.

Jamie worships his mother, Tia, but when the best-selling author she edits for dies unexpectedly, she uses her son as a conduit to get Regis Thomas's last book out of him, with Thomas dictating the novel's outline to Jamie, who in turn recites it for his mother, saving her publishing company and their small family from financial ruin. A few years later, Jamie's mother's former girlfriend and dirty cop, Liz Dutton, kidnaps Jamie when a serial bomber named Kenneth Therriault commits suicide, coercing Jamie to ask the dead man where his last bomb has been set in an attempt to save her own job and professional reputation. The damage to Therriault's body is horrifying and traumatic, including the exit wound of his self-inflicted gunshot, which "was almost as big as a dessert plate and surrounded by irregular fangs of bone."[46] While Jamie has seen dead people with traumatic injuries before, this is the first time he has been forced into such an interaction, against his will and with no consideration for his own thoughts, feelings, or ability to cope with such trauma. Liz's interest is self-serving and transactional, with Jamie strong-armed into the role of solving this mystery. While he understands the moral value of answering this question—finding Therriault's final bomb will save an inestimable number of lives—and actually gets some satisfaction in doing so as a result, this does not change the fact that Liz is abusing and exploiting Jamie for her own personal gain. While there are supernatural horrors in *Later*, including the restless dead Jamie encounters and a stronger monstrous entity that he faces later on, these supernatural horrors and the mysteries within which they are couched are compounded by everyday human evils as well, like Liz forcing Jamie into this detective role against his will. As Charles Yu writes, in *Later* "[t]here are hints of evil from another dimension. ... But mostly the horrors are familiar ones. Plain old human cruelty. The loss of loved ones to disease or old age. Alzheimer's. Also, less morbid though no less heavy: the loss of innocence. Growing up too fast. The unexplainable, the incomprehensible in our everyday lives."[47] This combination of horrors—the supernatural and the human—complicates Jamie's understanding and negotiation of his own experiences while also underscoring *Later*'s genre hybridity in its complex combination of mystery, horror, and coming of age.

Jamie's perspective is also unique and overtly foregrounded in *Later*. Jamie's narration bears some similarities to Devin's in *Joyland*, taking the position of a man looking back on days and experiences that have long since passed. However, while Devin is nearing middle age and looking back on the misadventures of his early twenties, Jamie is twenty-two, telling the reader about the experiences of his childhood self. Jamie's earliest recollections in the narrative took place when he was six years old, with additional moments recounted from his teen years as "the narrative shuttles between the immediacy of now and the hindsight of 'later' to tell a kind of coming-of-age-as-mystery story, an exploration of innocence and what's on the other side of childhood."[48] This perspective is central to both the style and narrative of *Later*, with Rob Merrill arguing that King "gets kids. Their fears, certainly, but also their voices, the way they see the world differently from adults."[49] As a result of this invested perspective and the complex negotiation of the hindsight Jamie possesses as an adult narrator, *Later* is narratively complex, highlighting Jamie's immediate experiences and first impressions at a range of ages from six to fifteen, in addition to his present-day self. In some ways, young Jamie's negotiations of the mysteries he encounters, from Mona Burkett's missing rings to Kenneth Therriault's final bomb and beyond, are mysteries of himself as well, as Jamie starts to gain an understanding of what he can do, who he can trust, and who he is, gaining confidence and self-awareness as he goes.

Jamie's understanding of his encounters with the dead and specifically with Therriault is also fundamentally grounded in the larger horror genre in general and King's body of work specifically. When Jamie challenges Therriault, the dead bomber becomes something more, possessed by an entity that is darker and more powerful when "something awful came into him and took him over."[50] While Jamie's ability to see and interact with the dead echoes that of young Danny Torrance in King's *The Shining* (1977), the power that possesses what remains of Therriault is aligned with King's *IT* (1986), a "deadlight" of inestimable destructive and supernatural force.[51] In further keeping with King's *IT*, Jamie's former neighbor Martin Burkett instructs the young man that the only way to best this power is through the Ritual of Chüd. As Burkett explains this ritual to Jamie:

> According to the stories, you and the demon bind yourselves together by biting into each other's tongues. ... Once this union has been accomplished, you and the demon have a battle of wills. This would occur telepathically, I assume, since it would be hard to talk while engaged in a ... mmm ... mutual tongue-bite. The first to withdraw loses all power over the winner.[52]

This echoes Bill Denbrough's showdown with IT in King's novel, though in Jamie's case this confrontation is a bit less metaphysical, as he embraces and battles the being trapped in Therriault's incorporeal body in the entryway of his apartment building. While time and space become diffuse and unfixed, Jamie is able to anchor himself within his own reality, rather than being cast out into the cosmos like Bill Denbrough, and Jamie claims victory. Jamie's final negotiation with the being that inhabited Therriault is grounded in earlier horror traditions as well, with Jamie telling this being "Now I'll haunt *you*. ... Oh, I'll whistle and you'll come to me, my lad."[53] This command is an echo of M.R. James's classic ghost story "Oh, Whistle, and I'll Come to You,

My Lad" (1904), in which an ancient whistle summons a terrifying specter. The touchstone of James's story further emphasizes the genre hybridity of *Later* in its combination of mystery and horror while the connections with King's larger body of work echo *The Colorado Kid*'s potential *Dark Tower* series connections, underscoring the ways in which King's fictions all take place within one expansive and interconnected universe.

At the intersections of mystery and the supernatural, Jamie's realization is that some mysteries really are not worth solving, while others may be solved only to leave just as many new, unanswered questions. Some of the mysteries he encounters have significant consequences of both large and small scales, including the lives that are saved by finding Therriault's last bomb and the satisfaction Jamie is able to give Burkett in finding his wife's rings. These mysteries carry great moral implications, and Jamie is confident that helping to solve these mysteries is the right thing to do. But there are other mysteries that are not worth risking one's safety, sanity, or soul to solve. These mysteries are morally bankrupt, undertaken by those who exploit Jamie not because solving this mystery is the right thing to do but because there is something they want, something they stand to gain from the mystery's resolution. The clearest example of this kind of morally reprehensible "detective work" is when Liz again kidnaps fifteen-year-old Jamie to help her find Donald Marsden's drug stash. Motivated by a combination of desperation, greed, and a need to get a fix herself, Liz takes Jamie to Marsden's house, where the horrors transcend the recently deceased with which Jamie is familiar and, to some degree, even comfortable. Instead of the usual disembodied spirit, Jamie encounters a living man who has been bound, gagged, and tortured, and who is then murdered right in front of him. Liz's demand that Jamie ask Marsden where the drugs are is morally compromised, and she kills Marsden for her own self-serving reasons: she wants the drugs for her own use and to sell. Marsden turns out not to have drugs of any significant weight or quantity in his house, leaving Liz enraged and empty-handed, while Jamie is drawn further into the moral degradation presented by both Liz and Marsden when he finds photographs of Marsden torturing and murdering his former wife, who had disappeared five years earlier.[54] This is one more mystery solved, but its resolution is neither comforting nor morally edifying. Liz, who at one point in her pre-addict life was a successful NYPD detective, takes a morally compromised approach to solving the mysteries that thwart her, with no regard for how seeing a man murdered or being exposed to drugs and violence might affect Jamie. In this instance, detection is a wholly traumatic experience for Jamie.

This also proves true in Jamie's attempt to understand himself and his strange abilities as he delves into his own personal mysteries. Jamie's mother, Tia, raised him alone, and his father has never been a part of his life. The only quasi-fatherly figure in his life is his Uncle Harry, a relationship which is compromised by Harry's early-onset Alzheimer's. Jamie's special gift offers him an opportunity to talk to his uncle that he would not otherwise have had, since after Harry's passing, Harry is both free of Alzheimer's and unable to lie. But when Jamie asks Uncle Harry who his father is, Harry responds with "I am,"[55] revealing that Jamie is the product of an incestuous union between his mother and her brother. In the shock of this realization, Jamie turns back to overt narrative construction, working to craft a story that will solve the mystery of himself and reconcile this new truth. He runs through multiple scenarios in his head, ranging from drunken comfort to rape, but in the end, he concludes, "That whole story is fiction."[56] The same is true of Jamie's attempt to figure out why he has his unique ability, a mystery that also remains impossible to solve. Whether in the mysteries he faces—willingly or not—with the recently deceased or the mysteries he tries to solve within himself, Jamie discovers that there are no easy answers and some mysteries are better left unsolved.

Ambiguity and the Moral Landscape of King's Hard Case Crime Novels

With *Joyland*, *The Colorado Kid*, and *Later*, King negotiates and subverts the traditional expectations of the mystery genre, reflecting just as much on the nature of mystery itself and the role of narrative construction as on the mysteries at the heart of each novel. In all three cases, readers are offered a story (or stories) within a story, including overt consideration of how we remember the past, how this storytelling works to make sense of the inexplicable, what stories we tell, and to whom we tell them. *Joyland* is Devin's story, but it is also Linda Gray's and Mike Ross's. *The Colorado Kid* is James Cogan's story, but it has also become Vince and Dave's, and is now Stephanie's as well. *Later* is the story of Jamie's childhood self, with its telling balancing the immediacy of his youthful experiences with the awareness and reflection of his adult perspective. Additionally, the detectives in these stories are not detectives at all in the professional sense, bringing the act of investigation into the realm of the everyday and inviting the reader to vicariously participate in the mystery story in a way that is distinct from the traditional reader engagement of following along with the detective as an expert. Finally, each of these novels leaves readers with unanswered questions to greater or lesser degrees: in *Joyland*, the restored moral order proves fleeting and illusory as the fundamental unfairness of reality reasserts itself, and in *The Colorado Kid*, order and resolution prove wholly unattainable, while *Later* leaves Jamie and the reader with unsatisfying answers and no clear sense of Jamie's ability, its continuation, or its impact on his adult life.

King's Hard Case Crime novels reinforce the ambiguity and uncertainty that the mystery genre frequently works to resolve, with King reveling in both the uncertainties of life itself and the possibility of unsolvable mysteries.

But as King posits in his afterword to *The Colorado Kid*, those mysteries themselves are the truth at the center of human existence. The unpredictable and uncontrollable nature of reality is certainly a significant part of why reading detective fiction is so enjoyable and cathartic, allowing readers to impose order and resolution in the face of disorder and ambiguity if only for a few moments in the mystery novel's final pages. While King writes mysteries, he also writes horror, in which the inverse is true: the inexplicable and terrifying are integral parts of the everyday, a foundational reality of the human condition. Whatever genre designation readers and critics may attach to King, whether as an author in general or in describing a specific work, his greatest skill lies in "his power to speak to us emotionally and imaginatively,"[57] which transcends genre, categorization, or narrative formula.

So where do *The Colorado Kid*, *Joyland*, and *Later* leave us as we survey the moral landscape of King's Hard Case Crime novels? In the moral philosophy of these novels, we cannot rely on answers, conventional justice, or life to treat us fairly. We can, however, rely upon one another. Devin, Vince, Dave, Stephanie, and Jamie keep asking questions and watching out for those they love. Devin saves a young girl and an old man; he refuses to let Linda Gray's murder go unsolved or the girl herself be forgotten, and he does everything he can to make a dying boy's greatest wish come true. Similarly, Vince and Dave work to solve the mystery of the Colorado Kid, to give Cogan's wife closure (if not answers), protect Cogan's memory and story from those who would not do it justice, and freely and generously share their lives, stories, and expertise with a young woman who will soon take on this story-keeping mantle herself. Jamie faces horrors beyond his comprehension and finds himself abused and exploited because of his ability, but in the end, his trust in and love for his mother are absolute, the foundation on which he builds his life amidst uncertainty and fear. The world may be cold and unforgiving, the bad guys might not always be brought to justice, and questions may even go eternally unanswered, but in caring for one another, there is a sense of order, safety, and reassurance in spite of it all, and in this way, King's mysteries are not too far afield from the emotional truth of his horror. In *The Colorado Kid*, *Joyland*, and *Later*, the mysteries matter. But in the end, solving the mystery matters less than who these unconventional detectives work alongside in the attempt and the moral imperative that drives them, with relationships transcending resolution.

Notes

1   J. Madison Davis, "Thoughts on a New Grandmaster," *World Literature Today* 81, no. 3 (May 2007): 16.

2   "Stephen King," in *Critical Survey of Mystery and Detective Fiction*, ed. E. Rollyson, revised edition (Amenia, NY: Salem Press, 2008), 1041.

3 Arthur Conan Doyle, "The Sign of the Four." In *The Complete Sherlock Holmes* (New York: Barnes & Noble, 1992), 111.
4 Nick Kolakowski, "The Uneasy Noirs of Stephen King," *Crime Reads* (June 22, 2020), crimereads.com/the-uneasy-noirs-of-stephen-king/, para. 9-10. Accessed October 29, 2021.
5 This theme is furthered in King's *The Outsider* (2018), a continuation that includes several key characters from the *Bill Hodges* trilogy.
6 Davis, "Thoughts," 19.
7 "Hard Case Crime," *Winterfall*, 2004–2023, http://www.hardcasecrime.com/, para. 1. Accessed March 9, 2023.
8 Just as the novels themselves engage with and subvert genre expectations, the cover art for each novel also requires complex negotiation. The cover of *The Colorado Kid* by artist Glen Orbik features a sultry woman in a low-cut dress with a recorder in one hand and the "come hither" expression of the traditional noir *femme fatale*, but "there's no one like her in the story" (Carol Memmott, "King's 'Colorado Kid': You Decide," *USA Today*, October 5, 2005, www.usatoday.com/story/life/books/2013/06/28/kings-colorado-kid-you-decide/2467563/, para. 11. Accessed November 1, 2021). Stephanie—the novel's central female protagonist—is significantly more down-to-earth, and her relationship with mentors Vince Teague and Dave Bowie is one of comfortable camaraderie rather than smoldering sexual tension. Similarly, the cover tagline of "Would she learn the dead man's secret?" is answered with a resounding no, once again subverting mystery and crime novel expectations. The cover of *Joyland* features another painting by Orbik, this one of a startled, open-mouthed beauty in a sexy green dress, one of Joyland's Hollywood Girls matching the narrative description of Devin's friend Erin Cook, though Erin and her fellow Hollywood Girls are never targeted by the park's dangers or hauntings. The cover tagline of "Who dares to enter the funhouse of fear?" is also sensational but a bit misleading since, while Linda Gray's ghost haunts the House of Horror, the funhouse itself is peripheral to the larger story. Devin enters it only twice (once with his friends and once on his own with the lights on to perform post-season maintenance), and the only one who sees Linda Gray's ghost within the funhouse is Devin's friend Tom Kennedy, an encounter which remains similarly tangential to the novel's larger mystery. Finally, the cover of *Later* is painted by Paul Mann, featuring a bombshell in stilettos and a low-cut blouse lounging against a car as an uncertain kid looks on, set against a smoldering orange background. This is again a sensational representation of the narrative within, blurring the lines between past and present to provide readers with a high-impact image. While Liz Dutton's beauty is remarked upon in earlier sections of the novel, by the time she kidnaps Jamie, she is addicted to drugs, has been fired from the police force, and has lost much of her prior glamour and sexiness. The tagline of "Only the dead have no secrets" is an accurate nod to one of the novel's main themes, as Jamie discovers that when he asks the recently deceased a question, they cannot lie to him; this tagline also more subtly underscores the various secrets the novel's living characters keep from one another. All three covers are gorgeous and executed in exquisite pulp art style,

but they definitely play on the expectations and subversion of the novels within. Alternate covers of later editions of these novels provide additional opportunities for visual and genre analysis.

9   Sandrine Berges, "The Hardboiled Detective as Moralist: Ethics in Crime Fiction." In *Values and Virtues: Aristotelianism in Contemporary Ethics* (Mind Association Occasional Series), ed. Timothy Chappell (Oxford: Oxford University Press, 2006), 217.
10 Rachel Haliburton, *The Ethical Detective: Moral Philosophy and Detective Fiction* (Lanham: Lexington Books, 2018), 123.
11 Ibid., 126.
12 Stephen King, *Joyland* (New York: Hard Case Crime, 2013), 112.
13 Keli Masten, "*Cherchez la Femme*: A Good Woman's Place in Hard-Boiled Detective Fiction," *Clues: A Journal of Detection* 36, no. 2 (Fall 2018): 32.
14 Kathryn Norlock, "Feminist Ethics," *Stanford Encyclopedia of Philosophy*, May 27, 2019, https://plato.stanford.edu/entries/feminism-ethics/, para. 29. Accessed November 14, 2022.
15 Anna Gotlib, "Feminist Ethics and Narrative Ethics," *Internet Encyclopedia of Philosophy*, https://iep.utm.edu/fem-e-n/, para. 4. Accessed November 14, 2022.
16 Masten, "*Cherchez la Femme*," 35.
17 King, *Joyland*, 63.
18 Carol J. Clover, *Men, Women, and Chain Saws: Gender in the Modern Horror Film* (Princeton: Princeton University Press, 1992), 35–41.
19 Norlock, "Feminist Ethics," para. 1.
20 Rebecca Frost, "A Different Breed: Stephen King's Serial Killers." In *Stephen King's Contemporary Classics: Reflections on the Modern Master of Horror* (Contemporary American Literature Series), ed. Philip L. Simpson and Patrick McAleer (Lanham: Rowman & Littlefield, 2014), 122.
21 *The Gingerbread Girl* was originally published in *Esquire* magazine in July 2007.
22 King, *Joyland*, 267.
23 Ibid.
24 Ibid., 239–40.
25 Ibid., 121.
26 Ibid., 278.
27 Ibid.
28 Davis, "Thoughts," 19.
29 King, *Joyland*, 85.
30 Angelina Stanford, "The Moral Universe of the Detective Novel," *CiRCE Institute*, August 13, 2016, https://circeinstitute.org/blog/blog-moral-universe-detective-novel/, para. 8. Accessed October 29, 2021.

31 Gotlib, "Feminist Ethics," para. 1.
32 Michael Perry, "Storytelling and a Story Told: Stephen King's Narrators in *From a Buick 8, The Colorado Kid*, and *Blaze*." *The Modern Stephen King Canon: Beyond Horror*, ed. Philip L. Simpson and Patrick McAleer (Lanham: Lexington Books, 2018), 26.
33 Stephen King, *The Colorado Kid* (New York: Hard Case Crime, 2005), 65.
34 Stanford, "The Moral Universe," para. 12. Emphasis added.
35 King, *The Colorado Kid*, 175.
36 Grady Hendrix, "The Great Stephen King Reread: *The Colorado Kid*," *Tor* (July 19, 2017), www.tor.com/2017/07/19/the-great-stephen-king-reread-the-colorado-kid/, para. 10. Accessed October 29, 2021.
37 King, *The Colorado Kid*, 182.
38 Ibid., 183–4.
39 Stanford, "The Moral Universe," para. 16.
40 King's *Dark Tower* series consists of eight books. *The Gunslinger* (limited edition 1982; expanded and revised 2003), *The Drawing of the Three* (1987), *The Waste Lands* (1991), *Wizard and Glass* (1997), *Wolves of the Calla* (2003), *Song of Susannah* (2004), and *The Dark Tower* (2004) comprise the original series, followed by an additional *Dark Tower* novel, *The Wind through the Keyhole* (2012), the action of which takes place between *Wizard and Glass* and *Wolves of the Calla*. The *Dark Tower* series features countless connections between worlds and realities as well as the possibility of passing between them, which is emphasized in the *Dark Tower* series' interconnections with King's larger body of work, including *'Salem's Lot*, *The Stand* (1978; revised and expanded 1990), *The Eyes of the Dragon* (1986), *Insomnia* (1994), *Desperation* (1996), *The Regulators* (1996, As Richard Bachman), *Hearts in Atlantis* (1999), and the two novels King coauthored with Peter Straub, *The Talisman* and *Black House* (2001). Within this metaverse, different realities are frequently described as taking place on different levels of the Tower. The mention of Cogan going to grab a Starbucks coffee in Denver in 1980 when the coffee chain did not have a franchise there until 1992 (Memmott, "King's 'Colorado Kid,'" para. 10) has led some readers and critics to speculate that *The Colorado Kid* may have some potential *Dark Tower* series connections (Bev Vincent, *The Dark Tower Companion: A Guide to Stephen King's Epic Fantasy* [New York: New American Library, 2013], 103). For further analysis of King's *Dark Tower* series, see my book *The Quest for the Dark Tower: Genre and Interconnection in the Stephen King Series* (Jefferson, NC: McFarland, 2021).
41 Stephen King, *The Dark Tower* (Hampton Falls, NH: Donald M. Grant, 2004), 818.
42 Ibid.
43 Stephen King, *Later* (New York: Hard Case Crime, 2021), 15.
44 Ibid., 22.

45 Ibid., 178.
46 Ibid., 108.
47 Charles Yu, "He Can See Dead People but 'Not Like in That Movie.' (OK, Sort Of)." *New York Times*, March 2, 2021, www.nytimes.com/2021/03/02/books/review/stephen-king-later.html, para. 5. Accessed October 29, 2021.
48 Ibid., para. 2.
49 Rob Merrill, "Review: King's New 'Later' Is Much More Than a Crime Story," *AP News*, March 1, 2021, apnews.com/article/entertainment-stephen-king-book-reviews-4eebf2a8fd0983f4bd212c7996ff469c, para. 1. Accessed October 29, 2021.
50 King, *Later*, 111.
51 Ibid., 159.
52 Ibid., 147.
53 Ibid., 159.
54 Ibid., 203.
55 Ibid., 243.
56 Ibid., 245.
57 Davis, "Thoughts," 19.

Bibliography

Berges, Sandrine. "The Hardboiled Detective as Moralist: Ethics in Crime Fiction." In *Values and Virtues: Aristotelianism in Contemporary Ethics* (Mind Association Occasional Series), edited by Timothy Chappell, 212–25. Oxford: Oxford University Press, 2006.

Clover, Carol J. *Men, Women, and Chain Saws: Gender in the Modern Horror Film*. Princeton: Princeton University Press, 1992.

Davis, J. Madison. "Thoughts on a New Grandmaster." *World Literature Today* 81, no. 3(May 2007): 16–19.

Doyle, Arthur Conan. "The Sign of the Four." In *The Complete Sherlock Holmes*, 87–158. New York: Barnes & Noble, 1992.

Frost, Rebecca. "A Different Breed: Stephen King's Serial Killers." In *Stephen King's Contemporary Classics: Reflections on the Modern Master of Horror* (Contemporary American Literature Series), edited by Philip L. Simpson and Patrick McAleer, 117–32. Lanham: Rowman & Littlefield, 2014.

Gotlib, Anna. "Feminist Ethics and Narrative Ethics." *Internet Encyclopedia of Philosophy*. https://iep.utm.edu/fem-e-n/. Accessed November 14, 2022.

Haliburton, Rachel. *The Ethical Detective: Moral Philosophy and Detective Fiction*. Lanham: Lexington Books, 2018.

"Hard Case Crime." *Winterfall*, 2004–2023. http://www.hardcasecrime.com/. Accessed March 9, 2023.

Hendrix, Grady. "The Great Stephen King Reread: *The Colorado Kid*." *Tor*, July 19, 2017. www.tor.com/2017/07/19/the-great-stephen-king-reread-the-colorado-kid/. Accessed October 29, 2021.
King, Stephen. *The Colorado Kid*. New York: Hard Case Crime, 2005.
King, Stephen. *The Dark Tower*. Hampton Falls, NH: Donald M. Grant, 2004.
King, Stephen. *Joyland*. New York: Hard Case Crime, 2013.
King, Stephen. *Later*. New York: Hard Case Crime, 2021.
Kolakowski, Nick. "The Uneasy Noirs of Stephen King." *Crime Reads*, June 22, 2020. crimereads.com/the-uneasy-noirs-of-stephen-king/. Accessed October 29, 2021.
Masten, Keli. "*Cherchez la Femme*: A Good Woman's Place in Hard-Boiled Detective Fiction." *Clues: A Journal of Detection* 36, no. 2 (Fall 2018): 29–39.
Memmott, Carol. "King's 'Colorado Kid': You Decide." *USA Today*, October 5, 2005. www.usatoday.com/story/life/books/2013/06/28/kings-colorado-kid-you-decide/2467563/. Accessed November 1, 2021.
Merrill, Rob. "Review: King's New 'Later' Is Much More Than a Crime Story." *AP News*, March 1, 2021. apnews.com/article/entertainment-stephen-king-book-reviews-4eebf2a8fd0983f4bd212c7996ff469c. Accessed October 29, 2021.
Norlock, Kathryn. "Feminist Ethics." *Stanford Encyclopedia of Philosophy*, May 27, 2019. https://plato.stanford.edu/entries/feminism-ethics/. Accessed November 14, 2022.
Perry, Michael. "Storytelling and a Story Told: Stephen King's Narrators in *From a Buick 8*, *The Colorado Kid*, and *Blaze*." In *The Modern Stephen King Canon: Beyond Horror*, edited by Philip L. Simpson and Patrick McAleer, 21–32. Lanham: Lexington Books, 2018.
Stanford, Angelina. "The Moral Universe of the Detective Novel." *CiRCE Institute*. August 13, 2016. https://circeinstitute.org/blog/blog-moral-universe-detective-novel/. Accessed October 29, 2021.
"Stephen King." In *Critical Survey of Mystery and Detective Fiction*, edited by Carl E. Rollyson, revised ed., 1041–6. Amenia, NY: Salem Press, 2008.
Vincent, Bev. *The Dark Tower Companion: A Guide to Stephen King's Epic Fantasy*. New York: New American Library, 2013.
Yu, Charles. "He Can See Dead People but 'Not Like in That Movie.' (OK, Sort Of)." *New York Times*, March 2, 2021. www.nytimes.com/2021/03/02/books/review/stephen-king-later.html. Accessed October 29, 2021.

4

"They've already killed him": Moral Ambiguity in *Chronicle of a Death Foretold*

Andrea Tinnemeyer

Published within a year of receiving the Nobel Prize for Literature, Gabriel García Márquez's *Chronicle of a Death Foretold* (1981) seemingly departs from his celebrated style as a magical realist by marking a return to his roots in journalism, a gesture reinforced by his decision to dedicate his prize money to founding a newspaper. García Márquez would go on to declare, "I am basically a journalist. All my life I have been a journalist. My books are the books of journalists, even if it's not so noticeable."[1] And, despite its title as a chronicle, and all that genre requires and restricts, *Chronicle* remains a novel and retains many of the author's tell-tale elements of style and his preoccupation with injustice. At its core, this novel considers an honor killing and its impact on a small community. García-Márquez subverts the conventional mystery associated with a murder plot by setting the novel's events twenty-seven years after the calamity. What remains a mystery, then, are the town's underlying colonialism, its racial tensions between its Spanish and Arab citizens, and the patriarchy's obsession with virginity for its female characters. Central to the Vicario twins' murder of Santiago Nasar is the identity of their sister Angela's lover. Indeed, Angela's ignominious return to her parents' home on her wedding night instigates the novel's events—the final hours of Santiago Nasar and Angela's brothers before their fatal meeting.

García-Márquez's novel opens with the following lines: "On the day they were going to kill him, Santiago Nasar got up at five-thirty in the morning to wait for the boat the bishop was coming on."[2] What follows is a rather belated investigation that mirrors a mystery novel, with its interviews of residents, eyewitnesses, and reconstruction of the fatal day's sequence of events. The identities of the culprits, however, are already determined; the Vicario brothers, briefly imprisoned, have pursued other lives and are no longer exclusively defined by the novel's focal point. Instead, the novel's pursuit of moral authority shifts focus to implicate everyone in the town who knew the murder was imminent (to include members of the Church and the police force) and who did nothing to actively prevent it. *The Chronicle of a Death Foretold* questions the structure of the mystery novel as well as institutions conventionally associated with moral authority to arrive at something altogether new and compelling, a work befitting a former journalist dedicated to social justice.

Solving the Mystery of Genre

Genre constitutes one of *Chronicle*'s most fascinating elements, with the question of structure or form an ongoing mystery. Solving this question of form seems essential to locating any moral quality. If *Chronicle* is a mystery novel, then determining the culprit satisfies its internal moral logic. If it is apocalyptic, as Lois Zamora believes, its morality is universal and widely held; it's the shared fate that we are all doomed to a "death foretold." As Zamora notes, "We hope, despite all evidence, that Santiago's death will be forestalled, perhaps because we recognize in his story the mortal weight of our own individual destiny."[3] If the novel resembles Apollonian or Dionysian tragedy, as John Carson Pettey posits,[4] then the moral element remains a passive and formulaic affair: witnessing Santiago's death reinforces the communal standards and values.

Unlike the shared, uniform values reinforced in witnessing Greek tragedy, Garcia Marquez' characters, residents of Riohacha, do not respond monolithically, either to Santiago's murder or to its cultural justification, honor killing. Prudencia, for example, hinges her marriage to Pablo on his fulfillment of his familial and cultural duty of returning honor to the Vicario family by murdering Santiago. Angela's mother beats her daughter when Bayardo returns her on their wedding night; she seems to gather up the wrath and shame into her cruel treatment of Angela, nearly killing her own flesh and blood. In the moments leading up to Santiago's death, citizens gather in the town square, hoping to witness the heinous act, unwittingly obscuring Cristo Bedoya's attempts to keep a watchful eye over his doomed friend. Those who line up for fictional milk, those who gather in the square, and those who read the novel are all implicated in Santiago's death because we know what is in store for him and we do not intercede. We find ourselves, like the crowds in Riohacha, guilty of sin by omission; we do not actively draw the knife, but we kill Santiago just the same by knowing and not acting to prevent it. The lawyer himself legitimizes this prejudicial practice by declaring the Vicario brothers guilty of "homicide by legitimate defense of honor."[5] As a fictionalization of the real-life crime that took place in Sucre, Colombia, in 1951, the text examines the antiquated cultural practice of honor killing and its concomitant preoccupation with the cult of female virginity. Lastly, considering whether or not *Chronicle* fits within García Márquez's body of magical realism is also a question the reader must decide. Determining which form or forms García Márquez follows provides clues essential to locating authority and morality within its narrative.

The fable, the tale of Santiago Nasar's final day, is separated from the plot, which is how García Márquez presents it to us, in the form of the chronicle. Traditionally, this form, the chronicle, exists outside of morality. Its purpose is to offer a "historical record, esp. in which the facts are narrated without philosophical treatment, or any attempt at literary style."[6] Given this definition, the novel's form deviates from the structure Todorov and others delineate, leaving us as readers to ponder where to locate morality.

Our narrator, intent on chronicling the novel's fatal events, has access to a "report," which has the potential to stand in as a moral document, and references the prior investigation.[7] Our chronicler notes gaps, such as the initial investigator offering a "marginal note" on why Santiago broke from his routine and exited the house from its front rather than back door, that are not "included in the report."[8] Considering the existence of an official report, the Vicario brothers' surrendering themselves and enduring imprisonment for their crime, all actions that were preceded by an investigation, one might question the chronicler's motivation. Additionally, the substantial time lapse between the murder and the chronicle, as much as twenty-seven years, undermines any moral claims the chronicler might boast.

If the conventional detective novel ends morally, with the reassertion of justice through the nabbing of a guilty party, we as readers find ourselves looking toward the conclusion for resolution. García Márquez frustrates that formula on multiple fronts: we never learn the identity of Angela's lover, the Vicario brothers are free, and one of the two enjoys the very civil and religious rite that initiated the novel's events; the wrong man (Santiago Nasar) is dead; and Angela Vicario, the woman whose unruly sexual appetites brought about this novel, finds love with the very man who would have been her husband, Bayardo.

Honor killings reside in the interstices between legal and moral authorities, and García Márquez's novel directly acknowledges what might be two, perhaps mutually exclusive, institutions that determine right and wrong. Santiago Nasar's murder coincides with the bishop's visit and another sacrament, the wedding between Angela Vicario and Bayardo San Ramón, who receives communion on his knees and helps with mass in Latin, and is reported to have golden eyes like the devil.[9] Santiago dresses for the occasion of the bishop's visit not because he is devout, but rather because he enjoyed the pomp of the Church, reminiscent of "the movies."[10] When the Bishop does sail past the village, just as Santiago's mother predicted, the narrator's sister notes that he made the sign of the cross "mechanically... without malice or inspiration."[11] Angela refused to be married by the Bishop because she is morally repulsed by his arbitrary cruelty of killing a rooster just for its comb, a butchery so vastly different from the Vicario brothers' occupation as butchers who name their pigs and use all of the carcass.

When it comes to the actual murder of Santiago, the novel continues to interrogate the Church officials' role. The Vicario brothers turn in themselves, and their weapons, to the local priest, Father Amador, and remain in jail simply for lack of bail. Furthermore, they are "absolved"—a term that carries spiritual weight.[12] Cristo Bedoya, fresh from a frantic search of Santiago Nasar at his home, runs into Father Amador and although this figure seems a God-send, the priest's thoughts are turned to a "frustrated mass," an indictment of the Bishop who didn't design to alight from the boat. Amador responds, indirectly, that he "didn't think he could do anything for Santiago Nasar except save his soul."[13] There's also the incredibly odd repurposing of this local priest: Father Amador must perform the autopsy on Santiago.

As for the local officials, such as the mayor and the like, their position as people rather than as officials works to undermine their authority to intercede, pronounce guilt or innocence, or serve as the arbiters of the novel's moral code. Some of these tautological bubbles, if you will, are shaped by an overreliance on their own perspective to shape reality. Father Carmen Amador didn't believe Santiago was in danger because he "'saw him safe and sound,'" and thus concluded the story "had all been a fib."[14] Santiago's mother, known for her dream interpretations, assures herself that all is well although she's misread his dream. Don Lázaro Aponte, town mayor, "had [his] own real reasons for believing [Santiago] wasn't in any danger anymore."[15] And perhaps that very self-assurance undermines what might have been a timely intervention—he dips into the social club to find out the time of a domino tournament and by the time he reemerges into the public sphere, "the crime had already been committed."[16] Aponte's notion of time, that he can act in his own interests as a private citizen before fulfilling his role as the ultimate civic authority, demonstrates the relative ease in which a moral authority (such as the town mayor) can undermine their very own position.

The significance any particular resident of Riohacha might exercise, intervening and preventing Santiago's murder, becomes a different issue for Grace Gomashie who attributes significance to the characters' names, arguing their similarity to biblical names key to the torment and death of Christ link Santiago to this narrative. If so, then Santiago's death should be cast as a sacrifice necessary for the greater good.[17] For Gomashie, Santiago's name, along with his Arabic surname, proves or solidifies his position as the sacrificial figure who brings or secures peace between the community's Arab and Hispanic citizenry.[18] His class status also makes him a prime candidate for sacrificial killing as Minu Susan Koshy also argues; Santiago's death alleviates some of the communal tension derived from class conflict.[19]

Honor and significant class distinctions compel both the wedding and the subsequent honor killing. Bayardo's arrival, his family's arrival, the use of superlatives to describe the guests' arrival to the wedding, as well as the additional buildings annexed to house their wedding presents—all attest to a material wealth, a surplus that overwhelms and intimidates the local villagers. On a personal note, the San Román family's renown is enough to compel Angela to marry Bayardo, with her own mother declaring, "a family dignified by modest means had no right to disdain that prize of destiny."[20] While it's certainly true that Santiago's class status breeds contemptible behavior (he actively seeks out virgins among the serving class to forcibly deflower), unfortunately the cult of virginity, along with machismo's robust tradition of moral double standards, creates an environment that, if not condoning of, is at least reluctant to openly chastise, the ruinous behaviors it gives rise to. Santiago, along with the narrator and other patrons of María Alejandrina Cervantes, the town's madam, exists in a moral grey area buttressed by patriarchy's infamous double standard.

Just as we as readers might dwell upon this particular topic, however, the narrator diverts our attention, returning to the data that chronicles amass: the wedding cost. Cristo Bedoya obtains figures at his grandparents' house, numbers that helped him calculate the party's cost. Along with the contraband alcohol and the forty "sacrificed turkeys," Cristobal's tallying invites readers to entertain the wedding party's role in Santiago's murder, perhaps even to account for his sacrificial death in the grand total. If turkeys can be sacrificed, as Gomashie argues that Santiago has been, then the direct link to Christ seems more distanced, if for no other reason than through irony. The Vicario Brothers, butchers, use the instruments of their trade in the honor killing. Butchery, sacrificial people and animals, all speak to the strained, subjective logic of morality among the villagers of Riohacha. The villagers absolve the Vicario brothers for killing the very pigs they raise, and give names to, by mentioning the significant caveat that their pigs retain the names of plants, not humans.

If Santiago's death does not signify as a sacrifice parallel to Christ's, then, as John Carson Pettey suggests, it references the classic tragedies, namely Sophocles' *Oedipus Rex* and Euripedes' *The Bacchae*. In and among the similar traits are the public's foreknowledge of the ending, ecstatic moments, and, above all else, fate's powerful role. Absent is the catharsis vital to Greek tragedies: the moment when the unfolding of events allows both the protagonist and the public to experience the purging of those emotions that have built up over the narrative's course. Santiago dies "without understanding his death."[21] The narrator offers a rare declaration of his own, proclaiming, on the heels of a description of Santiago's "bewilderment of innocence," that he expired unaware of the circumstances of his own demise.[22] Perhaps the chronicle serves this purpose: to offer meaning, context, and all the details a chronicle can marshal in the service of understanding. And yet, as critics have pointed out, the preponderance of evidence does nothing but offer accumulation. There's no distillation, no detail so crucial that it shifts or reframes what has happened already.

Denied a catharsis, Santiago, the villagers, and the reader alike must wrestle with the guilt that accumulates and never dissipates. García Márquez implicates us again and again in the text, with the reference to Riohacha as a "panopticon," an architectural term derived from Jeremy Bentham's blueprints for an eighteenth-century prison. Centered around a guard tower outfitted with Venetian blinds, Bentham's panopticon lives up to its name by providing the guard occupying the tower complete visibility into the prisoners' cells while denying the return of the gaze. Prisoners never know if a guard occupies the tower and so must always conjure him in their minds, internalizing the surveillance that may or may not be occurring externally. News of Santiago's murder, including the names of his murderers, functions like that guard tower, with knowledge, "omniscience," standing in for sight. If we occupy that position like the guard in Bentham's tower, surely we must feel a moral compunction to act, to intercede. And, returning to the Greek tragedy's important function of purging emotion, the "panopticon of Riohacha" may well draw us into the psychological self-policing Foucault famously investigated in *Discipline and Punish*. When that surveillance turns inward, and characters and readers alike engage in self-policing, the moral consequences of the novel are heightened.[23] Among the characters who model the kind of moral compunction we as readers experience is our chronicler, who operates less out of a duty to his village and its residents and more as a person who is conscientiously piecing together the "broken mirror of memory," not unlike his claim to recovering the majority of the pages from the magistrate's report.[24] Accountability is less to an individual like Santiago and more to a larger history, something comprehensive.

Narrator's mother, Luisa Santiaga, godmother to Santiago, is halted on her way to the Nasar home by news from the crowd that "they've already killed him."[25] She exists in a different moral plane than do other characters because she acts immediately on the premonition of his death, dresses herself accordingly, and "walk[s] with the determination she was capable of when a life was at stake."[26] García Márquez places us for a brief moment alongside the only character who seems actively invested, and yet, when we read further, we realize her purpose was to warn Santiago's mother, Plácida, not to intervene directly.

García Márquez transports us into the immediacy of the wedding and its festivities, and he does so even as we find ourselves carried by the hand by a mother who isn't quite aware she has a child in tow. As we dash along down the street, we are abruptly cut short in our narrative track and its pace when the crowd announces the futility of our haste: Santiago Nasar is already dead. Pedro and Pablo Vicario, Santiago's murderers, like the reader, are caught within a loop. We readers are likewise trapped as the narrative ends where it begins: in the kitchen with a fatally wounded Santiago declaring his own death as the narrator has on its opening page. Similarly, Pedro and Pablo publicly proclaim their intentions, announcing "we're going to kill Santiago Nasar," and privately reserve the motive, "Santiago Nasar knows why."[27] The two sentences, following closely on the heels of one another, create a macabre, circuitous dance. One thinks of the linguistic play: por qué and porque. Santiago Nasar is the why and the because. And, as García Márquez offers us with the title, his death is overdetermined, foretold. One would think the brothers, intent on honor killing, would maintain the most agency in this novel of predetermination and yet they themselves confess to one another, "There's no way out of this. It's as if it had already happened."[28] The past and present warp, merge when fate takes over, and the Vicario brothers, despite some small stumbles in fulfilling this destiny (having to replace the knives, falling asleep, missing the light signaling Santiago's return home), imagine looking backwards, having already performed the murderous deed.

Furthermore, Santiago's death echoes on, the reverberating death knell that doesn't cease. For the Vicario brothers, falling asleep prompts them to "commit the crime all over again."[29] The reader exists between the strike of the bell ("They're going to kill Santiago Nasar") and its echo ("Santiago Nasar is dead," "They've killed Santiago Nasar")[30] The phrase itself is not only temporally distanced from the moment, the chronicle takes place twenty-seven years after, but that distance, for some, has lost all meaning even in the moment it's uttered. The chronicler's brother, highly inebriated and incapable of remembering his own words from the time, casts doubt on the veracity of his own pronouncement: "[E]ven if I did remember, I wouldn't have believed it."[31] The rallying cry, the call for villagers of Riohacha to act, however directly or indirectly, becomes nonsense by a character close to the crime.

In *Understanding Comics*, Scott McCloud speaks to the reader's participation in the violence that transpires in the gutter, the space between the images. A character holding a knife (like the Vicario brothers) is followed by a panel of a corpse (Santiago pinned to his own front door). The in-between action, the actual violent crime, happens in the reader's head, making them a murderer or at least morally culpable. All the villagers of Riohacha are in that gutter, and many of them act (slipping notes under the door, walking to warn Plácida Linero, informing the mayor and the police, taking away the Vicario brothers' knives and plying them with hard liquor), and yet the death occurs regardless, in a time outside of their actions. Each pronouncement sets us with the scenario of McCloud's "blood in the gutter." We receive the bookends and, to achieve narrative closure, "mentally construct a continuous, unified reality."[32] In other words, we kill him.

There's also the prurient enticement of a "death foretold," where "fake customers buy milk they didn't need and ask for food that doesn't exist … with the purpose of seeing whether it was true that they were waiting for Santiago Nasar to kill him."[33] One might add the reader to this list of fake customers. We aren't making superfluous purchases, but we are curious, we are bystanders, and while one could complain that all readers are thus murderers, García Márquez reflects our culpability back onto us by his craft, the very structure of the novel.

People compelled to act outside their conventional roles add to the travesty, reminding one of the bumbling detectives whose incompetence stands as an obstacle, impeding the arrival of justice and a moral conclusion. And yet, according to the conventions of detective fiction, the novel should contain more than one death: the first committed by the murderer and the second by the detective.[34] Because García Márquez selects a chronicler instead of a detective, we witness a continuous series of deaths. Santiago's murdered more than twice. His brutal killing appears in the novel through his botched autopsy, just as reluctantly and perfunctorily performed as his honor killing. An aged priest (Father Amador), who studied medicine in Salamanca but entered the seminary before graduation, is one in a line of characters compelled to act as proxies, a dynamic García Márquez installs by having a chronicler instead of a detective. Beginning with the governor, orders trickle down within the village ranks, and characters begin to assume necessary roles. Santiago's body testifies to their ineptness. The autopsy, "a massacre," was performed with craftsmen's tools, and documented by Father Amador, who acted as both medical examiner and father confessor (the Vicario brothers turn themselves and their murder weapons into him).

The autopsy report, a staple of forensic science's contribution to detective novels, also factors into the violence inflected on Nasar's corpse. We read, clinically, of seven fatal wounds and precede to learn of the severity of the murder, knife wounds deep and sustained enough to "almost slice in pieces" the liver, and "destroy the pancreas."[35] Balancing the mimicry of medical terminology and reminding readers of the examiner's true vocation as a priest, García Márquez includes the biblical reading of one wound in particular: "It looked like a stigma of the crucified Christ."[36] The comment would be innocuous enough were it not for the more telling significance: Santiago Nasar himself, like all the other characters, is a proxy. He stands in for Angela Vicario's lover, the person named as having taken her honor.[37]

The apex of proxy, of people working outside of their designated roles, might be the result of absurdity when Santiago is implicated in his own death. As the chronicler recounts the three-day court case, he mentions the well-known prejudice held by all, villagers and the relatively unknown Bayardo alike. Because Santiago is imagined to be well aware of Bayardo's susceptibility to prejudice, Santiago's own disregard, "his refusal to worry" is tantamount to "suicide," as if no one could be held responsible for Santiago's death save for himself.[38] Even the investigating magistrate seems to corroborate this idea, writing in the margins of folio 416, "Give me a prejudice, and I will move the world."[39] Prejudice, a stand-in for honor killing, does "move the world" of Riohacha and of Sucre in the early 1950s.

Asi de simple/That simple

Critic Alexandra Fitts recounts Spain's and then Latin America's history with honor killings, noting that key historical events, such as the expulsion of Jews and the forced conversion of Moors (late fifteenth century), came to complicate the concept of honor so that it also included racial purity (limpieza de sangre), female sexual purity, and family name.[40] García Márquez briefly entertains this cultural preoccupation with racial purity in the novel; retaliation from the village's Arab community, based on Santiago Nasar's Arabic heritage, becomes a source of concern for the Vicario brothers. Villagers fear the brothers have been poisoned in jail in retaliation for Nasar's death, but the narrative quelches this potential racial-fueled fire by noting the insularity of the Arab community (only marry within their race), their assimilation (all were Catholic), and the key role an Arab villager plays in curing the Vicario brothers.[41]

The subject precipitating the novel's central concern—the murder of Santiago Nasar—is conventional, almost ahistorical: female virginity. And, like Prudencia Cotes, fiancée of Pablo Vicario at the time, women reinforce these antiquated cultural values. She confesses to the chronicler that she encouraged his killing of Santiago, vowing that she wouldn't marry him if he didn't kill for honor. Angela's confidantes, well versed in "men's tricks," offer her alum, to tighten the vaginal opening and "mimic virginity," as well as other stratagems to aid and abet her role as the virginal bride. Operating under her own moral authority, a topic addressed in more detail later in the article, Angela refuses any subterfuge.

Countless critics and journalists alike have recounted the real-life events that García Márquez recasts for this work. Miguel Reyes Palencia, who returns his first wife on their wedding night, was still living fifteen years after the actual event, which took place in Sucre, Colombia, in 1951, and delighted by the resurgence of notoriety and fame the publication of *Chronicle of a Death Foretold* brought to his case. García Márquez's family lived in Sucre, and the author was friends with the victim (Cayetano Gentile

Chimento) involved in this tale of love turned to violence, of a return to archaic traditions that sought to avenge family honor through bloodshed. Only one brother, not a twin, carried out the honor killing to reinstate the public standing of Margarita Chica Salas' family. Her brother Victor murdered Cayetano.

Similar to the *Chronicle*'s unnamed narrator, García Márquez was tangentially connected to the honor killing; both he and his family lived in the area at the time. Indeed, the novel's publication reignited interest in the newspaper story, and the real-life "wronged husband," Miguel Reyes Palencia, insisted, all these years after the actual events:

> en el momento exacto observé el detalle de que no era virgen. Entonces la sacudí violentamente y le dije: "¿Qué pasó? ¿Qué hay aquí? Usted me ha engañado, aquí hay un hombre. ¿Quién es que no soy yo?" A pesar de la oscuridad, observé que Margarita lloraba, que sus lágrimas rodaban y no alcanzaba a hablar. Estaba totalmente transformada. No era una mujer, era un ente. Pero la levanté a bofetadas tratando de hacerla hablar y diciéndole, 'Hable, hable, o la mato!'

> In the exact moment I observed that she wasn't a virgin. So I violently shook her and said, "What's happened? What do we have here? You have deceived me. I am the man here. Who am I not? Despite the fact that it was dark, I saw that Margarita cried, that her tears were rolling and she couldn't speak. Everything was completely changed. She wasn't a woman, she was a thing. But I slapped her, trying to get her to stand up, and I said to her, "Talk, talk, or I'll kill you."[42]

Mimicking the novel's own temporal remove from the events, this interview, fifteen years after the honor killing of Cayetano Gentile Chimento, nonetheless retains an emotional fervor and immediacy. In recounting the events of his fated wedding night, Miguel Reyes Palencia represents himself on the verge of committing murder ("Talk, or I'll kill you") when it is Margarita's brother, Victor, who commits the honor killing. Another interesting difference between the real-life event and García Márquez's fictional version is the intentional absence of the "wronged husband" in *Chronicle*. The novel's chronicler never interviews Bayardo San Ramón, the wronged husband; the chronicle elides this critical moment of discovery with Angela's mother's physical abuse of her daughter.

This first novelistic adaptation deserves further scrutiny, particularly as it relates to this article's preoccupation with morality within the text. García Márquez casts twins as the murdering siblings, Pedro and Pablo Vicario. Each has his own relationship to the twinned heated emotions at play, love and hate, which coalesce in honor killing. One suffers from gonorrhea, a condition directly attributed to his army years, and the other, Pablo, survives his brief stint in jail to marry his sweetheart, a foil for his sister's failed marriage.[43] Military service and the ravages of sexually transmitted disease mark Pedro's body, the very issues key to the honor killing, highlight the double standard at play. García Márquez further adds, in his retelling of the real-life events, that the two brothers were reluctant killers who did all they could, even to levels of absurdity, to be stopped, to have someone intervene, including one another. Just as one brother's resolve wans, the other's waxes, and so they are never morally aligned to prevent Santiago's murder.

"She recognized no other authority than her own"[44]

Angela Vicario prevails by the novel's end, having gained a confidence and independence from her mother that she lacked twenty years prior. The chronicler recalls spying her through her window, in a house near a beach, a form of self-exile that Pettey likens to the punishment characteristic of Greek tragedies. She magically sheds her years, becoming "almost as young as in [the chronicler's] memory."[45] In her newfound independence and vitality, she pursues Bayardo, the very man who sets the novel's actions in motion. She writes him copious letters, devotes herself to his image, to unfulfilled desires. Angela transforms into the "lucid, overbearing mistress of her own free will."[46] And, perhaps in the most magical of all transformations, Angela is revirginized, becoming "a virgin again just for [Bayardo]."[47] If she's able to undo the very state of being that instigated the novel's tragic turn of events, is the cult of virginity further upheld or is it scrutinized? When interviewed about *Chronicle*, García Márquez has stated that he wrote *Crónica de una muerte anunciada* in part as a denunciation of machismo, which he defines not as merely the aggressive assertion of one's own privileges but as "la usurpación del derecho ajeno. Asi de simple" (the usurpation of others' rights. That simple).[48] Rivalling Bayardo's relentless pursuit of her, Angela begins an earnest, steady campaign of her own, composing letters to Bayardo that, despite the lack of reply, she felt certain he was receiving.[49] To prove the ardor of her love for Bayardo, Angela continues her letter writing campaign for "over half a lifetime," for seventeen years.[50] As if to alert readers of the inverse of this dynamic, with Angela as the falconer,[51] García Márquez maintains the symmetry in each approaching the other's household: Angela had sent her mother for the valise equipped for her wedding night, and Bayardo appears "carrying a suitcase with clothing in order to stay and another just like it with almost two thousand letters."[52] Unlike Miguel Reyes Palencia, his fictionalized version in *Chronicle*, Bayardo reunites with his would-be bride and carries with him the manifestation of their improbable reconciliation (her love letters) in a significant container (the suitcase which, on their wedding night, was filled with various means to thwart the detection of her lost virginity).

Bayardo comes to Angela on different moral terms. The implications with his suitcases' contents are both that he'll "stay," and that such an arrangement exists outside holy matrimony. No one will bear witness to an exchange of vows, and the cult of female virginity no longer reigns as a moral institution. Angela's profession, making cloth flowers and embroidering, gestures to her remaking, her reflowering if you will, and to her ability to accomplish such a feat through weaving, sewing, a mastery of textiles not unlike the Fates of Greek lore. Given all the attention on Santiago and the Vicario brothers, Angela seems less a character than the occasion for the narrative, the catalyst for the death foretold. And yet, she writes her own narrative, woven just as magically and vibrantly as the tapestries she embroiders with her colorful threads. Angela's is a life unlike the others in Riohacha and while it is not one of community, that isolation provides her the ability to become the arbiter of her own morality. No one surveils her; she is no longer the topic of gossip. And she and Bayardo San Ramón may well upend the gender dynamics of honor killing, the cult of female virginity in the image of his appearance on her doorstep: the suitcase of unopened letters as the male hymen, intact.

Notes

1 Quoted in Dwight Garner, "Gabriel García Márquez, Journalist? A Book Revives the Novelist's First Calling," *New York Times,* May 6, 2019, https://www.nytimes.com/2019/05/06/books/review-scandal-of-century-gabriel-garcia-marquez.html, para. 18. Accessed February 28, 2023.

2 Gabriel García Márquez, *Chronicle of a Death Foretold* (New York: Vintage International, 2003), 3.

3 Lois Parkinson Zamora, "Ends and Endings in Garcia Marquez's 'Cronica de una muerte anunciada" ("Chronicle of a Death Foretold"), *Latin American Literary Review* 13, no. 25 (1985): 106.

4 John Carson Pettey, "Nietzsche's *Birth of Tragedy* and Euripedes's *Bacchae* as Sources for the Apollonian and Dionysian Aspects of García Márquez's *Chronicle of a Death Foretold*: A Speculative Reading," *Hispanófila,* no. 121 (1997), *JSTOR,* http://www.jstor.org/stable/43806977, 21. Accessed October 29, 2022.

5 García Márquez, *Chronicle,* 48.

6 *OED.* Hayden White distinguishes chronicles from novels, noting that the former "possess none of the attributes we normally think of as story; no

central subject, no well-marked beginning, middle, and end; no peripeteia" ("The Value of Narrativity in the Representation of Reality"), *Critical Inquiry* 7, no. 1 (1980), *JSTOR*, http://www.jstor.org/stable/1343174, 10. Accessed February 28, 2023.

7   And yet, our chronicler must rescue 322 out of the 500 pages of the magistrate's brief (99).

8   García Márquez, *Chronicle*, 12.

9   Ibid., 27, 28.

10 Ibid., 8.

11 Ibid., 17.

12 Ibid., 83.

13 Ibid., 108.

14 Ibid., 19.

15 Ibid.

16 Ibid., 110.

17 Grace Gomashie, "Preserving the Community in Gabriel Garcia Márquez' *Cronica de una muerte anunciada (Chronicle of a Death Foretold),*" *Onomastica Canadiana* 96 (2017): 37.

18 Ibid., 37.

19 Minu Susan Koshy, "Shards of a Gruesome Memory Commemorated: An Analysis of *Chronicle of a Death Foretold*," *Research Scholar: An International Refereed e-Journal of Literary Explorations* 2, no. 3 (August 2014), https://www.academia.edu/35193567/SHARDS_OF_A_GRUESOME_MEMORY_COMMEMORATED_AN_ANALYSIS_OF_CHRONICLE_OF_A_DEATH_FORETOLD, 469. Accessed February 28, 2023.

20 García Márquez, *Chronicle*, 34.

21 Ibid., 101.

22 Ibid.

23 Recalling the idea that the guard's absence can be the instrument of expanding the duty of policing onto everyone who resides in Riohacha's "panopticon," we as readers witness and experience this sense of moral compunction: we know that the Vicario Brothers are planning to murder Santiago Nasar. What are we to do with this knowledge?

24 García Márquez, *Chronicle*, 6.

25 Ibid., 24.

26 Ibid.

27 Ibid., 52, 69, 53.

28 Ibid., 61.

29 Ibid., 78.

30 Ibid., 52, 69, 71.

31 Ibid., 69.
32 Scott McCloud, *Understanding Comics: The Invisible Art* (New York: William Morrow Paperbacks, 1994), 67.
33 García Márquez, *Chronicle*, 63–4.
34 Tvetzan Todorov, *The Poetics of Prose* (Ithaca: Cornell University Press, 1977), 44.
35 García Márquez, *Chronicle*, 75.
36 Ibid.
37 Ibid., 47.
38 Ibid., 101.
39 Ibid., 100.
40 Alexandra Fitts, "The Persistence of Blood, Honor, and Name in Hispanic Literature: 'Bodas de Sangre and Crónica de Una Muerte Anunciada,'" *Confluencia* 22, no. 1 (2006), JSTOR, http://www.jstor.org/stable/27923187, 133–4. Accessed October 15, 2022.
41 García Márquez, *Chronicle*, 87.
42 Quoted in Alexandra Fitts, "The Persistence," 135–6.
43 García Márquez, *Chronicle*, 60.
44 Ibid., 93.
45 Ibid., 89.
46 Ibid., 93.
47 Ibid.
48 Jorge Olivares and García Márquez, "Garcia Márquez's 'Crónica de una muerte anunciada' as Metafiction," *Contemporary Literature* 28, no. 4 (1987): 159.
49 García Márquez, *Chronicle*, 93.
50 Ibid., 95.
51 *Chronicle*'s epigraph, a fragment of Gil Vicente's poem, follows the conventional fifteenth-century trope between romance and hunting: "the pursuit of love/is like falconry."
52 Ibid., 95.

Bibliography

Fitts, Alexandra. "The Persistence of Blood, Honor, and Name in Hispanic Literature: 'Bodas de Sangre and Crónica de Una Muerte Anunciada.'" *Confluencia* 22, no. 1 (2006):133–43. JSTOR, http://www.jstor.org/stable/27923187. Accessed October 15, 2022.

García Márquez, Gabriel. *Chronicle of a Death Foretold*. New York: Vintage International, 2003.

Garner, Dwight. "Gabriel García Márquez, Journalist? A Book Revives the Novelist's First Calling." *New York Times*, May 6, 2019. https://www.nytimes.com/2019/05/06/books/review-scandal-of-century-gabriel-garcia-marquez.html. Accessed February 28, 2023.

Gomashie, Grace. "Preserving the Community in Gabriel Garcia Márquez' *Cronica de una muerte anunciada (Chronicle of a Death Foretold)*." *Onomastica Canadiana* 96 (2017): 31–49.

Koshy, Minu Susan. "Shards of a Gruesome Memory Commemorated: An Analysis of *Chronicle of a Death Foretold*." *Research Scholar: An International Refereed e-Journal of Literary Explorations* 2, no. 3 (August 2014): 465–72. https://www.academia.edu/35193567/SHARDS_OF_A_GRUESOME_MEMORY_COMMEMORATED_AN_ANALYSIS_OF_CHRONICLE_OF_A_DEATH_FORETOLD. Accessed February 28, 2023.

McCloud, Scott. *Understanding Comics: The Invisible Art*. New York: William Morrow Paperbacks, 1994.

Olivares, Jorge, and García Márquez. "Garcia Márquez's 'Crónica de una muerte anunciada' as Metafiction." *Contemporary Literature* 28, no. 4 (1987): 483–92.

Pettey, John Carson. "Nietzsche's *Birth of Tragedy* and Euripedes's *Bacchae* as Sources for the Apollonian and Dionysian Aspects of García Márquez's *Chronicle of a Death Foretold*: A Speculative Reading." *Hispanófila*, no. 121 (1997): 21–34. *JSTOR*, http://www.jstor.org/stable/43806977. Accessed October 29, 2022.

Todorov, Tvetzan. *The Poetics of Prose*. Ithaca: Cornell University Press, 1977.

White, Hayden. "The Value of Narrativity in the Representation of Reality." *Critical Inquiry* 7, no. 1 (1980): 5–27. *JSTOR*, http://www.jstor.org/stable/1343174. Accessed February 28, 2023.

Zamora, Lois Parkinson. "Ends and Endings in Garcia Marquez's 'Cronica de una muerte anunciada" ("Chronicle of a Death Foretold")." *Latin American Literary Review* 13, no. 25 (1985): 104–16.

5

"What's luck got to do with it?": Privilege, Morality, and the Victim in Tana French's *Wych Elm*

Deirdre Flynn

Tana French's 2019 *The Wych Elm*[1] centers on the story of the privileged Toby Hennessy. By his own admission, he has always been "a lucky person." On the opening pages of the mystery, he notes that he has gone through life "without any of the standard misfortunes."[2] Hennessy comes from a stable, wealthy family and is totally oblivious to the inequalities of the world. Straight after university, Toby Hennessey walked into a job in PR and is in a relationship with the perfect and beautiful Melissa. He describes worrying "like a laughable waste of time and energy."[3] However, after a violent attack in his home that leaves him with a brain injury and physical repercussions, Hennessy must readjust to life without the swagger and confidence that have defined him. When a skull is then found inside the Wych Elm tree in the back garden of his uncle's sprawling Georgian home, Hennessy—now an unreliable narrator—has to face the reality of his position of privilege. He must confront the blind spots of his youth while dealing with memory loss. Hennessy becomes the antihero of the novel. Yes, he is the victim of a crime, but he has never realized how his gender, race, wealth, education, or looks have played a role in his success to date. He dismisses his friends' and their families' claims of oppression or prejudice, and he has none of the qualities of the hero. He is not "honest, idealistic, courageous, honorable, noble," and we come to realize his "moral compass is never firmly pointing north."[4] Toby Hennessy is not a likable guy.

French reconstitutes our expectations of the victim and asks us how we empathize if the victim is not a nice person. What happens to the moral codes when right and wrong become ambiguous? And what does luck have to do with it? In a *Guardian* interview with Alex Clark, French said that she wanted to think about what life was like if "you're too lucky. ... He's always taken for granted that his experience is the defining one—that's the only thing that counts or matters or has any bearing on reality. So he's got his own set of experiences and it hasn't occurred to him to question beyond those."[5] This chapter will investigate the relationship between morality, luck, and privilege, and how this impacts our need for vindication. How can we find order and clear verdicts when the victim is just too lucky?

Irish Crime Fiction

In the last two decades, critical work has flourished, matching the growth of Irish crime fiction. As Meier and Ross point out, "Irish writers ... have contributed to crime fiction since its emergence as a distinctive form of writing in the first half of the nineteenth century."[6] The genre decidedly expanded during the growth of the Celtic Tiger, a period of record economic growth in Ireland from 1996 to 2008. For the first time in Irish history, there were "unprecedented levels of inward migration, wealth, and consumerism" and "spending and consumption were at an all-time high during this period."[7] However, the global downturn exposed the "very, very shaky foundations" and the "whole edifice of the Irish economic miracle crashing to the ground in record time."[8] The corruption and greed underneath the rubble of the Tiger have been suggested as creating the ideal atmosphere for crime fiction to flourish. Rachel Schaffer explains, "With the boom-and-bust cycle and the social disruptions that accompanied it, dozens of writers, both Irish and international, began to see Ireland as a fruitful setting for their mysteries."[9] These conditions created "fertile ground," Schaffer says, for the "social commentary" of "emerald noir, aka Celtic crime and Hibernian homicide" that "has blossomed in the twenty-first century and continues to grow."[10] This social commentary is evident in Tana French's work, one of the most popular Irish crime fiction writers today.

Irish crime fiction has its own conventions and expectations, and it is known for "its journalistic links, its stubborn refusal to adopt an essential setting, and its generosity in fusing subgenres."[11] The boom-bust cycle of the Irish economy has had an influence on Irish crime fiction's interest "in contemporary discussions about confronting privilege."[12] Political corruption, very much a feature of the Celtic Tiger, and collapse feature heavily in Irish crime fiction, as Brian Cliff argues.[13] Also, the country's colonial past leaves a shadow on the genre with a strong focus on crime involving property and land development.[14] The "political, cultural, and historical specificity of the island" also means that Irish crime fiction cannot rely on the anonymity of the city, argues Brian Cliff.[15] "[I]n a landscape as intimate and compact as Ireland's, where can a mass serial killer hide the bodies? The scale of the stage, in other words, matters a great deal for the content and structure that are available to Irish crime fiction."[16] Place, politics, and privilege all play an important role in Irish crime fiction.

Tana French

The past two decades have seen Irish writers such John Banville (as Benjamin Black), John Connolly, Declan Burke, Ken Bruen, Arlene Hunt, Jo Spain, and Adrian McKinty make their names on the international stage. Tana French has emerged as one of the most successful Irish crime writers, with several international bestsellers under her belt, since her debut *In The Woods* in 2007. French's fiction refuses to be restricted by any genre, and her first-person narrator novels often blend crime, mystery, thriller, and gothic elements. Her work is often marketed as "both literary fiction and genre fiction," and she has won numerous awards domestically and abroad.[17]

Her oeuvre is dominated by her Dublin Murder Squad series, and these novels highlight certain trends in her work. French's style creates an "immersive quality," with unreliable first-person narrators who often "withhold, and even dissemble, or who remember only fragments, creating a problematic reliability that keeps the reader both immersed and off-balance."[18] Her novels depend on uncertainty, and she rarely allows for every element to be resolved at the end, most famously noted in *In the Woods*. Rosemary Johnsen ties this refusal to provide explanations to the uncertainty of the Celtic Tiger collapse: "Crime fiction has always allowed the possibility of the criminal going unpunished, but what French does goes beyond that to lay claim to some of the dark uncertainties concomitant with life in post-Tiger Dublin."[19] Her mysteries do not always follow a logical conclusion, "in which everything is explained, everything understood"; neither the characters nor the detectives are left with a clear verdict and conclusion to the crime.[20] There is no code of fair play at work in French's novels, and nowhere more so than *The Wych Elm*. The "whodunit" refuses to provide any satisfaction, and the moral code is certainly not restored but flouted by the "lucky" Hennessy. French's use of ambiguity in her fiction acts as a social critique and helps to build what Gudmundsdottir and Meany call "a new critical respect for the genre," ensuring that crime fiction is "no longer a historical and sociological symptom, neither is it a cure nor escape from social ills."[21] In fact, French draws attention to these social ills and does not offer easy solutions through neat conclusions.

This uncertainty is often associated with the home, which is exactly what we see *The Wych Elm*. Toby Hennessy returns to the Ivy House in the hope of finding stability and answers, but instead a dead body is uncovered in the garden. As Cliff posits, this focus on domestic property again relates to the shadow of the Tiger:

> This uncertainty is often illustrated in French's use of what should be the most stable elements of our lives: our homes. The Celtic Tiger centred in many ways on property, ... homes have at best a fragile role in the lives of the protagonists, most of whom are haunted by a desire to belong and by their own regrets, missed chances, and turning points. Along with this fragile hold on being at home, [there is a] gap between what the narrator regrets and the reader does not yet know.[22]

The house at the center of *The Wych Elm*, a sprawling Georgian home with extensive gardens, points to the historical wealth of the Hennessey family. Inhabited by the bachelor uncle Hugo, the future of the Ivy House becomes uncertain when Hugo is diagnosed with terminal cancer. With no direct heir, and his siblings still alive, the future of the valuable South Dublin city property also plagues the characters, torn between the nostalgia and the possible sale price. Each member of the family is eager to lay his or her claim to the property, or to the sale and division of the profits, all before the skull of Dominic Ganly is discovered by Toby's nephew, Zach, and the enclosed family home is swarmed by the Gardaí. Like the "homeowning bourgeois reading public," the Hennessy family wants "to see the dominant social order of which they are a part maintained, and their stake in it protected."[23]

In these circumstances, *The Wych Elm* plays out like a country house mystery, transported to Ireland's capital city. This oasis of calm, barely noticeable from the street and behind its mature gardens and high walls, contains many of the elements of the British mystery standard, including the locked room mystery. The body, discovered in the center of the Wych Elm tree, becomes the "hermetically sealed environment" in this case.[24] The death of Dominic Ganly, the cover-up, and the actual crime conform to the rules of the genre, only slightly reversed. In his discussion of Dickson Carr, John Scaggs explains the death in the locked room mystery is "in fact, a suicide intended to look like murder."[25] For mysteries that followed the rules, "[t]he locked-room mystery was immensely reassuring for the inter-war reading public, reducing the world, as it did, to self-contained, enclosed, manageable proportions and dimensions."[26] In this case, however, French presents us with the opposite: a murder intended to look like a suicide, ensuring that there is little reassurance in the resolving of the case.

The Antihero Protagonist

The protagonist of this novel is the 28-year-old Toby Hennessy, the victim, onetime suspect, and by the end of the novel, murderer. Hennessy comes from a stable, middle-class family, and everything has gone his way in life. In the opening lines, he explains that he has "managed to go through life without any of the standard misfortunes."[27] For Hennessy, it has been smooth sailing, and until his apartment is broken into, he felt a "satisfying sense that everything was going exactly as it should."[28] In an interview, French explains that for her protagonist "everything has conspired to make him a person for whom the world is set up."[29] When this facade comes crashing down, Hennessy's confidence and experience lead him to believe that he can solve the crime and that the social order will be restored. Despite receiving a head injury that has impacted his memory, and the physical implications of the assault, Hennessy maintains this belief that he can outsmart everyone.

Hennessy's worldview has been impacted by his "lucky" journey through life this far. As French explains in her interview, "He's always taken for granted that his experience is the defining one—that's the only thing that counts or matters or has any bearing on reality. So he's got his own set of experiences and it hasn't occurred to him to question beyond those"[30] The opening pages only serve to highlight Hennessy's privilege, as he remembers an exhibition on "representations of urban spaces by disadvantaged youths" at the gallery where he works.[31] Hennessy has no interest in the public service aspect of the exhibit; he only thinks of how it can further the galley's status and attract funding. He sees this exhibition as easy PR, with no consideration of the benefits for the at-risk community involved. He declares that "the only way that could have been easier to publicize was if some of the disadvantaged youth were also Syrian refugees and ideally trans."[32] Like everything he touched, the exhibition "went like a dream" and Hennessy is delighted with the "collection of satisfyingly scuzzy youths with low-grade criminal records" involved in the project.[33] Before the exhibition opens, Hennessy discovers that the exhibition coordinator, Tiernan, is the artist behind the most promising work. Tiernan created a front for his own work, called "Gouger," a typical inner-city Dublin nickname that connotes a working-class background. The "Gouger" character refused to do interviews and speak to anyone other than Tiernan. His most famous piece was "BoHerion Rhapsody," a spray-painted artwork based on clichés of inner-city working-class life. Despite the ruse, Hennessy's moral compass is nowhere to be seen. Choosing not to reveal the truth to the gallery owner, he continues to allow Tiernan to present work as the elusive "Gouger." He explains that he was on "Tiernan's side" and adds, "I've never got the self-flagellating middle-class belief that being poor and having a petty crime habit magically makes you more worthy."[34] Hennessy instead decides to spin "Gouger's anonymity into a sub-Banksy enigma," seeing ways to build more PR for the gallery:

> Tiernan and I did discuss, semi-seriously, getting an authentic skanger to be the face of the product, in exchange for enough cash to support his habit (obviously we would need one with a habit, for maximum gritty authenticity), but we decided against it on the grounds that a junkie skanger would be too short-sighted for reliability: sooner or later he would either start blackmailing us or start wanting creative control, and things would get messy.[35]

Hennessey's rhetoric and assumptions on class only serve to illustrate his own lack of self-awareness. The contents of the accounts are dependent on the negative classist archetypes which Hennessy holds. The pretense, we later find out, mirrors an email catfishing prank Hennessy played on his unsuspecting classmates while in school. Dominic Ganly was one of his victims, and his emails to Ganly encouraged Ganly to become more sexually aggressive toward Hennessy's cousin Susanna. Hennessy lacks empathy and cannot see the negative consequences of his actions.

Days later, when his boss the Gallery owner finds out, Hennessy is "startled" by how angry Richard is, suggesting that it was "out of proportion" for his misdeed.[36] He is sent home from work for a few days as punishment, something unfamiliar for Hennessy. He spends his days wondering about the consequences, and the "intensity of those moments [takes him] aback."[37] He tells his friends about the incident on a night out, expecting support, but they only point out how ethically wrong it was. His pal Dec asks if he ever thought about the other kids in the exhibition: "There they are, pouring their hearts out, and you're taking the piss out of their lives like they're a joke."[38] Hennessy dismisses Dec's arguments, suggesting he has a chip on his shoulder because he received a scholarship to the same school and joking with him about his "deprived background."[39] He adds that these people choose their fate: "They could have got jobs. The recession's over; there's no reason for anyone to be stuck in the muck unless they actually choose to be."[40] Hennessy's blinkered attitude to class and privilege set him as a deeply unlikable character.

The gallery event marks the beginning of Hennessy's luck changing. On the night out with his friends after his work punishment, he decides to return home to his apartment, rather than visit his girlfriend. That night he is awoken by two men in his apartment, and they attack him, leaving him in the hospital with a serious head injury and numerous physical impairments. After the attack, he becomes "a nervy, jittery wreck with a limp and a slur who gets lost in the middle of sentences."[41] This is all part of the exposition used to highlight Hennessy's character. His lack of empathy and his class privilege are illustrated through these incidents, which continue through the novel. His refusal to see the lived experiences of others adds to the blind spots in his memory when trying to solve the murder of Dominic Ganly. His lack of patience with his newfound medical situation and his failure to understand the extent of the damage leave him unreliable. He expects to have the same mental and physical capacity as before the attack and disregards his memory lapses, reliance on painkillers, mood swings, and extreme fatigue. Hennessy is, as Justine Jordan points in her *Guardian* review, "something rather different: a pin-sharp portrait of privilege, recounted not by a world-weary, wisecracking detective but by a crime victim who is also a suspect."[42] And Hennessey is one with "holes in [his] mind, blind spots shimmering nastily like migraine aura."[43] The attack only serves to highlight his privilege, as he fails to acknowledge that now he is dependent on the empathy of others and their memory.

The attack leads to his moving in with his uncle, recently diagnosed with terminal cancer. Justine Jordan is correct in her analysis that both are coming to terms with "changed horizons. ... Hugo deteriorates while Toby struggles to recover; the house becomes a haven for them both."[44] It is hard to categorize this overconfident citizen detective as a hero or antihero. Unlike Stewart and Peter's description of the antihero who seems "to have an endless struggle with the society that would have them crushed," Toby Hennessy is a lucky guy until now.[45] Cliff suggests that Irish crime fiction includes "the pronounced significance of empathy as an avowed motivation for protagonists," but this is where *The Wych Elm* departs from the rules again.[46] Hennessy has no empathy, other than for himself, as he struggles to adapt to the reality of his new mental and physical condition. Here the boundary between good and evil is blurred, as French forces us to focus on "subjects of social order, social morality and the various tensions between rich and poor" which Mary Evans suggests are not traditionally foregrounded by crime fiction.[47] The discovery of Dominic Ganly's body and his murder furthers this tension between the law and morality. Ganly is another deeply unlikable character. A schoolmate of Hennessy and his cousins Susanna and Leon, Ganly was a wealthy bully. Ganly had made unwanted and inappropriate advances on Susanna, and Leon was the target of his homophobic bullying. All of this went unnoticed to Hennessey during his school days, when he was "kind of oblivious" to it, as Susanna points out.[48] Leon explains that he had approached Hennessy to help him deal with Ganly's bullying: "Dominic was the only one who actually scared me. ... [H]e was a total sadist. Vicious ... you said I needed to learn to deal with my problems myself."[49] Hennessy shows that he was never an empathic person, and these incidents from his past only highlight his unlikability.

The Murder

When Dominic Ganly disappeared ten years previously, his death was treated as a suicide. He had received bad grades on his Leaving Certificate exams, precluding him from his university choices. A text was sent from his phone near the cliffs of Howth in Dublin one night in August to all his friends saying "sorry." However, when his body is discovered with a garotte in the core of the wych elm tree at the Ivy House, detectives quickly rule out suicide. To complicate matters, fiber from Hennessy's school hoodie, still hanging in the wardrobe of the Ivy House, is found on Dominic Ganly. Hennessy cannot remember what happened or if he was involved. His memory has been severely impacted, and his conversations with his cousins only add to how unreliable his recollections of those days are. Susanna and Leon remind him of events in his youth, which Hennessy has either forgotten or misremembered. Despite repeated examples of how his memory is flawed and impacted by his injuries, he maintains an unwavering confidence in his ability to solve the crime. He concocts reasons to invite Leon and Susanna to the Ivy House in the hope of securing confessions. As he prepares for one such evening, he feels very confident: "I had a good feeling about that night, though. It sparkled tantalizingly in front of me like a fourth date, a final interview, the big one with the prize waiting at the end and I was all pumped up and ready to ace it."[50] His anxiety and paranoia convince him that Leon organized the attack in his flat, but as more and more details about his past are revealed, Susanna starts to set him up as the chief suspect.

Throughout he refers to her "poker face," and she tells him about Ganly's sexual harassment. However, Hennessy cannot piece together her own motive. He is unable to see that she is keeping the attention off her and Leon. She builds her case against him further, telling Hennessy on the night Ganly disappeared he was nowhere to be seen. She builds up his paranoia, playing on the knowledge that he is unsure.[51] Hennessy cannot see through her actions even though his girlfriend Melissa is sure they have ulterior motives. Melissa tells him, "They're doing something too. ... [T]hey're trying to do something to you and I can't tell what it is but it's not good. And we need to go home."[52] Hennessy rejects her advice, saying, "Everything's fine. I know what I'm doing."[53] Just as when he was a teenager, or in his actions at the gallery, Hennessy is unable to accept he could be wrong. He is blindly confident that his theories are correct despite mounting evidence to the contrary. Mixing alcohol and weed with Xanax does not help his paranoia, and as he tries to get confessions from Susanna and Leon, he starts to see Detective Rafferty in the shadows: "I would have sworn it was human. Rafferty spying on us, clinging and listening, anywhere and everywhere."[54] French uses these incidents to increase ambiguity and build suspense around Hennessy. He cannot be trusted, and neither can his memory. At the same time, the misremembered memories and his cousin's disingenuous suggestions increase the unreliability of each of the stories. Susanna plants further doubt in Hennessy's already confused and paranoid mind to deflect from her own guilt.

Victims

Despite all of this, as Anne Diebel in the *London Review of Books* points out, Hennessy is a victim of a serious crime. He has been savagely beaten and will have repercussions for the remainder of his life. Diebel rightly comments that Hennessy has a "legitimate claim to victimhood" and French asks "how to judge which kinds of suffering are worse than others, which kinds of people more deserving of sympathy?"[55] Each of the characters put forward his or her case for victimhood. Leon tells Hennessy that Ganly "tortured" him for years: "I thought about killing myself all the time, you think getting beaten up fucked with your head—That was one night. Imagine what years of it would do to you"[56] Susanna offers up a similar story of Ganly's vile sexual harassment:

> Has there ever been someone who treated you like you weren't a person? ... Someone who did whatever they wanted to you. ... And you were totally powerless to do anything about it. If you tried to say anything, everyone thought you were ridiculous and whiny and you should quit making such a fuss because this is normal, this is the way it's supposed to be for someone like you.[57]

Both Leon and Susanna build these portraits of victimhood, so when the truth emerges about their calculated murder of Dominic Ganly, they can challenge the "villains-and-innocents fantasy."[58] Susanna and Leon claim a moral victory for the murder of Ganly, with Susanna claiming that "it made a difference. A concrete one."[59] To them, there is nothing ambiguous in their murder of Ganly; this was the right thing to do.

The information about the murder is only revealed after the ailing Hugo turns himself in to the detectives. He confesses to the crime and dies in police custody. Once the funeral is over, Susanna, and her accomplice Leon, feels safe enough to reveal the truth to Hennessy. Until that point, Hennessy thought he might have been responsible. Such is the power of Susanna's suggestion:

> "Toby," Susanna said, gently. "You didn't do anything. You never even knew about it."
> "But," I said, after a very long moment. My mind had been knocked totally blank. It wouldn't go in; was she lying, how much of this

whole story was made up, why would she—"You said. When we were stoned. You said you went to my room, that night, you said where was I—"

"Yeah, that was probably shitty of me. ... I was just trying to keep everything under control."[60]

Susanna, the chief instigator and planner, felt no remorse when she murdered Ganly and still feels secure in her decision. She, like Leon, justifies his murder through her victimhood. She was happy to allow Hugo to take the fall for Ganly and have his name ruined as a result. Now secure she will not be charged, she gloats in the perfection of her plan: "I went over it all in my head, to check if there was anything I'd missed, but there wasn't."[61] Leon's admission that it was "beautiful" and Susanna's moral justification for the murder add to the ethical ambiguity at play here. While they feel their victimhood outranks the murder, they still "come from privileged backgrounds and enjoyed many of the same advantages Toby did—a cozy, insulating family, financial security, educational opportunities."[62] The boundaries between right and wrong are ambiguous here because these two "believe that some aspect of their experience cancels out rather than complicates that privilege."[63]

This revelation, with its liminal position between good and evil, leaves Hennessy unsatisfied. He thinks he has finally "detected" the crime, but he does not feel "some kind of sense of achievement."[64] He has resolved the "whodunit" in the case, but the "answer that even big bad Rafferty hadn't been able to get his hands on" refuses to provide the clean conclusion.[65] He wonders "why all of this felt like such an enormous let-down."[66] Hennessy cannot be the traditional "single figure who takes on the forces of both evil" in this case because the boundaries are so blurred.[67] In the end, he envies the "kind of glory" the murder of Ganly confers upon Susanna and Leon, which helps to "define" them.

Detective Rafferty

Hennessy takes confidence in his belief that he has solved the crime ahead of Detective Rafferty. In reality, his cousins have confessed the murder, knowing they can no longer be charged. He has not, in his own words, "detectived" anything.[68]

Yet Hennessy's confidence remains, and when Detective Rafferty arrives at the Ivy House weeks later to see him, he is unsettled by Rafferty's "vitality."[69] Rafferty offers up his own theory of how Ganly's death came to pass, placing Hugo at the center of the crime thanks to a recent visit from Susanna. Rafferty details how Susanna was an eyewitness to Hugo "dragging something big across the grass" on the night of the murder, yet never realized it was Ganly until the body was discovered.[70] Susanna continues to secure her safety by acting behind the scenes to frame the dead Hugo. She has convinced Rafferty that she would not have been strong enough to carry out the murder alone. Her visit to Rafferty sparks his visit to Hennessy eager to tie up all the threads in the case. Hennessy, suddenly aware of how out of his depth he is, has a cold sweat. The visit from Rafferty only serves to highlight how unsure and unstable his memory is and remind him of his incapacitation. He realizes Rafferty has been playing him all along, using him "as bait."[71] Rafferty explains that Hennessy's injuries would convince a jury there was "something wrong" with him and used the threat of charging him to bait Hugo into confessing.[72]

This all proves too much for Hennessy, and he punches the detective. A protracted fight across the terrace and gardens of the Ivy House ensues until Rafferty's head hits a rock. Hennessy continues to punch him until the "holy rapture of it" has "lightning running through his bones" and he feels that the world was finally his again.[73] Yet the superhero feeling that Susanna and Leon had detailed failed to materialize, and Hennessy goes upstairs to take his own life with Xanax and vodka.

However, Hennessy's luck continues, and he lives. In court, the very things that would have convicted him for Ganly's murder, "the slurring and the jumpiness and the glazed look and the inability to focus, those were the things that saved me."[74] In the end, he serves two years in the psychiatric ward of the Central Mental Hospital and returns to the world with a new first name, still with luck running through "the secret tapestries of [his] DNA."[75] Hennessy's luck and privilege have helped him succeed in life. Despite all he goes through, he still manages to sail through a murder charge and use his attack to his advantage. His crime does not impact his prospects after he is released, and he retains his trademark confidence, quipping that he's "pretty sure" a young attractive colleague would go on a date with him if he asked.[76] He comes to realize how "smoothly and deliciously deceptive, how relentlessly twisted and knotted in on its own hidden places and how lethal" luck can be.[77] Luck rather than morality plays a vital role in Hennessy's court outcome.

Conclusion

Elena Alvarez posits that crime fiction can be transformative and instructive but notes that it also "offers a complex and very accurate portrayal of the society it is produced in, with each text becoming an exercise on reflection and morality."[78] With *The Wych Elm*, French proffers a theory that privilege and luck can impact the execution of justice. If crime fiction is expected to restore social equilibrium, that is exactly what *The Wych Elm* does, as Hennessy starts the story as he ends it, in a cushy job, living in an apartment paid for by his parents and overly confident that his luck will never run out.

Notes

1. Published as *The Witch Elm* in the United States.
2. Tana French, *The Wych Elm* (New York: Viking, 2019), 1.
3. Ibid., 13.
4. Fiona Peters and Rebecca Stewart, *Antihero* (Bristol, UK: Intellect, 2016), 7.
5. Alex Clark, "Tana French: 'Nobody with Imagination Should Commit a Crime. You Wouldn't Handle the Stress,'" *The Guardian*, February 16, 2019, www.theguardian.com/books/2019/feb/16/tana-french-powerful-mysteries-other-people-the-wych-elmm, para. 5. Accessed October 8, 2021.
6. William M. Meier and Ian Campbell Ross, "Editors' Introduction: Irish Crime since 1921." *Éire-Ireland (St. Paul)* 49, no. 1 (2014): 11, https://doi:10.1353/eir.2014.0010.
7. Deirdre Flynn, "Last Ones Left Alive: Zombies and Post-Celtic Tiger Ireland," in *Theorising the Contemporary Zombie: Contextual Pasts, Presents, and Futures*, ed. Scott Hamilton and Conor Heffernan (Cardiff: University of Wales Press, 2022), 185.
8. Gerry Smyth, "Irish National Identity after the Celtic Tiger," *Estudios Irlandeses* 7, no. 7 (2012): 133.
9. Rachel Schaffer, "Introduction: Tana French and Irish Crime Fiction," *Clues* 32, no. 1 (2014): 10, https://doi:10.3172/CLU.32.1.9.
10. Ibid., 10.
11. Elizabeth Mannion and Brian Cliff, *Guilt Rules All: Irish Mystery, Detective, and Crime Fiction* (Syracuse: Syracuse University Press, 2020), 2.
12. Ibid., 4.
13. Brian Cliff, *Irish Crime Fiction* (London: Palgrave Macmillan, 2018), 15.
14. Ibid., 15.
15. Ibid., 11.
16. Ibid.
17. Ibid., 88.
18. Ibid., 87–8.
19. Rosemary Erickson Johnsen, "Crime Fiction's Dublin: Reconstructing Reality in Novels by Dermot Bolger, Gene Kerrigan, and Tana French," *Éire-Ireland* 49, no. 1 (2014): 137, https://doi:10.1353/eir.2014.0009.
20. Cliff, *Irish Crime Fiction*, 91.
21. Gunnthorunn Gudmundsdottir and Gerardine Meaney, "Introduction: Noir in the North," in *Noir in the North: Genre, Politics and Place*, ed. Stacy Gillis and Gunnthorunn Gudmundsdottir (New York: Bloomsbury Academic, 2020), 6.
22. Ibid., 90.
23. John Scaggs, *Crime Fiction* (London: Routledge, 2005), 45.

24 Ibid., 51.
25 Ibid., 52.
26 Ibid.
27 French, *The Wych Elm*, 1.
28 Ibid., 1.
29 Clark, "Tana French," para. 3.
30 Ibid., para. 5.
31 French, *The Wych Elm*, 9.
32 Ibid., 9.
33 Ibid.
34 Ibid., 12.
35 Ibid.
36 Ibid., 13–14.
37 Ibid., 15.
38 Ibid., 19.
39 Ibid., 20.
40 Ibid.
41 Justine Jordan, "The Wych Elm by Tana French Review—A Portrait of Privilege," *The Guardian*, February 21, 2019, www.theguardian.com/books/2019/feb/21/the-wych-elm-tana-french-review, para. 2. Accessed October 8, 2021.
42 Jordan, "The Wych Elm," para. 1.
43 French, *The Wych Elm*, 105.
44 Jordan, "The Wych Elm," para. 3.
45 Peters and Stewart, *Antihero*, 8.
46 Cliff, *Irish Crime Fiction*, 16.
47 Mary Evans, *The Imagination of Evil: Detective Fiction and the Modern World* (New York: Bloomsbury Publishing, 2011), 2.
48 French, *The Wych Elm*, 321.
49 Ibid., 337.
50 Ibid., 304.
51 Ibid., 345.
52 Ibid., 340.
53 Ibid.
54 Ibid., 347.
55 Anne Diebel, "Hiss and Foam: The Wych Elm by Tana French," *London Review of Books* 41, no. 18 (September 26, 2019), www.lrb.co.uk/the-paper/v41/n18/anne-diebel/hiss-and-foam, para. 13. Accessed October 8, 2021.
56 French, *The Wych Elm*, 338.

57 Ibid., 453.
58 Diebel, "Hiss and Foam," para. 14.
59 French, *The Wych Elm*, 448.
60 Ibid., French 424.
61 Ibid., 441.
62 Diebel, "Hiss and Foam," para. 14.
63 Ibid., para. 14.
64 French, *The Wych Elm*, 448.
65 Ibid.
66 Ibid.
67 Evans, *The Imagination of Evil*, 81.
68 French, *The Wych Elm*, 460.
69 Ibid., 461.
70 Ibid., 471.
71 Ibid., 478.
72 Ibid., 480–1.
73 Ibid., 483.
74 Ibid., 493.
75 Ibid., 511.
76 Ibid., 509.
77 Ibid., 2.
78 Elena Avanzas Alvarez, "Criminal Readings: The Transformative and Instructive Power of Crime Fiction," *Journal of Comparative Literature and Aesthetics* 42, no. 3 (Winter 2019). *Gale Academic OneFile*, link.gale.com/apps/doc/A643530457/AONE?u=st42458&sid=googleScholar&xid=4fce63b5, para. 1. Accessed October 8, 2021.

Bibliography

Alvarez, Elena Avanzas. "Criminal Readings: The Transformative and Instructive Power of Crime Fiction." *Journal of Comparative Literature and Aesthetics* 42, no. 3 (Winter 2019). *Gale Academic OneFile*, link.gale.com/apps/doc/A643530457/AONE?u=st42458&sid=googleScholar&xid=4fce63b5. Accessed October 8, 2021.

Clark, Alex. "Tana French: 'Nobody with Imagination Should Commit a Crime. You Wouldn't Handle the Stress.'" *The Guardian*, February 16, 2019. www.theguardian.com/books/2019/feb/16/tana-french-powerful-mysteries-other-people-the-wych-elm. Accessed October 8, 2021.

Cliff, Brian. *Irish Crime Fiction*. London: Palgrave Macmillan, 2018.

Diebel, Anne. "Hiss and Foam: The Wych Elm by Tana French." *London Review of Books* 41, no. 18 (September 26, 2019). www.lrb.co.uk/the-paper/v41/n18/anne-diebel/hiss-and-foam. Accessed October 8, 2021.

Evans, Mary. *The Imagination of Evil: Detective Fiction and the Modern World.* New York: Bloomsbury Publishing, 2011.

Flynn, Deirdre. "Last Ones Left Alive: Zombies and Post-Celtic Tiger Ireland." In *Theorising the Contemporary Zombie: Contextual Pasts, Presents, and Futures*, edited by Scott Hamilton and Conor Heffernan, 185–206. Cardiff: University of Wales Press, 2022.

French, Tana. *The Wych Elm*. New York: Viking, 2019.

Gudmundsdottir, Gunnthorunn, and Gerardine Meaney. "Introduction: Noir in the North." In *Noir in the North: Genre, Politics and Place*, edited by Stacy Gillis and Gunnthorunn Gudmundsdottir, 1–20. New York: Bloomsbury Academic, 2020.

Johnsen, Rosemary Erickson. "Crime Fiction's Dublin: Reconstructing Reality in Novels by Dermot Bolger, Gene Kerrigan, and Tana French." *Éire-Ireland* 49, no. 1 (2014): 121–41. https://doi:10.1353/eir.2014.0009.

Jordan, Justine. "The Wych Elm by Tana French Review—A Portrait of Privilege." *The Guardian*, February 21, 2019. www.theguardian.com/books/2019/feb/21/the-wych-elm-tana-french-review. Accessed October 8, 2021.

Mannion, Elizabeth, and Brian Cliff. *Guilt Rules All: Irish Mystery, Detective, and Crime Fiction.* Syracuse: Syracuse University Press, 2020.

Meier, William M., and Ian Campbell Ross. "Editors' Introduction: Irish Crime since 1921." *Éire-Ireland (St. Paul)* 49, no. 1 (2014): 7–21. https://doi:10.1353/eir.2014.0010.

Peters, Fiona, and Rebecca Stewart. *Antihero*. Bristol, UK: Intellect, 2016.

Scaggs, John. *Crime Fiction*. London: Routledge, 2005.

Schaffer, Rachel. "Introduction: Tana French and Irish Crime Fiction." *Clues* 32, no. 1 (2014): 9–12. https://doi:10.3172/CLU.32.1.9.

Smyth, Gerry. "Irish National Identity After the Celtic Tiger." *Estudios Irlandeses* 7, no. 7 (2012): 132–7.

6

Beyond "Puzzles and Bugaboos": A Family Systems Interpretation of Dorothy L. Sayers's "Monster," *Gaudy Night*

Beth McFarland-Wilson

In *Gaudy Night*, early-twentieth-century detective fiction writer Dorothy L. Sayers frames mystery and meaning through multiple levels and unusual venues of intrigue. In the story, Harriet Vane, a detective fiction writer in London, has with much hesitation returned to her alma mater, Shrewsbury College, for a class reunion, a gaudy. Immediately after arriving, she finds malicious notes on the grounds of the College and more threateningly, a note in her own academic gown saying, "You dirty murderess. Aren't you ashamed to show your face?"[1] Harriet knows this message refers to her arrest for and accusation of the murder of Philip Boyes in London, with charges dropped only after Lord Peter Wimsey, an aristocratic sleuth, is able to solve who had really killed Boyes. Several months after the gaudy, however, Harriet learns that someone is maligning others at the College when the college dean, Letitia Martin, asks her to use her skills of detection to investigate the continuing malicious acts. Harriet will soon find it necessary to invite Lord Peter to help discover the perpetrator of the malevolence, and together, they will solve the case.

The novel's length, structural complexity, and absence of murder prompted some critics and readers not to regard *Gaudy Night* as any important effort at detective fiction, much less serious fiction.[2] For many, detective stories had one primary purpose, and that was for a detective to solve a crime rationally.[3] Even Sayers understood the problem with her novel: "I admit that when I had completed my monster, I felt some of the uneasiness of Count Frankenstein under the same circumstances."[4] Still, she answered contemporaries who condemned *Gaudy Night* "for lack of construction"; she argued that her novel "was obscured by the conviction ... in many people's minds, that a detective plot [could not] bear any relation to a universal theme."[5] Against much criticism, she had begun to think beyond the constraints of form in the detective story.

To show how Sayers moves beyond her readers' and her own generic expectations to integrate formal elements of detective fiction with universal themes of human experience, including virtue, truth, courage, and the value of community, I rely on family systems theory, a sociological model established during the 1960s and 1970s that holistically analyzes family in relationship and conflict. Within the generic frame of her mystery, Sayers structures the Shrewsbury characters' responses to untidy relationships, actions, and events within the College and among its members. The individuals who struggle against the mystery within the College, except for the perpetrator of the malevolence, will find what is true as they navigate the dysfunction imposed upon their academic family. Four fundamental family systems concepts especially help illumine *Gaudy Night*: transgenerational influence, triangulations, family secrets, and morphogenesis. These concepts illuminate Sayers's success in artistically unifying cultural, socio-psychological, philosophical, and generic concepts within a work of detective fiction and help show that a work of popular detective fiction may indeed bear universal themes.

Sayers's Fictional Approach in Writing *Gaudy Night*

While working to write more than the simple detective story in *Gaudy Night*, Sayers admitted feeling that she had cobbled the novel together.[6] She wanted to bring the detective story back to a place where it was more than "composed entirely without plot, without theme, or with the theme a mere incidental embroidery."[7] But in this work, she cogently integrates the cultural problem of the human value of men and women, the social and psychological problems of human relationships, the philosophical problem of human integrity, and the literary problem of artistic unity. Through understanding her approach to writing fiction and her commitment to write beyond the generic limits of the detective story, we may understand that Sayers, "in on the beginning of the genre,"[8] was aware of the artistic benefit of integrating cultural, socio-psychological, and philosophical matters in detective fiction.

In *The Woman Detective: Gender and Genre*, Kathleen Gregory Klein explains that for the nineteenth-century reader, detective fiction focused on a brilliant detective who systematically resolved a crime and restored order. For Sayers, however, as much as "puzzles and bugaboos" delighted individuals, detective fiction was about more than the mystery at hand.[9] Detective fiction provided a "form in which to experiment with serious questions about social relationships—human puzzles—and the interior note of essential mystery."[10] Sayers understood that the contemporary detective story was changing, noting that a "little more psychological complexity [was] allowed than formerly." She observed that "the villain [was not necessarily] a villain from every point of view; the heroine, if there [was] one, [was] not necessarily pure."[11] Moreover, "the falsely accused innocent need not be a sympathetic character."[12] And the "automata—the weeping fair-haired girl—the stupid but manly young man with the biceps—even the colossally evil scientist with the hypnotic eyes—[were] all disappearing from the intellectual branch of the art, to be replaced by figures having more in common with humanity."[13] Sayers had come to realize that detective fiction could no longer be a genre of amusement and gratuitous sensationalism; rather, it was a fiction that needed to explain.[14] Sayers's message was that "[truth] must be served—in scholarship, human relations, in living a life" and that *Gaudy Night* expressed this universal theme.[15] Sayers believed that detective fiction could provide a generic provenance beyond the formula of the time.

Recognizing Sayers's preeminence in writing detective fiction, Howard Haycraft acknowledged in 1941 that no "single trend in the English detective story of the 1920's [sic] was more significant than [Sayers's] approach to the literary standards of the legitimate novel."[16] He explained that Sayers's experimentation with psychological and characterological matters of fiction saved a genre "fast approaching its limits."[17] In *The Seven Deadly Sins in the Work of Dorothy Sayers*, Janice Brown explains that in Sayers's detective fiction, characterization had "depth and credibility, the internal conflicts take precedence of the external ones, the complex thematic structure is sound, and the city of Oxford—as a symbol of what is truly valuable—[was] a powerfully drawn image that [permeated] the entire work."[18] The secretive qualities of Oxford's closed communities, class distinctions, locked doors, high walls and fences, gardens, stone buildings, stairways, and quads, could not help but effectively stage the mysterious in Sayers's novel. But more, the setting metaphorically reflected the systemic setting of the family. As Harriet and her colleagues engaged with or against the family spaces and boundaries within Shrewsbury College, the novel's intrigue and suspense were framed.

The Shrewsbury Family System

A family systemic interpretation of Sayers's *Gaudy Night* allows a cultural, socio-psychological, philosophical, and generic investigation of the ambiguities, confusion, and consequences of human transactions within Shrewsbury College. As Sayers juxtaposes the integrity of the Shrewsbury family with the simpler truth of who has perpetrated malevolence upon that family, she shows that the detective story is about more than solving a puzzle; the detective story concurrently articulates the mystery of human relationships.

Within the mystery of *Gaudy Night*, four family systems concepts, including transgenerational influence, triangulations, secrets, and morphogenesis, especially invite detection as readers who observe and interpret the transactions of the Shrewsbury family engage in their own process of discovery. John V. Knapp explains that family systems theory provides a critical interpretive model that looks at individuals as they transact among family members: "family-systems analysis focusses as much on the shared ecosystem as it does on any individual within it and is, therefore, a social psychology and clinical therapy contrastive to the intra-psychic theories of Freud and Lacan."[19] Significantly, Sayers understood eighty years ago that "however complicated the problem, [writers of detective fiction] never present the story as an isolated episode existing solely in virtue of its relation to the mechanics of detection."[20] Instead, they are "interested in the social background, in manners and morals, in the depiction and interplay of character; their works have a three-dimensional extension in time and space; they all, in their various ways, offer some kind of 'criticism of life.'"[21] Her prescient words reflect systemic correlations that may be established in her detective fiction as she integrates cultural, socio-psychological, and philosophical structures with her mysteries.

Sayers thus expresses her concern that while mechanical elements of a detective story plot can be readily managed, writers of detective fiction have "yet to discover the best way of combining these [elements] with a serious artistic treatment of the psychological elements, so that the intellectual and the common man can find common ground for enjoyment in the mystery novel as once they did in Greek or Elizabethan tragedy."[22] In a letter to her friend, Muriel St. Anne Byrne, Sayers shared that it "seemed necessary to set the heart-mind problem against a wide background."[23] She understood that the artistic unity of detective writing depended heavily upon her characters'—and her readers'—humanity within the context of community; she understood that "one cannot write a novel unless one has something to say about life,"[24] and for Sayers, life was what happened when individuals were in relationship, or not, with others. Thus, we find Sayers's Harriet Vane finally agreeing to help solve a mystery at her alma mater, her soul's nourishing mother, Shrewsbury College. In that mystery, as Harriet puzzles her way through the series of crimes that plague and threaten her Shrewsbury family, she also faces the perplexing emergence of her own humanity.

Transgenerational Influences in *Gaudy Night*

Significant transgenerational influences have established an institutional myth of conduct that Harriet has internalized and assented to as she is groomed by Oxfordian ideals and expectations, and it is these ideals and expectations that contribute to the distress she initially feels about going "home." Harriet worries that the Shrewsbury community would not have expected one of their own to have lived with a man whom she had not married or to have been accused of murder. Her sense of guilt and momentary self-denigration prevent her from being able to trust that her academic family could welcome her again, but her sense of guilt and self-doubt also remark the value of this community to her.

While little is told to the reader about Harriet's early family life, the narrator does mention that when Harriet's parents died, they "left her penniless," making her "struggle to earn a livelihood" in London.[25] Sayers thus introduces the first level of tension and suspense in the story when the narrator tells us Harriet is troubled about going back to Oxford after "the bitter years that lay between" her college years and the present.[26] These bitter years refer to Harriet's trial for the murder of Peter Boyes, a former lover. As Harriet considers returning to Shrewsbury, she fears she will not be able to withdraw herself emotionally from the events of her trial in London.[27] She also fears that she will be judged against the traditions of the College. Even so, during the time that Harriet is in Oxford to solve the problem of the malicious pranks, and as the strength of the Shrewsbury academic family is evidenced in its response to Harriet's return and to the present malevolence, Harriet will come to "ignore the whimpering ghost of her dead youth and tell herself that she was a stranger and a sojourner, [and that now she is] a well-to-do woman with a position in the world."[28] She will appropriate Shrewsbury College as her family, and she will also come to love a man and commit with him to marriage. Despite her fears, Harriet's Shrewsbury family will effectively contribute to her relational resilience and strength, just as she contributes to reestablishing its relational health.

Froma Walsh explains that an "optimally functioning family provides a 'holding environment' for members, a context of security, trust, and nurturance to support individual maturation."[29] Within that environment, family myths are passed down. Vincenzo F. Di Nicola remarks that families "live at once in worlds they themselves build, while being shaped by the larger culture of which they form a part."[30] He further explains that there is "an increasing recognition that the family's construction of meaning, its myths and its memories, is bound up with, shaped by, and situated in the places where its members live and those they recall."[31] For Harriet, Di Nicola could suggest, this "includes the places where we actually live and those that have a hold on our hearts and minds through shared memories and symbols."[32] Shrewsbury College was this place of meaning for Harriet.

Walsh similarly recognizes the importance of significant relational networks besides the biological family.[33] She explains that all "individuals are members of kinship groups, whether formal or informal, living under the same roof, within a community, or scattered at a great distance."[34] Parallel to the biological family system Walsh describes, the strong generational hierarchy present in the Shrewsbury community's systemic dynamics contributes to the health, strength, and recovery of the Shrewsbury family in its time of crisis.[35] Even as families must negotiate challenges to the family system and work to move beyond dysfunction, the Shrewsbury family will negotiate the challenges of its own dysfunctional behaviors as it systemically navigates the harm that has come to it. The Shrewsbury community, as they relate to one another in response to the attack, will ultimately function as a "shock absorber"[36] against the harm. When Harriet returns to Oxford for the gaudy, the narrator reveals her initial eagerness "to distinguish herself as sharply as possible from the former undergraduate who would have had to be content with a packet of sandwiches and a flask of coffee beneath the bough in the by-lane."[37] Harriet will come to credit her college and Oxford for her self-discovery, laughing "suddenly, and for the first time confident."[38] She will discover that her past "can't take this [confidence and sense of place] away. Whatever [she] may have done this remains."[39] Harriet is securely a scholar and a member of her Shrewsbury family, and Oxford is for her "a place achieved, inalienable, worthy of reverence."[40] Despite her distress and through her return to her college at Oxford, Harriet will come to understand that she can "forget the wreck and chaos of the past, or see it, at any rate, in truer proportion."[41] For Harriet, the Shrewsbury family that once caused her concern, and despite its present dysfunction, is now a place of belonging, recognition, and great worth.

Within the frame of her detective fiction, Sayers desired to synthesize the larger concerns of *sensus communis*, what is considered virtuous and honorable by a community, and she accomplished this synthesis in *Gaudy Night* by placing Harriet within the Shrewsbury College family. Sayers understood that what tied the community together was "not a consciousness of common blood so much as a common law, a common culture, and a very long memory of national consciousness."[42] She believed that "the same intellectual honesty that is essential to scholarship is essential to life"[43] and that detective fiction was similar to scholarly pursuit, an understanding Harriet and Peter would come to discover within their emerging romance. For Sayers, at the core, detective fiction sought and affirmed truth and integrity within the frame of community.

Thematically and generically as a detective novel, *Gaudy Night* emphasizes the "supremacy of truth and honesty,"[44] qualities passed down within functional relational systems; without these virtues, the Shrewsbury academic family could not function well.

Creating Turmoil through Triangulations

Within Sayers's understanding of human transaction, Shrewsbury College becomes a rich generic medium through which Sayers creates and Harriet reflects the sustained turmoil and suspense of her return to Oxford. As the Shrewsbury family members come to feel the loss of community and stability, they begin to respond. Members of the College will especially participate in its dysfunction through triangulation, a family systems dynamic by which individuals in relationship co-opt someone or something else to distribute or alleviate distress or tension. Murray Bowen, a pioneer of family systems theory, explains that triangulations occur when a family member engages another individual against a third party.[45] Peter Titelman, a Bowenian family systems theorist, further explains that the Bowenian "triangle concept focuses on the myriad expressions of fusion and distance" among members within a family system.[46] In *Gaudy Night*, for example, a simple triangulation occurs when Harriet admits her need for help to solve the mystery of the poison letters. Thus, she writes to Lord Peter, telling him that she is "afraid something drastic may happen if [they] don't cope with it quickly."[47] Harriet and Lord Peter will work against the malevolence and its perpetrator to solve the case.

George Grella characterizes *Gaudy Night* as a comedy of manners;[48] the ensuing triangulations and unraveling of the mystery in the story beg his description. Reggie Pomfret, Harriet's junior by twenty years, maintains a crush on Harriet throughout the novel and assaults Lord Peter for being with her.[49] Miss Hillyard is enamored of Lord Peter and resents Harriet's involvement with him.[50] Triangulating with and among members of the Shrewsbury family against the perpetrator of the havoc, characters run through the College at all hours in pursuit of the Shrewsbury ghost. The perpetrator of the vandalism triangulates against Harriet and her academic family by leaving clues to misdirect them, as in the case with the bronze hairpins.[51] The perpetrator also introduces the potential for multiple triangulations as members of Shrewsbury College are positioned to wonder if one of their own colleagues has committed the acts against them.

Sayers creates these triangulations, comically or not, for the purpose of distraction and to create suspense. At a philosophical and moral level, however, the Shrewsbury family will courageously triangulate against the perpetrator of the vandalism as they seek the truth.

Driving Suspense through the Family Secret

Integral to triangulation is the secret through which one party hides some knowledge from someone or something else. A fundamental structural condition of detective fiction is established through the secret, which drives the plot, creates the suspense, and must be resolved to restore order. For self-protection and to set blame, a secret bearer often triangulates with the secret against another individual or entity. In time and through its manifestations, the secret becomes destructive as it generates anxiety in those who contend with harm without knowing who is doing the harm. Thus, through the triangulations generated by secrets in *Gaudy Night*, Sayers builds and sustains the generic imperative of suspense.[52]

Implicit in the College's request for Harriet to handle the matter is the need for "delicate interrogation,"[53] a triangulation sought because of the "extreme awkwardness of the situation," and the dean's hope that members of the College will cooperate "in getting the matter cleared up."[54] The dean warns, "Whatever any of us may think or feel, it is of the very greatest importance that we should dismiss, as far as possible, all vague suspicions from our minds, and be particularly careful how we may say anything that might be construed as an accusation against anybody at all."[55] She wisely asserts that in "a close community of this kind, nothing can be more harmful than an atmosphere of mutual distrust,"[56] intuiting what systemic theory demonstrates about the dangerous emotional liaisons, the triangulations, that may develop as a result of a miscreant's secret. She also understands that the reputation of the College may also be damaged and introduces a second secret into the fray. It is a secret about the secret; the College must keep things quiet. True to the nature of family systemic dysfunction, the secret that the College itself has agreed to perpetrate will provoke its members to begin to blame one another. Thus, as members of the College fear their secret may damage their reputations, these individuals systemically become enmeshed further within triangulations forced upon them by the perpetrator.

More problematically, in protecting the secret of what is happening in the College, the dons and scholars also protect the perpetrator of the maliciousness. As they protect the perpetrator, Annie Wilson, Annie gains the emotional advantage of a thorough revenge against Miss de Vine for exposing her [Annie's] husband's scholarly fraud; moreover, Annie blames her husband's suicide on Miss de Vine.[57] In *Secrets in Families and Family Therapy*, Evan Imber-Black demonstrates cases showing the destructive effects of secrets on family members.[58] In *Gaudy Night*, Annie's subtle emotional blackmail and her violence allow her to sustain control of Shrewsbury College through fear, and by what Maria Selvini Palazolli, founder of the Milan school of family therapy, calls "dirty games."[59] Blame is one of the dirty games Annie plays.

Annie knows enough of the College's fear for its reputation, of Harriet's shame over her past, and of Miss de Vine's sense of moral responsibility that when the secret of Annie's behavior comes to light, her hatred spills over.[60] After Miss de Vine tells Annie that it was her [Miss de Vine's] job to report Annie's husband's breach of scholarship, Annie responds by saying she wishes she could kill all the members of the Shrewsbury community. She seeks to destroy confidence in everyone in the room by revealing their failings, even spitting in Lord Peter's face as she blames men like him for making women do what she has done.[61] Annie's invective is so destructive that Harriet, who has throughout the novel shown strength and ability to negotiate the emotional distress of the mystery at Shrewsbury, becomes sick from the "shock of seeing so many feelings stripped naked."[62] Deborah Anne Luepnitz elaborates upon Selvini Palazolli's identification of the dirty games of secrecy, describing these games as "games of deceit and power."[63] The revelation of Annie's vengeance exposes her secrets, games of power, and maleficence.

While deceitful games may be created in detective fiction for the purposes of distraction and suspense, at a philosophical level, Harriet, Lord Peter, and the scholarly community of Shrewsbury College will participate in a final triangulation against the perpetrator of the vandalism through exposing the crimes, a true resolution of the story's conflict. From a philosophical and systemic perspective, the secret perpetrated by Annie against the members of the College motivates a search for truth.

Harriet's Morphogenesis in *Gaudy Night*

Only after the secret is exposed may the academic family return to stability. Mark A. Yarhouse and James A. Sells write that "families need balance, security and predictability in order to exist" and especially so when they face a crisis.[64] Within Annie's triangulations against the women of Shrewsbury College, Sayers shows that Annie's secret and her vengeance are sufficiently malevolent to destroy stability and the sense of belonging that members of Shrewsbury College value. Even so, through her experience with her Shrewsbury family, Harriet will find an independence that reflects the strength and value of an educated woman.

Family systems theorists and practitioners explain that the functional family system adjusts to its members' maturational process as it allows members to distance themselves from and then return to the system. In family systems theory, a person's growth despite the dysfunction of their family system is called morphogenesis. Knapp explains that "[not] all unsettling changes [in the family system] are ultimately negative. In a dysfunctional family, *morphogenesis* is the risk families must take."[65] It is thus possible for individuals not to be constrained by the boundaries of family dysfunction. Harriet's morphogenesis will become a positive movement toward personal liberation as she determines to move freely within the Shrewsbury family system, despite its dysfunction, as she engages with this community in their response to the malevolence it experiences, and then as she determines to move toward Peter in her decision to marry him. As she moves within the Shrewsbury family system and against its boundaries, Harriet and others within this system experience growth. Through the lens of family systems theory, it may be suggested that Sayers demonstrated an authentic liberation of women in *Gaudy Night*, not because of any societal trend but as a process of maturation occurring when an individual risked change and a willingness to break out of that which would constrain her.

Annie, in her mad games to avenge her husband's suicide, particularly capitalizes on the prejudice against women at Oxford. Annie argues with Harriet and other Shrewsbury women that there is something unnatural about an educated woman, that educated women are sexually and relationally starved, that educated women take away jobs from men and livelihoods from families, and that educated women still know fear.[66] And as negatively as Annie casts her view of educated women, so do Sayers's critics, both then and more recently.

Indirectly summing up Sayers's contemporary critics' generic problem with *Gaudy Night*, Klein describes nineteenth-century readers' expectations of the early detective novel:

> the prominent figure of the one [male] detective intelligently and unerringly picks his way through clues left by a limited group of suspects to find the villain who has killed, robbed, or blackmailed. As he uncovers evil, the detective is always able to provide an explicable motive for the crime. The fixed formula of the plot [requires] a three part ending: capture of the criminal, explanation of the crime, reestablishment of the social order guaranteed by the removal of the criminal from society. In its ability to create order out of chaos, the power of the detective intersecting with the plot is just short of godlike even if his personality does not always match.[67]

Even though in *Gaudy Night* the criminal is apprehended, the motive explained, and the social order restored, Harriet is a woman. Klein notes that detective fiction reflects an "unacknowledged sabotage of [women detectives]" and reinforces "a nostalgic mythology of women's [and criminals' secondary] position" in literature and society.[68] Elizabeth Trembley specifically articulates the negative response of more recent feminist readers and critics toward "Sayers's handling of Harriet [Vane]."[69] Their general dissatisfaction with the institution of marriage, Harriet's giving up her independence in agreeing to marry Lord Peter, and Harriet's abandonment of the feminist agenda help them justify the feminists' complaint against both the author and Harriet.[70] Trembley explains that for the feminist, "Sayers's potential to create a vibrant feminist character disintegrates with Harriet's final conventionality [of marrying Lord Peter]."[71]

Surprisingly, upon the publication of *Gaudy Night* in 1937, Sayers's male readers disagreed with her critics. While Sayers expressed her doubts to her publisher that men

> "would probably not be interested in a bunch of middle-aged academic women, and would find Harriet unattractive," the "'male reader' confounded [her] prophecy by not merely displaying interest in academic women, but by producing a strong 'pro-Harriet' party, which asserted, in the teeth of those female readers who complained of Peter's throwing himself away on Harriet, that Harriet, on the contrary, was completely thrown away on Peter."[72]

Sayers's contemporary male readers' interest in educated women can be explained. Identifying Sayers as the "first author to employ the detective story to write about important feminist issues," B. J. Rahn notes that Sayers thematically establishes the dons and scholars of Shrewsbury College as responsible, competent, caring, honest, and serious.[73] They are women of academic and personal integrity, with genuine motivations as they contend with the actions of a malcontent, a woman herself, who "disputes the importance of abstract truth and the value of scholarship."[74] Male readers could thus align themselves with the virtues that Sayers's academic women of Shrewsbury College signified.

On the other hand, in "Sayers and the Amazons," published in 1975, Nina Auerbach sharply criticizes Sayers' Shrewsbury women, inferring that they were like "impoverished old [Victorian] maids who inhabit the tucked-away little village, living on kindness and charity and memories of their parents' gentility" at the same time they gossiped at card parties.[75] Auerbach's inference is close in harshness but opposite to Annie Wilson's attack on academic women in their parochial communities. Annie scolds the Shrewsbury women, declaring that there is nothing about "life and marriage and children" in their books, that they "can't do anything for themselves," and that Harriet took a man, used him, and then threw him away.[76] Auerbach scolds that the "women of Shrewsbury are unique because they provide a haven from the self, not for it."[77] Sayers did not identify herself as a feminist, however; rather, she believed that "a woman [was] just as much an ordinary human being as a man, with the same individual preferences, and with just as much right to the tastes and preferences of an individual."[78] She was more concerned that women, especially women in colleges, may try to "copy" and assume the privileges of men[79] rather than recognize themselves as individuals.[80] She did not want women to be "reckoned always as a member of a class."[81] If this reckoning were the case, then women would admit to inferiority.[82] The Shrewsbury women would not ultimately admit to inferiority.

For Sayers, classifying human beings according to perceived failures of a particular class of individuals could put individuals at risk of losing the freedom "to think and act."[83] But in *Gaudy Night*, Sayers "show[ed] Oxford as a place where condescension towards women as such [was] not universal nor even typical."[84] The Shrewsbury community represented a place of learning, freedom, and growth, even as it faced, and because it faced, dysfunction. In the novel, Harriet Vane thus embodies Sayers' advocacy of the value of women to the educational institution and, in turn, the value of an education to a woman.

When a family systems interpretation is applied to Shrewsbury College, Annie's and Auerbach's analyses are rendered incomplete. Harriet actively chooses to leave and then return to and participate within her Shrewsbury family, indicating her ability to negotiate the family dynamics and its boundaries. The *family dance* is a systemic dynamic in which members of a family participate in "inevitable pushes and pulls to establish a balance between intimacy and self-independence."[85] The metaphor of the family dance can help the reader understand that Harriet's hesitations and advances within the Shrewsbury community are to be expected within the process of morphogenesis. Her character and disposition are shaped by, but not fused with, her Shrewsbury family. Also, at a dinner with Lord Peter in London, Harriet notes the number of "promising scholars, distinguished in their studies, [who were] subsequently extinguished by matrimony,"[86] reflecting Sayers's understanding that individuals were responsible for the consequences of their choices.[87] Harriet is aware of the possibility that educated women may become fused with and lost within a role, and particularly within the role of a wife. Even so, the story "makes a moving plea for the importance of [the academic family] for society as a whole."[88] These scholarly communities were "still centers where men and women [could] live self-examined lives, 'translating' ideas and concepts into other terms and testing them for truth."[89] The family dance of Shrewsbury College offered Harriet a place to move within, around, and beyond the Oxford community.

Harriet does initially struggle with a sense of inferiority in *Gaudy Night*, but, apart from several extreme events in the plot where she has reason to doubt herself, her good sense and intellect protect her from vulnerability to self-doubts and to Peter. Thus, Sayers could not easily "marry Peter off to the young woman he had ... rescued from death and infamy, because [she, Sayers,] could find no form of words in which [Harriet] could accept him without loss of self-respect."[90] Harriet would have been compelled to "live on gratitude" for what he had done for her in saving her from the lethal chamber.[91] Instead, through her ordinariness and authenticity within the context of her Shrewsbury family, Harriet's morphogenesis helps her reject a culture's misguided view of educated women and move toward a relationship with Peter.

Sayers creates relational balance between Harriet and Peter by characterizing them as human beings within the Shrewsbury family dysfunction. Sayers realized it was "the habit of intellectual integrity which is at once the foundation and the result of scholarship" and the "great permanent value in an emotionally unstable world" that could integrate the love interest within this detective narrative.[92] She explains that she could have thrown Peter and Harriet together easily, but as a writer, she "saw that [demanding this relationship] was in every respect false and degrading; and the puppets had somehow got just so much flesh and blood in them that [she] could not force them to accept [the marriage relationship]."[93] Sayers further tells her readers that she could also have simply ignored the problem—or she could change Lord Peter, make him "a complete human being, with a past and a future, with a consistent family and social history, with a complicated social psychology and even the rudiments of a religious outlook."[94] Sayers's allowance of instability and conflict within the relationship between Harriet and Peter would render it a flawed, yet authentic, relationship. Within that instability, conflict, and authenticity, growth could take place.

Out of this conundrum, Sayers allows Lord Peter to realize that Harriet "must come to him as a free agent, if she [comes] at all" and that she must be "independent of him before she [can] bring her dependence as a willing gift."[95] Sayers understood that Lord Peter and Harriet's relationship required the utmost integrity and the strength of living in community to succeed, fictionally and literally, if her perspective were understood by her readers. Such integrity is demonstrated when, after Harriet cannot say "Yes" to Lord Peter upon his last proposal of marriage, she can say to a man who has taken his scholar's hat off and "found the [words] for her": "*Placetne, magistra?. ... Placet*," she responds.[96] Through these words of approval and acceptance, two members of the Oxford community establish themselves in balanced, equal alliance. In this dialogue, Sayers performatively declares the equal humanity of Harriet and Peter as *magistra* and *magistri*. They are individuals whose relationship now stands as an equitable alliance that characterizes a functional relationship. Yarhouse and Sells write that "families need balance, security and predictability in order to exist" and especially so when they face crisis.[97] In Harriet's freedom to move toward

Lord Peter, she can paradoxically find balance, security, and predictability, even within crisis.

Harriet's morphogenesis in *Gaudy Night* brings her out of a past shame that could have kept her from growing as an individual with others she valued and cared for. Harriet returns to a community that encourages and needs her to act and think authentically and effectively in response to the malevolence that threatened to destroy it. At the same time, she willingly and knowingly establishes a balanced, functional relationship with Lord Peter. That fluidity allows her to move freely within and outside of the boundaries of the Shrewsbury family dance and then within and outside of the boundaries of her dance with Lord Peter.

Conclusion

One more return to the community in *Gaudy Night* must be noted. Within the Shrewsbury family system, Annie is not thrown out because of her behavior. When her great pain is revealed, she is kept within the family and cared for. The reader is told that the "Warden issued a brief and discreet announcement that the offender had been traced and the trouble ended."[98] In this forgiveness and understanding by those who had been offended in the community, Sayers seals her argument that the detective story is a place where humanity may be valued and preserved. David Coomes asserts that Sayers achieves her "ambitious goal of fusing social comment with detection."[99] She validated the detective story as more than a puzzle to be solved; for her, the detective story could articulate the range, mystery, and worth of people's experiences with and among others. As she broke the formulaic, gender-biased rules for writing detective stories, she raised the standard of writing detective fiction through addressing universal thematic concerns in *Gaudy Night*.

Family systems theory helps readers understand how Sayers achieved her goal. While a family systems approach helps readers piece together the "puzzles and bugaboos" of the Shrewsbury College mystery, this interpretive approach also helps confirm the themes of virtue, truth, courage, and *sensus communis* that the story evinces as it also evinces the betrayals and deceptions of dysfunction. Unlike the traditional psychoanalytic model that focuses on the pathology of an individual's behavior, family systems theory addresses the interrelationships and alliances among individuals as they contend with others in the everyday contexts of living, both good and bad. A good detective story could be written about the intrapsychic goings-on of a person, but Sayers shows that mystery remains ensconced in relationship.

In her Shrewsbury mystery, and well before family systems theory was formally recognized and then applied as a critical interpretive tool, Sayers successfully synthesized family dynamics with larger themes of life. As she structured the Shrewsbury family members' concern with the "supremacy of truth and honesty,"[100] the dysfunction introduced by the mystery's unraveling, the hope that an individual can move beyond family dysfunction, and the value of a family and community to an individual, Sayers articulated a high calling for the genre of mystery: to assert the importance and benefits of engaging genuinely within family and community for the good of self and others.

Notes

1   Dorothy L. Sayers, *Gaudy Night* (1935; New York: Harper Paperbacks, 1936), 58.
2   James Brabazon, *Dorothy L. Sayers* (New York: Charles Scribner's Sons, 1981), 153–4.
3   Michael Holquist, "Whodunit and Other Questions: Metaphysical Detective Stories in Post-War Fiction," *New Literary History* 3, no. 1 (1971): 139, 143.
4   Sayers, *Gaudy*, 89.
5   Ibid., 87–8.
6   Ibid., 75–95.
7   Ibid., 88.
8   Marjorie Lamp Mead, email communication to author, March 20, 2013.
9   Dorothy L. Sayers, "The Omnibus of Crime," 1928, in *The Art of the Mystery Story: A Collection of Critical Essays*, ed. Howard Haycraft (New York: Simon & Schuster, 1946), 71.
10 Dawson Gaillard, *Dorothy Sayers* (New York: Frederick Ungar Publishing, 1981) 10.
11 Sayers, "The Omnibus," 105.
12 Ibid., 105.
13 Ibid.
14 Gaillard, *Dorothy Sayers*, 7.
15 Carolyn G. Hart, "*Gaudy Night*: Quintessential Sayers," in *Dorothy L. Sayers: The Centenary Celebration*, ed. Alzina Stone Dale (London: Walker, 1993), 49–50.
16 Howard Haycraft, *Murder for Pleasure: The Life and Times of the Detective Story* (New York: D. Appleton-Century, 1941), 135.
17 Ibid., 137.
18 Janice Brown, *The Seven Deadly Sins in the Work of Dorothy Sayers* (Kent: Kent State University Press, 1998), 150.

19 John V. Knapp, "Family-Systems Psychotherapy and Psychoanalytic Criticism: A Comparative Critique," *Mosaic* 3, no. 1 (2004): 158.
20 Dorothy L. Sayers, introduction to *Tales of Detection*, ed. Dorothy L. Sayers (London: Dent & Sons, 1936), 9.
21 Ibid., 9.
22 Ibid., 13.
23 Barbara Reynolds, ed., *The Letters of Dorothy L. Sayers, 1899–1936: The Making of a Detective Novelist* (New York: St. Martin's Press, 1995), 353.
24 Sayers, *Gaudy*, 75.
25 Ibid., 2.
26 Ibid.
27 Ibid., 18.
28 Ibid., 4.
29 Froma Walsh, *Normal Family Processes*. 2nd edition (New York: Guilford Press, 1993), 36.
30 Vincenzo F. Di Nicola, *A Stranger in the Family: Culture, Families, and Therapy* (New York: Norton, 1997), 84.
31 Ibid., 84.
32 Ibid.
33 Walsh, *Normal Family Processes*, 104.
34 Ibid., 104.
35 Ibid.
36 Ibid., 141.
37 Sayers, *Gaudy Night*, 4–5.
38 Ibid., 8.
39 Ibid.
40 Ibid., 9.
41 Ibid., 17–18.
42 Dorothy L. Sayers, *The Mysterious English* (New York: Macmillan, 1941), 8.
43 Sayers, *Gaudy*, 217. Cushing Strout, "Romance and the Literary Detective: The Legacy of Dorothy Sayers," *The Sewanee Review* 109, no. 3 (2001): 427.
44 Marianne Thormählen, "The Idea of Academe in *Gaudy Night*—and How It Strikes a Contemporary," in *Studies in Sayers: Essays Presented to Dr. Barbara Reynolds on Her 80th Birthday*, ed. Christopher Dean (Hurstpierpoint, West Sussex, England: Dorothy L. Sayers Society, 1994), 21.
45 Murray Bowen, "Treatment of Family Groups with a Schizophrenic Member," in *Family Therapy in Clinical Practice* (Northvale, NJ: Jason Aronson, 1978), 3–15.
46 Peter Titelman, "The Concept of the Triangle in Bowen Theory: An Overview," in *Triangles: Bowen Family Systems Theory Perspectives*, ed. Peter Titelman (New York: Haworth Press, 2008), 16.

47 Sayers, *Gaudy*, 292.
48 George Grella, "Murder and Manners: The Formal Detective Novel," *Novel: A Forum on Fiction* 4, no. 1 (1970): 42.
49 Sayers, *Gaudy*, 422.
50 Ibid., 443–6.
51 Ibid., 479.
52 Ibid., 93.
53 Ibid., 88.
54 Ibid., 96.
55 Ibid.
56 Ibid.
57 Ibid., 485.
58 Evan Imber-Black, ed., *Secrets in Families and Family Therapy* (New York: Norton, 1993).
59 Quoted in Deborah Anna Luepnitz, *The Family Interpreted: Psychoanalysis, Feminism, and Family Therapy* (New York: Basic Books, 1988), 998.
60 Sayers, *Gaudy*, 473.
61 Ibid., 487–8.
62 Ibid., 489.
63 Ibid., 98.
64 Mark A. Yarhouse and James N. Sells, *Family Therapies: A Comprehensive Christian Appraisal* (Westmont: InterVarsity Press, 2008), 315.
65 John V. Knapp, "Family Systems Therapy and Literary Study: An Introduction," in *Reading the Family Dance: Family Systems Therapy and Literary Study*, ed. John V. Knapp and Kenneth Womack (Newark: University of Delaware Press, 2003), 18.
66 Sayers, *Gaudy*, 473.
67 Kathleen Gregory Klein, *The Woman Detective: Gender and Genre*, 2nd edition (Champaign: University of Illinois Press, 1995), 54.
68 Ibid., 1–2.
69 Elizabeth Trembley, "'Collaring the Other Fellow's Property': Feminism Reads Dorothy Sayers," in *Women Times Three: Writers, Detectives, Readers*, ed. Kathleen Gregory Klein (Bowling Green: Bowling Green State University Popular Press, 1995), 82
70 Ibid.
71 Ibid.
72 Sayers, *Gaudy*, 89–90.
73 B. J. Rahn, "The Marriage of True Minds," in *Dorothy L. Sayers: The Centenary Celebration*, ed. Alzina Stone Dale (London: Walker, 1993), 51, 57.
74 Ibid., 58.

75 Nina Auerbach, "Dorothy Sayers and the Amazons," *Feminist Studies* 3, nos. 1–2 (1975): 55.
76 Sayers, *Gaudy*, 487.
77 Auerbach, "Dorothy Sayers," 57.
78 Dorothy L. Sayers, *Are Women Human?* (Grand Rapids: Eerdmans, 1971), 24.
79 Ibid., 27, 30.
80 Ibid., 24.
81 Ibid.
82 Ibid., 30
83 Sayers, *Are Women Human?* 57.
84 Mary McDermott Shideler, introduction to *Are Women Human?*, ed. Dorothy L. Sayers (Grand Rapids: Eerdmans, 1971), 4–5.
85 Knapp, "Family Systems Therapy," 16.
86 Sayers, *Gaudy*, 67.
87 Sayers, *Are Women Human?* 35.
88 Alzina Stone Dale, *Maker and Craftsman* (1978; Wheaton, IL: Harold Shaw Publishers, 1992), 40.
89 Ibid.
90 Sayers, *Gaudy Night*, 79.
91 Ibid., 81.
92 Ibid., 82.
93 Ibid., 79.
94 Ibid., 79–80.
95 Ibid., 87.
96 Ibid., 501.
97 Yarhouse and Sells, *Family Therapies*, 315.
98 Sayers, *Gaudy Night*, 493.
99 David Coomes, *Dorothy L. Sayers: A Careless Rage for Life* (Oxford: Lion Publishing, 1992), 51.
100 Thormählen, "The Idea," 21.

Bibliography

Auerbach, Nina. "Dorothy Sayers and the Amazons." *Feminist Studies* 3, nos. 1–2 (1975): 54–62.
Bowen, Murray. "Treatment of Family Groups with a Schizophrenic Member." In *Family Therapy in Clinical Practice*, 3–15. Northvale, NJ: Jason Aronson, 1978.
Brabazon, James. *Dorothy L. Sayers*. New York: Charles Scribner's Sons, 1981.

Brown, Janice. *The Seven Deadly Sins in the Work of Dorothy Sayers*. Kent: Kent State University Press, 1998.
Coomes, David. *Dorothy L. Sayers: A Careless Rage for Life*. Oxford: Lion Publishing, 1992.
Dale, Alzina Stone. *Maker and Craftsman*. 1978. Wheaton, IL: Harold Shaw Publishers, 1992.
Di Nicola, Vincenzo F. *A Stranger in the Family: Culture, Families, and Therapy*. New York: Norton, 1997.
Gaillard, Dawson. *Dorothy Sayers*. New York: Frederick Ungar Publishing, 1981.
Grella, George. "Murder and Manners: The Formal Detective Novel." *Novel: A Forum on Fiction* 4, no. 1 (1970): 30–48.
Hart, Carolyn G. "*Gaudy Night*: Quintessential Sayers." In *Dorothy L. Sayers: The Centenary Celebration*, edited by Alzina Stone Dale, 46–50. London: Walker, 1993.
Haycraft, Howard. *Murder for Pleasure: The Life and Times of the Detective Story*. New York: D. Appleton-Century, 1941.
Holquist, Michael. "Whodunit and Other Questions: Metaphysical Detective Stories in Post-War Fiction." *New Literary History* 3, no. 1 (1971): 135–56.
Imber-Black, Evan, ed. *Secrets in Families and Family Therapy*. New York: Norton, 1993.
Klein, Kathleen Gregory. *The Woman Detective: Gender and Genre*. 2nd edition. Champaign: University of Illinois Press, 1995.
Knapp, John V. "Family-Systems Psychotherapy and Psychoanalytic Criticism: A Comparative Critique." *Mosaic* 3, no. 1 (2004): 149–66.
Knapp, John V. "Family Systems Therapy and Literary Study: An Introduction." In *Reading the Family Dance: Family Systems Therapy and Literary Study*, edited by John V. Knapp and Kenneth Womack, 13–26. Newark: University of Delaware Press, 2003.
Luepnitz, Deborah Anna. *The Family Interpreted: Psychoanalysis, Feminism, and Family Therapy*. New York: Basic Books, 1988.
Rahn, B. J. "The Marriage of True Minds." In *Dorothy L. Sayers: The Centenary Celebration*, edited by Alzina Stone Dale, 51–6. London: Walker, 1993.
Reynolds, Barbara, ed. *The Letters of Dorothy L. Sayers. 1899–1936: The Making of a Detective Novelist*. New York: St. Martin's Press, 1995.
Sayers, Dorothy L. *Are Women Human?* Grand Rapids: Eerdmans, 1971.
Sayers, Dorothy L. *Gaudy Night*. 1935. New York: Harper Paperbacks, 1936.
Sayers, Dorothy L. "*Gaudy Night*." In *Titles to Fame*, edited by Denys Kilham Roberts, 75–95. New York: Thomas Nelson, 1937.
Sayers, Dorothy L., ed. Introduction to *Tales of Detection*. London: Dent & Sons, 1936, 7–14.
Sayers, Dorothy L. *The Mysterious English*. New York: Macmillan, 1941.
Sayers, Dorothy L. "The Omnibus of Crime." 1928. In *The Art of the Mystery Story: A Collection of Critical Essays*, edited by Howard Haycraft, 71–109. New York: Simon & Schuster, 1946.
Shideler, Mary McDermott. Introduction to *Are Women Human?*, edited by Dorothy L. Sayers, 1–17. Grand Rapids: Eerdmans, 1971.
Strout, Cushing. "Romance and the Literary Detective: The Legacy of Dorothy Sayers." *The Sewanee Review* 109, no. 3 (2001): 423–36.

Thormählen, Marianne. "The Idea of Academe in *Gaudy Night*—and How It Strikes a Contemporary." In *Studies in Sayers: Essays Presented to Dr. Barbara Reynolds on Her 80th Birthday*, edited by Christopher Dean, 21–7. Hurstpierpoint, West Sussex, England: Dorothy L. Sayers Society, 1994.

Titelman, Peter. "The Concept of the Triangle in Bowen Theory: An Overview." In *Triangles: Bowen Family Systems Theory Perspectives*, edited by Peter Titelman, 3–64. New York: Haworth Press, 2008.

Trembley, Elizabeth. "'Collaring the Other Fellow's Property': Feminism Reads Dorothy Sayers." In *Women Times Three: Writers, Detectives, Readers*, edited by Kathleen Gregory Klein, 81–99. Bowling Green: Bowling Green State University Popular Press, 1995.

Walsh, Froma. *Normal Family Processes*. 2nd edition. New York: Guilford Press, 1993.

Yarhouse, Mark A., and James N. Sells. *Family Therapies: A Comprehensive Christian Appraisal*. Westmont: InterVarsity Press, 2008.

PART TWO

World Literature and Moral Ambiguity

7

Opaque Feminine Ethics in Kirino's *Out*

Aya Kubota and John J. Han

Upon publication in Japan in 1997, Natsuo Kirino's *Out: A Thriller* ("アウト" in Japanese; pronounced *a-utto*) created a publishing sensation, selling 300,000 copies. At a time when the phrase *disparity society* (格差社会, *kakusa shakai*) had yet to be coined, this novel allowed Japanese readers to understand their compatriots who lived on welfare and were neglected by society. Written by a female crime novelist, *Out* kept its readers on their tiptoes with its shocking yet thrilling plot. The novel earned a nomination for the Naoki Prize in 1997 but missed the prize because, according to *Ronza*, there was "too little hope in the world of the work."[1] In 1997, *The Mainichi Shimbun* predicted, "*Out* will be a long-lasting and memorable work as a harvest of this year's Japanese mystery."[2] In 2019, *The Asahi Shimbun* ranked the novel as the fourth among the thirty books of the Heisei era (1989–2019).[3] In addition, Kirino's novel garnered the Mystery Writers of Japan Award for Best Novel (1998), the Best Japanese Crime Fiction of the Year (1998), and a nomination for the Edgar Award for Best Novel (2004). Kirino's novel was also made into a movie in 2002 under the directorship of Hideyuki Hirayama.

Based on an actual crime,[4] the story includes uncomfortable details, such as cutting up human corpses, lust murder that pleasures both the killer and the killed, and the sexualization of schoolgirls. In addition to a suspenseful plot, *Out* offers a harsh criticism of contemporary Japanese society, including gender inequality, social alienation, clinical depression, and family breakdown. Works of mystery fiction tend to be dark, but *Out* is particularly dark in its mood and atmosphere. Set in contemporary Tokyo, the largest city in the world, the novel highlights the sordid underside of urban life. The novel hints that urban life is not entirely negative by mentioning the Tokyoites who watch out for criminal activities in their neighborhood and company employees who do their jobs. However, in its predominant focus on the seamy side of life, *Out* is a naturalistic novel—a novel of extreme realism. *Out* is also a psychological thriller that skillfully portrays the nervousness and anxiety that follow women's criminal activities.

The novel begins with the murder of an abusive and negligent husband, Kenji, by his 34-year-old wife, Yayoi Yamamoto. She works the night shift at a boxed-lunch factory in suburban Tokyo, where she has three close female co-workers: Masako Katori, a 44-year-old woman who is intuitive and even-keeled; Yoshie Azuma, a widow in her late fifties who looks after her bedridden mother-in-law; and Kuniko Jonouchi, a 33-year-old woman in constant debt due to her extravagant spending habits. Yayoi's homicide resulted from the grudges against Kenji's physical abuse, disinterest in her, gambling, and marital infidelity. After the murder, she contacts Masako, who, out of empathy, decides to help her cover up the crime. Masako manages to secure aid from Yoshie and Kuniko, who half-heartedly become accomplices after Masako tells them that she will have Yayoi pay them for their help.

A successful disposal of the body exonerates Yayoi from murder charges, and her friends feel relieved. Law enforcement, however, arrests the wrong person—Sadake, an ex-murderer and the owner of a club and an illegal casino. After around a month in jail, Sadake is released. By this time, however, he loses his entire business enterprise due to the rumors about his shady past. Intent on finding the real killer, he becomes a self-styled investigator. He kills Kuniko, whose body Masako and Yoshie are forced to cut up under his threats. Near the end of the novel, Sadake kidnaps Masako and attempts to kill her in the same way he killed another woman many years ago—during sex. After he rapes her repeatedly inside a deserted factory, the time comes for him to kill her. Although Sadake—a former gangster—is stout, she strikes first by slashing his face with a scalpel. Sadake dies a slow death, and Masako feels sympathy for him because she sees herself in him. The novel closes as she decides to leave Japan.

Critics and scholars in Japan have approached *Out* mostly from a feminist angle. For instance, Sachie Kitada writes,

> There is no doubt that *Out* was an expression of women's explosive anger towards a robust androcentric society. ... The monstrous nature of women's actions in this novel means that they reject the real "safe worldview and perfect order" and destroy it in search of a new life. ... The novel seems like a declaration of struggle for women to thoroughly push once for true survival.[5]

Certainly, *Out* is a radical departure from traditional Japanese fiction in which women are often portrayed as docile, submissive, and demure.

Out was first published in English translation in 2003 by Kodansha International, and a Vintage international edition came out in 2005.[6] Since its debut in the West, the novel has received extensive critical attention by periodicals, including *The New York Times*, *The Washington Post*, and *The Los Angeles Times*. Critical reception of the book has been marked by shock and surprise. Despite its excessively graphic nature, critics view Kirino's story as an exposé of contemporary Japanese society, especially the plight of women.[7] They also count *Out* among the best feminist murder mysteries of the world.[8]

As noted by many critics, the theme of feminism pervades *Out*, especially in the first half of the novel, where the author credibly portrays the plight of Japanese women. Seen from the perspective of morality, however, the author's feminist ideas lack consistency, which undermines the feminist ideals through questionable actions of the main character, Masako.[9] This chapter argues that, as a feminist novel, *Out* is only partially successful by portraying the malaise of contemporary Japan without providing a clear moral direction. The fact that Masako—the most important character in the novel—goes to another country implies escapism rather than a constructive solution.

Feminism in *Out*

In *Out*, the author expresses her empathy for women who fall victim to spousal abuse and neglect. In an interview with a magazine, Kirino stated, "Masako, Kuniko and the other female characters breathed in my head and shouted, 'Write quickly,' and it was about to explode."[10] As a graduate of a well-known university who seems to have a stable marriage, Kirino belongs to a social class higher than that of the women in the novel. In the story, however, Kirino almost becomes one of them by showing compassion for her female characters. After writing the last line of *Out*, her eyes were filled with tears. She felt the misfortune of the four women as her own to a great extent, and she might have felt like a victim of anomalous sexual behavior as displayed by Sadake.[11]

As Raman Selden notes, feminist criticism often "summons up the anger of the Furies in order to disturb the complacent certainties of patriarchal culture and to create a less oppressive climate for women writers and readers."[12] In *Out*, Kirino releases her fury against the deep-rooted male chauvinism and its debilitating effects on women in Japan. Yayoi endures Kenji's spousal abuse and neglect until, one night, she decides not to take them any longer:

> At that moment, her patience snapped. With lightning speed she slipped off her belt and wrapped it around his neck.

Kenji made choking sounds, trying to look around at her, but Yayoi pulled up and back, tightening the belt in one motion. Gasping, he tried to get his fingers around the belt, but it had already dug into his neck. Yayoi watched intently as he scratched at the leather, and then yanked even harder. His neck bent back at an odd angle, and his fingers twitched meaninglessly in the air. *He needs to suffer more*, she thought. *He's got no right to go on living like this!* … Strange that she'd never known she had such cruelty inside; still, she found this thrilling.[13]

After he dies, she assures herself that she did the right thing: "She had done something that was irreversible, but she felt absolutely no regret. So be it, she whispered to herself. She'd had no other choice."[14] In other words, her criminal act is accompanied by criminal intent.

In the novel, the four female characters are bound by a sense of female unity. Knowing that they all have a tough life, the women help each other. Despite the inhumane speed of factory work, for instance, Yayoi helps a newcomer who looks distressed because of her inability to keep up the pace. Having no money for her second daughter's school trip, Yoshie once asks in vain for an advance payment of her wages at the factory. When she asks Masako to lend her some money, Masako is thoughtful enough to bring it to her home. She does not want to accidentally shame Yoshie by handing her money at the factory, where other workers are present. Although her husband has died, Yoshie continues to care for her bedridden mother-in-law at her home, working the night shift and dreaming in vain of her daughter going to junior college.

Sisterhood power is exhibited when Yayoi tells her female co-workers that her husband squandered 5 million yen[15] the couple had saved to make a down payment for their own house. He wasted the money on baccarat and a bar hostess, Anna, and punches Yayoi in the stomach, making her "[topple] over, on the verge of losing consciousness from the pain."[16] Yayoi's colleagues comfort her, and, after Kenji's death, they help her hide the crime. They go against social norms because they know well that neither their families nor the workplace will protect blue-collar women like themselves. When Yoshie protests that it is unethical to dismember a corpse, Masako insists that Kenji attacked Yayoi first and that Yayoi is now left with two young children. Persuaded by Masako, Yoshie decides to help Yayoi. Yoshie's decision is not only due to the possibility of a monetary reward from Yayoi; she also acts out of her companionship with Masako and her sympathy for Yayoi.

The female ethics that drive these women's actions comes from three ideas: underprivileged women who are vulnerable in Japanese society should be united; a man who attacks a physically weaker woman is unforgivable; and it is more unethical to separate a mother who committed murder from her small children than to cut up a corpse. Without these three points, neither Masako nor Yayoi would have been able to convince themselves to be complicit in a crime. Masako used to be a competent full-time employee of a credit union. However, when she pointed out the mistake of her male boss, he suddenly struck her. It was one of the reasons why she left the credit union, where she had worked for twenty years. Butchering a corpse is illegal and violent, yet it seems to be the only option left for them in a male-dominated society.[17]

If males were the main characters of the novel, it would have been unnatural of them to voluntarily become involved in such a crime based on Masako's reasoning. By the same token, Masako would be unable to persuade a socially fortunate woman to get involved in the crime. Having no one else to protect Yayoi, the three working-class women in the novel decide to protect a fellow woman who committed an impulsive murder. Interestingly, men are killed in this novel, and only Kuniko, a cardboard character who does not have any redeeming qualities, is killed among women.

As the novel progresses, the women become bold in their self-perception and behavior. After murdering Kenji, Yayoi feels freed, independent, and self-assured. After cutting up and disposing of his body, her accomplices feel the same way. Masako tells her sullen teenage son, "You may think you can escape everything unpleasant in life just by keeping your mouth shut, but it does not work that way."[18] Then, armed with money from the crime, she decides to leave her loveless marriage: "She had made up her mind to leave this house, and the encouragement she'd needed was hidden beneath the bed she'd left, in a box among her nightclothes: five million yen in cash."[19]

Out also reveals women's sexual needs. In the story, women have erotic dreams and fantasize about men. In Masako's nightmare about Kenji and a stranger, fear and sexual pleasure are mixed. After Kenji's disappearance, a man begins to strangle her, and she becomes fearful: "But then, slowly, the warmth of his hands, the rough breathing on her neck, began to arouse a buried impulse in her: the urge to surrender, to relax and allow herself to die. Abruptly, her fear began to dissipate, as if floating weightlessly away, and in its place came a sense of blissful pleasure. She cried out in delight."[20] In Kuniko's case, she no longer passively awaits a man's advances. Rather, she initiates a romantic relationship with the new factory guard who looks masculine. Despite meeting him for the first time, she becomes immediately enamored of him and flirts with him: "She gave his arm a squeeze as she said this, and her heart skipped a beat as her hand met hard muscles."[21]

It was Yayoi's husband who exploited her most, which led to the incident of murder, but not only men are to blame in the novel. Kuniko physically and verbally abuses her live-in partner, who is younger than she. She is deep in debt because she compulsively buys brand items; readers can assume her appearance complex caused unaffordable shopping. Even though Yoshie is alone in caring for her mother-in-law, Yoshie's own daughter is too self-centered to give her mother a hand. The daughter is ashamed of her family's poverty and hopes to be surrounded by trendy things. In the novel, there is a suspicion that she might be working as a teenage sex worker without her mother's knowledge. Kirino is good at portraying those who are eager to fill the holes in their hearts with material things in modern society. In an interview article published in *Kinema Junpo*, Kirino said, "I was born as a woman in a male society, and I felt that my surroundings were full of enemies. It was difficult for me to go freely because it was always as if the world had approached and moved away from me all of a sudden."[22] Through her writing, Kirino has been fighting against all the enemies in the world as well as the male society. She knows the enemies sometimes hide in women themselves.

Kirino's novel also shows the maternal, gracious side of Masako, Yayoi, and Yoshie, which is a soothing aspect of this grisly novel. For instance, after the crime, Yayoi cuts her hair short with the intention of working hard on behalf of the family to raise her children who lost their father. When Masako visits Yoshie's poor home, where she is on welfare, she gazes at the vitality of red tomatoes in a tiny garden. Yoshie gives Masako a big tomato, pointing out its sweet taste. However, Yoshie's little grandson, who was left behind by his mother and is cared for by Yoshie, reaches his hand to the tomato Masako is holding. When Masako hands it over to him, he smells it, gently putting his cheek on it. Masako murmurs, "*Inochi no katamari dane*," which translates as "It's a lump of life."[23] The women know the importance of little human lives well and try to protect them.

As Loren Toussaint and Jon R. Webb note in "Gender Differences in the Relationship Between Empathy and Forgiveness," women tend to exhibit higher levels of empathy than men.[24] Yoshie's care for her bedridden mother-in-law even after her husband's death can be explained by not only the Japanese concept of familial duty[25] but also women's capacity for emotional and cognitive empathy. The immobilized mother-in-law takes Yoshie's service for granted, but Yoshie still looks after her and manages to live with her. Masako even shows her feminine empathy for the plight of her husband, Yoshiki, and of their son, Nobuki. Yoshiki suffers from depression, and Nobuki has disconnected himself from the world. The three family members live under the same roof but are emotionally detached from each other: "[T]hey seemed to have chosen their own separate burdens and inhabit their own solitary realities."[26]

Finally, as a social problem novel, *Out* shows that governmental inaptitude has made the life of Japanese women more difficult. In a recent interview, the author stated, "60% of women are non-regular employees and are becoming poorer. Looking at society from a feminist perspective, we can grasp how they have been exploited and deceived. I want them to change the situation by avoiding the grinning laughter of old men."[27] Furthermore, *Out* captures the incongruity and distortions of contemporary

Japanese society. In depicting various cruel incidents in the novel, Kirino exposes the monstrous reality of Japan and the need for changing it. In the criminal world of gangsters and illegal usury, women's desperate efforts for survival fail. Gangsters drive them out of normal life, and underworld moneylenders ruin their already tough lives. In addition, working conditions for non-regular female employees are poor. At the boxed-meal factory, where Masako and the other female characters work, a constant emphasis is on efficiency, and people are desperate to adjust to the speed of the conveyor belt. Incompetent people are not well-liked at work. An employee's relationship with the employer is not based on compassion, a traditional Japanese virtue. Instead, it is based on economic efficiency. The supervisor, Nakayama, yells at those who do not follow the production guidelines, such as Kuniko, who puts too much egg into a lunch box. No wonder Kuniko considers him an "asshole."[28]

Moral Ambiguity in *Out*

The story makes it clear Kirino's sympathy lies with the plight of working-class women. The question is whether there is a consistent moral message in the novel. Obviously, Kirino condemns men's sexism, abuse, incompetency, and lack of care, but there seems no real moral judgment in the story, either. The novel represents a harsh view of contemporary Japanese society, and all the main characters, at least in the second half of the book, seem to act out of a desire to survive (or outmaneuver those who try to harm them), not based on some moral principles. Masako—the ringleader among the four women—is admirable in her characterization, but she decides to leave Japan at the end of the story. What does that mean? She seems disillusioned with Japan and wants to start her life anew in another country. In this regard, *Out* mainly concerns the problems with Japanese society today, not how to solve them. It is hard to find a character in *Out* who speaks for the author, who portrays the depravity of humanity while offering a clear moral message. Except for Masako, Yoshie, and Yayoi, most of the characters are cardboard figures.

At the end of the novel, Sadake captures Masako and plots to kill her in a way that fulfills his sexual fantasy. After torturing her, he and Masako have aggressive sex that pleasures both. She has mixed feelings about him: he is disgusting yet understandable. After all, he is her own image: "[Sadake] wasn't a pervert or a madman; he was a lost soul in desperate search of something, and if he thought he could find it in her, then she might be able to play along with him ... and go on living."[29] At the height of their sexual pleasure, Sadake tries to kill her as he did another woman years ago: "Their bodies came together and their eyes met. Seeing nothing reflected there but her own image, she felt a wave of pure pleasure rise and break over her. She could die like this. But the glint of the blade in the corner of her eye pulled her back to earth."[30] As a woman of intuition and calm rationality, Masako acts first: she slashes his face with a scalpel. Blood spurts out of the wound: "[T]he blood began to gush from his face, pouring over his outstretched hand. The scalpel had made a deep incision from the corner of his astonished eye to the base of his chin."[31] She wants him—her own image—to survive: "Because I understand you now. I see that we're the same, and I want us both to live."[32] However, Sadake dies a slow death.

In the last scene of the novel, Masako decides to leave Tokyo—"Sadake's town, chaotic and steamily hedonistic"[33]—and go abroad. She renounces the place:

> She couldn't live her life as someone's prisoner the way [Sadake] had lived his, caught up in a dream of the past, with no way forward and no way back, forced to dig down inside oneself.
>
> ...
>
> The freedom she was seeking was her own, not Sadake's, or Yayoi's, or Yoshie's, and she was sure it must be out there somewhere. If one more door had closed behind her, she had no choice but to find a new one to open. The elevator moaned like the wind as it came to meet her.[34]

As the novel's title suggests, Masako is "out" of Japan and will start a new life elsewhere. She hopes to find a place that gives her true freedom. The ending of the story represents contemporary Japan as a stifling place where freedom is limited for both men and women.

Although feminism is a legitimate theme of *Out*, a lack of men's voice and questionable characterization of the main characters diminish the novel's credibility. For instance, readers do not hear what some of the negatively portrayed men think about their wives or their family lives. Masako's depressed husband does not come across as someone who is mean or abusive. He goes to work every day. The couple's sexual intimacy has been nonexistent for years, which is not entirely the husband's fault. He is irritated by Masako's smoking indoors but does not protest openly. Without men's voices, we hear only one side of the story—from the women. Most of the women seem to try their best to maintain domestic peace, but we never know what is really happening inside each household unless the men express their own feelings. Furthermore, Yayoi's and Masako's husbands hardly represent Japanese men. Finally, when authorities arrest Sadake as the main suspect, Masako and her friends are gleeful, thinking that they are not suspects. Their response is hardly moral, which the author does not condemn.

Indeed, it becomes harder for readers to empathize with Masako—the only main character that fully develops—in the second half of the novel. Her companionship with Yayoi fades. When Jumonji, a yakuza member, proposes that she make money by dismembering a corpse at night, she agrees to do that. Masako's son has refused to talk with her for months, and she slaps him in the face. In her single combat with Sadake, she comes across as someone who is as deviant as he—as a ruthless anomaly.

In the past, Japanese virtues did not allow financial gains to take priority, and in the country prone to natural disasters, the spirit of mutual aid was considerably strong. Nevertheless, since the end of the Second World War, individualistic thinking has become prevalent, and people have become more indifferent to other people's affairs than before the war. In *Out*, the female protagonists are portrayed as lonely losers in a society dominated by neoliberalism. In the first half of the novel, they—the cornered women—assist each other based on feminist ethics. In the second half, however, their actions depart from the ethics. There is no family love to support them, and their family members exploit them for money. Eventually, the women choose to discontinue their efforts to fulfill their familial responsibilities. They commit crimes as a means of getting money and leave behind their families who have become burdens. In their fight against the patriarchy, they become almost as brutal as men. Although the plot of *Out* is in an extreme form, Kirino shows in her novel how social changes deprive people of their sense of ethics.

Conclusion

Out is an intriguing mystery novel that depicts the violence, abnormality, and poverty that pervade a society that has lost its ethical sense. In particular, the novel sheds light on women who are forgotten at the bottom of society and halfway forgotten even by their families. Many female readers will be able to sympathize with Yoshie, Masako, and Yayoi to some extent.

As Kazunari Suzumura points out, "Kirino's men and women are in a state of war."[35] Born in 1951, Kirino knows the history of female subjugation in Japan. Japan has a long history of discrimination against women, and the voices of women like Kirino have helped improve Japanese social situations. However, the women's acts of revenge are often too overwhelming to sound convincing. They act like child abuse victims who become child abusers themselves: their words are harsh, and they act violently against others instead of finding a constructive way to overcome their painful childhood. The extreme gender inequality as described in Kirino's novel may not be relatable to younger people, who live in an environment where women are legally protected from domestic violence.

Indeed, despite its long history of male dominance, Japan has gradually improved in its gender equity since the Meiji era, particularly making significant progress in recent decades. For instance, in its 2008 edition of "To Victims of Spousal Violence," the Gender Equality Bureau of Japan's Cabinet Office offers information on the legal basis for the prevention of spousal violence and the protection of victims, spousal violence counseling and support centers, applicable welfare systems, the punishment of abusers, and protection orders.[36] Hyogo Prefecture aids victims of domestic violence, categorizing the various types of violence that happens at home: physical abuse, psychological abuse, sexual abuse, economic abuse, social abuse, abuse through children, abuse through procedures concerning visa status, and cultural abuse.[37] As in other nations, these governmental actions do not necessarily prevent domestic violence, but they evidence the country's concern for the welfare of women in general.

Out is not a moralistic story in the sense that Dostoyevsky's *Crime and Punishment* is. Besides Masako's interpretation of her hunger as punishment, her sense of guilt is manifested in the first half of the novel. Assisted by Yoshie, she dismantles Kenji's body in the bathroom of her own house. A few days later, Masako dreams of her dead father. The father, who stands in the garden, tells Masako that he is thinking of going out. Busily cleaning the house, Masako tells him that a guest is coming. The father worriedly says that, if so, they need to clean the bathroom. In her nightmare, Masako realizes that there is a tremendous amount of Kenji's hair in the bathroom. At that point, Masako has a strong sense of guilt. Nevertheless, especially in the second half of the novel, the women who commit crimes do not regret their crimes. Instead, they laugh them away, getting involved in more crimes. They seem to crave a distorted sense of accomplishment when they commit atrocities to shock the society. They are relieved that an innocent man becomes a prime suspect. Poverty plagues these women, but the characters in Dostoyevsky's nineteenth-century novel are much poorer and have fewer choices in life. In short, *Out* successfully exposes some of the societal problems in Japan and captures the attention of readers with suspense and gory details. Yet, in its overemphasis on the underbelly of society and its dichotomic approach to gender issues, *Out* undercuts its own artistic merit. The novel begins with realistic descriptions and a convincing moral tone but ends in a fantastical, bizarre, and morally confusing way.

One could interpret Masako's departure from Japan as something positive. Psychologically, corpses and murders in adolescents' dreams are known to symbolize the hearts seeking ways to throw away their old lives. *Out* seems to be a mixture of violent nightmares with corpses and murders. Amid a midlife crisis, Masako seeks a new birth in a foreign country, and, perhaps, Kirino wanted to show how a drastic change could be made to the social morals of Japan. As Masako abandons Japan, Kirino might be dreaming of a new Japan that would be reborn after the destruction of old

Japan. However, this interpretation seems not to be in tune with the author's concrete description of Masako's abandonment of her native country. She seems weary of Japan and would rather find rest and peace of mind elsewhere—as some East Asian women do even in the twenty-first century.[38]

Notes

1. Toshio Takahashi, "Auto wo saidoku suru (Rereading of *Out*)," *Ronza* 41 (September 1998): 269.
2. Tetsuya Shigesato, "Chumoku no josei-sakka (Notable Female Writers)," *Mainichi Shimbun*, December 19, 1997, 11.
3. "Asahishimbun 'Heisei no 30-satsu' o happyō (Asahi Shimbun Announces the '30 Books of the Heisei Era')," *Good Life with Books*, March 7, 2019, book.asahi.com/article/12182809.
4. In the actual murder case, dismembered body parts of a man were found at Inokashira Park in western Tokyo in 1994. The murderer was not caught, and the case remains unresolved. The victim was in his thirties, and Kirino did not alter this point in her novel. While collecting the details of the murder, she interviewed some of the residents, took pictures of the neighboring districts, and gauged the atmosphere of the crime scene. However, Kirino portrayed the crime of women without including the fact that two suspicious men reportedly walked in the park holding a plastic bag.
5. Sachie Kitada, "Kirino Natsuo sakuhin no onnatachi (Female Characters in Natsuo Kirino's Works)," *Journal of the Asia-Pacific Women's Studies Association* 35 (March 2011): 25–7. Other critics in Japan approached the novel from a psychological or sociological perspective. For instance, the reviewer for *Weekly Shincho* called *Out* "an unprecedented crime novel," adding, "The modeling of the four housewives is wonderful, and the psychology and process of their involvements in crimes are outstandingly persuasive" (Tempo Editorial Team 122). According to Sachi Komai, "*Out* can be positioned in the genealogy of 'social detective novels' which originates from Seicho Matsumoto in the 1960s and focuses on the importance of motives and the social nature of crime rather than tricks" (20). Meanwhile, Tetsuo Ota finds "staggered families" with time differences (62), and Masaru Inoue focuses on the "individual meals" that represent the incommunicability among family members (73).
6. The primary source's page numbers in parenthetical citations come from the 2005 Viking edition. In 2022, the translator—Stephen Snyder—published a revised translation of the novel with Vintage Crime/Black Lizard; James Ellroy, an American crime fiction writer, contributed an introduction to the new edition.
7. For instance, in his *New York Times* review, Howard W. French finds that, although the novel is "written somewhat in the manner of French detective

fiction," it is much more than that, "particularly to the legions of female fans who have snatched it up and read it as a scathing allegory about the subjugation of women in Japanese society and the secret lives this forces them to lead" (para. 3). Katy Munger states in her review for *The Washington Post*, "Forget about flower arranging and geisha girls. ... *Out* is not easy to read. The passages of violence, in particular, are hampered by an abruptness that borders on the choppy. ... But it is a fascinating tale nonetheless" (para. 3, 5). Meanwhile, Stephen Poole begins his *Guardian* review by pointing out how Japanese fiction and movies tend to be replete with sex and ultraviolence, adding that "it's even better if the killing and maiming is committed by women, as in *Audition* or *Battle Royale*. Thus *Out*, a lurid and bloody thriller whose heroines chop up bodies, is a logical choice for the first translation into English of a novel by Kirino, who has been described as the 'queen of Japanese crime'" (para. 1).

8   For instance, the website *Book Riot* considers it one of the top fifteen best feminist mysteries written during the last fifteen years. These novels are "a lot more interesting, diverse crime novels that challenge the status quo and look at crime fiction a bit more broadly. ... These 15 feminist mystery novels explore crime and feminist issues in new and exciting ways" (para. 1).

9   *Out* deals with not only feminist concerns. It also portrays the world of gangsters (yakuza), prostitution by high school girls, family breakdowns, abnormal and compulsive sexual behavior, a hostile work environment, spousal and parental negligence that fosters simmering anger, and the pervasive sense of loneliness and alienation. In this paper, however, we will primarily focus on the feminist issues in the novel.

10 Natsuo Kirino, "Auto toiu na no unmei (Destiny in the Name of Out)," *Mystery Magazine*, September 2004, anond.hatelabo.jp/20101003182909, para. 4.

11 Kirino's empathy recalls that of Truman Capote, who understood and shared the feelings of Perry Smith, one of the criminals he covered in *In Cold Blood*.

12 Raman Selden, *A Reader's Guide to Contemporary Literary Theory* (Lexington: University of Kentucky Press, 1985), 128.

13 Natsuo Kirino, *Out: A Thriller* (New York: Kodansha International, 2003; Vintage, 2005), 48.

14 Ibid., 49.

15 Equivalent of more than 37,762 USD as of February 2023.

16 Kirino, *Out: A Thriller*, 47.

17 In her celebrated book of cultural anthropology, *The Chrysanthemum and the Sword* (1946), Ruth Benedict defines Japan as a nation of "order and hierarchy" in which "taking one's proper station" is of prime importance (43). Masako and her friends violate this age-old social concept.

18 Kirino, *Out: A Thriller*, 296.

19 Ibid., 296.

20 Ibid., 292.

21 Ibid., 363.
22 Okada, 46.
23 Natsuo Kirino, アウト *Out* (Tokyo: Kodansha, 1997), 158; Aya Kubota's translation.
24 Loren Toussaint and Jon R. Webb, "Gender Differences in the Relationship between Empathy and Forgiveness," *Journal of Social Psychology* 145, no. 6 (December 2005), https://www.ncbi.nlm.nih.gov/pmc/articles/PMC1963313/, para. 8.
25 In *Japan: An Attempt at Interpretation* (1904), Lafcadio Hearn offers an insight into the family structure and culture of old Japan. The scope of a family reaches far beyond a man, his wife, and their children. Rather, it includes several preceding generations, which is part of the ancestral cult. In traditional Japanese society, the wives are expected to obey their husbands, and the younger members of a family are under the authority of the elder members (55–61). Hearn notes, "In a well-conducted household, … every act is performed according to the old forms of courtesy and kindness" (76).
26 Kirino, *Out: A Thriller*, 51.
27 Satetsu Takeda, "Nichibotsu wo mukaete (At Sunset)," *Sowing Seeds*, September 29, 2020, tanemaki.iwanami.co.jp/posts/4031, para. 48.
28 Kirino, *Out: A Thriller*, 18.
29 Ibid., 393.
30 Ibid., 395.
31 Ibid., 396.
32 Ibid., 398.
33 Ibid., 399.
34 Ibid., 400.
35 Kazunari Suzumura, *Warau Kirino Natsuo: aku wo egaku sakkagun* (*Laughing Natsuo Kirino: Novelists Writing the Evil*) (Tokyo: Genshisha, 2020, Kindle edition.), ch. 4, para. 12.
36 Gender Equality Bureau of the Cabinet Office, 2008, https://www.gender.go.jp/policy/no_violence/e-vaw/siensya/pdf/01english.pdf.
37 "Freedom from Domestic Violence," *Hyogo Prefectural Women and Family Consulting Center*, https://web.pref.hyogo.lg.jp/kf12/documents/101eigo.pdf.
38 In her November 2021 interview with Aya Kubota, Natsuo Kirino regretted the fact that the English translation of the novel omits some of her depictions of the female characters' psychology. Regarding the seemingly pessimistic ending of the story, the author stated, "Many Japanese women feel unfairly treated in a male-dominated society. Even now, amid COVID-19, the number of women who suffer from irregular employment and financial difficulties is increasing. I think many Japanese women feel suffocated living in Japan and want to get out of the country at least for a while" (Kirino, "Personal Interview"). Regarding the gruesome nature of her female characters' crimes, which seems to contradict the popular image of Japanese women as

being kind-hearted and gentle, Kirino responded, "Recently, more and more Japanese people cannot control their emotions. For example, violent incidents, such as skirmishes on crowded trains, often occur. In an inhumane modern society, Japanese people are becoming unbearable. Sensing the troubles brewing in the real world, writers have no choice but to portray violence in their works" (Kirino, "Personal Interview").

Bibliography

"Asahishimbun 'Heisei no 30-satsu' o happyō (Asahi Shimbun Announces the '30 Books of the Heisei Era')." *Good Life with Books*. March 7, 2019. book.asahi.com/article/12182809. Accessed November 23, 2021.

Benedict, Ruth. *The Chrysanthemum and the Sword*. 1946. Naples, Italy: Albatross, 2019.

"15 of the Best Feminist Mystery Novels." January 27, 2021. https://bookriot.com/best-eminist-mystery-novels/. Accessed November 23, 2021.

"Freedom from Domestic Violence." *Hyogo Prefectural Women and Family Consulting Center*. https://web.pref.hyogo.lg.jp/kf12/documents/101eigo.pdf. Accessed December 13, 2022.

French, Howard W. "A Tokyo Novelist Mixes Felonies with Feminism." *New York Times*, November 17, 2003. www.nytimes.com/2003/11/17/books/a-tokyo-novelist-mixes-felonies-with-feminism.html. Accessed June 27, 2021.

Hearn, Lafcadio. *Japan: An Attempt at Interpretation*. Boston: Tuttle, 1904.

Inoue, Masaru. "Setsudan to danpenka (Cutting and Fragmentation)." *Journal of Atomi University* 53 (2018): 73–90.

Kirino, Natsuo. "Auto toiu na no unmei (Destiny in the Name of Out)." *Mystery Magazine*, September 2004. anond.hatelabo.jp/20101003182909. Accessed May 29, 2021.

Kirino, Natsuo. アウト (*Out*). Tokyo: Kodansha, 1997.

Kirino, Natsuo. *Out: A Thriller*. Translated by Stephen Snyder. New York: Kodansha International, 2003. Vintage, 2005.

Kirino, Natsuo. Personal interview. November 21, 2021.

Kitada, Sachie. "Kirino Natsuo sakuhin no onnatachi (Female Characters in Natsuo Kirino's Works)." *Journal of the Asia-Pacific Women's Studies Association* 35 (March 2011): 22–8.

Komai, Sachi. "Kirino Natsuo *Out* no Kenkyu-doko (Natsuo Kirino's *Out* as Cross-genre World Literature)." *University of Tsukuba Repository* 21 (February 28, 2020): 17–31. tsukuba.repo.nii.ac.jp/records/54260#.YQD7NI77Qak. Accessed May 24, 2021.

Munger, Katy. "A Japanese Noir, a Pair of Northwest Mysteries and an Elegant Culinary Tale from Spain." Review of *Out*, by Natsuo Kirino [and of three other novels]. *Washington Post*, August 31, 2003. www.washingtonpost.com/archive/entertainment/books/2003/08/31/a-japanese-noir-a-pair-of-northwest-mysteries-and-an-elegant-culinary-tale-from-spain/780bf0e1-4c9a-4cea-897c-27ef2e080c39/. Accessed November 23, 2021.

Okada, Kazue. "Kirino Natsuo ga kataru Kirino Natsuo no sekai (Natsuo Kirino's World Told by Natsuo Kirino)." *Kinema Junpo*, October 2002, 44–6.

Ota, Tetsuo. "Kirino Natsuo *Out* wo megutte (On *Out* by Natsuo Kirino)." *J. F. Oberlin University Journal of World Literature* 2 (2006): 55–65.

Poole, Stephen. "Murder Sushi Wrote." Review of *Out*, by Kirino Natsuo. *Guardian*, November 26, 2004. www.theguardian.com/books/2004/nov/27/featuresreviews.guardianreview18. Accessed June 27, 2021.

Selden, Raman. *A Reader's Guide to Contemporary Literary Theory*. Lexington: University of Kentucky Press, 1985.

Shigesato, Tetsuya. "Chumoku no josei-sakka (Notable Female Writers)." *Mainichi Shimbun* (December 19, 1997): 10–11.

Suzumura, Kazunari. *Warau Kirino Natsuo: aku wo egaku sakkagun (Laughing Natsuo Kirino: Novelists Writing the Evil)*. Kindle edition. Tokyo: Genshisha, 2020.

Takahashi, Toshio. "Auto wo saidoku suru (Rereading of *Out*)." *Ronza* 41 (September 1998): 268–71.

Takeda, Satetsu. "Nichibotsu wo mukaete (At Sunset)." *Sowing Seeds*, September 29, 2020. tanemaki.iwanami.co.jp/posts/4031. Accessed May 28, 2021.

Tempo Editorial Team. "Barabara satsujin-jiken to yonin no shufu no tenraku (Torso Murders and Fall of Four Housewives)." *Weekly Shincho* (July 31, 1997): 122.

"To Victims of Spousal Violence." *Gender Equality Bureau of the Cabinet Office*, 2008. https://www.gender.go.jp/policy/no_violence/e-vaw/siensya/pdf/01english.pdf. Accessed December 13, 2022.

Toussaint, Loren, and Jon R. Webb. "Gender Differences in the Relationship between Empathy and Forgiveness." *Journal of Social Psychology* 145, no. 6 (December 2005): 673–85. https://www.ncbi.nlm.nih.gov/pmc/articles/PMC1963313/. Accessed December 13, 2022.

8

Moral Certainty or Ambiguity in Clerical Detective Novels: Discovering a Middle Way in F. H. Batacan's *Smaller and Smaller Circles*

C. Clark Triplett

There has recently been an enthusiastic interest in mystery novels that feature a clerical detective. With this interest in clerical detectives, questions have been raised about the significance of this subcategory of mystery novels. Rachel Haliburton argues that, although murder mysteries and philosophy—moral philosophy in particular—may seem like strange bedfellows, philosophers ought to take this genre very seriously and assign the best of the novels along with the usual philosophical texts.[1] She finds them to be a source of ethical insight and a tool to spark ethical imagination. Mystery fiction, perhaps more than any other genre, raises questions about good and evil and whether the world is just or unjust. Perhaps an even odder combination are those novels that feature a clerical detective, whether priest, rabbi, minister, or ecclesial sister or brother. Despite this strange avocation, there are numerous iconic characters in mystery fiction, including Father Dowling, Father Blackie Ryan, Father Mark Townsend, Rabbi David Small, Rabbi Daniel Winter, Brother Cadfael, Brother William of Baskerville, and, of course, the inimitable Father Brown, the quintessential clerical detective.

An obvious question that arises in reference to clerical detective novels is what this particular character adds to the detective story. Or rather, what does it contribute to the moral trajectory of detective fiction? Amy Wellborn believes it is important to understand that most mystery novels present a strong sense "of the confrontation between good and evil, an attempt to restore justice to creation, and to shed light into the darkness."[2] Many significant writers such as Graham Greene, Agatha Christie, W. H. Auden, G. K. Chesterton, and Dorothy L. Sayers assume a cosmic sense of justice and recognize the unique moral context of mystery stories. Auden argues, for example, that "completely satisfactory detectives are extremely rare ... the job of the detective is to restore the state of grace in which the aesthetic and ethical are as one."[3] He goes on to state that "since the murderer ... is the ethically deficient individual, his opponent, the detective, must be either the official representative of the ethical or the exceptional individual who is in a state of grace."[4] This does not shed light on what moral weight clerics bring to the table, but the inclusion of the clergyman, at least on the surface, brings some moral authority and draws attention to the importance of questions about good, evil, and justice in the universe.

Although clerical detective novels are unique because of the profession of the protagonist, they still use the same literary mechanisms and moral trajectories as other mystery novels. The reader can find the same complexity and variation in moral perspectives. These variations reflect different ways of arranging the events, time sequences, and characters in a story that are intentional and present a certain way of looking at the world. Carole Buggé argues that the moral of the story is something we should always keep in sight, like a lighthouse in a storm:

> When you tell a story, you are also saying to the reader, "Life is like this. People behave in this way, Nature is indifferent, (or, if you live in Los Angeles, cares deeply about your [well-being]), God and the Devil exist (or not, if you live in New York), and if you want to be good/happy/successful, this is what I have to teach you." You are sharing your vision of the world as it exists in your story, and the reader will come away knowing what that vision is—and what you value or don't value.[5]

In some cases, the moral is obvious—it is more on the surface of the story—but in other cases moral questions arise that are more complex and may tap into the mysteries of life itself. Buggé compares the moral universes of Agatha Christie and John le Carré. Agatha Christie's stories are pretty cut and dry. Murder is certainly an evil thing, but once the murderer is discovered and apprehended everything goes as it was before. In le Carré's work, however, no one can be trusted, and the world is constantly changing. The world of the story is a dark place, and it is not always clear who is the good guy or the bad guy. Everyone struggles with right and wrong, and there are always complex intersections of culture, social expectations, psychological ambiguities, and strange circumstances. Many contemporary mystery writers portray a world of moral ambiguity, sometimes without resolution. Raymond Chandler describes this nitty-gritty moral climate in his work *The Simple Act of Murder*:

> The realist in murder writes of a world in which gangsters can rule nations and almost rule cities … a world in which you may witness a hold-up in broad daylight and see who did it, but you will fade quickly back into the crowd rather than tell anyone. …
> It is not a very fragrant world, but it is the world you live in, and certain writers with tough minds and a cool spirit of detachment can make very interesting and even amusing patterns out of it.[6]

As has been discussed in some detail, there is considerable variation in moral perspective in mystery novels in particular and no less so in clerical detective novels. In some cases, the moral of the story is pretty much *prima facie* while others are more ambiguous with various layers of moral concerns in which the protagonist struggles with psychological and moral issues along with multiple social justice issues. In some cases, the moral view is "from above"—Tom Nagel's view from nowhere—and in other cases, the moral view is "from below"—a view from somewhere or, in some cases, anywhere. The question is whether there is a view that threads the needle and takes a middle path that recognizes the need for a grounded critical framework from above while respecting the local, historical-cultural context from below. Without a point of view or rationality that is anchored somewhere outside the particular social and cultural matrix, there is no means of determining moral flaw in psychological behavior and/or social practices. This is not a position that is ahistorical or atemporal (the view from nowhere) but rather a view that is transhistorical, transcultural, and/or transdisciplinary and intersubjective. Calvin Schrag suggests a new metaphor, *transversality*, that is designed to overcome the purely vertical viewpoint that assumes an atemporal, formal, universal invariant essence that is above any historical context.[7] Transversality locates critique, including moral critique, within a socially embedded rational context, so critique is not above critique itself, but at the same time, it does not devolve into a relativistic indifferentism or personal opinion.

This chapter will make the case that F. H. Batacan's *Smaller and Smaller Circle* provides this middle ground between certainty and ambiguity, between the view from nowhere or the view from anywhere in mystery fiction. This story reflects the two-way tension of Mark Johnson's concept of moral imagination. This is Batacan's debut mystery work and is one of the first mystery novels published in the Philippines. It was initially published by the University of Philippines Press in 2002 and then later, in 2015, by Soho Press in New York. The main protagonists in the novel are two Jesuit priests, Father Gus Saenz and Father Jerome Lucero, who are both academics. They are asked to use their expertise as forensic investigators to hunt for a serial killer who is mutilating young boys in Manilla's impoverished Payata slum. The novel is unique because it is not only a crime novel with a serial killer, but a scathing social commentary that is critical of the country's treatment of poverty, police corruption, impropriety in the Catholic Church, and the duplicity of the local media. The complex interweaving of these social concerns impacts the investigatory process and is even, to some extent, complicit in the horrible crimes of the killer. As the local priest Father Emil states, "I just hope you manage to find him soon. The people aren't stupid; they're already asking questions; the fear is growing. It's a poor community, and they're used to being ignored by the powers that be. If that fear turns to anger—well, you know very well what can happen."[8] Because of a corrupt government system and a lack of concern by local law enforcement, the two priests, along with a local tough-minded reporter Joanna Bonifacio, must take matters into their own hands. Almost from the beginning, they have to work against the local constabulary, the National Bureau of Investigation, and the Catholic hierarchy.

The story begins with the brutal face of violence when the local priest, Father Emil, is led by a group of slum kids up a mountain of garbage in a 50-acre landfill where the local kids scavenge for food and other goods. They lead the priest to the body of a young boy whose face has been peeled from his skull, his heart cut out, and his genitals removed. As is later discovered, he is the sixth child found murdered in a similar fashion. Batacan immediately gives the reader a vision of how cheap life is in the slums and how unfair and hopeless society is, especially for those who cannot speak for themselves. Violence leads to more violence in a social environment that is ripe for unspeakable evil. The particularly descriptive language of the novel sets the stage for a macabre series of murders: "The stench from the sea of garbage around them is overwhelming. It rained last night and now that the sun is out, the dump site is steaming, awful vapors rising lazily with the heat; wet paper and rot and excrement mixing in a soup around them."[9] This description becomes a scatological metaphor for the people who are being exploited by the social bureaucracy and the leadership of the church. It applies to the children of the slums who are the victims of the gruesome and ghastly machinations of the killer. The plight of the common people seems hopeless at times when they are victimized from all directions. Instead of helping, government institutions contribute to even more suffering through the misuse of funds provided for the poor, and instead of arresting lawbreakers, they engage in bribery and commit worse crimes themselves. Since law enforcement in the Philippines does not collect crime statistics on missing persons nationally, families of missing members are referred to local police where little or no effort is expended following up on cases. Officials seem satisfied with the status quo and placate their consciences with myths about the easygoing nature of the Filipino people. When Father Saenz attends a social, he talks with one of the law enforcement officials. He happens to mention his theory about the case, saying that he thinks it may be a serial killer. Smiling patronizingly, the police officer says, "You've been watching too many foreign movies. Father Saenz, there are no serial killers in the Philippines."[10] Father Saenz is both angered and amused at the reasons for this response: "Our neighborhoods are too congested, our neighbors too nosy, our families too tightly knit for secrets to be kept and allowed to fester. We have too many ways to blow off steam—the nightclubs, the karaoke bars ... We're too Catholic, too God-fearing, too fearful of scandal."[11]

Batacan paints a vivid picture of Philippine society and culture "from below." It is a perspective that was engendered in many Filipinos against the background of Marcos's brutal dictatorship. In the story, both Saenz and Lucero were brought in originally by the Director of the NBI to help bring solace to families who were victims of the regime. To add insult to injury to the people, the Catholic Church, which has insinuated itself into almost every aspect of life including the law enforcement bureaucracy, seems to find ways to interfere in the work of the two investigators even though they are priests. Part of the background of the story is an ongoing scandal in which a well-known local priest is accused of pedophilia and the hierarchy's unwillingness to responsibly sanction the priest. Saenz's outspoken criticism has put him on the cardinal's enemies list. Although both Fathers Saenz and Lucero have an unwavering sense of justice for the poor in the community, their moral perspective is not a "pie-in-the-sky" view. They are both scholars and teachers—Saenz is a forensic anthropologist and Lucero is a clinical psychologist, and they both understand the complications and vectors of influence that are the result of psychological and cultural injustice and failures. They must continually act despite the government, police, and church. Their moral vision is quite often "over-against" the expectations and short-sighted moralisms of social institutions.

This more realistic sense of justice and the part institutions play in their failures on behalf of the poor do not necessarily cause the priests to lose their faith. In a conversation, the Director of the National Bureau of Investigation, Francisco Lastimosa, says to Father Saenz, "You'll get him yet, you know."[12] Saenz is not sure what he is talking about. Lastimosa answers, "Your Monsignor Ramirez," referring to the priest accused of pedophilia.[13] The blood drains from the priest's face. Lastimosa asks, "Did you not think anyone else knew?"[14] In an angry voice, Father Saenz says, "Certainly no one else seems to care."[15] The man quotes the Scripture, from Ecclesiastes 3.1-2a: "To everything there is a season, and a time to every purpose under the heaven. A time to keep silence, and a time to speak."[16] (34). The conversation continues:

> "What are you trying to tell me, sir?"
> "Perhaps you've forgotten verse seventeen, Father."
> "I said in mine heart, God shall judge the righteous and the wicked: for there is a time there for every purpose and every work." ...
> "You're a man of God. You of all people must have faith in the possibility of a satisfactory outcome. Even if, sadly, long delayed."
> "Faith in God, yes. Faith in man—to be honest, I sometimes ..."
> Saenz's voice trails off.[17]

His faith seems to still be there, despite everything, but the actions of men have shifted his moral perspective. Instead of the rule-bound "morally correct" perspective of the ecclesial and social institutions, his values are driven and shaped by the needs of the Filipino people. This means that his sense of justice is influenced by the historical and cultural situation. At the same time, his sense of justice provides a critical framework that overrides the rigid and uncaring position of the church and government. This is not an absolutist position because it is determined by the needs of the people. This position is in keeping with the middle way that Tzvetan Todorov discusses, arguing for a balanced moral stance: "Consciously or not, everyone relies on criteria that permit distinctions to be made not so much between good and evil absolutely as between more and less good, more and less evil."[18]

As a result of the failures of human institutions, his critical moral stance leads the priests to continue his investigation, even though the resistance of authorities at times makes the effort seem futile. However, it is their awareness of the futility of the people living in the slums that eventually leads them to believe they are dealing with a serial killer who is acquainted with that part of the city, where life is cheap. It is in the context of the futility of things, that they get a hint of who it might be and why he might be doing what he is doing. Even the killer recognizes how futility leads to certain desperate behaviors:

> *It is depressing to read the paper or watch the news. Every day something bad happens—a bank gets robbed, a war breaks out, a child gets raped—and nobody can do anything about it. Not the police, not the press. Not the mothers and fathers, not the lawyers or the priests.*
>
> *We are all powerless in the face of evil.*
>
> *No, no, that's not true. We are powerless when we wait for other people to act on our behalf.*
>
> *Yes, that's it. The truly powerful man is the man who stands alone.*[19]

In the process of looking for clues, they discover that marks on the skulls of the children found in the dump could easily be made by a dental instrument. After looking at records located in the mobile dental clinic, they learn that Dr. Alex Cross, a local dentist, examined at least some of the victims. They also learn from Cross's parents that he had been raped by a P.E. teacher at school, but nobody ever talked about such things when he was a child. As is often the case, the killer had been a helpless victim himself; like the murdered children, he was "*powerless in the face of evil.*"[20]

In the book, the author interjects the killer into the narrative early in a first-person commentary that initially reflects a sense of power but gradually becomes a testimony of his own pain and despair and ultimately a feeling of paranoia as the detectives gradually get closer to him in their investigation: "*I can feel them. Scurrying in circles around me, smaller and smaller circles like rats around a crust of bread or a piece of cheese. Waiting, waiting, waiting for the right moment. The moment when I slip up, when I make a mistake, when I get careless.*"[21] Then later, as if a foregone conclusion, he says,

The priest knows. He's coming for me.

Let him come, then. Let him come soon. And then all this will be over.[22]

Finally, the killer becomes like a child victim himself:

They're coming to get me. Coming on their big, quiet feet they're coming.

I want my mother. I want my father.[23]

This is the inevitable outcome. It seems that in his own mind he has resigned himself to this fate. In a discussion with one of Cross's schoolmates, the detectives learn that seven or eight small boys were molested at the same time by the P.E. teacher at the Payatas District High School, Isabelo Gorosope. These were small boys about the same age as the boys who had been killed. Why did no one complain about Gorosope? "The mechanic sighs and shrugs, and they know what he would have said anyway: *Complain about what? To whom? We didn't want any trouble.*"[24] Later, the school friend explains that Alex was Gorosope's favorite, his special little boy. But Alex did not want to be special. He did not want to be seen as special either by the P.E. instructor or by the other boys. By killing the boys, in some perverse way Alex was erasing what the boys in his school knew about his special position—he blames them for his guilt and shame. When asked whether Alex will continue killing boys, Saenz predicts that he is escalating to a resolution, but in the end, "he'll destroy the one thing that keeps reminding him of the trauma ... "Himself'"[25] This does not necessarily mean he will end it by suicide, but that he will place himself in a position to end the violence one way or another: "And just as an authority figure started this whole mess, he's looking to an authority figure—the police, maybe even you—to bring it to an end. He knows he has to answer to *society's justice*, but only after he's extracted his own personal justice."[26]

So, what is the moral center in this extremely violent and disturbing story about the murder of young, poverty-stricken boys when the government, law enforcement, and the church have failed so miserably to protect them or even care what happens to them? What does Father Jerome mean when he says the killer knows he will have to answer to society's justice? In what way does society's justice reflect some *via media* between moral absolutism and moral relativism? The social institutions that both detectives are concerned about represent moral absolutism or moral correctness that Todorov discusses. This perspective tends to be rigid and univocal attempts to impose formal rules on diverse historical and social situations and, according to Mark Johnson, trivialize the features of a particular social situation and lack moral imagination. Johnson wants to make readers aware of the vast array of metaphors used to describe moral behavior in different situations and in various cultures. Jeffrey Stout argues that there are many "distinct moral languages, organized around different central concepts and at home in different social settings."[27] Although there may be some moral languages that transcend cultural and/or historical specificity, in most cases ethical and moral decision-making is culturally determined. Father Saenz's and Father Lucero's unwavering sense of social justice seems to be a very clear example of an intersubjective or transversal perspective that cuts across institutional and specific cultural expectations. It allows for a moral critique of the government, law enforcement, and the church as well as the passivity of the Filipino people when injustices are so much a part of their everyday life. Finally, the actions of the serial killer represent a form of moral relativism. While he has been the subject of a great injustice, his "personal ethic" is based on pathological behaviors based on personal grievances and arbitrary decisions about who is responsible for such injustices. His moral decisions are childlike and in the end lead to his own demise.

Batacan does an excellent job in this first novel balancing the moral concerns with the multiple social justice issues in the Philippines. The novel has all the elements of a fast-paced and thoughtful mystery story that stirs the conscience of the reader about the plight of the poor. Her characters, particularly the two detectives, are compelling and authentic. Her detailed descriptions of the country are vivid and clear and her descriptions of the slum in Payata are particularly lucid and colorful. The details of the notorious Payatas dump and the gruesome portrait of the child at the beginning of the book provide a face for the violence, victimization, and abuse in the rest of the story. The faceless boy in the dump becomes in one sense the face of Philippine society and as the story unfolds, the face of the serial killer. Batacan's willingness to take on the Catholic Church and other government institutions in the Philippines provides a crucial background for revealing nuanced moral and social issues that are addressed by the detective priests throughout the novel. This is a complex and dark story that raises multiple moral aporias that challenge the reader to struggle and participate with the victimization and injustice in the Philippine culture even from a privileged position.

Notes

1. Rachel Haliburton, *The Ethical Detective: Moral Philosophy and Detective Fiction* (Lanham: Lexington Books, 2020), ix.
2. Amy Welborn, "The Mystery of the Clerical Detective," accessed February 14, 2023, www.amywelborn.com/catholicmysteries/mysteries.html, para. 2.
3. W. H. Auden, "The Guilty Vicarage: Notes on the Detective Story, by an Addict." *Harper's Magazine*, May 1948, accessed November 2, 2021, harpers.org/archive/1948/05/the-guilty-vicarage/, para. 32.
4. Ibid.
5. Carol Buggé, "Moral in Mysteries." *Gotham Writers*, 2021, accessed October 23, 2021, www.writingclasses.com/toolbox/articles/moral-in-mysteries, para. 7.
6. Raymond Chandler, *The Simple Art of Murder* (Boston: Houghton Mifflin, 1950), 1.
7. Calvin O. Schrag, "Rationality between Modernity and Postmodernity," in *Life-World and Politics: Between Modernity and Postmodernity*, ed. Stephen K. White (Notre Dame: University of Notre Dame Press, 1989), 96.
8. F. H. Batacan, *Smaller and Smaller Circles* (Manila: University of the Philippines Press, 2002), 20.
9. Ibid., 8.
10. Ibid., 44.
11. Ibid.
12. Ibid., 33.
13. Ibid., 34.
14. Ibid.
15. Ibid.
16. Ibid.
17. Ibid.
18. Tzvetan Todorov, *Hope and Memory: Lessons from the Twentieth Century*, trans. David Bellos (Princeton: Princeton University Press, 2003), 138.
19. Batacan, *Smaller and Smaller Circles*, 121. Emphasis in original.
20. Ibid., 121. Emphasis in original.

21 Ibid., 255. Emphasis in original.
22 Ibid., 255. Emphasis in original.
23 Ibid., 271. Emphasis in original.
24 Ibid., 299. Emphasis in original.
25 Ibid., 302.
26 Ibid., 303. Emphasis added.
27 Jeffrey Stout, *Ethics after Babel: The Languages of Morals and Their Discontents* (Boston: Beacon Press, 1988), ix–x.

Bibliography

Auden, W. H. "The Guilty Vicarage: Notes on the Detective Story, by an Addict." *Harper's Magazine*, May 1948. harpers.org/archive/1948/05/the-guilty-vicarage/. Accessed November 2, 2021.

Batacan, F. H. *Smaller and Smaller Circles*. Manila: University of the Philippines Press, 2002.

Buggé, Carol. "Moral in Mysteries." *Gotham Writers*, 2021. www.writingclasses.com/toolbox/articles/moral-in-mysteries. Accessed October 23, 2021.

Chandler, Raymond. *The Simple Art of Murder*. Boston: Houghton Mifflin, 1950.

Haliburton, Rachel. *The Ethical Detective: Moral Philosophy and Detective Fiction*. Lanham: Lexington Books, 2020.

Johnson, Mark. *Moral Imagination: Implications of Cognitive Science for Ethics*. Chicago: University of Chicago Press, 1993.

Schrag, Calvin O. "Rationality between Modernity and Postmodernity." In *Life-World and Politics: Between Modernity and Postmodernity*, edited by Stephen K. White, 81–106. Notre Dame: University of Notre Dame Press, 1989.

Stout, Jeffrey. *Ethics after Babel: The Languages of Morals and Their Discontents*. Boston: Beacon Press, 1988.

Todorov, Tzvetan. *Hope and Memory: Lessons from the Twentieth Century*. Translated by David Bellos. Princeton: Princeton University Press, 2003.

Welborn, Amy. "The Mystery of the Clerical Detective." www.amywelborn.com/catholicmysteries/mysteries.html. Accessed November 2, 2021.

9

"Life's messy complexity": Moral Ambiguity, Compromise, and Vigilante Justice in Kishwar Desai's Simran Singh Trilogy

Nikita Gloria Pinto

In his article "Why Crime Fiction Is Good for You," Ian Rankin argues that contemporary crime writing is pervaded by "a sense of the incomplete and of life's messy complexity" where

> good [does not] always triumph over evil; evil [cannot] always be explained away ... the villains may escape justice altogether, or the reader may be invited to take sides with the criminal against the powers of law and order ... showing a world in which criminality, in the form of organized crime, operates openly and without apparent hindrance.[1]

This "messy complexity" of sympathetic criminals, deferred justice, and persistence of evil eschews the genre's escapist and cathartic inclinations, instead inviting readers to engage with the murkier and unsettling aspects of real life. Likewise, Kishwar Desai's crime fiction trilogy articulates the "messy complexities" of life in its incisive depiction of gender-based crime and its ambiguous view of justice.

Primarily set in India, the novels feature a middle-aged amateur detective and social worker, Simran Singh, who investigates and confronts various crimes and issues affecting women, such as female feticide and infanticide in *Witness the Night* (2010); commercial surrogacy in *Origins of Love* (2012); and sexual violence in *The Sea of Innocence* (2013). In the first novel, she is assigned the case of a fourteen-year-old girl, Durga Atwal, who is charged with murdering thirteen of her family members in one night. Simran, however, believes there is more to the case as Durga is found raped and bound at the scene of the crime. Simran's friend in the police force asks her to determine Durga's mental condition and elicit a confession out of her. Instead, Simran's investigation leads her to discover several unsettling crimes committed by the victims, who are guilty of decades of female feticide and infanticide. She learns that the Atwals had also cruelly oppressed their surviving daughters because of their gender.

In the second novel, Simran is tasked with helping her friends who run a surrogacy clinic investigate the suspicious deaths of their British clients Mike and Susan Oldham, parents to a baby born out of surrogacy. The baby, Amelia, is discovered to have HIV and is left abandoned at the clinic after the Oldhams' surrogate, Preethi, goes missing. In the course of her investigation, Simran also helps her friends locate their missing consignments of embryos, which, as she discovers later, are being used by their unscrupulous business partner, Dr. Ashok Ganguly, to conduct illegal experiments. Her third case deals with the rape and disappearance of a British teenager, Liza Kay, who goes missing on a trip to Goa. Asked by her police friend to investigate, Simran is sent mysterious videos of the girl's repeated molestation by unknown perpetrators. Eventually, Simran discovers that Liza has actually been dead for a year due to a brutal gang rape orchestrated by some of Goa's most powerful politicians.

Based on real-life cases,[2] the novels expose how political corruption coupled with deeply ingrained patriarchal beliefs interferes with Simran's quest for justice, driving her to seek alternative means to suture the violent ruptures brought about by these disturbing crimes. Despite her attempts to deliver justice, the punishment of perpetrators, restoration of order, and the possibility of catharsis, which characterizes most crime writing, are deliberately absent in these novels. Instead, the novels envisage a world built around ambiguity and uncertainty. While previous research on Desai's trilogy has delved into the postcolonial, feminist, and even biopolitical dimensions of her work,[3] the moral ambiguities within her novels and within her detective have not been fully explored. This paper, therefore, aims to examine the ways in which moral ambiguity informs Desai's trilogy and enhances its ethical value. I argue that Desai opts for ambiguity as a subversive tool, to interrogate the relationship between morality and the law, to critique the moral legitimacy behind Indian society's patriarchal values, and to cultivate moral engagement among readers.

The Detective as an Ethical Guide

To unearth the truth, Simran must navigate through a fractured society and a convoluted legal system which sustains what Desai refers to in her "Author's Note" as a "complicity of corruption."[4] She often discovers the tenuous lines between police and criminal as in *Witness the Night*, where Ramnath Singh, the Police Superintendent in charge of the case, is one of the chief conspirators behind the Atwal murders, driven by greed for their palatial property. Similarly, in *The Sea of Innocence*, Simran realizes that the influential minister Vinay Gupta colludes with the police, morgue technicians, and immigration officials to cover up Liza's murder. In *Origins of Love*, hospitals are also riddled with corruption; illegal experiments and exploitative practices go on unnoticed. Even the Health Minister exploits a desperate surrogate for political clout.

In *Witness the Night*, Simran finds the press to be equally complicit as they refuse to publish anything controversial about the Atwal family despite their ownership of illegal clinics to kill baby girls. They possess undue influence in their society, so much so that they get away with institutionalizing their daughter Sharda in a psychiatric hospital without being questioned by the police, press, or members of the public. The complicity that exists among mental institutions, hospitals, politicians, journalists, and law enforcement demonstrates that crime in India is ubiquitous. Crime feels all the more omnipresent due to the abominable values of society which in turn sustain illegal acts. Indian society's patriarchal values engender sexist practices and traditions such as dowry,[5] female feticide and infanticide,[6] and demeaning fertility rituals.[7] While these traditions are illegal, they are still widely practiced, and often reinforced by women themselves to gain social acceptance in a patriarchal society. In the face of such rooted and sustained sexism, the detective's ability to counter crime may be ineffectual because "the evil is of a kind that can only be solved by a change in society's attitudes."[8]

In spite of these social obstacles, Simran unfailingly condemns these discriminatory practices and, in doing so, typifies the notion of the detective as someone who refuses to "accept the given social order as a source of moral virtue and behaviour."[9] She actively challenges the righteousness attributed to these practices, instead relying on her own moral code which is founded on egalitarian and inclusive beliefs. Although she faces criticism, difficulty, and danger, her beliefs and emotional involvement in the case compel her to take action. In *The Sea of Innocence*, when the police, witnesses, and even family members of Liza give up on finding her, it is Simran who tirelessly soldiers on to discover the truth. When her life is threatened by Dr. Ashok's henchmen in *Origins of Love*, the plight of the HIV-infected baby Amelia motivates her to continue pursuing the case. In *Witness the Night*, Simran questions the narrative of Durga's guilt fed to her by the police. She worries that they were "trapping" a young girl for far too brutal a crime and therefore decides to protect Durga.[10] In all these instances, Simran's ability to empathize with the victims leads her to act morally and motivates her to act on their behalf.

At times, she is faced with moral dilemmas and must choose to set aside her own interests for the greater good. In *Origins of Love*, she learns that illegally procured embryos are being used to treat ailments and diseases at Freedom Hospital. Most of the embryos, as it turns out, are unfairly siphoned off from consignments belonging to the fertility clinic, Madonna and Child, which is run by her friends Dr. Anita and Subhash Pandey. As a result, many childless couples desperate for children are made to wait longer for treatment. Upon further investigation, she discovers that her childhood friend, Abhi, is a patient at Freedom Hospital. After a plane crash in 1978, Abhi is rendered paralyzed and comatose. However, at Freedom Hospital, with the help of stem cell surgery, his condition starts to slowly improve. Simran feels terribly conflicted, knowing that exposing the illegal activity at the hospital will also terminate her friend's treatment. She tells herself,

> I couldn't afford to be too sentimental about it all, or my investigation would get completely derailed. I had to force myself to stop wanting to know about Abhi and instead focus on the real issue before us. Freedom Hospital had been involved in bribing officials and conducting illegal experiments. ... There was also a human cost to this. I must remember that.[11]

Simran must either choose her friend or the couples and surrogates who are victims of a major scam. Although she chooses to expose the villain Dr. Ashok's crimes, she is unable to provide proper evidence to incriminate him. Regardless of the outcome, Simran does not waver from her objective to ensure justice. According to Rachel Haliburton, the detective serves as a "role model" for readers demonstrating the "virtues of honesty, courage and a commitment to justice."[12] By setting aside her personal interests for the needs of the vulnerable, Simran exemplifies Haliburton's assessment of the detective as a role model.

Her role as a social worker further cements her as an ethical guide as she fights for "the human rights of the downtrodden, the voiceless, faceless, nameless, and often blameless millions."[13] She says, "When I think there has been a miscarriage of justice, I get into the system, meet everyone, represent no one, and try and get to the truth."[14] Simran thus works in an inclusive manner, careful to examine all perspectives, while acting independently, indifferent to political influence or law enforcement. Furthermore, her quest for knowledge differs from that of the police; her concerns are more social than criminal as she is motivated more by the desire to protect vulnerable people than to incriminate them. For instance, when she meets Vishnu Braganza, the police's chief suspect in Liza's disappearance, she immediately observes his scarred body and broken speech. She finds herself moved to tears after hearing how he was falsely charged and tortured in prison by the police.[15] Instead of criminalizing him, she sympathizes with him, observing that poor men like him "were as much at the mercy of the police as women were."[16]

As a social worker, she is familiar with the failures of the police and the other disciplinary institutions that she encounters such as the juvenile home, which is rife with sexual exploitation, the mental asylum which inhumanely tortures its patients, and the women's prison which neglects the human rights of its prisoners. These institutions do not work to rehabilitate individuals but instead to control and further oppress. The patriarchal family, too, is criticized by Simran for creating social prisons for women. In *Witness the Night*, the Atwals suppress their daughters' individuality and subject them to cruel practices. The Atwals are also guilty of killing most of the baby girls in the family by either poisoning, drowning, or burying them alive. These crimes, within the family, prisons, and law enforcement, are acknowledged by Simran in her crusade against injustice. When the law fails to protect these vulnerable women from repressive structures, she becomes a refuge for them and is able to rehabilitate them. For instance, she learns that Sharda has been "missing" for years and neither the police nor the press "bothered" to trace her to the asylum.[17] Ultimately, it is Simran who finds, rescues, and rehabilitates her, using her own finances to heal her. Similarly, in *Origins of Love*, she protects abused surrogates at Dr. Ashok's clinic and ensures that they receive better treatment elsewhere.

She also acts as an ethical guide for the characters around her, particularly for her friend Dr. Anita Pandey who runs a surrogacy business at her fertility hospital. Although Simran disapproves of commercial surrogacy and sees it as an exploitative business, she is hired as an "unofficial adviser" on social and legal issues and works as a "facilitator" with the surrogates.[18] In this manner, she is able to "ensure the ethics" of surrogacy are met—that the poverty-stricken women opting to become surrogates are humanely treated and properly compensated.[19]

Simran also works to enact social justice, using her experience, resources, and contacts to protect those affected by the crimes. For instance, she rehabilitates both Sharda and Durga, adopting the latter while drawing on her own finances to provide care for the former. She oversees Durga's education and mental well-being with the hope that Durga's ambition to become a doctor will be the "real vindication" for her painful childhood.[20] Sharda also improves under Simran's care, as she begins to communicate properly and take up hobbies such as cooking in the sequels *Origins of Love* and *The Sea of Innocence*. In *Origins of Love*, she ensures that baby Amelia is adopted by a couple who will look after her and love her regardless of her illness. She also advises the Pandeys to make a deal with the health minister to revoke Dr. Ashok's license. In the third novel, she works with a journalist to ensure that Vinay is subjected to intense scrutiny on social media and is subsequently barred from engaging in political activities. Simran thus does not rely on the law for justice but takes on the responsibility herself. However, there are instances when she seems to endorse an ambiguous moral code, particularly in her attitude toward vigilantism and the compromises she makes with perpetrators.

Vigilantism as an Alternative Form of Justice

Although it is never explicitly revealed, Durga, under the influence of her tutor Harpreet, poisons, kills, and burns the thirteen members of her family in an act of vengeance. Throughout their childhood, Durga and her older sister, Sharda, are oppressed by their family members and are viewed as being inferior to their male relatives. When Sharda is discovered to be pregnant with Harpreet's child, her tutor and a lower-caste man, she is cast off into an asylum and violently tortured until she succumbs to madness. Harpreet plots revenge by seducing the younger sister, Durga, and manipulates her into killing her family members, an act that he claims to be just and "deserved" for their mistreatment of women.[21] Being wealthy and influential in their town, the Atwals rely on police, political, and media contacts to cover up their crimes of female feticide and infanticide. With their influence and impunity from legal punishment, traditional justice seems virtually impossible. In the face of such failures within the justice system, vigilantism, or rather murder, emerges as an alternative form of justice in the novel. Through the presence of vigilante justice, Desai raises many questions about morality and the law: As the law and its instruments fail to protect vulnerable girls like Sharda and Durga, can Durga's supposed act of murder be seen as morally justified? By allegedly killing her family, Durga prevents the feticide of her sister-in-law Binny's daughter. Can the deaths then of thirteen people to save one be justified? What if Durga was, in fact, insane or severely depressed? Can she be guilty? How much agency does Durga have in the murders if she was manipulated and groomed by Harpreet? These questions remain unanswered in the novel and are left for the reader to decide. However, Desai's detective, Simran, seems to take on a stance that is more morally relativist than absolutist.

Drawing on her experience as a social worker, she recalls instances of children being groomed by adults to commit crimes. She sympathizes with these children, suggesting that their crimes could have been avoided if they were counselled or cared for.[22] Simran also subscribes to a broader view of criminality, stating that there are instances where it can be "difficult to distinguish the criminal from his circumstances … life can really be unfair."[23] Her inclination toward moral relativism along with her experience working with vulnerable children allows her to demonstrate compassion for Durga. She approaches her with empathy instead of condemnation, saying,

> It made me angry to see a child so helpless, possibly caught in a trap. Who had laid it for her? Who was the mastermind? More and more, I was being irrevocably drawn to the conclusion that she was innocent. She was a hurt and angry child, no doubt, but ... Someone had used her and possibly continued to use her.[24]

Simran thus believes that Durga is a victim of negative influences and lacks the agency to be convicted of guilt. She also refuses to confront Durga with the truth and confesses to the reader that she does not (want to) know the extent of Durga's culpability. Likewise, in the sequel, *Origins of Love*, she maintains that Durga was "falsely accused of being a murderess."[25] She deliberately and unquestioningly accepts her innocence to spare her further trauma.

By treating Durga as a victim who is somewhat culpable of murder, Simran highlights the tension between "a moral code, which presents itself as omnipresent and relevant to all" and "the very considerable differences in social power."[26] These differences in social power such as Durga's age, her lack of access to legal protection, abuse at home, and grooming by her tutor upend the absolutism of murder as an indefensible act. The stark difference between Durga's intent and Harpreet's intent also contributes to an alternative understanding of murder and justice. Durga's conception of vigilante justice is one of vengeance and deterrence; she allegedly kills her family out of revenge for the crimes committed against her sister, but also prevents them from harming Binny's unborn daughter, whom they tried to abort. Binny recounts to Simran how she owes her life and that of her daughter's to Durga who cautioned her to leave before the murders.

Her alleged act of murder also grants Durga freedom from her oppressive family. While in prison, she notes in her diary that she is "finally freed" of her family members and wonders what kind of childhood she would have had if she had been "loved and wanted and cared for" and had a mother who did not "hate [her] because [she] was a girl."[27] Durga's actions reflect her powerlessness and victimhood, but also cast her in a heroic light in her self-liberation and protection of Binny. She is both victim and vigilante, hero and perpetrator.

Conversely, Harpreet's actions reflect his vile nature and selfish motives. He initially orchestrates the plot for revenge to hold the Atwals accountable for mistreating both girls. However, he impregnates Sharda when she is a teenager and later sexually exploits her sister Durga when she is still a minor. Towards the end of the novel, it is revealed that his intentions are far more sinister as he sought out the girls' inheritance and property. Despite this, Simran does not condemn him completely but views him in an ambiguous light, stating that he "avenged the death of their childhood … but at a terrible price."[28]

Simran's morally ambiguous perspective is also present in *The Sea of Innocence* when she commends Vishnu's hacktivism and vigilantism. As Liza's friend, he feels compelled to enact vengeance for her sexual assault, murder, and subsequent cover-up by the police and politicians. He hacks into the police's computers to obtain information about her cover-up and uses this information to terrify those involved while reopening the investigation into her disappearance. Later in the novel, it is revealed that he used to follow Liza and film her without her knowledge. Through the videos, Simran and a journalist, Dennis, are able to identify the main perpetrator behind Liza's disappearance, the influential minister Vinay Gupta. Although they cannot prove his culpability in her sexual assault and murder, they release one of the incriminating videos on social media and let the incensed netizens hold him accountable. Simran thus dubs Vishnu as the "real hero" of the case for bringing this information to light.[29] However, dubbing him as such casts his actions as ethically ambiguous, not just because of his hacktivism but also because of his stalking and voyeurism. Vishnu tells Simran that he wished to intervene when Liza was being raped but was held back by the fear that he would be killed, particularly because of his experience with police brutality. Furthermore, he claims, his death would ensure that the crimes committed against Liza would stay buried. Without his stalking of Liza, there would be no evidence to link her entrapment, assault, and murder to Vinay. Simran seems to approve of his actions, as she praises his "ingenuity," "loyalty," and "exceptional courage" in exposing the corrupt.[30] While his actions are morally questionable, she condones his acting outside the law as it generates some semblance of justice.

Crime and Compromise

Apart from her attitude toward vigilantism, the compromises Simran makes with the perpetrators highlight the "messy complexity" and moral ambiguity that is present in Desai's fiction. As a social worker who works with the dispossessed and disenfranchised, she is acutely aware that pursuing legal action is often ineffective with disappointing results.[31] Furthermore, there are many instances in which she cannot prove any criminal wrongdoing, even with police intervention. For instance, in *The Sea of Innocence*, she tries to work with an honest inspector to gather evidence against Vinay but is unsuccessful. For these reasons, Simran resorts to other means to achieve some semblance of justice. In *Witness the Night*, she works out a compromise with the mastermind(s) behind the Atwal murders. In exchange for the meagre evidence that she has, the corrupt police superintendent Ramnath agrees to release Durga and Sharda to her care. Simran also agrees (on Durga's behalf) to sell the Atwal property to Ramnath and Harpreet. The compromise that she makes mirrors reality as Desai explains in an interview with Namita Gokhale, "That is what the reality is in India ... you make a compromise, you do a deal. And that's what happens in cases where very powerful people are concerned. But if you're a poor person, you'll be picked up and thrown in jail immediately."[32] In other words, Durga's inheritance secures her freedom, as that is the chief reason—apart from evidence of Ramnath's and Harpreet's culpability—behind the sisters' release. While it is illegal and fairly unethical for her to make deals with criminals and murderers, Simran possesses limited choices. Her negotiations exemplify the impossibility of neat solutions and reiterate "life's messy complexity."

Similarly, in *Origins of Love*, Simran makes a compromise to protect her friends, Dr. Anita and Dr. Subhash Pandey. Simran suspects that Dr. Ashok is the orchestrator behind Mike and Susan's deaths and their surrogate Preethi's accident. However, she does not possess concrete evidence to prove his involvement in their deaths. She cannot prove his attempts to hurt the baby, Amelia, either. Nor can she alert the police to his illegal experiments as he threatens to plant evidence to incriminate the Pandeys for his offenses. The Pandeys therefore cannot file a case against him without receiving negative publicity and censure. Instead, with Simran's help, they negotiate a deal to break off ties with him. In both novels, the perpetrators go free and are held unaccountable for their crimes. By avoiding the restoration of order that comes from catching the perpetrator and subjecting them to the law, Desai's fiction goes against the typical tenets of crime writing.

Catharsis vs. Emotional Engagement

Traditionally in crime writing, the perpetrator is revealed by the detective and subjected to the law. In doing so, order is restored, closure is achieved, and the reader experiences catharsis from this materialization of justice. As Rankin affirms, "The tight three-act structure of the crime novel (crime–investigation—resolution) pays tribute to the fact that we humans hunger for form and a sense of closure."[33] Likewise, P.D. James suggests that in its resolution of crime, the detective story confirms that "we live in a rational, comprehensible and moral universe."[34] She notes that it also produces a "reassuring relief"[35] from the anxieties of the modern world and even though we encounter violence and murder in the text, we "remain personally inviolate both from responsibility and from its terrors."[36] In other words, the traditional crime novel becomes a restorative refuge, where justice—which may not be possible in the real world—is actualized within the text, thus offering the reader catharsis. In the closure and catharsis that it provides, the typical crime novel ensures that we are unaffected by the violence in the text. However, Desai's fiction with all its moral ambiguities and complexities departs from this neat notion of "reassuring relief" and ensures that readers shoulder the "responsibility" and experience the "terrors" of crime.

In all three novels, the perpetrators are exempted from punishment, either because of a lack of concrete evidence or because of the overwhelming presence of corruption within the government and justice system. In *Witness the Night*, Harpreet receives impunity for the Atwal murders while Ramnath's involvement is concealed from public knowledge. Similarly, in *Origins of Love*, Dr. Ashok goes unpunished for his role in Mike and Susan's deaths and the clinic responsible for the HIV strain in Amelia remains unaccountable. Likewise, Vinay cannot be charged with the murders of Liza and his employee Vicky due to a lack of evidence. The other politicians, government officials, police officers, and employees of Vinay who collude with him to cover up Liza's rape and murder also escape punishment. The lack of justice and closure that comes from their impunity closely reflects reality. Desai herself bases these crimes on real-life cases such as the horrific rapes and murders of Scarlett Keeling and Jyoti Singh in 2008 and 2012, respectively. In doing so, her fiction negates the "reassuring relief" that crime novels provide and instead demonstrates how victims in real life often do not get resolution, justice, or fully recover from the violence endured.

Desai's repudiation of neat solutions in her novels ensures that the affective aftermath of crime lingers beyond the text. Instead of experiencing catharsis, the reader is appalled, disturbed, and enraged by the absence of justice. This subversion thus forces us to "confront and reflect on the evil that we see every day (and ignore; otherwise, it would not be so omnipresent)."[37] As Desai admits in an interview with Steven Chan, she wrote *Witness the Night* out of "sheer rage" with the callous attitude toward female feticide in India. She explains, "I got tired of living in a country where murder could be atoned. You could kill your baby girl and nobody's going to put you behind bars."[38] Her intention then is to draw attention to these absurd injustices while also raising questions about the morality of the law and responsibility of society in perpetuating evil. She also expresses her hope that her fiction "disturbs and mobilizes" readers against gender-based crimes.[39] Desai's intent then behind the subversion of closure and catharsis is for readers to emotionally engage with the crimes text and be provoked into action in the real world.

By writing about social issues in the space of crime fiction, Desai encourages readers to think and behave ethically. Therefore, the moral ambiguities in her fiction—vigilantism, compromises with murderers, ethical dilemmas, blurred lines between victim and perpetrator, evasion of the killer's identity, and a detective who subscribes to a morally grey notion of justice—not only reflect life's messy complexity but force readers to imagine themselves in the unjust circumstances that prompted the very same ambiguity. The moral ambiguities coupled with the presence of a resolutely feminist detective ensure that readers confront the attitudes behind gender-based crime and then become inspired to make a difference.

Notes

1. Ian Rankin, "Why Crime Fiction Is Good for You," in *Howdunit: A Masterclass in Crime Writing by Members of the Detection Club*, ed. Martin Edwards (London: Collins Crime Club, 2020), 31.
2. *Witness the Night* is loosely based on the case of Ruchika Girhotra, a fourteen-year-old girl who was molested by a police officer in 1990. She committed suicide after she and her loved ones were harassed by the police for filing a complaint against the official. Desai also draws on accounts of female feticide and infanticide encountered during her time as a journalist. *The Sea of Innocence* is based on the 2008 murder of British teenager Scarlett Keeling in Goa. The novel also makes references to the "Nirbhaya case"—the brutal and fatal gang rape of Jyoti Singh on a bus in Delhi in 2012.
3. Neele Meyer closely examines Desai's detective in *Witness the Night* from a feminist perspective while Holly Morgan provides a feminist and postcolonial reading of all three novels. Neele Meyer, "Challenging Gender and Genre: Women in Contemporary Indian Crime Fiction," *Zeitschrift für Anglistik und Amerikanistik* 66, no. 1 (2018); Holly Morgan, "Kishwar Desai's Simran Singh series: Crime, Detection, and Gender," *The Journal of Commonwealth Literature* 57, no. 3 (2020): 706–21. Manali Karmakar and Avishek Parui's essay looks into the biopolitical ethics of surrogacy and presence of neoliberal eugenics in *Origins of Love*. Manali Karmakar and Avishek Parui, "'These were made-to-order babies': Reterritorialised Kinship, Neoliberal Eugenics and Artificial Reproductive Technology in Kishwar Desai's Origins of Love," *Medical Humanities* 46 (2019): 323–32.
4. Kishwar Desai, *Witness the Night* (New York: Penguin Books, 2010), 164.
5. Desai, *Witness*, 49, 62.
6. Ibid., 68.
7. Kishwar Desai, *Origins of Love* (London: Simon & Schuster, 2012), 16, 176.
8. Sandrine Berges, "The Hardboiled Detective as Moralist: Ethics in Crime Fiction," in *Values and Virtues: Aristotelianism in Contemporary Ethics*, ed. Timothy Chappell (New York: Oxford University Press, 2006), 224.
9. Mary Evans, Sarah Moore, and Hazel Johnstone, *Detecting the Social: Order and Disorder in Post-1970s Detective Fiction* (Cham: Palgrave Macmillan, 2019), 3.
10. Desai, *Witness*, 18.
11. Desai, *Origins*, 349.

12 Rachel Haliburton, *The Ethical Detective: Moral Philosophy and Detective Fiction* (Lanham: Lexington Books, 2018), xiv.
13 Desai, *Witness*, 16
14 Ibid.
15 Kishwar Desai, *The Sea of Innocence* (London: Simon & Schuster, 2013), 157.
16 Desai, *Sea*, 156.
17 Desai, *Witness*, 92.
18 Ibid., 95.
19 Ibid., 98.
20 Ibid., 162.
21 Ibid., 64.
22 Ibid., 60.
23 Ibid., 17.
24 Ibid., 120.
25 Desai, *Origins*, 17.
26 Mary Evans, *The Imagination of Evil: Detective Fiction and the Modern World* (London: Continuum International Publishing Group, 2009), 3.
27 Desai, *Witness*, 149.
28 Ibid., 158.
29 Desai, *Sea*, 219.
30 Ibid., 205.
31 Desai, *Witness*, 16. See also Desai, *Sea*, 26.
32 Kishwar Desai, "Writers etc. session 32 Kishwar Desai," interview by Namita Gokhale, French Institute in India, YouTube video, August 13, 2014, https://www.youtube.com/watch?v=JlQfrBmiqqY.
33 Rankin, "Crime Fiction," 37.
34 P.D. James, *Talking about Detective Fiction* (New York: Vintage Books, 2011), 14.
35 James, *Talking*, 174
36 Ibid., 14.
37 Berges, "Hardboiled Detective," 217.
38 Kishwar Desai, "Gender Roles in India, part of the 2013 SOAS Alumni & Friends Weekend," interview by Steven Chan, SOAS University of London, YouTube video, August 12, 2013, https://www.youtube.com/watch?v=QaMVAMUKJcU.
39 Kishwar Desai, "India Has Become Very Cruel towards Its Women," *South Asia @ LSE,* June 7, 2013, https://blogs.lse.ac.uk/southasia/2013/06/07/kishwar-desai/.

Bibliography

Berges, Sandrine. "The Hardboiled Detective as Moralist: Ethics in Crime Fiction." In *Values and Virtues: Aristotelianism in Contemporary Ethics*, edited by Timothy Chappell, 212–25. New York: Oxford University Press, 2006.
Desai, Kishwar. "Gender Roles in India, part of the 2013 SOAS Alumni & Friends Weekend." Interview by Steven Chan. *SOAS University of London*, YouTube video, August 12, 2013a. https://www.youtube.com/watch?v=.
Desai, Kishwar. "India Has Become Very Cruel towards Its Women." *South Asia @ LSE*, June 7, 2013b. https://blogs.lse.ac.uk/southasia/2013/06/07/kishwar-desai/.
Desai, Kishwar. *Origins of Love*. London: Simon & Schuster, 2012.
Desai, Kishwar. *Witness the Night*. New York: Penguin Books, 2010.
Desai, Kishwar. "Writers etc. session 32 Kishwar Desai." Interview by Namita Gokhale. *French Institute in India*, YouTube video, August 13, 2013c. https://www.youtube.com/watch?v=JlQfrBmiqqY.
Desai, Kishwar. *The Sea of Innocence*. London: Simon & Schuster, 2013d.
Evans, Mary. *The Imagination of Evil: Detective Fiction and the Modern World*. London: Continuum International Publishing Group, 2009.
Evans, Mary, Sarah Moore, and Hazel Johnstone. *Detecting the Social: Order and Disorder in Post-1970s Detective Fiction*. Cham: Palgrave Macmillan, 2019.
Haliburton, Rachel. *The Ethical Detective: Moral Philosophy and Detective Fiction*. Lanham: Lexington Books, 2018.
James, P.D. *Talking about Detective Fiction*. New York: Vintage Books, 2011.
Karmarkar, Manali, and Avishek Parui. "'These were made-to-order babies': Reterritorialised Kinship, Neoliberal Eugenics and Artificial Reproductive Technology in Kishwar Desai's Origins of Love." *Medical Humanities* 46 (2019): 323–32.
Meyer, Neele. "Challenging Gender and Genre: Women in Contemporary Indian Crime Fiction." *Zeitschrift für Anglistik und Amerikanistik* 66, no. 1 (2018). https://doi.org/10.1515/zaa-2018-0010.
Morgan, Holly. "Kishwar Desai's Simran Singh Series: Crime, Detection, and Gender." *The Journal of Commonwealth Literature* 57, no. 3 (2020): 706–21. https://journals.sagepub.com/doi/10.1177/0021989420912294.
Rankin, Ian. "Why Crime Fiction Is Good for You." In *Howdunit: A Masterclass in Crime Writing by Members of the Detection Club*, edited by Martin Edwards, 28–38. London: Collins Crime Club, 2020.

10

Mystery Pierced with Social Evil: Reading Caste and Class Issues in *The Quills of the Porcupine*

Debaditya Mukhopadhyay

By the time readers reach the conclusion of a mystery narrative (especially the mystery narratives featuring a detective), they are familiarized with various dos and don'ts, which the narrative establishes as essential for moral development. These dos and don'ts are not always representative of the ideal. Rather, they represent the ideological, that is, a set of moral codes observed and endorsed by a particular section of a society. In his seminal monograph *Bloody Murder*, Julian Symons touches on the matter pointing out that the various subgenres of mystery fiction or crime fiction represent the values of a class in society that felt it had everything to lose by social change[1] and calls the detective an "agent" of this particular class of the society, endowed with the responsibility to ensure that "those who tried to disturb the established order were always discovered and punished."[2]

In certain instances, as shown in Annette Wren's chapter on narratives featuring Hercule Poirot, the detective can indeed rise above the moral codes observed by a particular nation, society, or culture by way of possessing "an objective moral standard," a term Wren derives from Johnson's notion of "moral imagination." In this chapter, I will further explicate the dialogue between moral imagination and mystery narratives by taking up Saradindu Bandyopadhyay's *The Quills of the Porcupine* (1967; referred hereafter as *The Quills*) as a case study. Hercule Poirot's stance as an "international detective" might indeed endow him (or the narrative he is featured in) with a moral vision characterized by objectivity, but detectives positioned as representative of a specific nation, culture, or in more general terms, a specific group of a particular socio-cultural milieu is not necessarily informed by such absolute objectivity. However, it is important to note that this discussion is not aimed at underlining the absence of moral imagination in *The Quills*. Rather, my discussion will bring out the interplay between moral imagination and ideological baggage, that is, the moral standards of Bandyopadhyay's contemporary society set by a privileged class. As this chapter will explain, these codes, representative of a hegemonic group's interest and Bandyopadhyay's own moral imagination, contest each other within the novel creating an ambiguity of moral stance within the novel.

In *The Quills*, the Bengali detective Byomkesh Bakshi investigates a series of murders committed in Kolkata where the murderer pierced the victim's heart using a porcupine quill. During the investigation, he detects an intriguing connection between the murders and two major social problems of his time, namely inhibition against inter-caste marriage and denial of women's freedom, both supported by the dominant section of the contemporary Bengali society. Though the resolution of the novel does not at all deviate from a typical detective story in which mystery is solved and the criminal gets punished, Bandyopadhway's way of interspersing critiques of the status quo with the mystery narrative differentiates this novel from most other murder-mystery stories.

Instead of unfolding the mystery through a linear narrative focused solely on the detective's unraveling of the mystery, Bandyopadhyay offers three overlapping narratives that allow him to separate the authorial and the detective's points of view. Noting this layered nature of the novel, I analyze both these points of view in relation to the concept of moral imagination. Writers of mystery narratives are either aligned with the status quo, as suggested in Symons's observations cited above or understood as consciously critical of dominant groups, as explained by C. Clark Triplett's chapter in this collection, I locate Bandyopadhyay's novel between these two differing stances by explaining how and why Bandyopadhyay intercuts his detective's responses to the contemporary Indian society's casteist, classist, and patriarchal biases through other narratives exposing or critiquing these biases. In other words, I use *The Quills* to illustrate how moral imagination, in the Johnsonian sense, and ideological underpinnings that shape the detective into an agent of the dominant groups can co-exist in a mystery narrative, intercutting each other. I will explore this by reading closely the conflicting narratives of Bandyopadhyay's novel followed by an overview of existing critical responses on Byomkesh Bakshi stories that will explain the importance of viewing Byomkesh as a detective shaped by his socio-cultural and ethnic setup, which makes him differ significantly from a detective presented as an investigator above national-cultural-ethnic boundaries like Poirot.

Critical Engagements with Byomkesh's Identity

Though this section will be chiefly concerned with reviewing critical analyses of Byomkesh stories, it seems relevant to begin by referring to Bandyopadhyay's own brief write-up on detective fiction which shows Bandyopadhyay's eagerness to create a canon of detective stories characterized by ethnic distinctness. In this piece entitled "Detective Story" ("Detective Galpa" in Bangla), Bandyopadhyay shares his views on the genre, expresses his concerns about the devalued status of the genre in India, and defends his own detective Byomkesh against critics. For the present discussion, it is important to note that, while exploring the reasons for detective stories' maligned reputation, Bandyopadhyay critiques the trend of lifting plots from foreign detective stories which characterized his contemporary detective stories. In his opinion, these copied stories were "cheap like Japanese toys made of tin" (my translation) and were completely devoid of literary aspects that intrigue intelligent readers.[3] Bandyopadhyay does not explicitly state to what extent he differed from this trend he critiques while creating Byomkesh, but his emphatic disapproval of copying foreign detective stories in this write-up written immediately after he finished the first Byomkesh story and the subsequent observations of critics regarding the identity of Byomkesh show how Indianness or Bengaliness shaped Byomkesh.

The Bengali critic Sukumar Sen, renowned for his monograph on Crime Stories (which is arguably the first of its kind in Bengali language), draws attention to the differences between the universally popular Western detective Sherlock Holmes and Byomkesh, describing the latter as the ideal example of an intellectual Bengali young man of 1930s characterized by his intelligence, merit, alertness, politeness, and empathy, instead of the eccentricities or addictedness shown in Holmes[4] Subsequent analyses of Byomkesh added a postcolonial angle to Sen's insights, explaining Byomkesh as a manifestation of the empire's way of writing back to the Western canon of detective stories. Pinaki Roy's monograph *The Manichean Investigators* (2008) was the first to approach these stories from a postcolonial perspective. Comparing the Holmes canon with Byomkesh stories in his monograph, Pinaki Roy describes Byomkesh as "Saradindu Bandyopadhyay's answer to the imperial and Orientalist Sherlock Holmes,"[5] by referring to the various markers of Bengaliness in Byomkesh. As explained by Roy, despite being written with colonial India as backdrop, the Byomkesh stories highlight the Bengali community, the humble demeanor of Byomkesh sets him apart from typical Western adventurist-detective like Holmes, and the setting of Kolkata replaces the images of London frequently appearing in the Holmes stories.[6]

Subsequent analyses of the Byomkesh stories mostly mark a continuation of the critical approach found in Roy's monograph. In a recent analysis of

Byomkesh stories, Abhinaba Chatterjee maintains that the Byomkesh stories, together with Satyajit Ray's equally renowned Feluda series, manifest a resistance to the Anglo-centric detective story canon.[7] Likewise, Anindita Dey's monograph on Bengali detective stories reads the Byomkesh stories as a cultural resistance against Western dominance through the assertion of Bengali identity. Drawing attention to the overt display of cultural markers like the wearing of *dhoti* (a cloth used by the males of many ethnic groups of India for covering the lower portion of the body) in Byomkesh's appearance in an era culturally dominated by the popularity of Holmes stories, Dey argues, "When western detectives had complete authority over global acclaim, a dhoti-clad detective emerges to establish a paradigm shift with indigenous cultural traits in his personality as well as nationalist fervor in the adventures."[8] Though the Byomkesh stories indeed derive their cultural significance by pitting themselves against the Western detective stories, the emphatic stress on Byomkesh's Bengali identity aligns these stories with the dominant social group of Bandyopadhyay's contemporary society, yet this particular aspect of the Byomkseh stories remains less highlighted, except for Gautam Chakrabarti's article that connects Byomkesh with the figure of the *Bhadralok*.

Instead of accepting Byomkesh's wearing of *dhoti* essentially as a sign of his Bengaliness or viewing these stories as a manifestation of cultural resistance against the Western icons, Chakrabarti locates Byomkesh within the class of *Bhadralok*s, who, according to him, are a section of the Bengali society shaped by Western education and are characterized by Anglophilia, despite their tendency to oppose British colonialism[9] The very word *Bhadralok* as well as the class of people signified by it manifests Indian society's classist and casteist biases (more on this in the next section), and by connecting Byomkesh with the figure of the *Bhadralok*, Chakrabarti's discussion hints at the possible ways the Byomkesh stories are informed by the class-caste differences of the contemporary society. Since Chakrabarti's article primarily concerned itself with explaining Byomkesh as an "intersectional figure,"[10] locating him between Anglophiliac and nationalist cultures, his discussion does not take up Byomkesh's links with caste-class hierarchy or patriarchy. I will trace the impact of these ideologies in my close-reading and subsequent analysis of *The Quills of the Porcupine*, but, before that, I will explain the significance of the *Bhadralok* identity within the class-caste hierarchy of Bandyopadhyay's milieu.

Bhadraloks: Their Caste and Class

Two Bengali words *Bhadra*, meaning "gentle," and *lok*, usually signifying "adult males," are conjoined in the word *Bhadralok*. Since the 1990s, the term has emerged as a keyword in discussions about colonial Bengal, especially its intelligentsia or middle-class population. Though eminent historians like Partha Chatterjee and Sumit Sarkar have related the term primarily with the middle-class, historian Tithi Bhattacharya, referring to a nineteenth-century Bengali text's passages about *Bhadralok* class, has talked about the presence of three types of *Bhadralok*s in colonial Bengal, namely the rich, the middle-class, and the poor.[11] Pointing out the economic difference among the three types of *Bhadralok*s[12] and adding how some influential merchant families of Bengal (both Bengali and non-Bengali) were never categorized as *Bhadralok*s[13] Bhattacharya identifies intellectuality, especially the kind demarcated by an individual's grasp over books, newspapers, magazines, etc., to be the marker for the *Bhadralok* category.[14] Such qualities did not simply endow the *Bhadralok*s with a social position, but they also helped them foster "social power."[15] Despite the apparent differences between these three historians' views regarding *Bhadralok*, collectively their deliberations present the *Bhadralok*s as a revered social group characterized by their intellectuality and control of the moral codes of Bengali society.

Bhattacharya's views regarding the *Bhadralok*s' connection with intellectual knowledge, irrespective of economic status, recall Partha Chatterjee's translation of the term as "respected folk."[16] Though Chatterjee does not consider *Bhadralok* a category surpassing economic differences, his use of "respected" as a qualifier for the category indirectly shows the possible link between intellectual knowledge and the respectable position of the *Bhadralok*s. Chatterjee does not consider the possession of intellectual knowledge by the *Bhadralok* as a factor that enabled them to have an influence. Bhattacharya's views on the matter quoted above with Chatterjee's arguments about the *Bhadralok*s' "playing a pre-eminent role" in the creation of "the social institutions of Bengal,"[17] the impact of the *Bhadralok*s' intellectual knowledge becomes understandable. The *Bhadralok*s, according to Chatterjee, "laid down new criteria of social respectability" and "set new aesthetic and moral stands of judgement."[18] Seen in the light of Bhattacharya's views, such achievements appear as the outcome of the intellectual capacity of the *Bhadralok*s. Altogether, being a *Bhadralok* in Bengali society positioned an individual among the dominant groups. Naturally the category of *Bhadralok*s, as shown by Bhattacharya's study, was formulated through an "exclusionary mechanism,"[19] which refused to allow sharing of the grasp of the *Bhadralok*s over moral standards. Though Bhattacharya does not directly connect caste system with this exclusionary mechanism, the large presence of upper-castes among the *Bhadralok* category[20] is indicative of the possible ways caste-based differences informed the *Bhadralok* identity.

The caste system, at present identified as one of the major challenges against equality in Indian society, was founded along with the emergence of Brahminic domination in India. The Brahmins have been traced back to the invading Aryans who conquered the native population of India known as Dravidians and thereafter created the varna system (which later came to be known as caste system), placing the Aryans at the uppermost rank of the Brahmins.[21] Four major castes are mentioned in traditional Hindu literatures, and the entire system is characterized by a rigidity that prohibits mobilization of the people designated as lower castes which has disintegrated the Hindu community.[22] It is difficult within the limited scope of this discussion to determine to what extent the exclusionary mechanism formulating the *Bhadralok* group was shaped by the caste system's rigid structuring, but the resemblance between the two and the dominant presence of upper-castes among the *Bhadralok* category shows the plausibility of connecting the two. Besides, the long tradition of denying of educational opportunity to the lower caste in India[23] also points out a possible link between the caste system and the *Bhadraloks'* dominance over the intellectual world. In short, the *Bhadralok*s were a category of the Bengali society who benefitted significantly from the limited circulation of knowledge based on caste differences and on the caste system as a whole. Additionally, it is important to note the gendered nature of the term *Bhadralok* and its possible patriarchal overtone. As suggested above, the word *lok* conventionally means "male." Besides, the use of term *Bhadramahila* (*mahila* meaning woman in Bangla) excludes the women from the category of *Bhadralok*s, showing a reluctance to place women in the privileged position allocated for the *Bhadralok*s.

Primacy of the *Bhadralok*, however, underwent an interesting change during the twentieth century. Toward the early twentieth century a number of lower castes showed visible signs of upward mobility toward attaining the *Bhadralok* identity and attained the status despite belonging to a lower caste.[24] In post-independence India further changes ensued from the expansion of the city-space, increase in educational opportunity, and easy access to information media. In addition, the growing tradition of inter-caste marriages, which received legal sanction by the Special Marriage Act of 1954, also contributed significantly toward the undoing of caste-based differences in general, and the difference between *Bhadralok* and the inferior lower class pejoratively called *chotolok* ("choto" meaning lower in this context) was no exception.

Presently the term *Bhadralok* is no longer associated with the privileged group it previously signified. Instead, the term signifies an individual with commendable moral conduct and high educational qualification.[25] The erstwhile class of *Bhadralok*s has therefore disappeared, gradually witnessing the attempts of previously ousted sections of society gravitating toward their coveted and protected domain of knowledge and intelligence. *The Quills* captures both the anxiety of the *Bhadralok* class against attempts of the lower class to move upward and the impact of the *Bhadralok*'s supremacy over the sections dominated by the *Bhadralok*s' caste-class-gender position through its nonlinear narrative.

Layers Within: A Close Reading of the Novel

Twenty-seven of the Byomkesh stories (total thirty-three) are narrated by Byomkesh's assistant, Ajit, who is introduced as an aspiring writer in the first published Byomkesh story (1934) "Satyanneshi" ("Truth Seeker"). The typical pattern of detective stories informs the plot of these narratives. A visit or communication from a victim or potential victim of a crime opens these stories, and thereafter the narrative moves along with Byomkesh's investigation of the matter. In these stories, Ajit merely records Byomkesh's words and actions, rarely making any comment upon the situation Byomkesh deals with. Though the stories are narrated in first person, it is always Ajit who narrates not the writer Bandyopadhyay per se. In doing so, these stories distance the writer Bandyopadhyay from the stories through the facade of Ajit's narration, thereby minimizing the presence of Bandyopadhyay's comments regarding both the crimes and the criminals.

From the story "Room No. 2," completed three years before *The Quills*, Bandyopadhyay started experimenting with a new style of narration replacing Ajit by an omniscient narrator who uses a more colloquial form of Bangla, in comparison to Ajit's *Sadhu bhasha* (Sanskritized form of Bangla language predominantly used during the nineteenth century). In "Room No. 2" and "The Rhyme in the Deception," Bandyopadhyay limits his experimentation to changing the language of narration. Neither of these stories features any section disclosing the omniscient narrator or any other character's perspective, except for Byomkesh, nor do they use flashbacks. Interestingly, *The Quills* shows Bandyopadhyay using omniscient narration to capture multiple narratorial voices and moving beyond the limits of linear narration.

Instead of merely following the incidents within and outside the household of Byomkesh, the narrative of *The Quills* keeps offering glimpses of other households, often peeking into the depicted character's thought process. In sum, the novel narrates happenings in three households, namely the house of the newly married couple (Dipa and her husband Debashish Bhatta), the house of Dipa's parents (the Mukherjee family, dominated by Dipa's grandfather, brother, and father), and the house of Nripati Laha (a close friend of Dipa's brother, Bijoy Madhav). Each of these households is described and commented upon by the narrator in detail, and when a character starts ruminating, the narrative shifts to a thought-reading mode, bringing out the inner turmoil of the concerned character. Thus, the narrative is not just Byomkesh's response to the serial killings. In fact, the narrative is not just concerned with depicting the crime and the process of investigation. Byomkesh's investigation is surprisingly excluded from the central section of the plot, entitled as "The Tale." Instead, "The Tale" describes the three households, none of which are crime scenes, in detail. This sustained focus on these households shows how this novel is more concerned with detailing the social setup than the detective's feat.

The opening section of the novel, entitled "Prologue," begins describing three consecutive murders in South Kolkata. In each case, the omniscient narrator depicts the plight of the victim briefly commenting on the victim's life and identity. The murdered victims are shown as struggling individuals conventionally associated with the lower ranks of the society. Apart from building suspense through the portrayal of these individuals' hapless death by getting pierced in the heart from behind, this section subtly mocks the attitude of the upper class of South Kolkata.

In each case, the victim's body is discovered in public places, but neither the public nor the police bother much about the first two murders because the victims, a beggar named Phaguram and a day-laborer named Mangalram, are classless for the administration and the sophisticated urban population of Kolkata. In fact, their names hint at their non-Bengali identity which makes them further removed from the concerns of the Bengali upper class. The murderer is viewed as a serious threat only when he kills the Bengali shop owner Gunamay Das.

The same public of South Kolkata that simply ignored the deaths of a beggar and a laborer start critiquing the administration severely for being negligent. By depicting these differing reactions regarding the murders, the narratorial voice mockingly critiques the devaluing of lower sections of the society by the Bengali upper class and administration. It is even more significant to note that Byomkesh himself gets involved in the matter only after a person belonging to the gentry of South Kolkata is attacked by the murderer.[26] Byomkesh gets involved because the police inspector Mr. Rakhal requests him to visit the fourth victim. Though Byomkesh was quite curious about the murders, until the murderer attempts to kill a member of the gentry, Byomkesh does not visit the crime scenes, even though both the incidents were published in newspapers, nor do the police request him for guidance in these murder cases.

As the novel proceeds to the section "The Tale," the focus shifts to the impact of class-caste-gender-based domination on the society from the mysterious murders. First, this section describes the household of Dipa-Debashish where the newly wed couple lives together yet refrains from consummating their marriage. Suspense is maintained throughout the portrayal of the couple by not revealing the reason behind their charade despite their unwillingness to stay together. This episode shows both Debashish and Dipa suffering intensely from the situation. Debashish feels humiliated when Dipa turns down his offer of going to the cinema, which is interpreted by Debashish as Dipa's inability to rely on Debashish's vow to maintain physical distance.[27] Dipa remains restless throughout the episode. Toward the end of the episode, Dipa in particular is shown to break down, uttering "How long can this go on?"[28]

The second episode of this section uses flashback to explore the roots of the prison-like marriage Dipa and Debashish suffer from. Dipa's family members, especially the three male members—Dipa's elder brother Bijoy Madhav, father Nil Madhav, and grandfather Uday Madhav—are shown as staunch supporters of casteism and patriarchy. Uday Madhav sets their family honor above everything else, and despite being highly educated, both Nil and Bijoy followed Uday's flawed ideals blindly. Dipa is shown as a helpless victim of these men's biases. They deprive her from higher education, restrict her life strictly to the domestic sphere, and even deny the right to go out on her own. These suffocating dictums make Dipa eager to break free, and she aims to achieve that by marrying a man of her choice. Dipa's act of defiance creates further difficulties for her. She is severely rebuked by her grandfather,[29] and when she desperately attempts to elope with her beloved, she is physically assaulted by her brother in public.[30] After Dipa's failed attempt to elope, her family becomes desperate to get her married to a groom suitable to their family honor, and in this episode, Bandyopadhyay severely lashes at their family biases.

Bijoy's desperate search for a suitable boy takes her to Nripati's household who is shown as a liberal and progressive individual completely different from the Mukherjees. The following conversation between the two is significant for the present discussion:

> Nripati: You believe it is best to marry off the girl before she attains adulthood. So, what kind of groom are you looking for? Educated, well-off and handsome, right?
> "Yes," Bijoy affirmed, "but you forgot the most important point–he has to belong to the same caste."
> Nripati lit his cigarette and as he blew out the smoke, a fairly sardonic smile played on his lips. "Of course!" he said. "The family tradition must be perpetuated. Since you are Mukherjees, a Chatterjee, Banerjee, Ganguly or Ghoshal would do. Right? Would a sub-caste do?" Bijoy: I'm afraid not, Nripatida. You are aware that we still faithfully abide by the old family traditions.
> Nripati: I certainly am. The lot of you belong to the cockroach class of living creatures.
> Bijoy: How do you mean?
> Nripati: The cockroach is an ancient species that originated millions of years ago. Since then, the animal world has gone through many evolutions, but the cockroach has retained the original form and character. As a result, it doesn't command, much respect these days.[31]

The above conversation shows how little these patriarchs valued Dipa's happiness. For them, it is not at all important to find a man who would be liked by their daughter, who has been brought up with little to no liberty; they are eager to find literally any man from a suitable caste. In short, they are ready to sacrifice Dipa for their family honor. Their false family pride pushes Dipa into a relationship which upsets both Dipa and her husband Debashish's life. Debashish is not a regressive Brahminist like the

Mukherjees, and he proposes to end the marriage by applying for divorce. When Dipa turns it down, expressing concern over the impact the news of divorce is likely to have on a regressive old man like her grandfather, Debashish stops pressing further, realizing how probable it is for Dipa's grandfather to actually kill her if she tries to divorce her husband.[32] Dipa and Debashish therefore are left with no option, stuck in a lifeless marriage due to the dominance of people like the Mukherjees and their dead customs in society. Seen against the damage they cause to innocent young people like Dipa and Debashish, Bandyopadhyay's comparison of the casteist-classist-patriarchs like the Mukherjees with repulsive insects is justified and representative of the writer's stance against upper-caste families who had significant hold over his contemporary society.

The third household shown in this section is Nripati's house, which, as mentioned before, is characterized by his liberal mindset. Nripati is shown as a bachelor who freely mixes with people from all professions. His house is very popular in their locality as a place for informal gathering, and Bijoy's connection with such a place or Dipa's falling in love with a member of Nripati's gatherings named Probal Gupta shows how the new generations of the upper castes were provided with opportunity to end the irrelevant biases endorsed by their preceding generations. Yet, Bijoy refuses to embrace the change and uses his social influence which compels Nripati to find a groom for Bijoy's sister despite his disliking of the Mukherjee family's value system. It is evident from the fact that Bijoy does not bother giving Nripati a proposal to marry Dipa that Nripati was inferior to Bijoy for their caste differences which makes the whole episode of Bijoy pressing Nripati to find a groom more complicated. Nripati was held as inferior and therefore below their standard by Bijoy, and yet Nripati does Bijoy's bidding. Despite his progressive outlook, Nripati still complies with the domination of the upper caste and the maintaining of upper-caste customs.

In sharp distinction to Nripati's compliant attitude, the singer Probal Gupta refutes the upper caste's domination by daring to marry Dipa despite being a man of lower caste. In caste hierarchy, Probal or people with surname of Gupta in general represent the caste of *Baidya*s, placed below the Brahmins in the traditional caste system.[33] Probal's penchant for music and the romantic couplet he uses for proposing to Dipa show Probal's intellectuality which as suggested before he was associated with the *Bhadralok*s. Lack of financial strength plagues Probal, and in the episode where the novel shows the nocturnal activities of each member of Nripati's gathering, Probal is shown as a helpless artist unable to focus on composing tunes due to his financial crisis.[34]

Such sympathetic portrayal of Probal is however contested by the "Epilogue" section where Byomkesh exposes Probal as the murderer and analyzes his motives highlighting Probal's cruel as well as scheming nature. In Byomkesh's analysis, Probal was greedy and envious at birth,[35] and he never genuinely loved Dipa. Byomkesh further explains Probal's motive behind targeting Debashish by pointing out Probal's greed for Debashish's wealth.[36] Surprisingly, Byomkesh's analysis does not mention the way Dipa's family complicated the situation at all. Even if Probal was indeed a man guided solely by greed and envy, which is significantly absent from the episode depicting Probal's nocturnal life, it was the pressure of Dipa's family that created desperation in Dipa that obliged her to blindly fall in love. Yet, Byomkesh remains silent about this problematic impact of the Mukherjees. Only Byomkesh's wife Satyabati retorts about the Mukherjees' impact on Dipa after hearing Byomkesh's analysis. Co-existence of these differing takes regarding the actual reason behind Dipa's problems within the novel indicates a distancing between Byomkesh's narrative about Probal and the sections of the novel critiquing the Mukherjees.

Byomkesh and Bandyopadhyay: Analyzing Their Distances

The distance maintained by Bandyopadhyay with Byomkesh is to be understood taking into consideration Bandyopadhyay's own identity and his views regarding inter-caste marriages. As suggested by his surname, Bandyopadhyay himself was an upper-caste Brahmin and his educational background as a student of Law, his love for English literature, and his very identity as a writer aligns him with the *Bhadralok*s to a significant extent. Yet, he was not a blind supporter of the upper caste's ideals which most other *Bhadralok* significantly benefitted from. It is particularly relevant at this point to refer to Bandyopadhyay's journal entries (entitled "Mon-Konika" meaning "Fragments from the Mind") on May 2, 3, and 4, 1949, where he discusses his views regarding the warning against inter-caste breeding in *Bhagvad Gita*. Though Bandyopadhyay does not altogether reject *Gita*'s ideals, he criticizes vehement opposition against inter-caste unions arguing how mixing of groups has aided the progress of Western societies.[37]

It is significant to note that Bijoy refers to the section of *Gita* analyzed in Bandyopadhyay's journal entry in defense of his family's aversion to inter-caste marriages, and Nripati, who represents Bandyopadhyay's views to a great extent, simply ignores Bijoy's explanation of the *Gita* in response.[38] Bandyopadhyay's critiques about the Mukherjees are not simply creative choices; they represent his sense of right and wrong. Contrarily, Byomkesh the detective is bound by his obligation of being a typical *Bhadralok*, as suggested in Chakrabarti's analysis. The Mukherjees, representative of *Bhadralok*s' bias regarding caste, class, and gender, sought to see Dipa's marriage with Debashish thrive despite its forced nature, and Byomkesh, therefore, has to play the protector of this marriage, safeguarding the *Bhadralok* values.

Conclusion

In this section, I return to the concept of moral imagination as suggested by Johnson to explain why Bandyopadhyay's novel maintains the distancing explained in the previous section. It becomes difficult to determine whether caste-related bias (as shown by Mukherjees) is critiqued or safeguarded in the novel due to the co-presence of the two contrasting attitudes shown toward it. This co-presence, however, should not simply be treated as an ambiguity. Rather, it is reminiscent of the presence of contrasting and contesting moral values in a given society. Johnson provides an insight into the presence of these oppositional moral values while explaining the practical need for moral imagination. Johnson does not endorse the adoption of a fixed and exclusionary set of moral ideals while talking about the importance of moral imagination. Instead, he highlights how it endows one with an understanding of the multiplicity of moral values and the importance of taking multiple versions of such values into account. Rhetorically raising the question "How is having moral imagination going to tell me the right thing to do in a particular situation?," Johnson responds that his concept of moral imagination does not at all talk about "*the* right thing to do" at all.[39] According to him, in most cases it is not possible to determine a singular course of action while dealing with moral problems because the conflicting groups of any given society will have their respective "moral laws, motivations, and goals,"[40] and it is not morally correct to accept any one group's set of ideals as the ultimate one. In such situations, instead of prioritizing any one particular version of these values, laws, etc., Johnson recommends a critical approach regarding one's own "moral tradition," as well as the moral tradition of others, even if the former is contradicted by the latter ones.[41] He terms this critical approach as "reflective criticism" and adds that this critical stance enables one to recognize both the "values" and "limitations" of moral traditions in general (including one's own).[42] It is significant to note that Johnson also mentions the presence of "blind-spots" in moral traditions in this context.[43] The co-presence of conflicting attitudes to the caste-related discrimination in *The Quills* is reminiscent of one such blind-spots in Bandyopadhyay's moral imagination.

Bandyopadhyay wrote *The Quills* toward the very end of his literary career. Chronologically, it was written three years prior to Bandyopadhyay's demise, and it is the thirtieth of the thirty-three Byomkesh stories. Byomkesh did excuse individuals committing crimes against the so-called upper castes. A notable instance is the twenty-first story of the Byomkesh series "Thus Spake Poet Kalidasa" where the detective leaves Bhuban Das and his wife Mohini, who is described as a "lower class woman,"[44] to their fate despite identifying them as murderers of the upper-caste man, Pranahari. Besides, in the journal entries previously referred to, Bandyopadhyay unambiguously criticized the upper-caste people's antipathy to inter-caste marriages, stating,

"In world history mixing of castes is a negligible matter as the world has recurrently witnessed mixing of races" (my translation). He also condemned the Indian upper-caste people's aversion to inter-caste marriages by calling it "blind fundamentalism" (my translation).[45]

Yet in *The Quills*, readers find a conflicted take regarding caste-prejudices. Both the sarcastic comments on upper-caste families' obsession with caste by Nripati and Byomkesh's safeguarding of the upper-caste values mentioned above come from Bandyopadhyay's imagination, and yet they manifest oppositional views about right and wrong. In the light of Johnson's views referred to previously, it seems possible to read these oppositional views in two ways. First, these conflicting responses regarding caste-prejudices embody Bandyopadhyay's ability to recognize the multiplicity of moral values functional within his contemporary society. Second, Bandyopadhyay, himself being an upper-caste Brahmin, accepts his own limitations as an upper-caste individual by hinting how the society in general would prefer to support people like the Mukherjees. This acceptance is reflected in his decision to provide a critique of the caste-prejudices through a minor character like Nripati and reserving the safeguarding of upper-caste ideals, maintaining silence about the impact of Mukherjee family's obsession for marriage within the same caste on Dipa's life. Byomkesh clearly has a more important role to play in the novel in comparison with Nripati, and therefore Bandyopadhyay's decision to let Byomkesh unapologetically support to the Mukherjees' ideals seems to be reflective of Bandyopadhyay's realization—it is caste-prejudices that will have the last laugh. No matter what individual upper-caste people like Bandyopadhyay feel about the wrongness of caste-prejudices, the sting of caste-bias will go on piercing the society.

Read along the lines of Johnson's ideas, the first possible explanation mentioned above corresponds to Johnson's notion of accepting the moral traditions of others despite their conflicting nature, and the latter reminds of the possible existence of blind spots within one's own moral imagination. Bandyopadhyay and Johnson are indeed individuals positioned within different milieus, but the resonances in their ideas attest to the importance of recognizing the interconnection between mystery fiction and the concept of moral imagination.

Notes

1 Julian Symons, *Bloody Murder: From the Detective Story to the Crime Novel* (New York: Penguin, 1972), 21.
2 Ibid., 21.
3 Saradindu Bandyopadhyay, "Detective Galpa," in *Saradindu Omnibus* 12, ed. Pratulchandra Gupta (Kolkata: Ananda Publishers, 1957), 216.

4   Sukumar Sen, "Byomkesh Upanyas," in *Byomkesh Samagra*, ed. Saradindu Bandyopadhyay (Kolkata: Ananda Publishers, 2016), 11.
5   Pinaki Roy, *The Manichean Investigators: A Postcolonial and Cultural Rereading of the Sherlock Holmes and Byomkesh Bakshi Stories* (New Delhi: Sarup and Sons, 2008), 138.
6   Ibid., 138–40.
7   Abhinaba Chatterjee, "Nativizing Holmesian Tradition of Detective: A Reading of Select Stories of Byomkesh Bakshi and Feluda," in *Critical Essays on English and Bengali Detective Fiction*, ed. Debayan Deb Barman (Lanham: Lexington Books, 2022), 166.
8   Anindita Dey, *Sherlock Holmes, Byomkesh Bakshi, and Feluda: Negotiating the Center and the Periphery* (Lanham: Lexington Books, 2022), 89.
9   Gautam Chakrabarti, "The *Bhadralok* as the Truth-Seeker: Towards a Social History of the Bengali Detective," *Cracow Indological Studies* 14 (2012): 257.
10 Ibid., 261.
11 Tithi Bhattacharya, *The Sentinels of Culture: Class, Education, and the Colonial Intellectual in Bengal (1848–1885)* (Oxford: Oxford University Press, 2005), 38.
12 Ibid., 38.
13 Ibid., 39.
14 Ibid.
15 Ibid.
16 Partha Chatterjee, *The Nation and Its Fragments: Colonial and Postcolonial Histories* (Princeton: Princeton University Press, 1993), 35.
17 Ibid., 35.
18 Ibid., 36.
19 Bhattacharya, *The Sentinels of Culture*, 38.
20 Sumit Sarkar, *Writing Social History* (Oxford: Oxford University Press, 1997), 169.
21 Ebenezer Sunder Raj, "The Origins of the Caste System," *Transformations* 2, no. 2 (1985): 10.
22 M.D. Altekar, "Caste System and Its Relation to Social Life," *The Annals of the American Academy of Political and Social Sciences* 145, part 2 (September 1929): 183.
23 Ghanshyam Shah, "Caste, Class, and Reservation," *Economic and Political Weekly* 20, no. 3 (1985): 133.
24 Parimal Ghosh, "Where Have All the Bhadraloks Gone?" *Economic and Political Weekly* 39, no. 3 (January 17–23, 2004): 248.
25 Ibid., 252.
26 Saradindu Bandyopadhyay, "The Quills of the Porcupine," in *The Menagerie and Other Byomkesh Bakshi Mysteries*, translated by Sreejata Guha (New York: Penguin, 2006), 204.

27 Ibid., 208.
28 Ibid., 209.
29 Ibid., 212.
30 Ibid., 214.
31 Ibid., 216.
32 Ibid., 234.
33 The *Baidya*s, as researchers have shown, were a part of the influential section of the colonial society of Bengal and were often included in the category of *Bhadralok*s along with two other upper-caste communities (see, Sekhar Bandyopadhyay's book for more details). Considering this information, Bandyopadhyay's choice to show Prabal Gupta getting rejected by the visibly *Bhadralok* Mukherjee family does appear historically inaccurate to a great extent. However, it is important to note that the Mukherjees (as shown in Bijoy's conversation with Nripati quoted above) sought *only* a Brahmin bridegroom, which may be interpreted as a reflection of the conflict between various upper castes lumped together as *Bhadralok*s.
34 Bandyopadhyay, "The Quills of the Porcupine," 268–9.
35 Ibid., 306.
36 Ibid., 307.
37 Ibid., 359.
38 Bandyopadhyay, "Mon-Konika," 349–50.
39 Mark Johnson, *Moral Imagination: Implications of Cognitive Science for Ethics* (Chicago: University of Chicago Press, 1993), 187.
40 Ibid., 186.
41 Ibid., 187.
42 Ibid.
43 Ibid.
44 Saradindu Bandyopadhyay, "Kahen Kabi Kalidas/Thus Spake the Poet Kalidasa," in *Byomkesh Samagra*, ed. Saradindu Bandyopadhyay (Kolkata: Ananda Publishers, 2016), 712.
45 Bandyopadhyay, "Mon-Konika," 349.

Bibliography

Altekar, M.D. "Caste System and Its Relation to Social Life." *The Annals of the American Academy of Political and Social Sciences* 145, part 2 (September 1929): 183–7.

Bandyopadhyay, Saradindu. "Detective Galpa." In *Saradindu Omnibus* 12, edited by Pratulchandra Gupta, 216. Kolkata: Ananda Publishers, 1957.

Bandyopadhyay, Saradindu. "KahenKabi Kalidas/Thus Spake the Poet Kalidasa." In *Byomkesh Samagra*, edited by Saradindu Bandyopadhyay, 674–715. Kolkata: Ananda Publishers, 2016.

Bandyopadhyay, Saradindu. "The Quills of the Porcupine." In *The Menagerie and Other Byomkesh Bakshi Mysteries*, translated by Sreejata Guha, 200–312. New York: Penguin, 2006.

Bhattacharya, Tithi. *The Sentinels of Culture: Class, Education, and the Colonial Intellectual in Bengal (1848–1885)*. Oxford: Oxford University Press, 2005.

Chakrabarti, Gautam. "The *Bhadralok* as the Truth-Seeker: Towards a Social History of the Bengali Detective." *Cracow Indological Studies* 14 (2012): 255–72.

Chatterjee, Abhinaba. "Nativizing Holmesian Tradition of Detective: A Reading of Select Stories of Byomkesh Bakshi and Feluda." In *Critical Essays on English and Bengali Detective Fiction*, edited by Debayan Deb Barman, 164–72. Lanham: Lexington Books, 2022.

Chatterjee, Partha. *The Nation and Its Fragments: Colonial and Postcolonial Histories*. Princeton: Princeton University Press, 1993.

Dey, Anindita. *Sherlock Holmes, Byomkesh Bakshi, and Feluda: Negotiating the Center and the Periphery*. Lanham, MD: Lexington Books, 2022.

Ghosh, Parimal. "Where Have All the Bhadraloks Gone?" *Economic and Political Weekly* 39, no. 3 (January 17–23, 2004): 247–51.

Johnson, Mark. *Moral Imagination: Implications of Cognitive Science for Ethics*. Chicago: University of Chicago Press, 1993.

Raj, Ebenezer Sunder. "The Origins of the Caste System." *Transformations* 2, no. 2 (1985): 10–14.

Roy, Pinaki. *The Manichean Investigators: A Postcolonial and Cultural Rereading of the Sherlock Holmes and Byomkesh Bakshi Stories*. New Delhi: Sarup and Sons, 2008.

Sarkar, Sumit. *Writing Social History*. Oxford: Oxford University Press, 1997.

Sen, Sukumar. "Byomkesh Upanyas." In *Byomkesh Samagra*, edited by Saradindu Bandyopadhyay, 7–12. Kolkata: Ananda Publishers, 2016.

Shah, Ghanshyam. "Caste, Class, and Reservation." *Economic and Political Weekly* 20, no. 3 (1985): 132–6.

Symons, Julian. *Bloody Murder: From the Detective Story to the Crime Novel*. New York: Penguin, 1972.

PART THREE

Faith, Certainty, and Doubt in Mystery Fiction

11

Between Faith and Nihilism: Greene's Moral Imagination in *The Third Man*

John J. Han

Graham Greene's noir novelette *The Third Man* appeared in 1950, one year after the release of the movie version. *The Third Man* tells the story of a private investigator, Rollo Martins (Holly Martins in the movie). He pursues the mystery surrounding the death of his old friend, Harry Lime, who reportedly died when he was hit by a car. Martins's investigation reveals that Lime is alive and is a notorious racketeer on the blacklist. Martins ends up killing Lime in the name of justice.

Greene's story is characterized by mystery, suspense, and thrill. He classified *The Third Man* as a work of "entertainment," not a literary work.[1] In his *New York Times* article, he recalls the time when he collaborated with Carol Reed, a movie director, on the production of the film version of the story: "We had no desire to move people's political emotions: we wanted to entertain them, to frighten them a little, to make them laugh."[2] Greene also recalled, "I held the view that an entertainment of this kind was too light an affair to carry the weight of an unhappy ending."[3] In the screenplay, Greene accommodated Reed's suggestion not to make the ending contradict the moral message the story delivers. In the book version, the story closes in a melodramatic way; Martins and his friend's mistress, Anna Schmitt, become new lovers as they leave Lime's funeral: "her hand was through his arm."[4]

However, all of Greene's works of "entertainment" include moral underpinnings in the same way his serious works of fiction include elements of entertainment. In *The Third Man*, Major Calloway, who investigates the "death" of Harry Lime, narrates the story. His storytelling focuses on Rollo Martins's arrival in Vienna, confusion, determination to avenge Lime's death, encounter with the truth related to Lime's criminality, amorous interest in Lime's mistress, pursuit and execution of Lime, and initiation of a relationship with Anna Schmitt.

The setting of the story is Vienna under occupation by four Allies—Great Britain, the United States, France, and the Soviet Union—which divide the city among themselves. It is part of "Greeneland," the seedy, squalid place that characterizes Graham Greene's fiction.[5] At the beginning of the story, Rollo Martins—a second-rate American novelist of Western fiction—arrives in Vienna at the invitation of Harry Lime, his childhood friend who has offered him a job. What awaits Martins is the news that Lime died in an auto accident one day before his arrival. Martins grieves at his friend's funeral but becomes suspicious of his death. He soon learns that Harry is alive and is hiding. Martins also learns that Lime was a big-time criminal who stole penicillin from military hospitals, diluted it, and sold it on the black market, causing the brain damage or deaths of many patients, including children. Indignant at his friend's crime against humanity, Martins decides to chase him to bring him to justice. Lime shoots and kills Sergeant Paine, but Calloway shoots Lime. Badly wounded, Lime disappears into the sewers, which in a way symbolize his depravity. Martins picks up Paine's revolver, pursues Lime, and shoots him to death. The scene recalls the ending of John Steinbeck's *Of Mice and Men* (1937), in which George kills his best friend Lennie. However, George acts out of mercy, whereas Martins's action is based on a sense of righteousness. Hit by Martins's first bullet, Lime murmurs two words before he dies, which confuse Martins:

> For a moment I thought he was dead, but then he whimpered with pain. I said, "Harry," and he swivelled his eyes with a great effort to my face. He was trying to speak, and I bent down to listen. "Bloody fool," he said—that was all. I don't know whether he meant it for himself—some sort of act of contrition, however inadequate (he was a Catholic)—or was it for me—with my thousand a year taxed and my imaginary cattle-rustlers who couldn't even shoot a rabbit clean? Then he began to whimper again. I couldn't bear it any more [sic] and I put a bullet through him.[6]

Martins has a character flaw: he is a philanderer who tends to make a girlfriend wherever he goes.[7] However, he is also morally astute enough to bring justice to Lime, whom he calls an "appalling trafficker" in an interview with Marie-Françoise Allain.[8] Martins is a typical sinner-saint who roams Greene's fiction and serves as a mouthpiece for the author.

This paper examines Greene's moral imagination as reflected in *The Third Man*, which the narrator calls a "strange, rather sad story,"[9] with particular emphasis on the contrasting ways in which Martins and Lime view right and wrong. After a brief review of literature, we will examine the conventions of mystery fiction, especially historical mystery, in *The Third Man* and then examine Martins and Lime as figures embodying Catholic morality and functional nihilism, respectively. A cursory impression of the novel is that Greene sides with Martin, but Martins is a complex character whose ethically dubious conduct undercuts his words of Christian morality. This will lead to discussion of Greene's moral position that seems to waver between Catholicism, to which he converted to marry Vivien Dayrell Browning, and functional nihilism, which reflects the hopeless world of "Greeneland."

Charles J. Rolo was one of the early critics who drew attention to the theological nature of Greene's serious novels and thrillers. In his *Atlantic* article "Graham Greene: The Man and the Message" (1961), he notes,

> Greene's theology uncompromisingly rejects the natural world as a realm of imperfection and corruption, and it admits of no human solutions to the problem of evil. The drama which is the storm center of Greene's work is a drama of allegiance. Man has the liberty to love God and to recognize that grace is always in pursuit of him. This is his God-given power and glory, and if he repudiates or ignores it and lives by the values of corrupted nature, he reduces himself to a kind of "stubborn non-existence."[10]

Along similar lines, Gwenn R. Boardman notes in *Graham Greene: The Aesthetics of Exploration* (1971), "Obviously, none of Greene's entertainments should be read as 'simply' amusing. ... *The Third Man* [is] enriched by hidden, deeper meanings."[11] Indeed, the story offers entertainment yet delves into the theological issue of what is right and what is wrong—where to draw the line between ethical and unethical—in a morally confusing time period.

Meanwhile, in *The Labyrinthine Ways of Graham Greene* (1973), Francis L. Kunkel places Graham Greene as a thriller writer among the likes of G. K. Chesterton, Herman Melville, and Fyodor Dostoyevsky:

> Unlike Edgar Wallace's old-fashioned thrillers, Graham Greene's modern thrillers expose, in addition to a murderer, a profound problem. Like Chesterton, Greene uses the detective story to dramatize a moral problem of far-reaching significance. Greene's Ishmaelites are so alive to the immense combat of heaven and hell that they are doubly pursued. ... By placing the moral problem at the core of the narrative, Greene modernizes the standard thriller. ... In associating morality with the traditional detective story, Greene follows the example of Dostoyevsky in *Crime and Punishment*.[12]

In *Graham Greene: The Entertainer* (1972), Peter Wolfe goes one step further by considering Greene's entertainments a form of prayer. According to him, Greene "makes his literary labors a function of prayer by executing his themes as human dramas."[13]

All of these critical comments are valid. In this chapter, we will dig deeper into the issue of morality in *The Third Man* by examining Harry Lime as an allegorical character who advocates functional nihilism, Rollo Martins as an example of what Martin Luther calls *simul justus et peccator* (at the same time saint and sinner), and finally, Graham Greene as a novelist who persists in believing Christian theology despite his lingering doubts.

The Third Man as a Mystery

Greene conceived *The Third Man* as a thriller.[14] In 1947, two years before the release of the film version of the story, he wrote to Catherine Walston, "I believe I've got a book coming. ... I saw the three characters, the beginning, the middle & the end, & in some ways all the ideas I had—the first sentence of the thriller about the dead Harry who wasn't dead, the risen-from-the-dead story, & the one the other day in the train—all seem to come together."[15] Indeed, *The Third Man* meets the conventions of the mystery genre. Violent crimes take place, the pursuit of a criminal pushes the story forward, the mystery surrounding the death of a supposedly innocent person intrigues the reader, a surprising turn of events happens, and an objectified woman—Anna Schmitt—"passes through the story."[16] The title of the story suggests the mysterious man whose identity will solve the mystery surrounding Lime's supposed death. There are conflicting reports on whether two men moved Lime's body or three men did after the car accident and on whether Lime died at the scene or later. To add intrigue, Herr Kock, the eyewitness who saw three people move Lime, is murdered.

Rollo Martins, an American author of Western novels, serves as a private detective in this novella. Chapter 6 of *The Third Man* begins with the advantages he has as an "amateur detective."[17] Unlike the law enforcement officers, he is not bound by time constraints and is free from rigid thinking. Indeed, he is more astute and incisive than they:

> Rollo Martins was not confined to the eight-hour day: his investigations didn't have to pause for meals. In his one day he covered as much ground as one of my men would have covered in two, and he had this initial advantage over us, that he was Harry's friend. He was, as it were, working from inside, while we pecked at the perimeter.[18]

Although not licensed, Martins has elements of hard-boiled detectives, the characters created by such American authors as Dashiell Hammett (1894–1961) and Raymond Chandler (1888–1959): he meets violence with violence, is a solitary man, and has the capacity to fall in love with a woman without compromising his duties.[19] Martins is also in line with what P. D. James calls the Golden Age (1920s–30s) detective writers of England. These authors, including E. C. Bentley, Nicholas Blake, and Monsignor Ronald Knox, used detectives with a profession or with some connection with the police.[20] Golden Age detective stories are "concerned with bringing order out of disorder," and therefore they are "a genre of reconciliation and social healing."[21] Likewise, Greene's story reflects the traditional British respect for "a religious and moral code based on the Judeo-Christian inheritance [which is] buttressed by social and political institutions" in the name of sociopolitical stability.[22]

More specifically, *The Third Man* belongs to the subgenre of the historical mystery (also called the historical "whodunit"), which combines the elements of historical fiction and mystery fiction.[23] According to Peter Lovesey, the historical mystery presents a historical event "as a murder mystery, complete with twists, discoveries, and a surprise ending."[24] In their article "Fake penicillin, *The Third Man*, and Operation Claptrap" (2016), Paul N. Newton, a physician, and Brigitte Timmermann, a historian, uncover the story behind *The Third Man*, which they call a "pharmaceutical story."[25] According to them, "In April 1946, in the bleak aftermath of the Second World War, American and British intelligence services arrested seven men and three women in Berlin on charges of manufacture, possession, and sale of fake penicillin."[26] In addition to the Allied information, Greene used multiple sources in yarning his story, such as Peter Smollett, the *Times* correspondent in Vienna and a Soviet agent, and his own spying activities for the Secret Intelligence Service.[27] Greene was not only a novelist and a secret agent but also a journalist who converted contemporary events into fictional stories with moral implications.

Catholic Morality and Functional Nihilism in *The Third Man*

The Third Man embodies the universal literary theme of appearance and reality. Martins comes to Vienna with only good memories of his childhood friend whom he considered immature yet heroic. Martins strives to clear Lime's name when Kurtz, one of Harry's local friends, tells him that the police believe that Harry was involved in racketeering. He tells Kurtz, "I'm going to stay [in Vienna] until I prove them wrong. ... I'm going to start working back from his death."[28] Like King Oedipus, who genuinely tries to find the killer of his father without knowing the truth, Martins begins his private investigation until he discovers that Lime is not the kind of man he used to know. What Martins finds disgusts him. Finally, in Chapter 14, Martins and Lime meet for the first time in Vienna and have a conversation about the implications of Harry's criminal activities. This conversation not only reveals the gap in the two characters' life philosophies but also hints at Greene's moral vision.

Martin's Catholic moral consciousness and Lime's functional nihilism are highlighted in the dialogue the two former friends have in Chapter 14. Here Martins confronts Lime, reminding him, "You used to be a Catholic."[29] In response, Lime insists that he retains his Catholic faith while rationalizing his crime at the same time:

> "Oh, I still *believe*, old man. In God and mercy and all that. I'm not hurting anybody's soul by what I do. The dead are happier dead. They don't miss much here, poor devils," he added with that odd touch of genuine pity, as the car reached the platform and the faces of the doomed-to-be-victims, the tired pleasure-hoping Sunday faces, peered in at them.[30]

Here, Lime denies the Torah commandment not to kill. Instead, he plays God, defending his supposed right to terminate the lives of those who suffer. Perhaps affected by the tragedies of war he witnessed in Vienna, Lime has become numb to human suffering and has fallen into despair, which makes him think that being dead is better than living in misery. The claim that he does not hurt anyone's soul with his criminal activities is an absurd, twisted self-defense. Unsurprisingly, his funeral is attended by only three people: Martins, Anna Schmitt, and Calloway. In the final chapter of the story, Calloway describes the scene of Lime's funeral as follows: "It was almost as warm as a spring day when Harry Lime had his second funeral. I was glad to get him under earth again, but it had taken two men's deaths. ... And there weren't any tears."[31] However, the way Lime rationalizes his own criminality exudes nihilism, which strives to overcome the meaningless of life by creating values or beliefs that provide some significance to life.

Read as a moral story, *The Third Man* is based on traditional moral principles. Lime's crime reflects his diabolical cunning, and Martins executes Lime based on his moral consciousness. As Ruth Franklin rightly notes, Greene's "impassioned and tortured relationship with his faith is the backbone of his best work."[32] In his interview with Anthony Burgess, Greene states, "The theme of human beings lonely without God is a legitimate subject."[33] In an interview with Shiv K. Kumar, Greene also states that his conversion to Catholicism was an act of renunciation: "Protestantism was too critical, too questioning, and too rational. I had come to a stage in my life when I wanted to surrender my reasoning faculty to a Will above and beyond any ratiocination. And this is what I found in Catholicism ...."[34] As in the case of Greene himself, the Christian doctrine of good and evil is engrained in the psyche of Martins: "[Christopher] Marlowe's devils wore squibs attached to their tails: evil was like Peter Pan—it carried with it the horrifying and horrible gift of eternal youth."[35]

In contrast, Lime is a functional nihilist. As Alan Pratt notes, "A true nihilist would believe in nothing, have no loyalties, and no purpose other than, perhaps, an impulse to destroy."[36] In the preface to *The Will to Power* (1901), Friedrich Nietzsche proclaims the coming of nihilism, "the radical repudiation of value, meaning, and desirability," a philosophical trend that will dominate the world for the next two centuries.[37] According to Nietzsche, life is without meaning and purpose, and absolute moral truths do not exist. The realization of the nothingness of this world is the first step toward truth: "The deeper one looks, the more our valuations disappear—meaninglessness approaches! We have *created* the world that possesses values! Knowing this, we know, too, that reverence for truth is already the consequence of an illusion—and that one should value."[38]

Despite his outward profession of Christian faith, Lime thinks somewhat along the lines of Nietzsche's philosophy. The German philosopher does not encourage criminal acts, such as the one committed by Lime. Nietzsche's philosophical aim is to critique traditional European values—as related to religion, morality, and philosophy—and to offer a new philosophical paradigm for the future. Lime may or may not be familiar with Nietzsche's philosophy. What is certain is that his dialogue with Martins sounds nihilistic. Nevertheless, it is hard not to empathize with Lime when he says that life is a misery and that, for some people, dying is perhaps better than living. As Peter Wolfe observes, "Lime had to be stopped. But if we do not sympathize with him, neither do we approve the society that stops him. Organized society has no moral right to butcher anybody."[39]

Similar to Greene's other entertainment stories, *The Third Man* is ostensibly grounded in Christian ethics. However, it is important to note that Greene's moral vision is complex and ambivalent. To borrow Marie-Françoise Allain's words, as a Catholic, Greene "reflects the image of a tormented, wavering but ineradicable faith, the product of his paradoxical universe."[40] As mentioned earlier, Martins is not particularly moral in his personal conduct. For example, "he always tried to dismiss women as 'incidents,' things that simply happened to him without any will of his own, acts of God in the eyes of insurance agents."[41] Likewise, Greene's own relationships with women were far from the Church's teachings. Greene's decades-long affair with Catherine Walston (1912–91)—his goddaughter and the wife of Henry Walston—is well documented. Having Catherine as his mistress was not an isolated case. In his investigative article "The Decadent World of Graham Greene—The High Priest of Darkness," Michael Thornton reports,

> [Greene's] family and friends were aware that his conversion to Catholicism was not a matter of genuine faith but an act of expediency to enable him to marry a woman he loved and wanted to get into bed.
> Once he had achieved his object and his wife was pregnant, he broke his marriage vows and became a serial adulterer with at least 47 prostitutes whose identities are known and with dozens more who remain unknown.
> An alcoholic, he abandoned his wife and two children for affairs with a series of married mistresses.[42]

More importantly, Greene did not write for the Catholic Church. He insisted that he was "a novelist who happen[ed] to be a Catholic," not "a Catholic novelist."[43] Furthermore, as expressed in his 1971 interview with Alex Hamilton, he lost interest in theology in his later life. Hamilton records, "[Greene] no longer has any interest in theology, having done his homework on Newman, Bonhoeffer, St John of the Cross and the only book he liked of Father D'Arcy, 'The Nature of Belief.' Trying to talk of the pathology of the urge to martyrdom was something of a cul-de-sac."[44] Meanwhile, in a book-length interview with Marie-Françoise Allain, which was published in French in 1981, Greene reveals that he does not believe in some of the key Catholic doctrines—such as the Holy Trinity, mortal sin, hell, and eternal damnation—although he embraces the probability of God, miracles, and the historicity of Jesus.[45] Regarding mortal sin, he states, "I find the idea difficult to accept because it must by definition be committed in defiance of God. I doubt whether a man making love to a woman ever does so with the intention of defying God."[46] He characterizes his religious conversion as "purely intellectual"—he converted to "the idea of Christianity" unaffected by emotions.[47] Finally, in 1986, he confessed, "Mind you, I'm not entirely sure what God is," declaring himself to be "a Catholic agnostic."[48]

As Ian Hunter put it, however, Greene was "always God-haunted," and his favorite Bible passage was "Lord, I believe, help thou my unbelief."[49] *The Third Man* shows that his fiction is grounded in a moral vision, yet it also reflects Greene's paradoxical, nihilistic vision of the world. Rollo Martins lacks sexual integrity yet holds himself to higher standards regarding the matters that affect people's lives and wellbeing. As Peter Wolfe points out, "Calm and lucid, rash and extravagant, Martins becomes the forked inconsistency God and the Devil both use in Greene to carry out their wills."[50]

Conclusion

In this strange way, *The Third Man* is a twentieth-century moral story that is informed by theology. The twentieth century saw not only unprecedented heights of human achievement but also unprecedented depths of human tragedy, as exemplified by the First and Second World Wars, the Communist revolutions, the Korean War, the Vietnam War, the Cambodian genocide, and the Bosnian War. Greene's story unfolds in a complex environment in which people easily lose moral direction, showing that there are fundamental values in life that deserve to be defended. His perspective is grounded in Christian theology no matter how nuanced it is.

In Greene's fiction, the heroic characters who stand on the side of the Church or justice tend to be unheroic and sinful. He once stated, "The greatest saints have been men with more than a normal capacity for evil, and the most vicious men have sometimes narrowly evaded sanctity."[51] In Greene's *The Power and the Glory* (1940), for instance, the "whisky priest" is an alcoholic and a fornicator chased and executed by the Police Lieutenant, a stoic atheist whose life mission is to eradicate the Church from his state. By the end of the story, however, the Church, which is represented by the imperfect priest, survives, whereas the Lieutenant feels empty once the priest is killed. Like the whisky priest, a morally unfit believer who dies as a martyr, Martins exhibits his belief in human decency by executing an incorrigible criminal.

In his influential book *On Moral Fiction* (1978), John Gardner writes that

> true art is moral: it seeks to improve life, not debase it. ... [T]rivial art has no meaning or value except in the shadow of more serious art, the kind of art that beats the back the monsters and, if you will, makes the world safe for triviality. That art which tends toward destruction, the art of nihilists, cynics, and merdistes, is not properly art at all.[52]

The Third Man fits the definition of moral fiction. In addition to providing entertainment, it "seeks to improve life, not debase it," as Gardner puts it. Greene's story embodies morality through Martins, a character who is flawed yet principled. It is often difficult to envision Martins as a reliable character and narrator, yet one can understand the moral ground on which he executes Lime. In contrast, Lime is a cynical nihilist. He insists that he believes in God and his mercy although his criminal records indicate that he is a man of no moral consciousness, which makes Lime's characterization not entirely convincing. Indeed, he is a cardboard character not fully humanized or developed. His reasoning is absurd, and his actions are diabolical. Greene once stated that the name of Lime has the connotation of "quicklime, the disposal of bodies,"[53] thereby acknowledging the allegorical nature of Lime's characterization.

Notes

1 In 1995, the members of the Mystery Writers of America rated *The Third Man* the forty-eighth best mystery novel of all time. Greene's *One Man in Havana* and *Brighton Rock* are ranked sixty-first and sixty-ninth, respectively (Penzler and Friedman 19). Meanwhile, as a work of espionage/thriller, *The Third Man* is ranked the tenth best text of all time (Penzler and Friedman 109).

2 Graham Greene, "'The Third Man' as a Story and a Film," *New York Times*, March 19, 1950, https://archive.nytimes.com/www.nytimes.com/books/00/02/20/specials/greene-astory.html?scp=15&sq=Preface%2520to&st=cse, para. 10.

3 Graham Greene, *Ways of Escape* (London: Bodley Head, 1980), 124.

4 Graham Greene, *The Third Man* in *The Third Man and The Fallen Idol* (1950; New York: Penguin, 1971), 119. In *Ways of Escape*, Greene recalls, "Reed on his side felt that my ending—indeterminate as it was, with no words spoken, Holly [Rollo Martins] joining the girl in silence and walking away with her from the cemetery where her lover Harry was buried—would strike the audience who had just seen Harry's death and burial as unpleasantly cynical" (124). Considering the moral underpinnings of the story, both the screenplay and the novelette could have ended in a less cynical way so that Martins could serve as a more convincing moral voice. The fact that Anna Schmitt leaves the funeral without looking at him would not mean that the two figures can never initiate a romantic relationship.

5 According to Gloria Emerson, Greene "thought the term 'Greeneland' had been first used by a man who used to write rather good novels, who was at Oxford the same years he was there" (para. 3). Greene had an intense disliking for the term (para. 2).

6 Greene, *Third*, 117–18.

7 Martins is somewhat akin to Graham Greene himself, who had a penchant for women. As Heather Moreland McHale notes in her 2011 Ph.D. dissertation written at the University of Maryland, *Erotic Transgression: Sexualities and Companionship in Graham Greene's Fiction*, "Greene employs one of fiction's most commonly developed centers of energy—the erotic—as the site of moral complexity. His use of sexuality brings vigor back to moral consideration. This reading of Greene makes his novels relevant for today's reader; while the specific political problems or religious settings of the novels may grow dated, Greene's engagement with sexuality remains ultimately modern" (179–80).

8 Greene, *The Other Man*, 23.

9   Greene, *Third*, 13.
10 Charles J. Rolo, "Graham Greene: The Man and the Message," *The Atlantic*, May 1961, https://www.theatlantic.com/magazine/archive/1961/05/graham-greene-the-man-and-the-message/658049/, para. 38. Accessed February 13, 2023.
11 Gwenn R. Boardman, *Graham Greene: The Aesthetics of Exploration* (Gainesville: University of Florida Press, 1971), 120.
12 Francis L. Kunkel, *The Labyrinthine Ways of Graham Greene* (Mamaroneck, NY: Paul P. Appel, 1973), 60–1.
13 Peter Wolfe, *Graham Greene: The Entertainer* (Carbondale: Southern Illinois University Press, 1972), 4.
14 The terms "mystery fiction," "thriller," and "crime fiction" used to be interchangeable. *The Crown Crime Companion* (1995), annotated by Otto Penzler and compiled by Mickey Friedman, divides mystery fiction into ten categories: classics, suspense, hardboiled/private eye, police procedural, espionage/thriller, criminal, cozy/traditional, historical, humorous, and legal/courtroom (9). These days, however, mystery fiction, thriller, and crime fiction are generally not synonymous genres.
15 Richard Greene, introduction to *The Third Man and Other Stories*, ed. Graham Greene (London: Collector's Library, 2011), 8.
16 As Dana King states, in detective fiction, which is a male-dominated genre, women "merely pass through the story, such as the secretary in an office or the waitress who brings coffee" ("Portrayal").
17 Greene, *Third*, 45.
18 Ibid., 45.
19 In their introduction to *The Great American Detective* (1978), William Kittredge and Steven M. Krauzer trace the development of the private detective since the days of Edgar Allan Poe's detective stories. Poe's detective is an intellectually superior amateur who "perceives his cases as puzzles more than as crimes" (xii). Unlike Poe's classical detective, Carroll John Daly's type of private eye is "the hard-boiled dick," who solves mysteries "through persistence, legwork, and trial and error, not through a near-mystical power of logical process" (xv). Typically, this detective is "a tall, handsome young man who is fast with his fists, his wit, and his women" (xvii). Rollo Martins fits the mold of the hard-boiled dick.
20 P. D. James, *Talking about Detective Fiction* (New York: Vintage Books, 2011), 62.
21 Ibid., 82.
22 Ibid., 78–9.
23 Alan Furst (b. 1941), the author of *Night Soldiers* (1988), is credited with establishing the subgenre of what he calls *historical espionage fiction*. He has acknowledged writing in the tradition of Graham Greene, Joseph Roth, and Eric Ambler (David Seed, "American Spy Fiction," in *The Cambridge Companion to American Crime Fiction*, ed. Catherine Ross Nickerson

[Cambridge: Cambridge University Press, 2010], 91–2). *The Lacuna* (2009) by Barbara Kingsolver, *Running the Rift* (2010) by Naomi Benaron, *The Trinity Six* (2011) by Charles Cumming, and *An Officer and a Spy* (2013) by Robert Harris are some of the recent historical mystery thrillers.

24 Peter Lovesey, "The Historical Mystery," in *The Crown Crime Companion*, ed. Otto Penzler and Mickey Friedman (New York: Crown, 1995), 127.

25 Paul N. Newton and Brigitte Timmermann, "Fake Penicillin, *The Third Man*, and Operation Claptrap," *BMJ: British Medical Journal*, December 13, 2016, doi.org/10.1136/bmj.i6494, para. 2.

26 Idid., para. 3. Indeed, the *Daily Telegraph* included a special report from Berlin in its April 22, 1946, edition. Entitled "Last of Berlin Gang Arrested: Bogus Penicillin," the article states,
    The last members of a gang of ten who have been flooding the Berlin black market with bogus penicillin ampules have now been arrested. The "penicillin," which would have brought in over £3,007,000 in German marks has been seized.
    The gang, which includes three women, began selling stolen ampules of glucose labelled "penicillin." Later a few milligrams of a mixture of face powder and the drug atebrin was used. An American medical expert stated this mixture injected in solution would be dangerous to life and health (qtd. in Davies para. 4 and 5).

27 Ibid., para. 3.

28 Greene, *Third*, 37.

29 Ibid., 106.

30 Ibid., 106–7. Italics in original.

31 Ibid., 119.

32 Ruth Franklin, "God in the Details: Graham Greene's Religious Realism," *New Yorker*, September 26, 2004, https://www.newyorker.com/magazine/2004/10/04/god-in-the-details, para. 7.

33 Graham Greene, "God, Literature, and So Forth: Interview with Anthony Burgess," in *Graham Greene: The Last Interview and Other Conversations*, ed. John R. MacArthur (New York: Melville House Publishing, 2019), 12.

34 Shiv K. Kumar, "Conversations with Graham Greene," *Punch Magazine*, November 30, 2018, https://thepunchmagazine.com/the-byword/interviews/conversations-with-graham-greene, para. 25. Accessed February 13, 2023.

35 Greene, *Third*, 104.

36 Alan Pratt, "Nihilism," *Internet Encyclopedia of Philosophy: A Peer-Reviewed Academic Resource*, https://iep.utm.edu/nihilism/, para. 1. Accessed December 3, 2022.

37 Friedrich Nietzsche, *The Will to Power*, trans. Walter Kaufmann and R.J. Hollingdale and ed. with commentary, by Walter Kaufmann (New York: Vintage Books, 1968), 3, 7.

38 Ibid., 326. Italics in original.

39 Wolfe, *Graham Greene*, 129.

40 Greene, *The Other Man*, 152.
41 Greene, *Third*, 16.
42 Michael Thornton, "The Decadent World of Graham Greene—The High Priest of Darkness," *Daily Mail*, March 19, 2008, www.dailymail.co.uk/news/article-539011/The-decadent-world-Graham-Greene–high-priest-darkness.html, para. 9–11. Accessed April 8, 2021.
43 Greene, "God," 12.
44 Alex Hamilton, "Saving Graces," *Guardian*, September 11, 1971, reprinted September 11, 2017, https://www.theguardian.com/books/2007/sep/11/fromthearchives.britishidentity, para. 42. Accessed December 4, 2022.
45 Greene, *The Other Man*, 154–8.
46 Ibid., 158.
47 Ibid., 154.
48 Graham Greene, "I'm an Angry Old Man, You See: Interview with Anthony Burgess," in *Graham Greene: The Last Interview and Other Conversations*, ed. John R. MacArthur (New York: Melville House Publishing, 2019), 34.
49 Ian Hunter, "Graham Greene: A Saint Who Would Be Sinner," *Catholic Register*, February 3, 2021, https://www.catholicregister.org/features/arts/item/32674-graham-greene-a-saint-who-would-be-sinner, para. 13, 10.
50 Wolfe, *Graham Greene*, 124.
51 Quoted in Ian Hunter, "Graham Greene," para. 9.
52 John Gardner, *On Moral Fiction* (New York: Basic Books, 1978), 5–6.
53 Greene, "God," 10.

Bibliography

Boardman, Gwenn R. *Graham Greene: The Aesthetics of Exploration*. Gainesville: University of Florida Press, 1971.

Emerson, Gloria. "Graham Greene: Our Man in Antibes." *Rolling Stone*, March 9, 1978. https://www.rollingstone.com/culture/culture-features/graham-greene-our-man-in-antibes-44997/3/. Accessed February 13, 2023.

Franklin, Ruth. "God in the Details: Graham Greene's Religious Realism." *New Yorker*, September 26, 2004. https://www.newyorker.com/magazine/2004/10/04/god-in-the-details. Accessed December 8, 2022.

Gardner, John. *On Moral Fiction*. New York: Basic Books, 1978.

Greene, Graham. "God, Literature, and So Forth: Interview with Anthony Burgess." In *Graham Greene: The Last Interview and Other Conversations*, edited by John R. MacArthur (New York: Melville House Publishing, 2019a), 5–16.

Greene, Graham. "I'm an Angry Old Man, You See: Interview with Anthony Burgess." In *Graham Greene: The Last Interview and Other Conversations*, edited by John R. MacArthur, 27–40. New York: Melville House Publishing, 2019b.

Greene, Graham. *The Other Man: Conversations with Graham Greene*, edited by Marie-Françoise Allain. Translated by Guido Waldman. New York: Penguin, 1984.
Greene, Graham. "The Third Man." In *The Third Man and The Fallen Idol*, 13–120. 1950; New York: Penguin, 1971.
Greene, Graham. "'The Third Man' as a Story and a Film." *New York Times*, March 19, 1950. https://archive.nytimes.com/www.nytimes.com/books/00/02/20/specials/greene-astory.html?scp=15&sq=Preface%2520to&st=cse. Accessed November 23, 2021.
Greene, Graham. *Ways of Escape*. London: Bodley Head, 1980.
Greene, Richard. Introduction to *The Third Man and Other Stories*, edited by Graham Greene, 7–16. London: Collector's Library, 2011.
Hamilton, Alex. "Saving Graces." *Guardian*, September 11, 1971, reprinted September 11, 2017. https://www.theguardian.com/books/2007/sep/11/fromthearchives.britishidentity. Accessed December 4, 2022.
Hunter, Ian. "Graham Greene: A Saint Who Would Be Sinner." *Catholic Register*, February 3, 2021. www.catholicregister.org/features/arts/item/32674-graham-greene-a-saint-who-would-be-sinner. Accessed April 8, 2021.
James, P.D. *Talking about Detective Fiction*. New York: Vintage Books, 2011.
Kittredge, William, and Steven M. Krauzer, eds. *The Great American Detective: 15 Stories Starring America's Most Celebrated Private Eyes*. New York: Mentor, 1978.
Kumar, Shiv K. "Conversations with Graham Greene." *Punch Magazine*, November 30, 2018. https://thepunchmagazine.com/the-byword/interviews/conversations-with-graham-greene. Accessed February 13, 2023.
Kunkel, Francis L. *The Labyrinthine Ways of Graham Greene*. Mamaroneck, NY: Paul P. Appel, 1973.
Lovesey, Peter. "The Historical Mystery." In *The Crown Crime Companion*, edited by Otto Penzler and Mickey Friedman, 127–31. New York: Crown, 1995.
McHale, Heather Moreland. *Erotic Transgression: Sexualities and Companionship in Graham Greene's Fiction*. Ph.D. diss., University of Maryland, 2011. drum.lib.umd.edu/bitstream/handle/1903/11783/McHale_umd_0117E_12291.pdf?isAllowed=y&sequence=1. Accessed February 13, 2023.
Newton, Paul N., and Brigitte Timmermann. "Fake Penicillin, *The Third Man*, and Operation Claptrap." *BMJ: British Medical Journal*, December 13, 2016. doi.org/10.1136/bmj.i6494. Accessed February 13, 2023.
Nietzsche, Friedrich. *The Will to Power*. Translated by Walter Kaufmann and R.J. Hollingdale and edited, with commentary, by Walter Kaufmann. New York: Vintage Books, 1968.
Penzler, Otto, and Mickey Friedman, eds. *The Crown Crime Companion*. New York: Crown, 1995.
Pratt, Alan. "Nihilism." *Internet Encyclopedia of Philosophy: A Peer-Reviewed Academic Resource*. https://iep.utm.edu/nihilism/. Accessed December 3, 2022.
Rolo, Charles J. "Graham Greene: The Man and the Message." *The Atlantic*, May 1961. https://www.theatlantic.com/magazine/archive/1961/05/graham-greene-the-man-and-the-message/658049/. Accessed February 13, 2023.

Seed, David. "American Spy Fiction." In *The Cambridge Companion to American Crime Fiction*, edited by Catherine Ross Nickerson, 86–95. Cambridge: Cambridge University Press, 2010.

Thornton, Michael. "The Decadent World of Graham Greene—The High Priest of Darkness." *Daily Mail*, March 19, 2008. www.dailymail.co.uk/news/article-539011/The-decadent-world-Graham-Greene–high-priest-darkness.html. Accessed April 8, 2021.

Wolfe, Peter. *Graham Greene: The Entertainer*. Carbondale: Southern Illinois University Press, 1972.

12

Brother Cadfael, Social Justice, and the Medieval Mystery Novels of Ellis Peters

Jane Beal

Under the pen name Ellis Peters, award-winning English writer Edith Mary Pargeter (1913–95) wrote twenty mystery novels between 1977 and 1994 featuring an extraordinary detective: Brother Cadfael. Cadfael was a twelfth-century Benedictine monk of St. Werburgh's Abbey on the Welsh border who, before taking his vows, was a lover, soldier, and fighter in the First Crusade. Like Cadfael, Ellis Peters had Welsh ancestry, served as a soldier in wartime, and, as a long-time chemist's assistant, had special knowledge of herbs, plants, and pharmaceutical drugs. In understanding the extraordinary character of Cadfael, Ellis Peters's most famous detective, it is important to understand the author's life.

Both Cadfael and his creator reflect a strong commitment to social justice. This is evident in a specific book that she wrote, the fifth novel in the Chronicles of Brother Cadfael, *The Leper of St. Giles* (1981). In it, readers can see Ellis Peters's particular penchant for emphasizing the need for social justice in the world. The author's medieval settings, plots, and characters speak clearly to modern readers of moral matters. Ellis Peters firmly believed that crime and mystery fiction ought to be moral: "It is, it ought to be, a morality. If it strays from the side of the angels, provokes total despair, willfully destroys … the innocent and the good, takes pleasure in evil, that is an unforgivable sin. I use the word deliberately and gravely."[1] Literary analysis of *The Leper of St. Giles* reveals much of value, including characters who are transformed when the plot places their lives between the proverbial hammer and anvil, so that the importance of truth and honor emerges victoriously in the end. Film analysis enriches literary analysis when considering the television adaptation of the story, an episode also entitled "The Leper of St. Giles" (1994), starring Derek Jacobi in the lead role.

Whether on the page or in the film, the story of *The Leper of St. Giles* is particularly worthy of attention because of the subtle but poignant critique of social injustice pictured through the treatment of Lazarus, a leper, who is actually a lord and a Crusader who has assumed a secret identity to conceal the shame of his disease from his surviving family.

The Life of Ellis Peters

Ellis Peters[2] was born Edith Mary Pargeter on September 28, 2013, in Horsehay, Shropshire, England, the daughter of Edith Hordley and Edmund Pargeter. Her father was a clerk at the local ironworks, and her mother, Ellis Peters has said, was "artistic, musical, and interested in everything."[3] The young author grew up with both parents; an older brother, Ellis; an older sister, Margaret; and her grandmother, a Welsh woman. Her maternal family origins in Wales influenced much of her writing, for many of her stories have Welsh settings and Welsh characters. Interactions between the Welsh and the English on the borderlands are a repeated motif in her mystery novels featuring Brother Cadfael.

Ellis Peters attended school at Dawley Church of England School and the Coalbrookdale High School for Girls. She excelled in her classes in English, Latin, and History. After completing secondary school, she did not continue at the university but became a self-educated scholar as she pursued her life as a writer. In recognition of her dedication to scholarship, she was awarded an Honorary M.A. from the University of Birmingham in 1994.

Despite the economic hardships of the 1930s, she found work as a pharmacist's assistant. Then, from 1940 to 1945, she served as a petty officer in the Women's Royal Navy Service (WRNS). In 1944, she was awarded the British Empire Medal for her bravery and meritorious service. Ellis Peters enriched her imagination through both of her early professions.

While working as a pharmacist and then an officer, she began publishing both mystery and realistic fiction: her first crime novel, *Murder in the Dispensary* (as Jolyon Carr), was published in 1938 and her realistic novel *She Goes to War* (as Edith Pargeter) in 1942. Her protagonist in the latter, Catherine Saxon, resembles Ellis Peters herself, and through her, the author advocated for equality of treatment and pay for women. The author subsequently wrote a trilogy of novels set during the Second World War, featuring protagonist Jim Benison. Like Catherine, Jim shares much in common with the author, despite the difference in sex. Ellis Peters's ability to share her own perspectives through a male lead would later be further developed in her other well-known protagonists, Detective Sergeant George Felse and, of course, Brother Cadfael.

When she was demobilized from the WRNS, Ellis Peters returned to her home in Shropshire, where she lived with her brother, with whom she was close all her life. She had become a famous novelist by this point, having published a number of novels and short stories.[4] She used her voice in *The Sunday Chronicle* in March 1947 to advocate for women:

> By the time our particular base was closed down after VE day, it was being run almost entirely by women under the Admiral's immediate staff. Women have discovered what they could do, and I suspect in most cases it was more than they had thought likely. They discovered also what they could not do, and it was less than they had feared. Women could and can afford to acknowledge it. It is no longer necessary for them to assert that they are the equal with men; they know it to be true.[5]

Ellis Peters herself rejected some traditional expectations of women of her time, choosing not to marry so that she could more easily continue her career as a writer. Instead of living with a husband, children, and other domestic obligations, she embarked on non-traditional adventures, including visits to other parts of England, Wales, and even India. With her brother, she visited Czechoslovakia after the Second World War many times. She learned the language of the country, which she loved passionately and called "my other country."[6] She also became a prodigious translator of Czechoslovakian poetry and prose into English, introducing many Czech writers to English readers for the first time.[7] In recognition of this achievement, she received a Czech Gold Medal. After Czechoslovakia fell to Communist Russia's regime, she became a champion of Czech independence. In 1989, after twenty-one years of waiting and hoping, she celebrated Czech and Slovak freedom right alongside other Eastern European patriots in England and abroad.

In her later years, after the death of her brother in 1984, Ellis Peters moved to another home and lived near her cousin, Mavis, and Mavis's husband, Roy Morgan. With Roy Morgan, Ellis Peters co-authored two books about her shire, *Shropshire* (1992) and *Strongholds and Sanctuaries* (1993).[8] Then in 1995, she was hospitalized at age eighty-two due to a stroke. She was able to return home to Madeley, Shropshire, where she passed away peacefully. Her memorial was subsequently held at Shrewsbury Abbey. As the home of her fictional Brother Cadfael, it was a suitable place to remember her life and contributions to literature and society. On September 14, 1997, Ellis Peters was again honored: at Shrewsbury Abbey, a glass window depicting St. Benedict was installed and dedicated to her memory.

Throughout her life, Ellis Peters received many honors for her writing. For her novel *Death and the Joyful Woman*, the Mystery Writers of America gave her the Edgar Allan Poe Award of 1963 for best mystery novel. For *Monk's Hood*, a Brother Cadfael novel, the British Crime Writers Association (CWA) gave her the Silver Dagger of 1980. In 1993, the CWA recognized Ellis Peters for her outstanding lifetime contribution to crime and mystery writing by awarding her the Cartier Diamond Dagger. In 1999, the CWA established the Ellis Peters Historical Dagger (later called the Ellis Peters Historical Award) for best historical crime novel—the genre that she pioneered and popularized—of the year. As in life, so in her writing, Ellis Peters subtly but clearly emphasized the need for social justice for women and people living under political oppression.

Brother Cadfael and the Medieval Mysteries of Ellis Peters

Brother Cadfael did not spring to life out of thin air. Rather, he had older brothers in English detective fiction who came before him: Sir Arthur Conan Doyle's famous Sherlock Holmes, who featured in quintessentially Gothic stories like "The Adventure of the Speckled Band" and *The Hound of the Baskervilles,* and G. K. Chesterton's lesser-known Father Brown (a priest), who shares religious profession with Brother Cadfael (a monk). Both of these crime detectives certainly can be included in a small group of antecedents for Brother Cadfael. Although never set in the Middle Ages, the mystery novels of Agatha Christie, starring her detective Miss Marple, are consistently realistic, developed with an insightful understanding of geographical and historical contexts, which certainly could have provided Ellis Peters with some inspiration. Overall, however, Brother Cadfael is a singular character uniquely inspired by the imagination of his creator.

Brother Cadfael appears in the first medieval mystery novel of the Chronicles of Brother Cadfael, *A Morbid Taste for the Bones* (1977), fully formed, a whole person, straight from the mind of his maker, Ellis Peters. He is a sixty-year-old Benedictine monk of Shrewsbury Abbey, a Welshman living on the border, in the tumultuous twelfth century when King Stephen and Empress Maud vie for the rulership of England. He maintains a fragrant garden of herbs and a shed where he makes medicine, and he serves his Benedictine brothers and the local people with his healing gifts. His past, however, is less peaceful: he previously served as a soldier in the First Crusade, when called upon to do so with many others by Pope Urban II, to recover the Holy Land from the Islamic Seljuk Turks. In the course of the series, readers learn that Cadfael was present at the siege and sack of Jerusalem on July 15, 1099.

Clearly, Brother Cadfael came to a turning point in his life's road, leaving the active life of the military for the contemplative life of the monastery. In *A Rare Benedictine: The Advent of Brother Cadfael* (1988), Ellis Peters reveals the moment of her protagonist's turn toward Benedictine monasticism in her short story "A Light on the Road to Woodstock" (1985). In her preface to the story, Peters remarks, "What happens to him on the road to Woodstock is simply the acceptance of a revelation from within that the life he has lived to date, active, mobile, and often violent, has reached its natural end, and he is confronted by a new need and a different challenge."[9] The moment of surrender to his calling is beautifully depicted in the story itself as Cadfael stands before an altar in a church:

> It was the light touch of a small hand on the hilt of his sword that startled him out of his profound isolation. He looked down to see a little acolyte, no higher than his elbow, regarding him gravely from great round eyes of blinding blue, intent and challenging, as solemn as ever was angelic messenger.
> "Sir," said the child in stern treble reproof, tapping the hilt with an infant finger, "should not all weapons of war be laid aside here?"
> "Sir," said Cadfael, hardly less gravely, though he was smiling, "you may very well be right." And slowly he unbuckled the sword from his belt and went and laid it down, flatlings, on the lowest step under the altar. It looked strangely appropriate and at peace there. The hilt, after all, was a cross.[10]

This is the moment of Cadfael's conversion from the active life to the contemplative life. It is also the beginning of a new career, not only as a Benedictine monk but also as an investigative detective who will seek to right wrongs and reveal murderers in his ongoing quest for justice in his society. His motive may be partially penitential, but it is also devotional: the Cross calls him into a new life in which, without the weapons, he will fight for truth and for those who have been silenced, side-lined, victimized, or unjustly killed.

In the short story, this is told as one of the moments occurring in the "present." However, throughout the novels and short stories concerned with Brother Cadfael, Ellis Peters typically uses flashbacks that reveal more of Cadfael's life before he joined the Benedictine Abbey of St. Peter and St. Paul in Shrewsbury, interweaving these with her intricate medieval mystery plots. Readers learn from the first novel that Cadfael is Welsh and fluent in the language of his native country; from *Monk's Hood*, that he loved and left a lady named Richildis when he was young and went to fight in the Crusades; from *The Virgin in the Ice*, that he had as a lover a woman in Antioch, a dark-haired widow named Miriam, who, unbeknownst to him until decades later, bore him a son, Olivier de Bretagne.

Cadfael also served in the First Crusade under Godfrey de Bouillon in the battles for Antioch and Jerusalem. Afterward, he became a ship's sea captain for ten years, traveling throughout the Mediterranean. He joined Roger Marduit as a man-at-arms in Normandy, which was then under the rulership of King Henry I, and he went with him across the Channel to England. At the Church of St. Mary Magdalene in Woodstock, he laid down his sword at the altar. Then he took up his new vocation as a Benedictine monk, joining Abbot Heribert and his brothers at Shrewsbury Abbey.

There Brother Cadfael is surrounded by a colorful cast of characters that Ellis Peters carefully develops through many novels: Robert Pennant, Prior; Brother Richard, sub-prior; Brother Jerome, Robert's clerk; Brother Paul, master of the novices; Brother Anselm, the precentor; Brother Edmund, the infirmarer; Brother Dennis, the hospitaller; Brother Matthew, the cellarer; and Brother Benedict, the sacristan. Brother Mark is a monk who becomes a priest, and Brother Oswin is a clumsy but cheerful brother who becomes Cadfael's aide in making and delivering medicine (when he is not breaking pots!). Old Abbott Heribert is eventually replaced by stern Abbott Radulfus.

One of the most significant characters that Ellis Peters develops is not a brother but a sheriff: Hugh Beringar of Maesbury. At first an under-sheriff to Gilbert Prestecote, Hugh eventually becomes sheriff himself. At the beginning of their acquaintance, Cadfael and Hugh are cautiously wary of one another, but they eventually become allies. Both men work together to solve crimes in several of the mystery novels. Over time, they become such good friends that when Hugh and his wife, Aline, have a child, they ask Brother Cadfael to be the godfather, and he accepts.

In each story, Brother Cadfael repeatedly stands up for truth, defends the innocent, and supports young lovers whose love is needlessly forbidden or hindered by various obstacles. Cadfael is dedicated to justice, and from justice, he does not swerve. Through twenty mystery novels, Ellis Peters leads him on adventures from year to year, proceeding chronologically from 1137 to 1145, and she represents Brother Cadfael's moral thoughts and deeds as occurring in a realistic, historical context. To do so, she relied (at least in part) on the Cartulary of Shrewsbury Abbey, a historical register, which was edited and published in 1975 by the National Library of Wales.[11]

For finer details about Cadfael's plants and herbs, she was known to draw on such books as Culpeper's *Illustrated Herbal,* John Harvey's *Medieval Gardens,* and Tony Hart's *Plant Names of Medieval England,* as well as her own personal knowledge and experience as a chemist's assistant. Ellis Peters loved to do research, which for her was not work but pleasure. Her historical accuracy in her books is a point of pride, and her historical consistency has been acknowledged by academics.[12] More important to Ellis Peters, however, was the impact of the Chronicles of Brother Cadfael on readers for, as she said, "They offer a degree of hope and consolation, and leave people feeling better, not worse, about their fellow creatures and their situation in this imperfect world."[13]

The Leper of St. Giles

The fifth mystery novel in the Chronicles of Brother Cadfael, *The Leper of St. Giles* (1981), is a significant book for revealing the talents of Ellis Peters as an author, Brother Cadfael's abilities as a detective, and the importance of social justice not only in the twelfth century but in our own. To understand how, it will be useful to consider a summary of the story and an ethical analysis of its themes before considering the television film adaptation directed by Graham Theakston (1994). Through the latter, Ellis Peters reached not only readers but viewers with hope and consolation through her critique of social injustice. Her book sends a clear message that whoever the "leper" may be, whoever the sick person isolated and mistreated for no other reason than illness may be, that person has a right to dignity, privacy, honor, and justice.

The Leper of St. Giles is the story of two young lovers, Lady Iveta de Massard and a squire named Joscelin Lucy, who are thwarted in love by Iveta's guardians, Godfrid and Agnes Picard. The Picards are forcing Iveta, barely eighteen years old, into an arranged marriage with a man much her senior, Huon de Domville. Huon, at sixty years old, is a wealthy, powerful man who behaves cruelly toward others, as becomes apparent when he uses the lash of his whip on Lazarus, who is a leper of St. Giles, a hospital near Shrewsbury Abbey run by the Benedictine brothers. In due course, readers learn that Huon also has had many affairs with other women, including a long-time mistress named Avice of Thornbury, so it is clear that he hardly knows and barely cares for his betrothed bride. In brokering this May–January marriage contract, Iveta's guardians have dowered her with only part of her inheritance from her grandfather—a grandfather whose identity is vital to the story—in order to retain the rest for themselves.

Guimar de Massard, Iveta's grandfather, was a hero of the First Crusade. He was known to Cadfael, and much admired by him, when Cadfael was a knight fighting the battles for the Holy Land. When the death of Guimar was reported, his sword and armor were sent back honorably by his Islamic enemies to his family in England. Iveta still has these keepsakes and cherishes them. Cadfael, seeing the unhappiness of the bride as she comes to the Abbey to be married, is convinced her grandfather would have wanted better for her. When Brother Cadfael subsequently learns from Joscelin Lucy that Iveta's guardians are forcing her to marry against her will, he asks for the help of Abbot Radulfus.

In medieval England, as elsewhere, children of the nobility were often betrothed by their families in their infancy or youth, and they were pressured into alliances fundamentally based on the retention or transfer of the wealth and power of noble families. Yet the Catholic Church championed marriage as a sacrament that should not be entered into lightly or under compulsion. The free consent of both bride and groom was considered necessary as were a contract, a duly witnessed public marriage ceremony, and the sexual consummation of the union. Without these elements, a marriage would be considered invalid.

So, when Brother Cadfael approaches Abbot Radulfus, he asks the Abbot to inquire with Iveta de Massard about whether she is marrying Huon de Domville of her own free will. The Abbot does speak to Iveta, but under pressure from her guardians, the young woman does not admit to loving Joscelin Lucy or wanting to escape from the forced marriage contract to Huon de Domville. Since she does not speak, the Abbot does not pursue any further objection to the alliance. Brother Cadfael acutely feels the injustice of the situation.

At issue, morally, is the greed and exploitation of Godfrid and Agnes Picard, who are using their legal ward to financially benefit themselves. The issue of free will and of free choice of love is also at issue. Ellis Peters does not hesitate to indicate whose side she is on in these issues. Through Brother Cadfael's thoughts and deeds, she critiques social injustice.

Yet when Huon de Domville turns up dead, murder becomes the main issue. Other matters of social justice seem to pale before the degree of moral depravity involved in murder. Joscelin Lucy, with the obvious motive, becomes the prime suspect. He had even said to Brother Cadfael that he wished the would-be husband dead so that Iveta de Massard might be free to make her own choice of whom to marry. Joscelin flees pursuit by the local sheriff, Gilbert Prestcote, and escapes capture, making a daring leap into the River Severn. After hiding in the Bishop's garden, he goes to ground in the most unlikely spot: the hospital of St. Giles, where he dons a leper's robe and conceals his identity, befriended by other lepers, including Lazarus, whom Huon de Domville earlier in the story had lashed with his whip.

Yet there is another young man, a squire like Joscelin and supposedly Joscelin's friend, one Simon Aguilon, who also had a motive, hidden from others: he, too, wished Huon de Domville, his uncle, dead. Simon, as heir, did not wish his uncle to conceive a child with the young Iveta de Massard, a child who might supplant him. Charming and ambitious, the death of his uncle renders him rich, and he actually asks for Iveta's hand himself, though he had promised to help both her and Joscelin in their desire to be united.

Eventually, Cadfael ferrets out the facts, which clearly point to Simon as the murderer: he strangled his uncle with his bare hands when his uncle was returning from a last night with his long-time mistress, Avice of Thornbury. The impression of Simon's ringed finger remains in the flesh of his uncle's neck. With this, and Avice's testimony, Brother Cadfael is able to clear the accusations against Joscelin Luc—though not before Godfrid Picard is murdered and his wife, Agnes, accuses Simon Aguilon of her husband's death, since Godfried suspected Simon as the murderer of Huon de Domville and was rash enough to say so to Simon. So, two murders are laid at Simon's feet.

Yet, as Brother Cadfael discovers, though both Huon de Domville and Godfrid Picard died by strangulation, they were not killed by the same man. Huon de Domville was murdered, but Godfrid Picard was killed after he was called out by another nobleman who had a just quarrel with him. The other nobleman is none other than Guimar de Massard, whose other name in the story is Lazarus, the leper of St. Giles.

In her book, Ellis Peters is intent upon contrasting Huon de Domville, who is outwardly well-dressed and powerful but inwardly craven, with Guimar de Massard, who is outwardly clothed in rags and poverty but inwardly noble. One man looks good on the outside, but inside, he is morally bad. The other man looks bad on the outside, but inside, he is morally good. As Lazarus, Guimar de Massard defies Huon de Domville on the road when he mocks the other lepers. He befriends Joscelin Lucy when the young squire hides at St. Giles. He executes a knight's justice against Godfrid Picard and does not let the greedy man continue to exploit his granddaughter.

Brother Cadfael goes to Iveta's grandfather at the leper hospital and urges him to reveal himself to his family and be reunited with them. But Guimar, satisfied that his granddaughter's marriage will no longer be coerced by conniving relatives—that her will and her happiness will be taken into consideration and her wealth will follow her to a marriage, most likely, to Joscelin Lucy—does not wish to take up his old identity again. Cadfael reminds him of the Lazarus of the New Testament story who was resurrected from the dead and welcomed back by his sisters, Mary and Martha. But this is not convincing to Guimar. Briefly, he removes the cloth that hides his face, ravaged by leprosy, and asks, "And was this the face that made his sisters glad?"[14]

Later, Guimar de Massard, called Lazarus, leaves the hospital of St. Giles to continue his wandering pilgrimage and does not ever return to Shrewsbury. Yet his figure casts a powerful shadow over the whole story Ellis Peters tells. At the beginning of the novel, Huon de Domville violently lashes Lazarus, and Cadfael and others clearly see this as unnecessary cruelty. When Iveta de Massard comes down the road next, in bridal procession to the abbey following her affianced, she gives generously of her coins to the lepers who are begging and does not speak harshly to them. These two characters are foils as well, and their actions speak to the readers about what choices the readers themselves will make in the future: will they avoid and spurn those who are diseased, out of fear or spite, or will they give to them and bless them as their fellow human beings?

In late-medieval England, lepers had to cry out, "Unclean!" to all passersby on the road. They had to beg that they might eat, kept as they were from entering towns or cities lest other people contract their contagion. They were isolated from their families and had as their friends only other sick people, lepers like them, and the caregivers willing to put their own lives at risk to minister to their medical needs. Ellis Peters shows these customs in her book, not only to be historically accurate, but to cause the readers to enter imaginatively into the experience of being sick and cast out from society. Not for the leper the bonds of friendship or the embrace of family! They have no safe place to call home, and their homelessness and their poverty make their vulnerability to illness all the more extreme.

To draw readers in even further to the issues of social justice, Ellis Peters designs her plot specifically so that at least two healthy men, Brother Mark and Joscelin Lucy, will enter into the experience of the lepers of St. Giles. Brother Mark, called to ministry to the sick, tends their open sores and makes sure they receive good care in the hospital. Cadfael recognizes that one day, Brother Mark may become a leper just like those he cares for and that the tender-hearted brother is not afraid of the eventuality.

For different reasons than Brother Mark, Joscelin takes refuge with the lepers. While in hiding, he shows his lack of prejudice against the sick when he stays close to Lazarus and also befriends a little leper-boy. The boy, Bran, is desperately vulnerable because his father is absent, his mother is ill in the hospital, and he himself has a terrible growth on his neck called leprosy, though obviously it is not the same leprosy that is destroying the body of Guimar de Massard. Joscelin promises to make the boy his squire when he himself is made a knight.

When fulfilled, this promise will give the boy hope and a future. Clearly, Ellis Peters advocates for the sick and the outcast, and especially for children. She wants her readers to make the moral connection between what is going on in her story and what is going on in the world—and what readers can do about it.

The Leper of St. Giles (dir. Theakston, 1994)

Overall, the film adaptation of *The Leper of St. Giles* is faithful to the plot, themes, and character development Ellis Peters establishes in her mystery novel.[15] Through the techniques of film, the director, Graham Theakston, is able to emphasize important moral points from Ellis Peters, beginning with the opening credits.

Like most television shows, the Brother Cadfael series has a theme song paired with a set of images that recur at the beginning of every episode. The song for this series is a Latin chant, which begins with the words

Veni, Spiritus Sanctus ("Come, Holy Spirit"). As the chant rises over eerie music and the sound of a bell tolling, the camera pans over an elaborate, medieval-looking wooden carving, ending at a figure of King Death: a skeleton wearing a crown and holding a scepter.[16]

Clearly, this will be a story set in the Middle Ages. Viewers are meant to understand the symbolic iconography so prominently displayed in the allegorical figure of Death. This is not just a story, but a murder mystery! Yet most viewers will not understand the Latin words *Veni, Spiritus Sanctus*. The words speak consciously only to educated viewers who know the language or to curious ones willing to look up their translation into English. However, subconsciously, the words speak to all viewers, whether they understand Latin or not, about the role of the Holy Spirit in the revelation of truth.

In the Middle Ages, the Catholic Church taught that the Holy Spirit was the Advocate, the Spirit of Jesus, the Spirit of Truth. These teachings about the role of the Holy Spirit were based on the words of Jesus to his disciples at the Last Supper.[17] He said to them, "But when the Spirit of truth comes, he will guide you into all truth."[18] After Jesus was crucified, died, and was buried, and resurrected three days later, he spoke to his followers again before he ascended into heaven, and he promised his followers that the Holy Spirit would come. The coming of the Holy Spirit in tongues of fire over the disciples' heads is dramatically depicted in Acts 2 in the Bible.

By inviting the coming of the Holy Spirit through the theme song at the beginning of the "The Leper of St. Giles" episode (and all episodes in the series), director Theakston is not only creating a medieval ambiance appropriate to the story, which features a Benedictine monk as the detective-protagonist and Shrewsbury Abbey as the primary setting, he is also speaking to a key theme essential to the plot: the need for the revelation of truth facilitated by divine intervention.

While Brother Cadfael is a smart detective, his knowledge is more than once helped along by small revelations of truth that eventually lead him to correctly deduce the causes of two murders. One symbol in the story (and the film adaptation) is a rare flower from a patch of gromwell. Avice of Thornbury puts a sprig of this in Huon de Domville's cap before he leaves her—and is murdered. Brother Cadfael, looking for the flower that he discovered on Huon's body, finds it at Huon's hunting lodge. From there, he is able to find Avice herself, who reveals that Simon Aguilon, Huon's nephew, is the only man who knew the path Huon de Domville would ride to come to her at the lodge—and she thus reveals the murderer.

Following the flower to find the truth, and finding it revealed through the testimony of Avice of Thornbury, is a powerful motif in the story. Theakston films more than one close-up shot of the tiny, purple gromwell flowers in Cadfael's hand to allow viewers to realize their importance as a clue to Brother Cadfael's later discoveries. Theakston later portrays Avice of Thornbury on-screen as Ellis Peters did in her novel: as a man's mistress who, after her lord's death, chose to take vows and become a nun. Dressed in symbolic white in the film, she becomes Sister Magdalen of the Benedictine nunnery at Godric's Ford.[19] Avice, for all her socially unacceptable past, is dedicated to truth-telling. Her forthrightness and lack of fear of the repercussions for herself are what allow justice to come to pass. Joscelin Lucy is freed from false accusations, and Simon Aguilon is held accountable for his actions.

Conclusions

The life of Ellis Peters and her extraordinary medieval detective, Brother Cadfael, have had a profound impact on the genre of historical mystery fiction. This is because readers and viewers alike are fascinated not only by the compelling plots of these stories, but by their edifying themes that bring hope and consolation. In *The Leper of St. Giles,* Ellis Peters emphasizes the importance of social justice for lepers, the outcasts of society.

At the same time, she shows the importance of the exercise of free will in matters of love and marriage, especially for women, and of truth-telling in the revelation of wrongdoing. Brother Cadfael feels profound concern that Iveta de Massard freely consent to any marriage into which she may enter. Brother Cadfael shows considerable respect for Avice of Thornbury as an ally in revealing the truth to find a murderer, models the same respect Ellis Peters clearly expects her readers to have for all women, regardless of their sexual past. Likewise, Brother Cadfael's great honor for Guimar de Massard, called Lazarus, the leper of St. Giles, which models the treatment Ellis Peters wants her readers to show to all social outcasts who are shunned because of their supposed contagion.

Ellis Peters published *The Leper of St. Giles* in 1981 at the beginning of the worldwide AIDS crisis. In a sense, AIDS was the leprosy of the 1980s: many people stricken with the disease were cast out of society and badly treated by others when they were sick and dying. Ellis Peters wrote a book that addressed this terrible reality. Her popular medieval detective, Brother Cadfael, shows great concern in her story for the dignity, privacy, honor, and justice due to lepers.

Today, as we face the worldwide coronavirus pandemic, Ellis Peters's story remains relevant. Terrible injustice has befallen many people who are ill and isolated from their families because of their sickness, whose only companions are other sick people like themselves or the doctors and nurses willing to put their own lives at risk to help them. Many of the poor who are sick have no access to any help, and people with underlying conditions are more vulnerable and dying as a result. We live in a fortunate time because new treatments may help to prevent the spread of the novel coronavirus. In the Middle Ages, there was neither an effective treatment nor a cure for leprosy.

In our world today, leprosy still exists but is curable. Many other diseases continue to ravage human bodies, especially in the developing world, where there is little access to adequate medical care. Ellis Peters told a moral parable in her medieval mystery, *The Leper of St. Giles*, to speak to issues of social injustice in the hopes that people who suffer from diseases would receive the love and care that they need. She told it in hopes that justice would be done, daily, by those who can stand up, like Brother Cadfael, for what is good, true, and necessary. The lesson of her story is worth remembering.

Notes

1. Quoted in Sue Feder, "Ellis Peters," in *Twentieth-Century Crime and Mystery Writers*, ed. Lesley Henderson, 3rd edition (Chicago: St. James Press, 1991), 848.
2. Edith Mary Pargeter also wrote under other pen names as well as her actual name, so she was not exclusive to Peters. She did write Brother Cadfael under Ellis Peters, however, and is most well-known by that name.
3. Margaret Lewis, *Edith Pargeter: Ellis Peters* (Chester Springs, PA: Seren, 1994), 10.
4. For a list of the numerous novels, short stories, and translations of Ellis Peters, see the bibliography in Margaret Lewis's biography of the author. Ellis Peters wrote thirty-six realistic fictional novels, twelve by 1945 when she returned to Shropshire from her service with the WRNS—hence her fame. From 1951 to 1979, she wrote thirteen Felse crime novels. From 1977 to 1994, she wrote twenty Brother Cadfael mysteries. She published three short story collections (in 1958, 1965, and 1988, respectively), the last featuring Brother Cadfael in all stories included in the volume, which was entitled *A Rare Benedictine*. She wrote three nonfiction books, two co-authored with her nephew Roy Morgan, about Shropshire. She also translated sixteen volumes from Czech into English. Her essay "The Thriller Is a Novel," published in 1973, is both a defense of the genre and a revelation of the author's own techniques. In total, Ellis Peters wrote seventy-five books and translated sixteen more.
5. Quoted in Lewis, *Edith Pargeter*, 37.
6. Suzanne Bray, "'Continually Walking a Tightrope': Edith Pargeter's Literary Crusade for Czechoslovakia," *Études britanniques contemporaines*, no. 52 (2017), https://doi.org/10.4000/ebc.3638, 1. Accessed March 3, 2023.
7. Ibid., para. 6–8, 13–15.
8. To see an excellent series of photographs of Shropshire, with attendant explanations connected to the Chronicles of Brother Cadfael, see Rob Talbot and Robin Whiteman, with introduction by Ellis Peters, *Cadfael Country: Shropshire and the Welsh Borders* (London: Little, Brown, 1992).

9   Ellis Peters, "A Light on the Road to Woodstock," in *A Rare Benedictine: The Advent of Brother Cadfael* (Brentwood: Warner Books, 1988), 7. This may echo something of Ellis Peters's own life experience; she was sixty-four herself when the first Brother Cadfael novel was published.
10 Ibid., 52–3.
11 Lewis, *Edith Pargeter*, 94.
12 As biographer Margaret Lewis notes,

> History professors accept Peters's creation of a medieval world that functions on its own terms. By removing her location from the center of power to the borders, the author can be sparing with actual political detail, providing just enough to give a realistic sense of the world of affairs whose influence can still affect even the smallest corners of the unhappy kingdom. The details that she incorporates are carefully checked, but historical accuracy would amount to very little if the characters in her novels were not interesting and attractive. The approval of the academics is, however, encouraging for a professional who has always taken pride in her historical reliability. (Ibid., 96)

   For more analysis of the historical and cultural accuracy of the world that Ellis Peters created in her medieval mystery novels, see Catherine Lanone, "From St. Winifred's Translation to Medieval Whodunnit: Ellis Peters and the Cadfael Chronicles," *Caliban: French Journal of English Studies*, no. 29 (2011), https://journals.openedition.org/caliban/844.
13 Quoted in Lewis, *Edith Pargeter*, 113.
14 Ellis Peter, *The Leper of St. Giles* (London: Macmillan, 1981), 191.
15 For further analysis, see Neil McCraw, *Adapting Detective Fiction: Crime, Englishness, and the TV Detectives* (New York: Bloomsbury, 2011), especially "Chapter 6: Cadfael, Medievalism, and Modern Nationhood," 92–107.
16 It was carved in oak by Hugh Wedderburn, a master woodcarver, specifically for the series. See The Gentle Author, "Hugh Wedderburn, Master Woodcarver," *Spitalfields Life*, October 14, 2010, spitalfieldslife.com/2010/10/14/hugh-wedderburn-master-woodcarver/.
17 See John 16:7-15.
18 See John 16:13.
19 Robin Whiteman, *The Cadfael Companion* (New York: The Mysterious Press, 1995), 223–4.

Bibliography

Bray, Suzanne. "'Continually Walking a Tightrope': Edith Pargeter's Literary Crusade for Czechoslovakia." *Études britanniques contemporaines*, no. 52 (2017). https://doi.org/10.4000/ebc.3638. Accessed March 3, 2023.

Feder, Sue. "Ellis Peters." In *Twentieth-Century Crime and Mystery Writers*, edited by Lesley Henderson, 3rd edition, 846–9. Chicago: St. James Press, 1991.

The Gentle Author. "Hugh Wedderburn, Master Woodcarver." *Spitalfields Life*, October 14, 2010, spitalfieldslife.com/2010/10/14/hugh-wedderburn-master-woodcarver/. Accessed October 25, 2021.

Lanone, Catherine. "From St. Winifred's Translation to Medieval Whodunnit: Ellis Peters and the Cadfael Chronicles." *Caliban: French Journal of English Studies*, no. 29 (2011). https://journals.openedition.org/caliban/844. Accessed October 25, 2021.

The Leper of St. Giles, directed by Graham Theakston, performed by Peter Copley, Jonathan Firth, Tara FitzGerald, Sarah Badel, Jamie Glover, Jonathan Hyde, Danny Dyer, and John Bennett. London: Central and Carlton Media, 1994. Movie.

Lewis, Margaret. *Edith Pargeter: Ellis Peters*. Chester Springs, PA: Seren, 1994.

McCraw, Neil. *Adapting Detective Fiction: Crime, Englishness, and the TV Detectives*. New York: Bloomsbury Academic, 2011.

Peters, Ellis. *The Leper of St. Giles*. London: Macmillan, 1981.

Peters, Ellis. "A Light on the Road to Woodstock." In *A Rare Benedictine: The Advent of Brother Cadfael*, 5–42. Brentwood: Warner Books, 1988.

Talbot, Rob, and Robin Whiteman, with introduction by Ellis Peters. *Cadfael Country: Shropshire & the Welsh Borders*. London: Little, Brown, 1992.

Whiteman, Robin. *The Cadfael Companion*. New York: The Mysterious Press, 1995.

13

A Vocation of Truth: The Pursuit of Moral Certainty in the Detective Fiction of Dorothy L. Sayers

Andrew J. Spencer

Dorothy L. Sayers was a founding member and longtime president of the Detection Club, an organization whose ranks also included figures like G. K. Chesterton and Agatha Christie. At the heart of the Detection Club was a vocation of truth: a requirement that mysteries be written honestly. The oath of initiation of the president required an affirmative answer to this loaded and ponderous question: "Do you promise that your Detectives shall well and truly detect the crimes presented to them, using those wits which it may please you to bestow upon them and not placing reliance upon nor making use of Divine Revelation, Feminine Intuition, Mumbo Jumbo, Jiggery-Pokery, Coincidence or Act of God?"[1] After the stirring desire to use the word *jiggery-pokery* in casual conversation, the next most striking element of this oath is its commitment to truthful construction as a necessary aspect of detective fiction. This vocation of truth characterized all of Sayers's work, but especially the mysteries she wrote toward the beginning of her career.

Despite her abiding concern for the truthful integrity of her work and her vigorous Christian orthodoxy, Sayers demonstrated a willingness to accept moral ambiguity if it served the greater truthfulness of the story. Janice Brown argues that the whole of Sayers's work can be analyzed along the framework of the so-called seven deadly sins.[2] The deadly sins serve as a taxonomy for morality that dates to at least the fifth century CE in the Christian tradition. The list of seven deadly sins evolved over time, but the most commonly recognized list includes lust, gluttony, greed, sloth, wrath, envy, and pride. Notably, murder, which is the central crime in many mysteries, is not a primary sin on this list. However, the willingness to kill another human can be the outcome of any of those deadly sins. Part of the vocation of truth in Sayers's work is the demonstration that the motivation for an act is as important as the act itself, which lends itself to a certain level of moral ambiguity.

Detective fiction is full of moral ambiguity and often intentionally transgresses social moral norms. One attractive aspect of contemporary mysteries is the way that social observation of these stories gives keen insight into the surrounding world. Through the sometimes-exaggerated behaviors of fictional characters, we can come to a better understanding of ourselves and our neighbors.[3] Sayers used the patterns of sin in the world to illustrate her certainty that immorality has consequences, which are often the natural result of deviating from the good[4]. Sayers's understanding of the nature of good was grounded in her Christianity, which she considered the best explanation for reality. In her essay "Creed or Chaos?" she argues, "Religious dogma is in fact nothing but a statement of doctrines concerning the nature of life and the universe."[5] Judgment for sin thus becomes "the inevitable consequence of man's attempt to regulate life and society on a system that runs counter to the facts of his own nature."[6] There is moral certainty because the laws of the universe are the basis of reality, but there is ambiguity because humans often attempt to establish patterns of life contrary to those natural laws.

In Sayers's fiction, the detective serves as a human agent to ensure consequences for significant departures from the good that might have otherwise gone unresolved. A vocation of truth is at the heart of Sayers's detective stories, as her characters eschew easy solutions in pursuit of the truth, sometimes at their own peril. The source of this vocation of truth is not found in self-righteousness or an *ad hoc* personal code of conduct. Instead, for Sayers, it is framed by the moral clarity that can be found in the nature of the universe itself.

Moral Clarity of Dorothy L. Sayers

Sayers was the only daughter of an Anglican clergyman. She was confirmed into the Church of England against her better judgment while a teen at boarding school. This dissatisfaction with the religion of her youth may have contributed to a period of moral rebellion early in adulthood. As a young woman, Sayers lived with a lover with whom she quarreled, fell for a mechanic who fathered her only, secret child, and eventually married a divorcee against social precedent and the teaching of the Anglican church. And yet, shortly after her son was born, she returned to her childhood Christian faith and eventually became a creative force for an orthodox vision of the universe and an apologist for the Christian faith. She remained vigorously and openly committed to doctrinally orthodox Christianity with its morally absolute ethical system.

At the same time, Sayers was a vocal critic of the morality of popular Christianity which tended toward legalism divorced from true ethical virtue. As she notes in her essay "Christian Morality," many Christians have "succeeded in placing strangely restricted interpretation on such words as *virtue, purity,* and *morality*."[7] Rather than robustly applying a biblical paradigm that interrogates all of life through a moral lens, Sayers believed that the Christians of her day "firmly believe that Christian morals, as distinct from purely secular morality, consist of three things and three things only: Sunday observance, not getting intoxicated, and not practicing—well, in fact, not practicing immorality."[8] Sayers made a distinction between "warmhearted sins," which were really excesses or misuses of otherwise good things, and "coldhearted sins," which were calculated rejections of the goodness of the universe.[9]

There is little doubt that, although she kept her son's out-of-wedlock birth a secret, she did so because of the reduction of "sin" to simplistic terms, meaning specifically sexual immorality, which is usually a warmhearted sin. In her essay "The Other Six Deadly Sins," she argues that sex was the only deadly sin that Christians still recognized.[10] Her frustration at the myopic focus on sexual sin as the primary concern of environmental ethics is, perhaps, why she makes her detective hero, Lord Peter, rather loose on that front. It may also help to explain why the hypocrisy of the social acceptance of Gerald Wimsey's infidelity in *Clouds of Witness* is emphasized by Sayers; she was, perhaps, undermining the improper moral certainty of her readers, which was often filtered through classist lenses. According to Downing, one of Sayers's major efforts in her fiction was to subvert an improper moral certitude among contemporary Christians, which she seems to have carried out consistently through her detective fiction.[11]

Unlike some critics of social morality, however, there is clarity in Sayers's vision. Lord Peter is promiscuous because it helps convey the complexity of his character: the sleuth is dedicated to the truth above all but capable of sinning and letting justice be meted out by a criminal's cudgel rather than by the court.[12] The moral ambiguity of characters in Dorothy L. Sayers's fiction serves to illustrate the damaging effects of sin and, in turn, demonstrates the moral clarity Sayers had in light of her rigorous Christian belief in the moral order of the universe.

Truth as a Vocation

The pursuit of truth at any cost is a trademark Lord Peter mystery. It shows Peter Wimsey's certainty about his role in the investigation: to determine the truth whatever the cost. In *Clouds of Witness*, there is tension between a vocation of truth and Peter's duty to protect his family's honor. There is both moral and social ambiguity as Lord Peter balances his pursuit of truth and his social duty to his family. In this novel, the body of Lady Mary's (Peter's sister's) fiancé is found in the garden shortly after an argument with the Duke of Denver (Peter's older brother). The Duke declares himself innocent, but he is reticent to explain his activities. Although he claims to have been out for a constitutional in miserable weather, the Duke finds himself the primary suspect. A peer of England is imprisoned, awaiting trial as a suspect for the murder, and unwilling to provide a real alibi. His brother's pursuit of absolute truth—a form of moral certainty—ends up imperiling the Duke's life before the end of the case.

After some intense investigation, Peter flushes out an unknown man who left footprints at the scene of the crime, who turns out to be the secret love interest of his sister, Lady Mary. The information gained from the night visitor, however, ends up eliminating uncertainty about a mysterious figure, without implicating the actual killer. In short, Peter discovers a piece of the truth, but it puts his brother's life and the family's honor at risk. The truth comes at a great personal cost, as this discovery earns Lord Peter a bullet to the arm. Despite Peter's personal sacrifice, the family lawyer, Sir Impey Biggs, is less than thrilled at the results of the inquiry. Their exchange reveals some of the moral ambiguity in defending clients in a criminal trial:

> "Well, Lord Peter," said Mr. Murbles slowly, "I congratulate you and Mr. Parker [the Scotland Yard detective working with Peter on the case] on a great deal of industry and ingenuity in working the matter out."
>
> "I think we may say we have made some progress," said Parker.
>
> "If only negatively," added Peter.
>
> "Exactly," said Sir Impey turning on him with staggering abruptness. "Very negatively indeed. And, having seriously hampered the case for the defense, what are you going to do next?"
>
> "That's a nice thing to say," cried Peter indignantly, "when we've cleared up such a lot of points for you!"
>
> "I daresay," said the barrister, "but they're the sorts of points which are much better left muffled up."
>
> "Damn it all, we want to get at the truth!"
>
> "Do you?" said Sir Impey drily.

"I don't. I don't care two-pence about the truth. I want a case. It doesn't matter to me who killed Cathcart, provided I can prove it wasn't Denver. It's really enough if I can throw reasonable doubt on its being Denver. Here's a client who comes to me with a story of a quarrel, a suspicious revolver, a refusal to produce evidence of his statements, and a totally inadequate and idiotic alibi. I arrange to obfuscate the jury with mysterious footprints, a discrepancy as to time, a young woman with a secret, and a general vague suggestion of something between a burglary and a *crime passionel*. And here you come explaining the footprints, exculpating the unknown man, abolishing the discrepancies, clearing up the motives of the young woman, and most carefully throwing back suspicious to where it rested in the first place. What *do* you expect?"

"I've always said," growled Peter, "that the professional advocate was the most immoral fellow on the face of the earth, and now I know for certain."[13]

Throughout Sayers's detective fiction there is the constant tension between the desired outcome of the case and the pursuit of truth. She brings that to the forefront in *Clouds of Witness* as Lord Peter's pursuit of truth imperils the doubt surrounding his brother's guilt. It was not enough for Peter to see his brother declared not guilty because of ambiguity around the facts, a fate that would leave a cloud hovering over the family's honor. Instead, he pursues moral certainty in defiance of social norms and at the risk of his brother's own life.

In *Strong Poison,* Sayers again shows Wimsey's concern for moral clarity in the pursuit of truth, even when it threatens the life of a romantic interest. Readers meet Harriet Vane as the judge is summarizing the facts of the case in her murder trial. It is clear from the narration that everyone expects a quick guilty verdict from the jury. But the jury ends up hung, in part due to the presence of Miss Climpson, an industrious woman who often does investigative work for Lord Peter. There is more doubt about Vane's guilt than the crowd will allow, which serves to give Peter a chance to investigate in an attempt to clear a woman that he had previously never met. Though Peter later becomes infatuated with Harriet and awkwardly proposes to her on his first visit to see her in prison, he still risks her life in his investigation of the murder by clearing up ambiguity that seems better left muddied.

In the course of his investigation, Lord Peter finds a witness who saw the murder victim stumble into a pub and take a white powder in an unmarked packet—perhaps the poison that finished off Harriet's former lover. Though Wimsey is working to undermine the Crown's case, which his friend Chief Inspector Parker was overseeing, the two gamely cooperate in pursuit of truth. Peter sets Parker to work to find the mysterious packet. Surprisingly, the gumshoes of Scotland Yard succeed, and the contents of the packet are determined to be bicarbonate of soda. This is a devastating blow for the defense.

Even before this discovery, the potential damage of being certain of the contents of the packet did not escape Lord Peter or the defense attorneys. When informed of Peter's cooperation with the police to find a witness and pursue the packet, Mr. Croft, makes clear his hope for ambiguity in his legal defense:

> "[B]ut don't you see that the police won't rest now till they've found this precious packet?"
> "Well?" [replies Lord Peter.]
> "Well, and suppose it isn't arsenic at all? If you'd left it in our hands, we could have sprung the thing on them at the last moment, when it was too late to make enquiries, and then we should have knocked the bottom out of the prosecution. Give the jury Mrs. Bulfinch's story as it stands and they'd have to admit there was some evidence that the deceased poisoned himself. But now, of course, the police will find or fake something and show that the powder was perfectly harmless."[14]

When the packet is discovered and the contents determined to be perfectly harmless, the result is exactly what might be expected: "Mr. Crofts, excusably enough, said, 'I told you so'; Sir Impey Biggs observed curtly, 'Very unfortunate.'"[15] With time ticking away until the retrial, the lawyers for the defense are saddened to find certainty where ambiguity is to the advantage of their client.

Though doubt about the white powder could save her life, there is a greater doubt that ambiguity will serve Harriet's best interests. Peter remains convinced she is not guilty of murder and pursues proof of innocence rather than seeking to leave sufficient doubt to save her from the hangman's noose. After having been chastised for cooperating with the police, Lord Peter states his interest in seeing Vane cleared:

> "Look here," said Wimsey, "I'm not out for a verdict of 'Not Proven.' As far as Miss Vane's honour and happiness are concerned, she might as well be found guilty as acquitted on a mere element of doubt. I want to see her absolutely cleared and the blame fixed on the right quarter. I don't want any shadow of doubt about it."[16]

There is a moral idealism here that runs counter to the pragmatism of our age, which acts as if it does not matter what the truth is as long as the consequences go the way we like. Part of the beauty of Sayers's detective fiction is the moral clarity in the pursuit of truth.

In fact, it is the premier place of truth that provides the justification for Wimsey's chosen vocation as an amateur detective. This is clear from the first introduction to the independently wealthy sleuth in *Whose Body?* that truth is his primary interest over other factors like financial gain, vengeance, or a sense of guilt. If anything, Lord Peter, the unpaid sleuth, wrestles more to justify the pursuit of truth than a paid professional. As he muses about his participation in the identity of an unknown body, Peter talks with his friend Charles Parker as he wrestles with liking a businessman, Milligan, who had motive to kill a missing man and with whom Peter has become friendly:

> "S'pose old Milligan has cut Levy's throat and plugged him into the Thames. It ain't my business."
> "It's as much yours as anybody's," said Parker, "it's no better to do it for money than to do it for nothing."[17]

Peter objects to this line of thinking but eventually comes to the deeper point of self-criticism. He is pursuing truth and seeking to find the murderer because it is a sort of a game to him, which he feels is disingenuous. As he continues to discuss with Parker,

> "I don't feel I'm playing the game somehow."
> "Look here, Peter," said the other with some earnestness, "suppose you get this playing-fields-of-Eton complex out of your system once and for all. There doesn't seem to be much doubt that something unpleasant has happened to Sir Reuben Levy. Call it murder, to strengthen the argument. If Sir Reuben has been murdered, is it a game? and is it fair to treat it as a game?"
> "That's what I'm ashamed of, really," said Lord Peter. "It is a game to me, to begin with, and I go on cheerfully, and then I suddenly see that somebody is going to be hurt, and I want to get out of it."
> "Yes, yes, I know," said the detective, "but that's because you're thinking about your attitude. You want to be consistent, you want to look pretty, you want to swagger debonairly through a comedy of puppets or else to stalk magnificently through a tragedy of human sorrows and things. But that's childish. If you've any duty to society in the way of finding out the truth about murders, you must do it in any attitude that comes handy. You want to be elegant and detached? That's all right, if you find the truth out that way, but it hasn't any value in itself, you know. You want to look dignified and consistent—what's that got to do with it? You want to hunt down a murderer for the sport of the thing and then shake hands with him and say, 'Well played—hard luck—you shall have your revenge tomorrow!' Well, you can't do it like that. Life's not a football match. You want to be a sportsman. You can't be a sportsman. You're a responsible person."[18]

Even in this earliest of Sayers's stories about Lord Peter we see the commitment to truth above all. He does care despite having little reason to comply with social norms or take an interest in the goings-on of the populace (since Peter is seemingly immeasurably wealthy). But there is ambiguity because the social expectations for his position include being uninterested in matters of life for the *hoi polloi*. As Parker notes, though, he is a "responsible person," which commits him to the duty to do his bit to see truth come to light. In the fictional universe of Sayers, the pursuit of truth is a vocation even for those, like Lord Peter, for whom it is only an avocation, not a paying job.

The Vocation of the Amateur Detective

Many stories of private detectives, both professional and amateur, rely on alternating cooperation and conflict with the police as a plotline to move the story along. In *Whose Body?* Sayers introduces a comedic character, Inspector Sugg, who acts as a police foil to Wimsey. In later books, she drops the Sugg plotline and brings in the sympathetic friend, Charles Parker, who eventually becomes Peter's brother-in-law. Similarly, in Agatha Christie's novels, Poirot sometimes competes against and sometimes complements Inspector Japp, while her Miss Marple often plays across from Inspector Slack. And, of course, there is the iconic relationship between Lestrade and Holmes in the fiction of Arthur Conan Doyle. A relationship with law enforcement officials is a vital plot device because it grants access to a wider range of data and the seemingly unlimited investigative manpower of the police. Sayers explores how that public-private alliance and confusion about the nature of vocation can create social tensions when the amateur detective is found asking too many awkward questions.

Wimsey's alliance with the police in the pursuit of truth risks friendships in *The Five Red Herrings*. While on vacation recuperating from the mental strain of solving another mystery, Wimsey and Bunter can be found living in rented lodgings in Kirkudbright, Scotland. Based on the unfolding of the narrative, Wimsey has been a repeat visitor to that small town and has been largely accepted by natives and long-term residents, many of whom are artists. When the quarrelsome drunkard, Sandy Campbell, is found dead in a stream after having given most of the town's residents a reasonable motive for murder, Lord Peter first convinces the local police that the death is murder before helping them to solve the case.

The clues soon lead Wimsey to conclude Campbell's murderer is an artist, which gives him six suspects, five of whom, as the novel's title indicates, are red herrings. As he seeks to help solve the mystery, Lord Peter treats innocent people as suspects. This suspicion raises the ire of several residents of Kirkcudbright, including Gilda Farren, the weaving wife of Hugh Farren.

Campbell was seemingly infatuated with the lovely Gilda, which inspires jealousy in Hugh. Farren disappears from the region on the night he was angrily seeking after Campbell and just before the lout is found dead. Thus, he becomes an obvious suspect. Wimsey offends Gilda by first seeking to know if she had any affection for Campbell and then inveigling information of Hugh's whereabouts from her. Though Lord Peter gets the information he needs to find Farren and clear him, Gilda accuses him of violating their hospitality:

> I resent this inquisitiveness about my private affairs extremely. The police I can forgive, Lord Peter, but what business is it of yours? ... Have you ever thought how contemptible you are? We have received you here in Kirkcudbright as a friend. Everybody has shown you kindness. And you repay it by coming into the houses of your friends as a police-spy.[19]

Truth, however, is more important than being polite company, even for the aristocratic Wimsey. As a result, he continues investigating his friends and neighbors until the actual killer is found.

The pursuit of truth often puts the detective at odds with friends and relations, creating moral ambiguity of another sort as the innocent are treated as suspects, wheedled and interrogated for information that might lead to their downfall. Before the moral certainty that comes when the solution to the crime is finally solved, the detective must work through lists of possible culprits. Sometimes the list of suspects includes friends, family, or other individuals who should be considered above suspicion according to the social norms of the day. The commitment to truth, which must characterize every successful detective, will sometimes lead to uncomfortable situations and, more significantly, to moral ambiguity when the social order of relationship is breached by suspicion. The social order is challenged by the moral claims of truth in ways that can make both detective and suspect uncomfortable.

Readers see this in *The Unpleasantness at the Bellona Club* where Lord Peter comes to suspect his old friend George Fentiman. The discomfort of the investigation is broader, of course, as the club members complain about Wimsey's asking questions and interviewing the servants so the members cannot get the attention they deserve. As one club officer complains, "They find your everlasting questions an intolerable nuisance, old boy, and I can't stop them from thinking there must be something behind it."[20] In his pursuit of certain truth, Wimsey is forced to violate the social norms of his club.

But the more direct violation of social norms comes when Wimsey has to investigate George more directly since George was one of the last to see the dead man alive, was financially strapped, and stood to benefit from the dead man's estate. Wimsey demonstrates a reluctance to suspect George because of their past friendship and a sense of compassion for the younger Fentiman's mental illness, which is a product of Post-Traumatic Stress Disorder from the First World War.[21] As it turns out, George Fentiman is not the culprit, despite suspicious behavior, but the truth must be brought to light to fulfill Wimsey's vocation. This is costly to Wimsey's comfort and place among friends.

In addition to the ire of his fellow club members over the investigation, Wimsey also has to deal with Robert Fentiman's (George's older brother) violent outburst and attempt to keep Wimsey from following the line of evidence. This interchange reveals a significant difference between Wimsey's calculated suspicion and Robert Fentiman's darker concerns. The exchange demonstrates that Wimsey's main concern is truth. He says, "You think your brother murdered your grandfather. I don't know whether he did or not. But the worst thing you can do for him is try and destroy evidence. And the worst thing you can possibly do for his wife is to make her a party to anything of the sort."[22] Truth must be the central pursuit for the righteous, especially for the amateur detective.

Beyond the criminal suppression of evidence, Wimsey also faces opposition along social lines due to his preoccupation with the truth as an amateur. In *The Unpleasantness at the Bellona Club,* he is insulted by a lawyer for being an aristocrat who is meddling in the pursuit of public truth. The plot of the novel revolves around determining the time of an old man's death because a few hours either way could determine the distribution of a large fortune to one of several different beneficiaries. Peter has been asked by the Fentiman's lawyer to pursue the truth of the matter, to their benefit or detriment.[23] However, after finding facts in the case difficult to uncover, Wimsey approaches the lawyer of the other possible heir to encourage a settlement and is accused of making the suggestion for his own gain—he is accused of being a detective for hire. In part, no doubt, because of his noble title and also because of his considerable wealth, but also because the accusation of being employed to broker a resolution offends his chosen vocation of truth, Lord Peter bristles at the accusation: "You will perhaps permit *me*, Mr. Pritchard, to inform you that I am not 'employed' by anybody. I have been requested by Mr. Murbles [the Fentiman's lawyer] to ascertain the facts."[24] Having come to the point of accepting his vocation as truth-seeker, Wimsey objects to it being seen as less virtuous than it is. For Sayers, there is moral clarity in the pursuit of truth in the vocation of the amateur detective.

Sayers's connection between vocation and work is not unique to her fiction. One of Sayers's most famous essays is "Why Work?" which has become a staple in ongoing discussions of the doctrine of vocation. In this essay, she argues for truth in labor as a central goal, writing, "No piety in the worker will compensate for work that is not true to itself; for any work that is untrue to its own technique is living a lie."[25] Later, Sayers laments that the Church "has lost all sense of the fact that the living and eternal truth is expressed in work only so far as that work is true in itself, to itself, to the standards of its own technique."[26] Moreover, echoing Parker's words to Peter, she argues, "You cannot do good work if you take your mind off the work to see how the community is taking it."[27] The same themes on the importance of truthfulness and integrity in vocation come through in her play *The Zeal for Thy House*, in her nonfiction book *The Mind of the Maker*, and as a subtext woven through her detective fiction.

The intersection of truth and vocation becomes most clear in what was meant to be the last of the Wimsey novels, *Gaudy Night*. Sayers puts the connection between the pursuit of truth as a vocation and detecting in stark relief as the semi-autobiographical Harriet Vane is being challenged by a progressive professor for participating as an amateur in an investigation that saw a man hanged for murder:

> "Did you like the idea of sending a man to the dock and the gallows?" [asked Miss Burton]. ... "I have met so many murderers when visiting prisons; and most of them are very harmless, stupid people, poor creatures, when they aren't definitely pathological."
> "You might feel differently about it," said Harriet, "if you'd happened to meet the victim. They are often still stupider and more harmless than the murderers. But they don't make public appearance. ..."
> "And," went on Harriet to Miss Barton, "you don't see the murderers actively engaged in murdering. You see them when they're caught and caged and looking pathetic. But the Wilvercombe man was a cunning, avaricious brute, and quite ready to go on and do it again, if he hadn't been stopped."
> "That's an unanswerable argument for stopping them," said Phoebe, "whatever the law does with them afterwards."
> "All the same," said Miss Stevens, "isn't it a little cold-blooded to catch murderers as an intellectual exercise? It's all right for the police—it's their duty."
> "In law," said Harriet, "it is every citizen's obligation—though most people don't know that."
> "And this man Wimsey," said Miss Barton, "who seems to make a hobby of it—does he look upon it as a duty or as an intellectual exercise?"
> "I'm not sure," said Harriet, "but, you know, it was just as well for me that he did make a hobby of it. The police were wrong in my case—I don't blame them, but they were—so I'm glad it wasn't left to them."[28]

The entire scene, which comes near the beginning of Harriet's voluntary investigation into a poison pen mystery at her *alma mater*, puts a relative bookend on Sayers's vision for the centrality of truth for the amateur detective—at least insofar as the amateur detective is working in her fictional universe. There is a duty to pursue truth and justice, whether one is paid to do so or not.

Shades of Gray

The centrality of a duty to truth makes it more striking in the cases where Wimsey does not see fit to expose the truth fully. There are obvious degrees of concern for truth in Sayers's fictional world. There is ambiguity around the moral certainty of truth, which stems from the nuanced difference between warmhearted and coldhearted transgressions of the order of the universe.

For example, Wimsey feels no shame in covering up the mischievous poaching of fish to gain facts toward solving a murder.[29] In a more striking example, Peter allows a murderer's identity to be kept secret for the sake of his son and soon-to-be widow's reputation. In *Murder Must Advertise*, Wimsey goes undercover as Death Bredon to work as a junior copywriter at Pym's Publicity. Evidence discovered after the tragic death of an employee, Victor Dean, suggests that something sordid is being coordinated out of the advertising agency. As he helps to discover how seemingly harmless ads are being used to coordinate cocaine smuggling, Wimsey discovers who killed the unlikeable Victor. It is the boorish mid-level manager Tallboy, who, as it turns out, is helping to coordinate the cocaine distribution, even though he is blind to the details. However, at the end of the novel, Wimsey takes pity on Tallboy who fell into a spiral of increasing crime as a result of warmhearted extravagances. Wimsey spares him the embarrassment of a public trial and allows the drug-smuggling gang to provide justice instead. Rather than turning in Tallboy to the police, Wimsey sends him out to walk down a dark London street alone to be clubbed by one of the gang's henchmen.[30]

The ambiguity causes strain for the truth-loving detective. Though Wimsey has been deeply involved in helping break up the gang's operation, he is too depressed to celebrate when Parker calls to let him know the arrests have been made. One gathers that sorrow over the brokenness of the situation, which leaves a young father dead and the truth of his guilt hidden despite the overall resolution of a crime on a grander level, is a source of mental anguish for Lord Peter. A vocation of truth in a world that is not always consistent with the natural order of the universe is a significant burden to bear.

As Sayers wraps up *Murder Must Advertise*, we get the idea that despite the pain, she sees Lord Peter's commitment to truth as a moral duty. This comes into relief as Wimsey says farewell to a co-worker at Pym's Publicity after having his identity revealed. Miss Meteyard commends Wimsey even as she admits her own deficiency, arguing, "I shirk responsibility, that's all. I just let things rip. I don't make it my business to interfere. But I don't blame the people who do interfere. In a way, I rather admire them. They do make something, even if it's only mischief. My sort make nothing. We exploit other people's folly. It's not admirable."[31] It is better to pursue truth than to simply go along to get along. Moral certainty comes in the form of the pursuit of truth in the face of moral and social ambiguities, which is a central theme in the detective fiction of Dorothy L. Sayers.

Conclusion

Sayers's detective fiction is remarkable for its clear prose, engaging plots, and delightful character development. She wrote novels that are true to the craft of fiction, even as she catered to the market's demand for mystery stories. Sayers's novels, in particular, are enjoyable for their excellence in storytelling and language, which helps to explain their continued circulation despite their being set in an increasingly foreign Britain between the World Wars. But along with the quality of the literature itself, Sayers's mysteries also convey deep truths about the tension between moral certainty and ambiguity.

Sayers's detective fiction necessarily plays with moral ambiguity—readers are intended to forgive a little fornication when the case is about murder—but it also reveals the deeper moral certainty that all humans seem to share innately: murder is wrong; truth must be prized. Given that Sayers was also an essayist and theologically committed Christian, her detective fiction serves as an illustration of the pursuit of virtue within the Christian worldview, which is a worldview that has space to recognize moral ambiguity even while pursuing the moral clarity of the ideal good. Sayers uses an amateur detective, who needs no financial gain from his work, to demonstrate that truth is more to be prized than gold or silver. It is the proper vocation of the amateur detective to uncover truth without considering the costs and rewards because there is moral clarity in truth that points beyond the immediate human experience into greater realities of the natural order of the universe.

Notes

1 James Brabazon, *Dorothy L. Sayers* (New York: Scribner's Sons, 1981), 144.
2 Janice Brown, *The Seven Deadly Sins in the Work of Dorothy L. Sayers* (Kent: Kent State University Press, 1998), 25.

3   Aaron Elkins, "The Art of Framing Lies: Dorothy L. Sayers on Mystery Fiction," in *Dorothy L. Sayers: The Centenary Celebration*, ed. Alzina Stone Dale (London: Walker and Company, 1993), 102–3.
4   Crystal Downing, *Subversive: Christ, Culture, and the Shocking Dorothy L. Sayers* (Minneapolis, MN: Broadleaf, 2020), 76–9.
5   Dorothy L. Sayers, "Creed or Chaos?" in *The Whimsical Christian: 18 Essays* (New York: Collier, 1987), 37.
6   Ibid., 47.
7   Dorothy L. Sayers, "Christian Morality," in *The Whimsical Christian* (New York: Collier, 1987), 152.
8   Ibid., 152.
9   Brown, *The Seven Deadly Sins*, 33–9.
10 Dorothy L. Sayers, "The Other Six Deadly Sins," in *The Whimsical Christian* (New York: Collier, 1987), 157–8.
11 Crystal Downing, *Subversive*, 96–9.
12 Dorothy L. Sayers, *Murder Must Advertise* (1933; New York: Bourbon Street Book, 2014), 331–2.
13 Dorothy L. Sayers, *Clouds of Witness* (1926; New York: Bourbon Street Book, 2014), 170–1.
14 Dorothy L. Sayers, *Strong Poison* (1930; New York: Harper, 1995), 113.
15 Ibid., 175.
16 Ibid., 113–14.
17 Dorothy L. Sayers, *Whose Body?* (1923; New York: Harper, 1995), 128.
18 Ibid., 129–30.
19 Dorothy L. Sayers, *The Five Red Herrings* (1931; New York: Harper, 1995), 202–3.
20 Dorothy L. Sayers, *The Unpleasantness at the Bellona Club* (1928; New York: Harper, 1995), 83.
21 Ibid., 82.
22 Ibid., 191.
23 Ibid., 19–22.
24 Ibid., 71.
25 Dorothy L. Sayers, "Why Work?" in *Letters to a Diminished Church* (Nashville, TN: Word, 2004), 139.
26 Ibid., 139.
27 Ibid., 143.
28 Dorothy L. Sayers, *Gaudy Night* (1935; New York: Harper, 1995), 31–3.
29 Sayers, *The Five Red Herrings*, 246–50.
30 Sayers, *Murder Must Advertise*, 330–2.
31 Ibid., 336–7.

Bibliography

Brabazon, James. *Dorothy L. Sayers*. New York: Scribner's Sons, 1981.

Brown, Janice. *The Seven Deadly Sins in the Work of Dorothy L. Sayers*. Kent: Kent State University Press, 1998.

Downing, Crystal. *Subversive: Christ, Culture, and the Shocking Dorothy L. Sayers*. Minneapolis, MN: Broadleaf, 2020.

Elkins, Aaron. "The Art of Framing Lies: Dorothy L. Sayers on Mystery Fiction." In *Dorothy L. Sayers: The Centenary Celebration*, edited by Alzina Stone Dale, 99–108. London: Walker and Company, 1993.

Sayers, Dorothy L. "Christian Morality." In *The Whimsical Christian*, 151–6. New York: Collier, 1987.

Sayers, Dorothy L. *Clouds of Witness*. 1926. New York: Bourbon Street Book, 2014.

Sayers, Dorothy L. "Creed or Chaos?" In *The Whimsical Christian: 18 Essays*, 34–52. New York: Collier, 1987.

Sayers, Dorothy L. *The Five Red Herrings*. 1931. New York: Harper, 1995.

Sayers, Dorothy L. *Gaudy Night*. 1935. New York: Harper, 1995.

Sayers, Dorothy L. *Murder Must Advertise*. 1933. New York: Bourbon Street Book, 2014.

Sayers, Dorothy L. "The Other Six Deadly Sins." In *The Whimsical Christian*, 157–79. New York: Collier, 1987.

Sayers, Dorothy L. *Strong Poison*. 1930. New York: Harper, 1995.

Sayers, Dorothy L. *The Unpleasantness at the Bellona Club*. 1928. New York: Harper, 1995.

Sayers, Dorothy L. *Whose Body?* 1923. New York: Harper, 1995.

Sayers, Dorothy L. "Why Work?" In *Letters to a Diminished Church*, 125–46. Nashville, TN: Word, 2004.

14

"What if a war was what he was waiting for?": Graham Greene, Patrick Hamilton, and the Writing of Crime between the Wars

Michael Hallam

In this chapter, I will argue that a strand of British interwar writing, exemplified by the important and widely read work of Patrick Hamilton and Graham Greene—in particular Hamilton's *Rope* (1929) and *Hangover Square* (1941) and Greene's *Brighton Rock* (1938)—uses the popular conventions and techniques of crime fiction to pose the sort of serious moral and philosophical questions more traditionally associated with the best literary fiction. Gill Plain suggests that one essential function of crime fiction, particularly detective fiction, is "confronting and taming the monstrous."[1] I will argue here that Hamilton's and Greene's works simultaneously parody and exploit the conventions of the crime thrillers and detective stories that were so much in vogue in the interwar period, and that they do so with the intent of addressing the realities of violence that the popular crime novel, with its ultimately triumphant detective figure, seemed to have domesticated and "tamed." The examination of "evil" and the moral and political ambiguities offered by crime narratives is also, I will suggest, strongly bounded by the specific historical experience generated by the period between the World Wars. Marina Mackay has recently argued that "there are few corners in the 1930s novel into which the threat of violent upheaval does not intrude."[2] Hamilton's and Greene's works are especially colored, I will argue, not only by the knowledge of the enormous scale of death and destruction caused by the First World War (both writers were children during the War) but also by the criminal and violent potential of the new forms of politics represented by the growth of Fascist parties in the late 1920s and 1930s. For Hamilton, in particular, "fascism" is often used not just in a literal sense (plenty of his characters are admirers of Hitler) but also as a metonym for violent crime and murder—a growing social problem in interwar Britain—and perhaps more unusually for a range of bullying attitudes he felt was part of the British psyche, and class system, in the period. Both writers use the destabilizing potential of crime narratives to raise difficult questions about the nature of order and disorder—questions which can have a theological, political, and sociological dimension. Specifically, both writers seem concerned by the ways in which people can treat each other as mere objects vulnerable to violent manipulation—just as a detective story might use a corpse as a plot device—and their texts question whether the instrumentality of this type of thinking is part of a permanently flawed human condition or a characteristic of the specific time in which they are living. As Valentine Cunningham persuasively argues, the "torrentially popular cult" of the crime novel in the interwar years could be seen as a condition of *post* and *pre*war psychology: "It was easy, in fact, to feel that war's parenthesis marks had expanded so as to join up, close a circle, and so utterly smother and imprison the period and all its doings as a condition of violence."[3]

The Popularity of Crime in the Interwar Period

In the 1920s and 1930s, the status of crime fiction in British culture was high. This was the Golden Age of detective fiction in which Agatha Christie and Dorothy L. Sayers were household names.[4] Not only did detective novels have a large readership, but critics and commentators of the interwar period, such as Marjorie Nicholson, often emphasized the "genre's status as the popular reading matter most beloved of intellectuals."[5] T. S. Eliot's praise for Victorian crime fiction, and in particular his 1929 panegyric for the Sherlock Holmes stories—"every writer owes something to Holmes"—is often cited in writing about detective fiction.[6] Yet, some intellectuals had reservations about quite how fashionable crime fiction was becoming in the years following the First World War. Virginia Woolf was uncomfortable that commercially successful fiction (she uses the term "middlebrow") could generally conform to genre conventions but also have some pretensions to literariness. This fiction was subversive because, in Woolf's opinion, it was "betwixt and between" the more stable and easily classifiable categories of highbrow and lowbrow literature and had a broad appeal that undermined the traditional distinctions between literary and popular fiction and indeed between social classes. Woolf's essay "Middlebrow" (written as a letter in 1932 and published in 1942) suggests that fiction that simultaneously panders to lowbrow and highbrow tastes is almost as duplicitous as a double-agent in a spy thriller: "The middlebrow ... saunters now on this side of the hedge, now on that, in pursuit of no single object, neither art itself nor life itself, but both mixed indistinguishably, and rather nastily, with money, fame, power, or prestige."[7] Woolf's essay reveals how much the period's committed highbrows were preoccupied by the cultural "problem" of middlebrow fiction, as well as how, as Isobel Maddison puts it, "cultural anxiety sometimes tips over into intellectual snobbery."[8] The fact that the Golden Age of detective fiction was a commercial as well as a cultural phenomenon meant that, as D. J. Taylor suggests, the unease about the new middlebrow was not confined to just "Bloomsbury and Mrs. [Q. D.] Leavis" but was also felt by

> book-trade insiders, distressed by what they saw as a blurring of lines between critic and publisher, writer and reviewer, a tearing down of fences that had the effect of hoodwinking the impressionable reader into grotesque lapses of taste and annoying the serious writer who had little respect for the judgement of critics who reviewed his books.[9]

As British publishers became increasingly professional in pursuing advertising and marketing strategies in this period, including the use of uncritical newspaper "puff pieces" that Taylor refers to, it was possible that the industry was not just catering for middlebrow taste but helping to *create* it.

Another important issue in the cultural debate about the popularity of crime and detective fiction was the prominence of lethal violence in so many novels of the period. What did it say about the "political unconscious" of the 1920s and 1930s that its reading public wanted to read so consistently about murder? Even if the killing occurs "off-stage" or before the narrative begins, the plot of many Golden Age detective stories turns on an act of murder rather than on the theft of jewels or blackmail plots of much Victorian and Edwardian crime fiction. It could be argued that this was a straightforward development of the genre, that the pleasure of solving the "whodunit" puzzle relies on the central transgression being serious enough to warrant the reader's sustained concentration on clues within the narrative, but several contemporary writers sought a more psychological and historicized explanation. Edmund Wilson suggested the popularity of the crime story could be seen as "reflecting a collective desire to exorcise a sense of guilt arising from the war,"[10] and Wyndham Lewis, as Cunningham explains, "repeatedly linked the First World War and the prevailing political destructive element with the thriller's world."[11] For Lewis, the cult of this new type of crime writing was tied to the psychological legacy of the war recently ended and the anticipation of the next, a collective "'blood psychosis' helping prepare for the next gigantic blood-letting."[12] The violence of crime writing was part of a larger "working through" of the cataclysmic violence of the First World War but also a mirror to the various social and political aggressions of the late 1920s and 1930s—political polarization, the emergence of fascism, the rise of violent and organized crime, and what Lewis saw as a gangster mentality permeating society and validated by fashionable culture.[13]

Murder had been, of course, a staple subject of popular writing in its various descriptions—"lowbrow," "sensation," "pulp fiction"—since the late eighteenth century. But in the 1920s and 1930s, violence and potential homicide were foregrounded in a very wide range of narrative styles and settings. The comfortable country-house environment of an Agatha Christie novel bears little resemblance to, say, James Curtis's gritty depictions of crime in working-class London in novels like *The Gilt Kid* (1936) and *They Drive by Night* (1938), yet both these interwar writers create narrative situations in which characters are vulnerable to sudden violence. To varying degrees, the threat and enactment of violence is also an element of the "war stories" that competed with mystery novels at the top of bestseller lists at the end of the 1920s.

Robert Graves's memoir *Good-Bye to All That* (1929), for example, combines moments of recollection that are solemn but also vividly aesthetic—"The colour of the dead faces changed from white to yellow-grey, to red, to purple, to green, to black, to slimy"[14]—to an anecdotal form that uses theatrical and comic effects in its treatment of violence and death.[15] There is some similarity in this regard between Graves's work and the Golden Age detective stories, especially Christie's Poirot novels, which often introduce an element of levity or even light farce. Indeed, Chris Baldick suggests that the "most important" transformation of reading and writing tastes in the period was shown not by the persistence of murder in the plotting but rather "the widespread tone of frivolity and facetious high spirits in the handling of both murder and detection."[16] (144). Perhaps rendering death as a lightly comic affair was a kind of escapist coping mechanism from the recent past. Samuel Hynes's *A War Imagined* (1990), for example, makes a strong case for thinking about the literature of the 1920s and 1930s as being "haunted" by the First World War, even when the work does not directly represent or even mention the War. Some crime writers, such as Dorothy L. Sayers, did make war experience an explicit part of characterization and plot. Sayers's detective, Lord Peter Wimsey, is generally a more serious character than Christie's Poirot. Although he possesses some of the affectations of an aristocratic playboy, his status as a shell-shocked veteran of the War provides the moral force for his sleuthing; he is working, as Charles Rzepka puts it, to "make the society [soldiers] died to defend worth their sacrifice."[17] Rzepka suggests that the Wimsey characterization and narratives are subtler than some previous critics have allowed. In particular, he argues that Wimsey is not so much a caricature of a superficial twenties aristocrat but rather a way for Sayers to "rehabilitate the idea of social responsibility for her own 'lost generation' by embodying it in a member of England's ostensibly least responsible and currently most superfluous class."[18] The argument is persuasive and shows how the sort of middlebrow novels that Woolf disliked could imbue rather clichéd characters and situations with an element of social and political commentary. However, Wimsey's upper-class dilettantism (his name, of course, puns on "whimsy") and enjoyment of crime as a kind of puzzle that could be measured in aesthetic terms still suggests, in my view, that classic interwar crime fiction was sublimating the raw experience of the First World War—the violence, the killing, the grief—into more ritualized and palatable forms and generally attempting to *contain* rather than confront the potential meanings of its dark subject matter.

There are several writers of the 1920s and 1930s who productively combine genre writing and literary fiction to create a more complicated picture of violence and its moral implications.[19] Patrick Hamilton and Graham Greene are, I believe, particularly significant examples of writers using the crime novel in ambitious and reflective ways. Their interaction with popular culture, especially the atmosphere and narrative world of thrillers, is self-conscious and shaped by the interwar critical debates about literary value. In an unusual step for a major writer, Greene famously labeled some of his novels "entertainments" to indicate that they were (merely) a thriller rather than one of his more literary and psychologically rich "novels"—a division that has often underpinned critical discussion of his work.[20] Hamilton gained significant fame and financial reward for his stage plays, especially *Rope* (1929) and *Gas Light* (1938)—from which the term *gaslighting* derives—but considered his less well-known novels more "valuable." Hamilton writes, for example, in a preface to *Rope*, "I should like to say that *Rope* is not intended to be a highbrow play—and that, supposing my ordinary writing to be designated as highbrow, then it bears no relation to the rest of my writing."[21] This self-consciousness about popular, or at the least non-highbrow culture, makes the use of it in these writers' work particularly interesting. It suggests a tension in their novels between an "authentic" evocation of the style, atmosphere, and setting of thrillers and something which is more like parody or pastiche. Writing, to use Woolf's phrase, "betwixt and between" literary modes is perhaps a way for the novelist to exploit the crime genre's power to create a symbolic world of right and wrong, order and disorder, whilst simultaneously exposing the genre's falsities, in particular its expectations of resolution and moral certainty.

There are two further features of Hamilton and Greene's explorations of crime writing that make their work significant. First, both Hamilton's *Hangover Square* (1941) and Greene's *Brighton Rock* (1938), as Stephen Knight explains, "strongly emphasize the consciousness of the criminal."[22] This was not entirely new, of course, but it aligns their work with important antecedents in the tradition of the psychological novel—Dostoyevsky's *Crime and Punishment* (1866), for example—rather than the detective-centered narratives of their period. *Hangover Square*'s George Bone and *Brighton Rock*'s Pinkie are deeply complex and ambiguous central characters in whom the reader is invited to take an almost psychiatric interest (indeed, *Hangover Square* is subtitled "The Man with Two Minds"). This focus on the subjectivity of the malefactor makes it hard for the reader to make clear moral judgments; their motivations, albeit sometimes obscure even to the characters themselves, are at least made more visible and contextualized by "circumstances" in ways that generally elude conventional thrillers. Second, both writers' works interact not just with the conventions of crime writing in the period but also with the cinema's growing influence on interwar popular culture, most especially how film in the age of the "talkie" was representing crime and wrongdoing. Laura Marcus describes how Greene's "involvement with cinema"—he was a film critic through the 1920s and 1930s, a prolific script-writer, and experimented with cinematic techniques in his novels—"was perhaps the most extensive of any twentieth-century British writer."[23] Greene generally embraced cinema's popularity, writing in 1937 that cinema "has got to appeal to millions; we have got to accept its popularity as a virtue, not turn away from it as a vice."[24] Later, he differentiated literature and film by suggesting that an audience's approval at the cinema was a way of measuring quality in a way that book sales were not: "A good film is seldom a flop. Whereas a book can be very good and still be a flop."[25] Hamilton was apparently less convinced by cinema's cultural importance, writing in 1948, "Films are fundamentally no good because they are ephemeral, *ephemeral*. You must write either *printed books* or *printed plays*."[26] But on a formal and thematic level, his work is also infiltrated by the new "ways of seeing," and indeed hearing, that cinema had popularized. *Hangover Square*, for example, uses an extended film metaphor to describe the texture of Bone's bipolar moods: "Life, in fact, which had been for him a moment ago a 'talkie,' had all at once become a silent film."[27]

These different formal issues—the self-conscious use of genre, the emphasis on the criminal's psychology, the influence of film—show how these writers were not just interested in exploring the meanings of crime *per se*, as a sociologist might, but also in the narrativization of crime, and indeed the potential interdependence of "real life" crime and crime storytelling.

Rope and the "Decline of the English Murder"

The relationship between crime and narrative is particularly pertinent to Patrick Hamilton's *Rope* as the stage play was loosely based on a "true story." First performed in 1929, the same year in which Graves's memoir was published, *Rope* was a critical and popular hit that played on contemporary fears about the potential moral nihilism of the postwar generation. It draws on the infamous Leopold and Loeb murder case of 1924 in which two American students, excited by their reading of Nietzsche and feeling invulnerable to authority, attempted to commit the proverbial "perfect murder" by killing a boy they selected at random (a fourteen-year-old called Bobby Franks—they bungled the cover-up and were quickly identified by the police). Leopold and Loeb were Jewish and were suspected of being lovers which added to the sensational nature of the case; the media reporting of the murder and the trial often linked their Jewishness and homosexuality to their murderous actions: "Their actions were not those of college kids who happened to commit a terrible act but those of persons who were completely anomalous and utterly foreign."[28] In *Rope*, two young friends, Brandon and Granillo, murder their fellow student, Ronald Kentley, purely for the "sake of danger and the sake of killing."[29] The play does not make much of the potential homosexuality of Brandon and Granillo—or indeed of potential Jewishness—but this would have been an important subtext for contemporary audiences familiar with the Leopold and Loeb case. At the start of the play, it is hinted that the corpse is being placed in a chest. The victim's family and some friends, unaware yet that Ronald is dead, are then invited to take a meal on the chest during a dinner party: "have we not already agreed the entire beauty and piquancy of the evening will reside in the party itself?"[30] Rupert Cadell, a former tutor of the three students, takes on the role of detective and discovers the body at the end of the play. Earlier in the evening, however, Cadell has enjoyed mildly scandalizing the other guests by dismissing redundant notions of "herd" morality such as the Ten Commandments. A veteran of the War, Cadell echoes the fashionable language of late 1920s "disillusion": "It is simply a question of scale. You, my friends, have, paradoxically, a horror of murder on a small scale, a veneration for it on a large. That is the difference between what we call murder and war."[31] But by the end of the narrative, *Rope* dramatizes the hypocrisy of Cadell. His sense of traditional morality no longer fitting a postwar world, his intellectual interest in Nietzschean ideas of the superior individual, the "superman" who can "live freely," and his pontificating about the appeal of motiveless murder—or rather, a "murder of vanity"[32]—have helped provide a rationale for the younger men to act out their murderous fantasy: "You have brought up my own words in my face."[33] At the play's conclusion, Cadell's *volte-face* allows him to passionately denounce the "cruel and scheming pleasure" of the killing, the "sin," "blasphemy," and "bad jest" of Brandon and Granillo's ruse with the chest, and suggests they will now face the retributive justice of the Old Testament that he had earlier dismissed: "It is not what *I* am going to do, Brandon. It is what society is going to do. ... You are going to hang, you swine! Hang!—Both of you!—Hang!"[34] Hamilton's insistence that *Rope* was only a "sheer thriller," "first class" dramatically but "ideologically ... nothing,"[35] underestimates how effectively the play articulates the problematic moral environment of the interwar years. The play certainly exploits the conventions of popular crime culture, utilizing the clue-puzzle element and potential for dramatic irony inherent in narratives of detection, as well as echoing some of the melodramatic and deliberately retrograde language of the form.[36] But it also comments on the origins of a "modern" sensibility regarding crime and wrongdoing not only by excoriating the hedonism and nihilism of the younger "lost generation" but also by exposing how the jaded cynicism and intellectualizing of a disillusioned war veteran could not provide the kind of authoritative moral education that might have been possible before the First World War.

Even as it makes a significant contribution to interwar popular culture, *Rope* manages to distance itself from that culture. Hamilton saw the violence of the "ordinary thriller and Grand Guignolism of this decade" as "aimless and sickening."[37] *Rope* portrays no actual violence on the stage and the contents of the chest are not exposed; the horror of Rupert's discovery is registered only by the expression and movement of the actor, as indicated by the stage directions: *The thing has obviously appalled him more than he could have imagined.*[38] Of course, keeping both the crime and its physical results hidden from the audience heightens the dramatic tension—the play takes place in real time with the chest constantly in view of the audience—but it also suggests that the play's meanings operate on the level of ideology as well as "sensation." The play also takes aim at what Hamilton saw as the vapidity of the dominating mass medium of the cinema: "That other film was good though, wasn't it?"—"Yes, wasn't it good?"—"Yes, it was good, wasn't it?"[39] The balancing act, between using the techniques of the crime genre whilst simultaneously repudiating the excesses of its "lowbrow" appeal, is carefully managed in Hamilton's play, and this was the main reason the writer was deeply unhappy with the sensationalizing aspects of the 1948 film version of *Rope*. Directed by Alfred Hitchcock and famous for being shot in what appeared one continuous take, the film opens with the murder scene itself along with a series of running jokes about the killing ("I could strangle you!"). Worst of all, to Hamilton's perspective, Hitchcock transplanted the setting to New York and charged the relationship between the two murderers with homoeroticism, therefore making explicit the dangerous subtext of the play that Hamilton had preferred to leave submerged, the connection between, as Sean French puts it, "forbidden acts of sexuality and the forbidden act of violence, the complicity of lovers and the complicity of criminals."[40] The issue, of course, is differing attitudes toward *representation*: leaving the more sensational elements hidden, as it were, in the locked chest, the play's meanings are more indeterminate and open to interpretation. Opening the chest, as Hitchcock's film does, might resolve some of these tensions, and in Hamilton's view pander to the prurient curiosity of the audience, but it might also allow the film to get closer to the transgressive enigma—the character and relationship of the two murderers—at the heart of the narrative.

Hamilton's antipathy toward the more overt style of storytelling found in films was shared by other writers of the period. In his short essay "Decline of the English Murder" (1946), George Orwell suggests that the "false values of the American film" were having a deleterious effect on murder itself. In the mode of Thomas De Quincey's "On Murder Considered as One of the Fine Arts" (1827), Orwell's essay ironically conflates actual murder and its narrativization. Famous Victorian and Edwardian murders "have given the greatest amount of pleasure to the British public," because of a "strong family resemblance" which allowed them to be "made into novels and re-hashed over and over again by the Sunday papers."[41] These murders provide narrative satisfaction and closure because their motivations were knowable and recognizably rooted in a stable social system:

> In the last analysis he should commit murder because this seems to him less disgraceful, and less damaging to his career, than being detected in adultery. With this kind of background, a crime can have dramatic and even tragic qualities which make it memorable and excite pity for both victim and murderer.[42]

Orwell contrasts such "traditional" English murder with the "cleft chin murder" of 1944 in which an American army deserter and a young English waitress meet in a café and form an instant "Bonnie and Clyde" relationship, committing acts of violence on randomly selected victims and finally killing a taxi driver "almost [by] chance."[43] This murder, Orwell suggests, "has no depth of feeling in it."[44] Orwell's essay is clearly part of a wider discourse regarding the ongoing Americanization of British culture, of which the seemingly arbitrary nature of gangster violence was a visible element. By the end of the Second World War, American popular culture was firmly embedded in Britain. Sales of American authors were high and the hard-boiled detective fiction of a writer like Dashiell Hammett—with its urban settings, use of slang, and stylized noir—made Golden Age detective novels seem outdated, even quaint. But the earlier *Rope*, based on a real American crime with "no depth of feeling," is part of this discourse, too. Like Orwell's essay, *Rope* explores the conflation between crime and narrative satisfaction.[45] Halfway through the evening, as Cadell becomes more suspicious, he teases Brandon about his adolescent reading and "chest complex": "Whatever the story was—piratical, detective, murder, adventure or ghost—it always contained a marvelous *dénouement* with a bloody chest containing corpses. You had a perfect mania for it, don't you remember?"[46] *Rope* is an important text in interwar crime writing because it speculates on whether the attractiveness of "meaningless" violence in the period (particularly to the younger generation who had just "missed out" on fighting in the War) was not just being reconstituted in crime narratives but *shaped* by them—a dramatization of the prevailing "blood psychosis." In *Rope* (and it is important it is a play rather than one of Hamilton's novels), the act of murder is a kind of *performance*, and thus both formally and thematically the text addresses the nihilistic impulses that were challenging conventional morality between the wars.

Hangover Square

The younger writers who emerged in the late 1920s and 1930s were, of course, children during the First World War; Hamilton and Greene, for example, were both fourteen at the War's end in November 1918. Discussion of the interwar period has noted the psychological issues that this generation might have faced absorbing the violence of the War, mainly via stories and propaganda, but without the outlet of direct experience at the front line experienced by individuals sometimes just a few years or months older.[47] Recalling his youth in *Ways of Escape* (1980), Greene suggested, "We were a generation brought up on adventure stories who had missed the enormous disillusionment of The First World War, so we went looking for adventure."[48] Several other male interwar writers framed the issue as a problematic gap in the formation of their masculine identity. Orwell suggested that those who "had been 'just too young,' became conscious of the vastness of the experience they had missed. You felt yourself a little less than a man, because you had missed it"[49]; Christopher Isherwood described being

> like most of my generation ... obsessed by a complex of terrors and longings connected with the idea "War." "War," in this purely neurotic sense, meant The Test. The test of your courage, of your maturity, of your sexual prowess: "Are you really a Man?" Subconsciously, I believe, I longed to be subjected to this test.[50]

As Marina Mackay explains, this "sense of misdirected masculinity, or middle-class manliness with nowhere to go in this pretended peacetime, is common in 1930s writing,"[51] and it provides one important sociological frame for attempting to understand both George Harvey Bone, in Hamilton's *Hangover Square*, and *Brighton Rock*'s teenage gangster Pinkie, the "Boy" who is aggressively virginal but also a killer.

Hangover Square is a crime thriller but one that has a "Condition of England" dimension—George Bone's initials, G.B, are a clear state-of-the nation hint—combined with a case study of damaged male psychology. In his mid-thirties, unemployed and an alcoholic, Bone's sense of himself as a sexual failure and social misfit, even a "nonentity,"[52] is inscribed with a sense of family loss or remembered trauma that is never made explicit in the narrative but which the reader assumes is connected to his childhood during the War. He has no real sense of purpose except that provided by his obsession with the unobtainable *femme fatale* Netta Longdon, a "brooding" and "self-absorbed" failed actress who manipulates Bone's affections and takes a "cold delight in his humiliation."[53] He is teased and bullied by Netta and the feckless group of London drinkers who surrounds her, but he also feels trapped in this corrosive lifestyle—dependent on drink, infatuated and unable to move: "Netta. The tangled net of her hair—the dark net—the brunette. The net in which he was caught. ... He was netted in hate just as he was netted in love."[54] The novel is set in "darkest Earl's Court" in 1939 (it begins in December 1938), and Bone's personal stasis is therefore set against the larger backdrop of a country waiting for war. Indeed, Bone feels that war might actually be what he needs to free himself:

> A filthy idea, but what if a war was what he was waiting for? That might put a stop to it all. They might get him—he might be conscripted away from his drinks, and smokes, and Netta. At times he could find it in his heart to hope for a war—bloody business as it all was.[55]

The nexus between war, sex, and masculinity has been a theme in British literature since around the time of the First World War, especially in stories inflected by Freudian ideas. We might think, for example, of the connection made between libido and violence in D. H. Lawrence's story "England, My England" (1922). But *Hangover Square* signals throughout that Bone's final enactment of violence will not be a liberation from the "net" in which he is trapped into a more fully realized manhood but ultimately an act of self-destruction. This is partly because, in an unusual and darkly comic plot device, Bone is not only an alcoholic but also has a split personality. His "normal" self is motivated by finally "possessing" Netta—"Not necessarily to sleep with her—just to have a look at, to talk to, quietly"[56] or perhaps "make love to her like a man."[57] He also experiences sudden "dead moods" in which he behaves like a "somnambulist" or "automaton"[58] and in which he has one compulsion: "To kill Netta Longdon. ... He was going to kill her, and then he was going to Maidenhead, where he would be happy."[59] Maidenhead, a small market town in the South of England, is a place where Bone remembers feeling content during a holiday with his sister Ellen: "the peace, Ellen, the river, the quiet glass of beer, the white flannels, the ripples of the water."[60] Bone is shown as a man whose intrinsically gentle and almost childish nature is out of step with the times in which he is living; at school he was a "noticeably uncruel boy in that cruel and resounding atmosphere."[61] He is psychologically disturbed by the insecurity of modern life in Britain in the era of global war and the bullying and casual violence they seem to have ushered in. His "dead moods," announced by a loud "*Click!*"[62] in his brain, are compared to "watching a talking film, and all at once the sound-track had failed. The figures on the screen continued to move, to behave more or less logically; but they were figures in a new, silent, indescribably eerie world"[63]—an evocative simile for contemporary readers who would have witnessed the recent transition from silent to sound cinema. His desire to kill the person he believes is trapping him—even Netta's physical presence was "a halo, a field of physical and magnetic influence"[64]—to enable him to return to a site of childhood *innocence*, is of course highly paradoxical and, to the reader at least, doomed to fail. But by the end of the novel, Bone has indeed murdered Netta as well as her "scornful, ultra-masculine" friend Peter.[65] On one level, this has seemed a foregone conclusion to the reader who has been given access to Bone's violent fantasies, but this feeling of inevitability has also been comically undercut by comic prevarication: "It was too cold to kill Netta yet. That sounded silly, but it was a fact."[66] As Lee Horsley argues, Bone's vacillation can be read as a wider comment on British national identity before the War: "Bone's 'shilly-shallying' about killing Netta and Peter is, like the delays and evasions in Greene, an image of the state of mind of decent, kindly Britain in the aftermath of Munich."[67] The deferral of forceful action ends for both Bone and "kindly Britain" on September 3, 1939. Minutes before Neville Chamberlain announces the "state of war" between Britain and Germany on the radio, Bone overcomes his apparent harmlessness and indecision by drowning Netta in a bathtub and then killing Peter with a single blow from his golf club. The linking of the new war to violent, personal fulfilment is made bathetic by Bone's befuddled and naïve interpretation of his actions and ultimately the novel suggests that enacting fantasies of violence is not cathartic but self-destructive. At the end of *Hangover Square*, Bone kills himself in the rural town of Maidenhead after realizing that it was not the idyll of innocence he imagined but suffers much the same problems of modernity as everywhere else.

After the double murder, the net metaphor that has run through the narrative is actualized as Bone ties the dead bodies and the furniture in the room together so that the corpses are enmeshed in an intricate crisscrossing network: "A real net. Netta. Poor Netta—don't worry—nothing should be disturbed: nothing should be disturbed until the police came."[68] As with *Rope* (indeed, Robert Browning's poem "Porphyria's Lover" [1836] which seems to be a thematic influence), the murder scene becomes a kind of ritualized performance in which the male protagonist is attempting to gain control through violence. The misogyny inherent in these male fantasies is made quite overt in the text. After Bone has been humiliated by Netta and her cronies (he's been left to pay a hotel bill), he thinks: "They were a dirty lot, and Netta was the dirtiest. He felt he would like to beat her up, do her some physical damage, smash her face and tell her to go to hell. He could understand men wanting to hit women."[69] Yet, the novel dramatically challenges the normal moral judgments we would expect to make of these desires; rather than condemning Bone, the reader is encouraged to see his point of view, indeed to sympathize with it. Introducing a 1972 edition of the novel, J. B. Priestley suggests that despite Bone's "idle and stupid existence," his "schizophrenia," and his acts of murder, it is "impossible to deny him our sympathy."[70] This is not simply because he is the victim of bullying but because his bullies, Netta and Peter, seem to "represent some principle of evil."[71] Peter is a fascist who "desired to single himself out from the herd and wear a 'uniform.'"[72]; Netta was "supposed to dislike fascism, to laugh at it, but actually she liked it enormously."[73] She wears her own sexual attractiveness "as a murderous utensil with which she might wound indiscriminately"[74] and, Bone thinks, is "probably, sexually stimulated" by the macho iconography of fascism: "the uniforms, the guns, the breeches, the boots, the swastikas, the shirts."[75] Their fascism is not really ideological—they were supposed to laugh at "people with strong opinions"[76]—but takes the form of a general fascination with cruelty and the belief that strong people should dominate the weak: "... she was dimly aware of the class content of all this: she connected it with her own secret social aspirations and she would have liked to have seen something of the same sort in her own country."[77] Bone is treated like an object to be exploited—"If you're *going* to make use of me, you might give me *something* in return—a little kindness of some sort"[78]—and they show a disregard for human life (Peter has carelessly killed a man whilst drink driving).[79] The novel suggests that the forces of evil, for which "fascism" stands as a metonym in the text, might not just be outside the country, to be confronted in the coming war, but also exist at home, residing in the snobbery, casual viciousness, and apathy that surround the "netted" Bone. One crucial irony of the text is that these insights are focalized through the "damaged" mind of Bone who, outside of his "dead moods," is fully aware of Netta's problematic nature and begins himself to make the connections between her "loathsomeness of character"[80] and deeper ethical questions: "You *must* be human somewhere."[81] It is the brilliantly painted mental worlds of Bone's conflicted existence—self-destructive and vulnerable yet straining to do something worthwhile and good—that make *Hangover Square* such a compelling account of crime in the 1930s, raising, if not resolving, the central moral question of the novel: do the malevolent and dehumanizing attitudes of Peter and Netta finally justify Bone's violence, is their killing just one more incarnation of the period's "necessary murder"?[82]

Brighton Rock

To escape claustrophobic London and "go to Brighton with Netta" is, for Bone, the "old dream of dreams,"[83] even though he is self-conscious about taking her to a "seaside town with a reputation."[84] Brighton, about an hour's train ride from London, was a popular seaside resort in the Victorian era. By the 1930s, it was firmly associated in the public imagination with the pursuit of pleasure, both licit and illicit. The town's reputation for potential criminality was confirmed by the sensational "Brighton Trunk Murders" of 1934 in which the body parts of two murdered women were discovered in abandoned trunks in the town, including one at Brighton's train station.[85] Hamilton understood the social dynamics of the town very well—he spent part of his childhood in nearby Hove—and Brighton is the setting of *The West Pier* (1952), his later novel about a local conman. But it is not surprising that Greene, too, would be drawn to the "seedy" seaside for his *Brighton Rock*—"why did I ever popularize that … adjective?"[86]—a novel which in its very first sentence would play on public recognition of Brighton as "The Queen of Slaughtering Places": "Hale knew, before he had been in Brighton three hours, that they meant to murder him."[87]

Greene's account of the novel's setting in *Ways of Escape* (1980) reveals some of the aesthetic tensions in a work that combines detective fiction, allusions to "real life" crime, and an ambiguous "moral fable of sin and damnation."[88] Responding to critics who had suggested that by creating an outpost of "Greeneland" in Southern England he had overplayed the danger and criminality of Brighton, Greene suggests that many of the places and crimes he describes "certainly did exist."[89] But he also admits that it belonged to an "imaginary geographic region"[90] and that his desire for verisimilitude was thwarted by the emergence of a more psychological narrative: "I had every intention of describing it, but it was as though my characters had taken the Brighton *I* knew into their consciousness and transformed the whole picture."[91] The sense of characters growing to dominate an author's intentions is a common enough explanation for writers when discussing their own work. But Greene's account does hint again at the self-consciousness with which certain interwar writing used the conventions of genre fiction, and popular culture more generally, and how this complicated the "realism" of their work. Greene had originally conceived of *Brighton Rock* as "an Entertainment," changing his mind before publication and then much later attempting to distance the text from genre fiction: "The first fifty pages of *Brighton Rock* are all that remain of the detective story; they would irritate me, if I dared to look at them now."[92] Brian Diemert argues that Greene's claim is "disingenuous" because the detective story is "woven into the fabric of the novel," including in the way it thematizes reading as a form of detection.[93] Not only does a detective story underpin the plot, which revolves around Ida Arnold's dogged pursuit of Fred Hale's murderer, but the entire social world of the novel is shaped by modern "entertainments"—advertising, drinking, gambling, music, film. In ways that articulate some of the main cultural and political preoccupations of the period, the characters' experiences are shown as strongly mediated by their interactions with this popular culture. The sentimental and sexualized singing of "the crooner" at the dancehall is "like a dictator announcing victory" and even Pinkie, with all his loathing of earthly pleasure, "surrendering himself to the huge brazen suggestion."[94] As Laura Marcus's reading of this scene suggests, "the seductions of popular culture and the mass media ... had become inextricably linked to mass culture, propaganda, and the words of 1930s dictators."[95] Greene's novel, like *Hangover Square*, suggests that the era's language, demagoguery, and politics of power were infiltrating all levels of British society. The potential for crime fiction to dramatize "secret" operations of power, for example, is embodied in *Brighton Rock*'s Mr. Colleoni, the gang-leader who controls his crime empire from a suite in a grand hotel:

> [S]itting there in the rich Victorian room, with the gold lighter in his pocket and the cigar-case on his lap, he looked as a man might look who owned the whole world, the whole visible world that is, the case registers and policemen and prostitutes, Parliament and the laws which say "this is right and this is wrong."[96]

The dominating presence of Colleoni provides a sense of latent corruption running through every level of the state. Because Colleoni himself is tipped to become a Conservative MP, Pinkie is not just up against a rival gangster but an entire apparatus of money, influence, and even "the Law." That Colleoni is an Italian (he's partly based on the real-life gang-leader Charles "Darby" Sabini, who ran a protection racket at Brighton racecourse) emphasizes Mafia connections but would also chime with contemporary readers worried about the "underground" influence of foreign individuals subverting the state. For example, a couple of years after the publication of *Brighton Rock*, Italian nationals living in Britain were interned for periods at the start of the Second World War. In the original 1938 British edition, Colleoni, his henchmen, and female hangers-on are Jewish and are described in disparaging ways—"old Semitic face," "little bitches"—until Greene removes the Jewishness and anti-Semitic descriptions after the Second World War.[97] The feeling of wealthy and powerful "outsiders" subverting British justice and lording it over the local boy gangster is emphasized even by the hotel in which they are residents, the suggestively named Cosmopolitan, where suites are designed in foreign styles but Pinkie and Rose are refused a room on their wedding night. As Cedric Watts suggests, "The Cosmopolitan is true to its name: it has a Louis Seize Writing Room, a Pompadour Boudoir, an American Bar—the aliens are invading Brighton."[98] Pinkie himself, however, is both an insider and an outsider—not welcome at the Cosmopolitan hotel but not entirely at home in his hometown. He is a local, striving to become the dominant criminal player in Brighton, but as a working-class Catholic he is also an outsider, not only to the traditional networks of British power but even to other members of his local community. As he competes for position and status with the expatriate Colleoni, Pinkie's motivations, the novel suggests, are more profound and mysterious than the sordid gangster world he inhabits.

Indeed, it is the characterization of Pinkie and his Catholicism where *Brighton Rock* really transgresses against the normal paradigms and presentations of morality found in conventional crime fiction. The inclusion of overtly Catholic characters is used by Greene, on a social level, to explore the equivocal status of Catholics living in Britain and, on a literary level, to provide a metaphysical dimension to crime writing; as Greene wrote in a 1938 article, "Murder, if you are going to take it seriously at all, is a religious subject."[99] Both Pinkie and Rose—the girl he is eventually forced to marry to prevent her from testifying against him—grew up in a Catholic ghetto in Brighton (around the Carlton Hill area).[100] When Pinkie asks Rose whether she is a Catholic, he uses the phrase "a Roman."[101] with overtones of foreignness, even foreign allegiance. Their childhood experience of Catholic church services, a "whole lost world"[102] of music, incense, and ceremony, and their belief in things "[l]ike Hell,"[103] affiliates the characters together as social outsiders in a modern and relativistic world. Crucially, Pinkie's theological vision also deeply inflects the language, imagery, and "feeling" of the novel. Colleoni looks like he owns the world, but only the "visible world." As he conducts his grim business dealings, Pinkie always feels the pressure of the *invisible* world, not as intimation but as reality: Eternity, Hell, though not really Heaven: "Heaven was a word: hell was something he could trust."[104] The narrative voice, which often employs aphoristic statements with a biblical tone and rhythm—"This was not one of the damned: he watched with horrified fascination: this was one of the saved"[105]—is very often echoing Pinkie's conceptions and angry religiosity, his sense of modernity as something degraded, over-sexualized, and tawdry. Ida does not believe in Heaven or Hell, to her "death was the end of everything" and so she takes "life with deadly seriousness."[106]

Her commitment to the temporal world and sensuous experience—"Life was poor Fred's mouth pressed down on hers in the taxi"[107]—makes her a natural antithesis to Pinkie who abhors "the game" of earthly pleasure. Ida is also "cheery," "healthy," "honest," and "kindly."[108] She is desired and desiring (she "liked a good time") and belongs "to the great middle law-abiding class";[109] "You can tell all the world's dandy with her,"[110] as Rose puts it. Ida's innate decency and tenacious interest in justice being served should make her the moral center and force for "good" in the novel—and yet, strangely, the narrative focalized through Pinkie's vision of the world stops that being straightforwardly the case. Ida's humanist conception of "right and wrong" is largely eclipsed by Pinkie's belief in "good and evil." Her interest in spiritualism—ghosts, Ouija boards, séances, etc.—is cast as superstitious silliness ("the squeak of a board, a piece of ectoplasm in a glass cupboard")[111]—that can only offer a pale, attenuated imitation of real religious feeling.[112]

The theological explanation for Pinkie's behavior—his "evilness"—does predominate the narrative. But this might be due to the intensity of Pinkie's self-visioning which at times is almost humorously exaggerated—when, for example, he gives his telephone number as 666. But there are also sociological and psychological factors that the text offers the reader as competing ways of interpreting his character and, consequently, the moral picture of the novel. Pinkie's deprived and violent childhood in the slums, his victimization at school, and his outsider status as a Catholic could all be seen as constitutive elements of the seventeen-year-old murderer: "Man is made by the places in which he lives" as the narrative puts it.[113] Like Bone, Pinkie is also a case study in threatened masculinity: "He had been insulted. He had to show someone he was—a man."[114] The gangland world of the 1930s was peopled by veterans of the First World War, whereas Pinkie, "the Boy," missed out on the "Great Adventure," on Isherwood's "Test" of manhood. Pinkie's wish to avenge the death of his mentor, Kite, also seems to reflect the larger, systemic distress of a younger generation responding to the violent death of older relatives and friends whilst having to prematurely assume their social and familial roles. Pinkie's aversion to pleasure and desire is partly derived from the ascetic Kite—a gangster who only drinks grapefruit juice—but is also weighted with competing explanations: does Pinkie recoil from having sex, for example, because he sees it as a path to damnation, or because of the disgust he felt as a child overhearing his parents' aggressive intercourse, or perhaps even because of repressed homosexuality? The text's persistent ambiguity is maintained even at the point of Pinkie's death. The scene is both filmic and impressionistic: a chase across the cliffs on a stormy night, initially by car and then on foot until Pinkie is suddenly over the edge: "It was as if he'd been withdrawn suddenly by a hand out of any existence—past or present, whipped into zero—nothing."[115] The reader is left to interpret, or perhaps just wonder, whether Pinkie has committed suicide, slipped to his death, or finally faced divine retribution. At the conclusion of the novel, Rose is returning home to listen to "the worst horror of all,"[116] the gramophone disc which has recorded Pinkie's vituperative disavowal of Rose: "God damn you, you little bitch, why can't you go home for ever and let me be?"[117] This, too, is given both a religious and satiric dimension: Rose is returning home from the confessional booth whilst the gramophone recording seems to serve as a modern, synthetic capturing of Pinkie's last "confession." Even though both characters are shaped by the conditions of modernity and the penetration of violence into everyday life that seems characteristic of interwar culture, Pinkie and Bone remain anomalies in their narrative "worlds." Likewise, *Hangover Square* and *Brighton Rock* are both "crime novels" but ones that strongly test the limits and certainties of the genre and, ultimately, frustrate easy moral judgment.

Notes

1   Gill Plain, *Twentieth Century Crime Fiction: Gender, Sexuality and the Body* (Edinburgh: Edinburgh University Press, 2001), 3.
2   Marina Mackay, "Literary Fiction," in *The Cambridge Companion to British Literature of the 1930s*, ed. James Smith (Cambridge: Cambridge University Press, 2019), 44.
3   Valentine Cunningham, *British Writers of the Thirties* (Oxford: Oxford University Press, 1988), 77.
4   For an account of the Golden Age of Detective Fiction and periodization, see Stephen Knight's "The Golden Age," in *The Cambridge Companion to Crime Fiction*, ed. Martin Priestman (Cambridge: Cambridge University Press, 2003), 77–94. The discussion in this section of my chapter draws particularly on Isobel Maddison's "The Middlebrow and Popular," in *The Cambridge Companion to British Literature of the 1930s*, ed. James Smith (Cambridge: Cambridge University Press, 2019), 81–97.
5   Laura Marcus, "Detection and Literary Fiction," in *The Cambridge Companion to Crime Fiction*, ed. Martin Priestman (Cambridge: Cambridge University Press, 2003), 261. As Marcus explains, Nicolson's 1929 article "The Professor and the Detective" analysed the "appeal of detective fiction to intellectuals as a reaction *against* literature" ("Detection," 248).
6   In "Sherlock Holmes and His Times," T. S. Eliot writes,
    > But every writer owes something to Holmes. And every critic of The Novel who has a theory about the reality of characters in fiction, would do well to consider Holmes. There is no rich humanity, no deep and cunning psychology and knowledge of the human heart about him; he is obviously

a formula. He has not the reality of any great character of Dickens or Thackeray or George Eliot or Meredith or Hardy; or Jane Austen or the Brontës or Virginia Woolf or James Joyce: yet, as I suggested, he is just as real to us as Falstaff or the Wellers.

See *Criterion* (April 1929), reprinted in *The Complete Prose of T. S. Eliot: The Critical Edition: Literature, Politics, Belief, 1927–1929*, ed. Frances Dickey, Jennifer Formichelli, and Ronald Schuchard (Baltimore: Johns Hopkins University Press, 2015), 605.

7   Virginia Woolf, "Middlebrow," in *Collected Essays* 2 (London: Hogarth, 1966), 199.
8   Isobel Maddison, "The Middlebrow and Popular," in *The Cambridge Companion to British Literature of the 1930s*, ed. James Smith (Cambridge: Cambridge University Press, 2019), 83.
9   D.J. Taylor, *The Prose Factory: Literary Life in England since 1918* (New York: Penguin, 2017), 92.
10 Brian Diemert, *Graham Greene's Thrillers and the 1930s* (Montreal: McGill-Queen's University Press, 1996), 18.
11 Cunningham, *British Writers*, 74.
12 Ibid., 74. The "blood psychosis" theory is put forward by a character in Lewis's satirical novel *The Roaring Queen* (1937).
13 See, for example, Lewis's mocking account of the French novelist François Mauriac:

> The fighting man is the flower of mankind: the human intelligence only reaches its perfection when it plunges its sword into a human body, or blows it up with a bomb. If no war is going on at the moment, and an exceptionally intelligent man is waiting (rather wearily) for the peace to stop, he can always pick a quarrel with a stranger in the street, and try to bash his face in. (Wyndham Lewis, *The Writer and the Absolute* [London: Methuen, 1952], 90.)

14 Robert Graves, *Goodbye to All That* (1929; New York: Penguin, 2000), 137.
15 See, for example, the anecdote in which Graves describes an officer warning his soldiers of the dangers of grenades:

> "Now lads, you've got to be careful here! Remember that if you touch anything while you're swinging this chap, it'll go off." To illustrate the point, he rapped the grenade against the table edge. It killed him and the man next to him and wounded twelve others more or less severely. (Ibid., 159)

For an examination of the tone of Graves's memoir, see Paul Fussell, *The Great War and Modern Memory* (Oxford: Oxford University Press, 1975), 202–20.

16 Chris Baldick, *Literature of the 1920s: Writers among the Ruins* (Edinburgh: Edinburgh University Press, 2012), 144.
17 Charles J. Rzepka, *Detective Fiction* (London: Polity, 2005), 162.

18 Ibid., 165.
19 For example, there has been recent academic interest in the work of 1930s spy novelists such as Eric Ambler. See Robert Snyder, *The Art of Indirection in British Espionage Fiction: A Critical Study of Six Novelists* (Jefferson: McFarland, 2011); Phyllis Lassner, *Espionage and Exile: Fascism and Anti-Fascism in British Spy Fiction and Film* (Edinburgh: Edinburgh University Press, 2016).
20 For an account of how Greene's entertainment/novel distinction has influenced criticism of his work, see Diemert, *Graham Greene's Thrillers*, 3–47.
21 Nigel Jones, *Through A Glass Darkly: The Life of Patrick Hamilton* (1991; London: Black Spring Press, 2008), 167.
22 Stephen Knight, *Crime Fiction, 1800–2000: Detection, Death, Diversity* (London: Palgrave Macmillan, 2004), 102.
23 Laura Marcus, *The Tenth Muse: Writing about Cinema in the Modernist Period* (Oxford: Oxford University Press, 2007), 428.
24 Ibid., 428.
25 Quoted in Gene D. Phillips, "Graham Greene: On the Screen," in *Graham Greene: A Collection of Critical Essays*, ed. Samuel Hynes (Englewood Cliffs: Prentice-Hall, 1973), 169.
26 Sean French, *Patrick Hamilton: A Life* (London: Faber, 1993), 198.
27 Ibid., 15.
28 David S. Churchill, "The Queer Histories of a Crime: Representations and Narratives of Leopold and Loeb," *Journal of the History of Sexuality* 18, no. 2 (May 2009): 305.
29 Patrick Hamilton, *Rope* (1929; London: Constable, 1961), 10.
30 Ibid., 12–13.
31 Ibid., 60.
32 Ibid., 63.
33 Ibid., 84.
34 Ibid., 85–6.
35 French, *Patrick Hamilton*, 103.
36 Ibid., 103.
37 Ibid.
38 Hamilton, *Rope*, 82.
39 Ibid., 34.
40 French, *Patrick Hamilton*, 202.
41 George Orwell, "Decline of the English Murder," in *The Complete Works of George Orwell, vol. 18—Smothered under Journalism: 1946*, ed. Peter Davison (London: Secker & Warburg, 1998), 108.
42 Ibid., 109.

43 Ibid.
44 Ibid.
45 For more on the connections between Orwell and Hamilton, see Peter Widdowson's "English Fiction in the 30s," in *Culture and Crisis in Britain in the 1930s*, ed. Jon Clark et al. (London: Lawrence and Wishart, 1979), 117–37.
46 Hamilton, *Rope*, 45.
47 For a seminal account of writers born in the early 1900s, and strongly associated with traditional accounts of 1930s British literature, see Samuel Hynes, *The Auden Generation: Literature and Politics in England in the 1930s* (United Kingdom: Bodley Head, 1976). For a recent overview of the psychological legacy and anticipation of war in the period, see Marina Mackay's "Total War," in *A History of 1930s British Literature*, ed. Benjamin Kohlman and Matthew Taunton (Cambridge: Cambridge University Press, 2019), 362–76.
48 Graham Greene, *Ways of Escape* (London: Bodley Head, 1980), 37.
49 Hynes, *The Auden Generation*, 21.
50 Christopher Isherwood, *Lions and Shadows: An Education in the Twenties* (New York: New Directions, 1947), 76.
51 Mackay, "Total War," 369.
52 Patrick Hamilton, *Hangover Square* (1941; New York: Penguin, 2001), 248.
53 Ibid., 53.
54 Ibid., 27, 29.
55 Ibid., 369.
56 Ibid., 114.
57 Ibid., 140.
58 Ibid., 18.
59 Ibid., 39.
60 Ibid., 280.
61 Ibid., 96–7. *Brighton Rock* also mentions Pinkie experiencing cruel treatment at school. Indeed, the bullying and violence of late Victorian and Edwardian schooling, and by implication, its lasting effect on adult psychology, are an underlying theme of much interwar writing by male authors. See, for example, Graves's account of his unhappiness at Charterhouse School: "From my first moment at Charterhouse I suffered an oppression of spirit that I hesitate to recall in its full intensity" (*Goodbye*, 37); and Greene's recollections in *The Old School* and *A Sort of Life*, where he describes his father, the Headmaster at Berkhamsted School, caning a pupil "for some offense which was never made clear to any of us, but we were accustomed at that age to the moral confusion of adults and we didn't trouble to ask him the reason" (Greene, *Sort,* 49).
62 Ibid., 15.

63 Ibid.
64 Ibid., 41.
65 Ibid., 104.
66 Ibid., 19.
67 Lee Horsley, *The Noir Thriller* (London: Palgrave Macmillan, 2001), 86.
68 Hamilton, *Hangover Square*, 275.
69 Ibid., 178.
70 J.B. Priestley, foreword to *Hangover Square*, ed. by Patrick Hamilton (1972; New York: Penguin, 2001), 9.
71 Ibid., 10.
72 Hamilton, *Hangover Square*, 104.
73 Ibid., 129.
74 Ibid., 104.
75 Ibid., 129.
76 Ibid.
77 Ibid.
78 Ibid., 80.
79 Hamilton was seriously injured after being hit by a car in January 1932 and automobile driving often features in his work as a symbol of a reckless or malignant form of modernity. For a discussion of this aspect of Hamilton's writing, see Ian Davidson's "Movement and Mobility in Patrick Hamilton," *Textual Practice* 30, no. 4 (July 2015): 1–19. For an account of the dangers faced by pedestrians in the interwar period, see Michael John Law's "Speed and Blood on the Bypass: The New Automobilities of Interwar London," *Urban History* 39, no. 3 (August 2012): 490–509.
80 Hamilton, *Hangover Square*, 79.
81 Ibid., 81.
82 W.H. Auden, "Spain," in *Selected Poems* (London: Faber, 1979), 54.
83 Hamilton, *Hangover Square*, 114.
84 Ibid., 139.
85 Newspapers often reported on these sensational crimes using similar language and themes from popular crime fiction. For example, "Is the Brighton Trunk Murder the perfect crime? Has the murderer covered his tracks so well he will never be caught? Up to the present, he does not appear to have made that one fatal slip which in other cases has led to detection and conviction, and he has had a long start" ("Is It the Perfect Crime?" June 25, 1934, 7).
86 Greene, *Ways*, 60.
87 Graham Greene, *Brighton Rock* (1938; New York: Penguin, 1970), 5.
88 Bernard Bergonzi, *A Study in Greene: Graham Greene and the Art of the Novel* (Oxford: Oxford University Press, 2006), 80.
89 Greene, *Ways*, 61.

90 Ibid., 61.
91 Ibid., 63. Emphasis in original.
92 Ibid., 60.
93 Diemert, *Graham Greene's Thrillers*, 134–5.
94 Greene, *Brighton Rock*, 51.
95 Marcus, *Tenth*, 429.
96 Greene, *Brighton Rock*, 89.
97 For a full discussion of Greene and Jewishness, see Andrea Freud Loewenstein, *Loathsome Jews and Engulfing Women: Metaphors of Projection in the Works of Wyndham Lewis, Charles Williams, and Graham Greene* (New York: New York University Press, 1993), 241–311.
98 Cedric Watts, *A Preface to Greene* (London: Pearson, 1997), 174.
99 Quoted in Cunningham, *British Writers*, 73.
100 Under British law at this time, wives were not permitted to give testimony against their husbands in criminal cases except in cases where the husband had been accused of violence against her. See Colin Manchester's "Wives as Crown Witnesses," *Cambridge Law Journal* 37, no. 2 (1979): 249–51.
101 Greene, *Brighton Rock*, 53.
102 Ibid., 53.
103 Ibid., 92.
104 Ibid., 248.
105 Ibid., 190.
106 Ibid., 36.
107 Ibid., 36.
108 Ibid., 81.
109 Ibid.
110 Ibid., 92.
111 Ibid., 36.
112 In a review of Greene's Catholic novels, Orwell criticizes the way that "Hell is a sort of high-class night club, entry to which is reserved for Catholics only, since the others, the non-Catholics, are too ignorant to be held guilty, like the beasts that perish." See George Orwell's "The Sanctified Sinner," in *Graham Greene: A Collection of Critical Essays*, ed. Samuel Hynes (Englewood Cliffs: Prentice-Hall, 1973), 107.
113 Greene, *Brighton Rock*, 35.
114 Ibid., 87.
115 Ibid., 245.
116 Ibid., 250.
117 Ibid., 179.

Bibliography

Auden, W.H. "Spain." In *Selected Poems*, 51–5. London: Faber, 1979.
Baldick, Chris. *Literature of the 1920s: Writers among the Ruins*. Edinburgh: Edinburgh University Press, 2012.
Bergonzi, Bernard. *A Study in Greene: Graham Greene and the Art of the Novel*. Oxford: Oxford University Press, 2006.
Churchill, David S. "The Queer Histories of a Crime: Representations and Narratives of Leopold and Loeb." *Journal of the History of Sexuality* 18, no. 2 (May 2009): 287–324.
Cunningham, Valentine. *British Writers of the Thirties*. Oxford: Oxford University Press, 1988.
Davidson, Ian. "Movement and Mobility in Patrick Hamilton." *Textual Practice* 30, no. 4 (July 2015): 1–19.
Diemert, Brian. *Graham Greene's Thrillers and the 1930s*. Montreal: McGill-Queen's University Press, 1996.
Eliot, T.S. "Sherlock Holmes and His Times: A Review of *The Complete Sherlock Holmes Short Stories*, by Sir Arthur Conan Doyle [and] *The Leavenworth Case*, by Anna Katharine Green." In *The Complete Prose of T. S. Eliot: The Critical Edition: Literature, Politics, Belief, 1927–1929*, edited by Frances Dickey, Jennifer Formichelli, and Ronald Schuchard (Baltimore: Johns Hopkins University Press, 2015), 601–10.
French, Sean. *Patrick Hamilton: A Life*. London: Faber, 1993.
Fussell, Paul. *The Great War and Modern Memory*. Oxford: Oxford University Press, 1975.
Graves, Robert. *Goodbye to All That*. 1929; New York: Penguin, 2000.
Greene, Graham. *Brighton Rock*. 1938; New York: Penguin, 1970.
Greene, Graham. *A Sort of Life*. London: Bodley Head, 1971.
Greene, Graham. *Ways of Escape*. London: Bodley Head, 1980.
Hamilton, Patrick. *Hangover Square*. 1941; New York: Penguin, 2001.
Hamilton, Patrick. *Rope*. 1929. London: Constable, 1961.
Horsley, Lee. *The Noir Thriller*. London: Palgrave Macmillan, 2001.
Hynes, Samuel. *The Auden Generation: Literature and Politics in England in the 1930s*. London: Bodley Head, 1976.
"Is It the Perfect Crime?" *Portsmouth Evening News*, June 25, 1934: 7. https://www.britishnewspaperarchive.co.uk/viewer/bl/0000290/19340625/124/0007. Accessed March 12, 2023.
Isherwood, Christopher. *Lions and Shadows: An Education in the Twenties*. New York: New Directions, 1947.
Jones, Nigel. *Through a Glass Darkly: The Life of Patrick Hamilton*. 1991; London: Black Spring Press, 2008.
Knight, Stephen. *Crime Fiction, 1800–2000: Detection, Death, Diversity*. London: Palgrave Macmillan, 2004.
Lassner, Phyllis. *Espionage and Exile: Fascism and Anti-Fascism in British Spy Fiction and Film*. Edinburgh: Edinburgh University Press, 2016.
Law, Michael John. "Speed and Blood on the Bypass: The New Automobilities of Interwar London." *Urban History* 39, no. 3 (August 2012): 490–509.

Lewis, Wyndham. *The Writer and the Absolute*. London: Methuen, 1952.
Loewenstein, Andrea Freud. *Loathsome Jews and Engulfing Women: Metaphors of Projection in the Works of Wyndham Lewis, Charles Williams, and Graham Greene*. New York: New York University Press, 1993.
Mackay, Marina. "Literary Fiction." In *The Cambridge Companion to British Literature of the 1930s*, edited by James Smith, 32–46. Cambridge: Cambridge University Press, 2019.
Mackay, Marina. "Total War." In *A History of 1930s British Literature*, edited by Benjamin Kohlman and Matthew Taunton, 362–76. Cambridge: Cambridge University Press, 2019.
Maddison, Isobel. "The Middlebrow and Popular." In *The Cambridge Companion to British Literature of the 1930s*, edited by James Smith, 81–97. Cambridge: Cambridge University Press, 2019.
Manchester, Colin. "Wives as Crown Witnesses." *Cambridge Law Journal* 37, no. 2 (1979): 249–51.
Marcus, Laura. "Detection and Literary Fiction." In *The Cambridge Companion to Crime Fiction*, edited by Martin Priestman, 245–69. Cambridge: Cambridge University Press, 2003.
Marcus, Laura. *The Tenth Muse: Writing about Cinema in the Modernist Period*. Oxford: Oxford University Press, 2007.
Orwell, George. "Decline of the English Murder." In *The Complete Works of George Orwell, vol. 18—Smothered under Journalism: 1946*, edited by Peter Davison, 108–10. London: Secker & Warburg, 1998.
Orwell, George. "The Sanctified Sinner." In *Graham Greene: A Collection of Critical Essays*, edited by Samuel Hynes, 105–9. Englewood Cliffs: Prentice-Hall, 1973.
Phillips, Gene D. "Graham Greene: On the Screen." In *Graham Greene: A Collection of Critical Essays*, edited by Samuel Hynes, 168–75. Englewood Cliffs: Prentice-Hall, 1973.
Plain, Gill. *Twentieth Century Crime Fiction: Gender, Sexuality and the Body*. Edinburgh: Edinburgh University Press, 2001.
Priestley, J.B. Foreword to *Hangover Square*, edited by Patrick Hamilton. 1972, 7–11. New York: Penguin, 2001.
Rzepka, Charles J. *Detective Fiction*. London: Polity, 2005.
Snyder, Robert. *The Art of Indirection in British Espionage Fiction: A Critical Study of Six Novelists*. Jefferson: McFarland, 2011.
Taylor, D.J. *The Prose Factory: Literary Life in England since 1918*. New York: Penguin, 2017.
Watts, Cedric. *A Preface to Greene*. London: Pearson, 1997.
Widdowson, Peter. "English Fiction in the 30s." In *Culture and Crisis in Britain in the 1930s*, edited by Jon Clark et al., 117–37. London: Lawrence and Wishart, 1979.
Woolf, Virginia. "Middlebrow." In *Collected Essays*, vol. 2, 196–203. London: Hogarth, 1966.

15

The Restorative Vision of Justice in G. K. Chesterton's Father Brown

Matthew Bardowell

Father Brown, G. K. Chesterton's bumbling, clerical sleuth, presents a striking contrast to other detectives of the late-nineteenth and early-twentieth centuries. Consider his difference from the Golden Age detective *par excellence*, Sherlock Holmes. While Holmes is relentlessly deductive, Father Brown is an oddly intuitive figure whose knowledge of human nature arises from his experience in the confessional booth. Because of his understanding of the sacrament of reconciliation, Father Brown's aim in hunting down and bringing criminals to justice is markedly different from that of his contemporaries. While some detectives are driven by retribution, deterrence, or simply the pleasure of puzzle-solving, Father Brown seeks the repentance and restoration of his quarry. This chapter centers on three stories collected in *The Innocence of Father Brown* (1911) in which Father Brown pursues the French criminal mastermind Flambeau. While other law enforcement officers focus their efforts on capturing the notorious thief, Father Brown engages in a series of discussions with him on the nature of reality and one's obligation to it. Chesterton's acquaintance with the writings of St. Thomas Aquinas and Jacques Maritain impressed upon him reason's role in uniting the mind with external objects, and this idea looms large in Father Brown's discussions with Flambeau. Flambeau's narrative arc ends not with his imprisonment but with his repentance and restoration to society because of Father Brown's commitment to the claims reality makes on humanity.

The emphasis Father Brown places on justice through repentance emerges over the course of his interactions with Flambeau, and there is one scene in the third story collected in *The Innocence of Father Brown* that illustrates the priest's particular interest in restoring the criminal. The tale is "The Queer Feet," in which Flambeau's target is a set of ornate cutlery used at the annual dinner of the elite club The Twelve True Fishermen. I will discuss this story at some length later, but for now, it is the story's conclusion that illustrates most succinctly Father Brown's ethos as a crime solver. Father Brown manages to confront Flambeau prior to his escape and to convince the thief to give back what he has stolen. As Father Brown returns with the silver cutlery, he tells one of the diners, Colonel Pound, that he has led the man who stole these valuables to repentance. Colonel Pound, desiring to get to the heart of the matter, is confused by the priest's story and asks, "Did you catch this man?"[1] Father Brown replies: "Yes, ... I caught him, with an unseen hook and an invisible line which is long enough to let him wander to the ends of the world, and still to bring him back with a twitch upon the thread."[2] To what can Father Brown be referring as the "unseen hook" and the "invisible line"? While the priest may be speaking of their latest interaction in the cloakroom where he confronts Flambeau, I think it more likely that Father Brown refers to an acquaintanceship that was started between the two men in the first story of the collection, "The Blue Cross." Since that meeting, Father Brown's ongoing discussions with Flambeau have all been of a piece. This essay aims to examine those discussions to reveal the nature of Father Brown's restorative vision of justice and offer further explanation for how such a seemingly hardened criminal can change in such fundamental ways.

Chestertonian Epistemology and the Moral Imagination

While it is Einstein's definition of insanity that has lodged itself in the modern mind—i.e., doing the same thing again and again and expecting a different result—it is perhaps G. K. Chesterton's definition of the same term that is better suited to a society even more decadent than the one to which he was writing. Insanity, Chesterton explains in *Orthodoxy*, "is reason used without root, reason in the void."[3] In context, Chesterton here addresses the habits of thought that fail to proceed from fundamental truths and which, as a result of this dislocation from first principles, lead to absurd conclusions. Without a firm conceptual anchor, any chain of logic, however linear and concatenated, will ultimately be suspended over the very abyss to which Chesterton refers. To illustrate this predicament, he conjures the image of the ouroboros—the Egyptian symbol for eternity that depicts a serpent eating its own tail.⁴ For Chesterton, the serpent perpetually consuming itself—a rather "unsatisfactory meal," he wryly observes—is very much like those who are guided through life by an unwavering belief in themselves. According to Chesterton, the serpent that dines on its own tail is "a degraded animal who destroys even himself,"⁵ and the man who believes in himself as a first principle is similarly degraded. The person who believes in himself as a guiding principle lacks a connection to external reality—to things as they are rather than things merely as one perceives them. If one cannot achieve a knowledge of reality outside one's own mind, then one falls into the same mental trap as the solipsist. Chesterton calls these characters "individualists" and prophesies for them a grim fate:

> Then when this kindly world all round the man has been blackened out like a lie; when friends fade into ghosts, and the foundations of the world fail, then when the man, believing in nothing and in no man, is alone in his own nightmare, then the great individualistic motto shall be written over him in avenging irony. The stars will be only dots in the blackness of his own brain; his mother's face will be only a sketch from his own insane pencil on the walls of his cell. But over his cell shall be written, with dreadful truth, "He believes in himself."⁶

Here Chesterton describes a man untethered from truth—a man whose mind has been severed from reality. For Chesterton, such a disseveration results in devaluing the reality of the "kindly world" all around. Failing to see the objects in the world and to perceive our proper relationship to them leads to solipsistic madness. Thus, a proper evaluation of the world and a proper awareness of our place within it constitute for Chesterton a crucial anchor to all rational thought. To be sane, therefore, one must operate within sound first principles. As Chesterton notes, "The man who begins to think without the proper first principles goes mad; he begins to think at the wrong end."⁷ Without beginning from solid, bedrock principles, the human mind will link ideas together in some logical way, but while the connections between discrete ideas may be sound, the premises on which they are founded will be faulty. Furthermore, without a reliable and meaningful connection to reality, one cannot check one's work, so to speak—to allow the external world to correct and teach us where and how we have erred in our first principles. This profile of the madman will be helpful in understanding the philosophical underpinnings of the conversations between Father Brown and Flambeau.

In his writings about religion and politics, Chesterton shows a strong affinity for building a philosophical argument by interrogating first principles. Writing about Chesterton's politics, Sheridan Gilley remarks on "Chesterton's gift for fundamental thought," observing that for Chesterton to think well and clearly "he had to go back to first principles: above all to the very first principles of recognizing reality and the existence of the moral order."[8] Here Gilley notes the relationship between true perceptions of reality and the acknowledgment of a moral order. The phrase "recognizing reality" is apt because to recognize reality is not to create meaning dependent upon the subject who perceives it. We do not, as Immanuel Kant might say, create the signification of objects, but instead, we surrender our perceptions to the concrete and tangible world. It is this epistemic process that leads to Chesterton's first principles, and it is out of these first principles that Chesterton's notion of the moral order flows.

Alison Milbank discusses this idea of recognizing reality when considering Chesterton's penchant for the defamiliarization technique popularized by Viktor Shklovsky.[9] Yet, unlike Shklovsky, whose notion of defamiliarization "problematizes understanding in order to empower its reach by the subject's mind, Chesterton does so to empower the object."[10] Chesterton privileges the external object over the mind of the perceiving subject. When an object has been defamiliarized, it is not we who, through the power and ingenuity of our minds, have created that fresh significance. Rather, it is we who surrender ourselves to external reality and so become transformed by it. Milbank describes the intellectual heritage of these ideas in Chesterton's thought and observes that Chesterton knew through intuition much of what would become more focused through reading Aquinas and Maritain.[11] In their works, we see that proper orientation to the world stems not from foisting ourselves upon it, not from believing in ourselves, but in believing in everything else, thereby allowing our minds to be expanded by that which surrounds us.

One such fruitful place to begin understanding Aquinas and Maritain's influence on Chesterton is Chesterton's own biography of Aquinas. Reading the biographies penned by Chesterton, one comes away with the feeling that one knows less about the subject than one has learned about the author. This may simply be the consequence of learning about one towering figure of human history from the vantage point of another towering figure. But it is because of rather than despite this quality in Chesterton's biographies that examining them serves to clarify the nature of his own thought. By his own admission, what Chesterton offers in this book is only a sketch, and sketches are, by their very nature, brief and partial. Even so, a sketch reveals what the artist thought to be the most essential elements of its subject. In Chesterton's sketch of Aquinas, there are two major contours Chesterton is most interested in articulating, and those are Aquinas's role in the Aristotelian revival and its subsequent answer to that perennial and shape-shifting heresy, Manicheanism. For the purposes of this study, I focus mainly on how these aspects of Aquinas's legacy bear on Chesterton's own philosophy of knowing as well as how such a philosophy helps to illuminate the error of Flambeau and the ministry of Father Brown.

For Chesterton, Aquinas's work in reviving Aristotle's philosophy and his answer to the Manicheans both center on the value of Being. Here, "Being" should be understood in its Thomistic sense. It is *ens*—"that which is."[12] Being is everything that participates in the existence of God, who is perfect Being. Chesterton acknowledges the centrality of Being for Aquinas when he observes that "nobody will begin to understand the Thomist philosophy ... who does not realise that the primary and fundamental part of it is entirely the praise of Life, the praise of Being, the praise of God as the Creator of the World."[13] The central claim of the Thomist philosophy according to Chesterton is that God's creation possesses Being and that which exists is intelligible to human senses. Chesterton observes that this notion is often regarded as an appeal to both Aquinas and Aristotle but could also be called "the appeal to Reason and the Authority of the Senses."[14] Such an epistemology differs from the pure transcendentalists like Plato in that it allows for knowledge formation based on sensory experience rather than on the claim that understanding of the world comes, as it were, pre-loaded and already formed in the mind as an "uplifted and abstracted sort of intellect."[15] In Chesterton's words, Aquinas "insisted that the senses were the windows of the soul and that the reason had a divine right to feed upon facts."[16] The authority of the senses further explains why Chesterton's insane self-believer goes so far astray. Belief in oneself is not grounded in the world God has made but rather in the private world of one's own mind. To believe in oneself is to place subjectivity above the objective and external world, which severs one's connection to Being by blocking out all that exists outside of oneself. In such a condition, the self-believer is intellectually impoverished, unable to learn from the senses and unable to permit any external influence to contradict whatever one happens to believe subjectively. Therefore, the self-believer is indeed locked away within and, failing to admit the evidence of the sense, has effectively draped the windows, blocking out all light.

Aquinas's argument enables the "recognition of Ens or Being as something definitely beyond ourselves."[17] For Aquinas, the world possesses Being because it proceeds from the creative act of God, which has been pronounced good. The world, though fallen, retains its goodness in participation with the goodness of God, its maker, and when one recognizes that goodness, one perceives God, through whom all creation receives its Being and has life insofar as it participates in divine existence. What is crucial here for Chesterton is that participation in God's being is not limited to humanity as God's creation but extends to eggs and horses, and trees and rocks. The goodness of Being includes all matter in which the external world consists. If all objects in the world participate in some measure with the Being of God, then this ontological status has implications for the humans who move about within creation and who are themselves a part of it. Aquinas's insistence on the essential goodness of nature provided a Christian "motive" for studying the material world—"for the study of facts" and for beginning such inquiry with "the most material, and even the meanest of things."[18] Aquinas asserts the goodness of the created world as well as the authority of the senses in perceiving those external objects. This idea yields a theory that links our treatment and perception of objects to a Christian moral vision of the created world. If objects exist outside of us and have their own Being, then what we think about them and how we treat them redound to our ability to treat them justly.

Chesterton and Maritain seem to have felt a mutual appreciation for one another based on their shared appreciation for Aquinas. Chesterton mentions Maritain's book, *Theonas*, in his biography of Thomas.[19] Maritain's text is composed of a series of conversations featuring such characters as Philonous, Theonas, and an assortment of other respectable personages.[20] Chesterton singles out a fruitful metaphor that describes the effect of an object upon the human mind. In Chesterton's summation, Maritain argues that "external fact *fertilises* the internal intelligence, as the bee fertilises the flower."[21] Chesterton understands this metaphor as a kind of marriage between humanity and the world and acknowledges its Thomistic roots: "God made Man so that he was capable of coming into contact with reality; and those whom God has joined, let no man put asunder."[22] In both Maritain and Chesterton, Kant's epistemology is charged with such an attempted separation. Maritain writes that the process whereby an object fertilizes the human mind is the process of[23]

> being rightly subjected to the real. This is precisely what Kant did not see and what St. Thomas saw quite clearly. Kant had a profound feeling of the spontaneity of the intellectual nature but because he believed that the act of knowing consists in *creating* the other, not in *becoming* the other, he foolishly reversed the order of dependence between the object of knowledge and the human intellect and made the human intellect the measure and law of the object.[24]

Here, Kant stands in for Chesterton's insane self-believer. Chesterton aligns this argumentative thread in *Theonas* with Aquinas's epistemology in perhaps his most forceful terms when he writes that "according to Aquinas, the object becomes part of the mind; nay, according to Aquinas, the mind actually becomes the object."[25]

The object therefore shapes the mind, and its effect is likewise entirely opposite to the intellectual condition of the self-believer. Instead of being hemmed in by the constituting effects of one's own mind, the adherent to Aquinas's epistemology is "enlarged"—made expansive even as it yields to the object.[26] One may be tempted to frame Aquinas's theory of the mind as essentially passive whereas Kant's theory is essentially active. It certainly seems that the mind's submission to the external world and its subsequent transformation into the object it contemplates suggests passivity, whereas Kant's notion of the mind creating the object is much more active. Yet this dichotomy is not accurate. Aquinas agrees with Aristotle that to understand is "in a way to be passive" because the intellect "has an operation extending to universal being."[27] In other words, the human reason, insofar as it is limited and not infinite, is always in a state of potentiality to what it knows. Yet, to be fair to Kant, Aquinas also acknowledges that this potentiality is only to be passive "in a way." There is indeed an active power of the intellect. This power does not create the object but is active in its ability to become that which it perceives. Thus, in the process of becoming the object, human reason demonstrates its "power to make things actually intelligible."[28] This broadening of the mind enables the subject to come into real contact with the world in a way that imparts confidence in one's senses and in the material world. Chesterton views this philosophy as truly constructive—a sturdy foundation on which to build ever-expanding conclusions about reality.

Flambeau in the Confessional Booth

These arguments, proffered by Aquinas and Maritain, are embedded in Father Brown's encounters with Flambeau and bring to light the moral problem that lodges itself in Flambeau's mind like a fishhook. Flambeau is indeed a master criminal, and yet he does not commit any crime indiscriminately. The narrator explains that "his real crimes were chiefly those of ingenious and wholesale robbery."[29] Flambeau sees himself as an artist-criminal, and he often uses his amazing dexterity and acrobatic skill in the service of his art. After his repentance, Flambeau characterizes his crimes for the reader in his own voice when he calls his final act of theft "beautiful."[30] Indeed, Flambeau targets objects that are not merely valuable but beautiful. In the three stories I consider here, he aims to steal a silver cross inlaid with blue sapphires, a set of silver cutlery cast in the shape of fish, and three large diamonds. Later in their acquaintanceship, Father Brown shows that he understands how Flambeau views himself and urges him to consider the degrading effects of a life of crime. He will not always be able to stay on the right side of the boundaries he has drawn. He will not remain "an honest outlaw, a merry robber of the rich."[31] While he may not be able, as Father Brown says, "to keep on one level of evil,"[32] this persona is intact upon their first meeting. By contrast, Father Brown is seemingly hapless and befuddled. Chesterton tells us, his face is "as round and dull as a Norfolk dumpling" and that he "did not seem to know which was the right end of his return [train] ticket."[33] A restaurateur who has spent only a few moments in his company calls him "a slower coach altogether,"[34] and Flambeau, after spending the entire day with him disguised as a priest, calls him a "turnip" and a "bumpkin."[35] To the observer, Father Brown seems utterly ill-equipped to handle his sophisticated adversary, and yet, when the two fall into conversation together, Father Brown shows that he is every bit Flambeau's equal.

In "The Blue Cross," the reader follows the antics of what appears to be a pair of priests recently in town for The Eucharistic Congress to be held in London. The reader follows this tandem alongside the head of the Paris police, Valentin, who is, if not precisely a "thinking machine," "the most famous investigator in the world."[36] We follow this detective down a series of fox and rabbit holes in pursuit of the most notorious criminal in the world, Flambeau. The reader learns that one of these priests is indeed the criminal mastermind who has adopted an elaborate disguise so that he can steal the silver cross from Father Brown. Father Brown, however, is far less hapless than he would appear to be at first and surreptitiously contrives to send a parcel containing the cross to a friend in Westminster.

When Valentin finally catches up with these two, he brings several police officers along with him and approaches the pair stealthily to take Flambeau by surprise and rescue the poor prelate from harm. As he draws near, Valentin can hear brief snatches of their conversation, but he picks out the word *reason* "recurring frequently in a high and almost childish voice"—the voice of Father Brown.[37] In this way, Chesterton carefully develops the theme of their discussion, and, good disciple of Aquinas that he is, Chesterton makes reason the crucial point on which Flambeau's repentance turns. The epistemology of Aquinas, which Chesterton explores in his biography, holds that reason is sound because of the authority of the senses—the ability of the human mind and body to encounter the external world and learn true and reliable things. To recall Maritain's phrasing, reason enables the mind to be "rightly subjected to the real."[38] As the two men sit in conversation, the day slowly turns to evening: "The gorgeous green and gold still clung to the darkening horizon; but the dome above was turning slowly from peacock-green to peacock-blue, and the stars detached themselves more and more like solid jewels."[39] Chesterton's description of the setting will mirror the setting of their final conversation, which I will discuss later. On this night, the stars appear as jewels. On that future night, jewels will stand out from the night sky like flying stars.

The ensuing conversation unfolds like a Socratic dialogue with Father Brown playing the role of teacher and Flambeau serving as the student. Flambeau believes that he can speak enough like a priest to fool Father Brown, but his attacks on reason give him away as an imposter. Flambeau first commits an intellectual sin that any adherent to Aquinas's epistemology would see a mile off: he violates the law of non-contradiction. As Father Brown looks up to the heavens and remarks upon the Medieval notion of their incorruptibility, Flambeau attempts to agree with the priest by saying, "Ah, yes, these modern infidels appeal to their reason; but who can look at those millions of worlds and not feel that there may well be wonderful universes above us where reason is utterly unreasonable?"[40] Flambeau's strategy is clear enough. He believes that flattering the priest's assumed antipathy for modern thought will help to prolong the ruse, but he fails to understand the role of reason in Father Brown's theology. An infinitude of universes could never invalidate the eternal laws of intelligibility if such a trait existed through God, the efficient cause of all things.[41] Flambeau fails to understand the law of non-contradiction by postulating a reality in which reason could at once be itself and its opposite. Indeed, Father Brown reasserts the law of non-contradiction when he rejects Flambeau's argument. "No," says the other priest, "reason is always reasonable."[42]

This first conversation between the priest and the thief centers on reason, and such a foundational concept touches upon the moral differences of each man. Flambeau adheres to a skeptical epistemology that stupefies his moral imagination. The thief continues to argue that the night sky into which they are gazing may yet contain a universe that deviates from reason simply by virtue of its infinitude: "Yet who knows if in that infinite universe—?"[43] In other words, who can know what infinity holds? Perhaps it contains a universe in which our rationality is turned on its head, and, if it does, then our reason is made relative—only one choice among others—and it and its fruit can be discarded at will. Father Brown's response makes a rather Thomistic distinction between physical space and ontology: "'Only infinite physically,' said the little priest, turning sharply in his seat, 'not infinite in the sense of escaping from the laws of truth.'"[44] Ever the sensitive minister, Father Brown offers an incisive reading of Flambeau's argument as though he were a penitent at confession. Flambeau seeks an escape from reason and, therefore, from reality. If he can achieve this, then all is lawful, or, at least, nothing is lawless.

In the next portion of their conversation, Father Brown makes an explicit connection to the reliability of reason and the moral imagination. Father Brown also articulates a clear relationship between a failure to embrace reason and Flambeau's crime of choice: theft. Given the influence of Thomistic thought on Chesterton, it is no surprise to see Father Brown suggest that this disjunction from reality will lead to the vice of stealing. If, as Maritain claims, reason represents the act of submitting to the real—to the external world through the authority of the senses—then theft is a clear repudiation of such a process. Rather than subjecting himself to the object, Flambeau subjects the object to himself. He takes what does not belong to him. His mistake is akin to what Maritain accuses Kant of making—he forces himself on the object to create its meaning rather than submitting himself to the object and thereby allowing some external influence into the hermetically sealed universe of his own will. Here is what Father Brown says:

> Reason and justice grip the remotest and the loneliest star. Look at those stars. Don't they look as if they were single diamonds and sapphires? Well, you can imagine any mad botany or geology you please. Think of

forests of adamant with leaves of brilliants. Think the moon is a blue moon, a single elephantine sapphire. But don't fancy that all the frantic astronomy would make the smallest difference to the reason and justice of conduct. On plains of opal, under cliffs cut out of pearl, you would still find a notice-board, "Thou shalt not steal."[45]

The priest delivers a homily that includes an object lesson in morality. By drawing Flambeau's attention to the stars and likening them to diamonds, the priest foreshadows his final crime: a theft of diamonds. In speaking of the moon as a "single-elephantine sapphire," Father Brown references the sapphires set in the silver cross that Flambeau plots to steal. Father Brown's speech reveals that Flambeau has a disordered relationship not merely to the law but to the world, and Aquinas's influence on Chesterton helps to explain the nature of this disorder. Father Brown's lesson is that how we think of the external world influences how we act toward the objects that surround us. One's ability to reason rightly and one's inclination toward justice are inextricably linked. This Thomistic vision of reason and the authority of the senses allows the external world to impinge on the sealed-off world of the self-believing solipsist. At this point in his narrative arc, Flambeau is the self-believer. If reality can differ in nature as radically as he believes in "The Blue Cross," then all that remains is to be an individual strong enough and willing enough to shape the world in whatever way seems best. For Father Brown, however, this conclusion is a failure of reason, and because Flambeau fails in his reason, he also fails in his morality. This notion is the fishhook that Father Brown speaks of in "The Queer Feet," and the fishing line runs through their next two encounters.

The next story in which Flambeau appears is "The Queer Feet." Here, Chesterton begins by emphasizing a theme of exclusion that further develops Father Brown's vision of repentance. In this story, Father Brown finds himself taking confession from a waiter at an upper-class club called The Twelve True Fishermen, a reference to the twelve Apostles whom Christ charges with being "fishers of men."[46] The name of the club and Father Brown's dramatic declaration that he has indeed caught the thief at the end of the story show that Father Brown's vision of justice differs from that of the others present at the dinner. The kind of restoration Father Brown seeks is not only to restore the criminal to those whom he has offended but also to restore the criminal to a right relationship to the objects he appropriates to himself in the act of theft. Such a restoration is presented in this story as a radical act of inclusion in the face of the club's exclusivist bent. Likewise, Chesterton's understanding of Aquinas's epistemology in which the mind becomes the object is itself a kind of inclusion. Chesterton's biography of Thomas explains that when the mind submits to the external object the effect is to "enlarge the mind of which it becomes a part."[47] Thus, the mind expands because of that which it includes. If this mode of knowing is characterized as inclusion, then its opposite may be justly characterized as exclusion. The mind that aims to impose its own meaning on the world only succeeds in separating itself from reality.

In "The Queer Feet," we see this theme of exclusion in the formalities of the club's annual dinner. As Chesterton describes the event into which Father Brown has unwittingly wandered, he conveys a sense of exclusivity and separation based primarily on class. Every aspect of this dinner accentuates a class division, beginning with the venue: The Vernon Hotel. Chesterton explains that this hotel is "small ... and very inconvenient. But its very inconveniences were considered as walls protecting a particular class."[48] The "inconveniences" only serve to enhance the desirability of the venue. Chesterton calls them "walls," and in this instance, the walls serve as an obstacle for keeping unwanted people out. Even more explicit is the essential exclusivity of The Twelve True Fishermen itself, which exists, rather improbably, to profit by exclusion: "[the club] was that topsy-turvy product—an 'exclusive' commercial enterprise. That is, it was a thing which paid not by attracting people but actually by turning people away."[49] The difference between the club's namesake and its *raison d'etre* cannot be overstated. The members of this club have no interest in fishing for men. Chesterton is at such pains to emphasize the class difference in this story that he addresses the reader directly to make such a separation personal. In describing the hotel, he remarks upon the unlikelihood that the reader would be sufficiently well-connected to warrant entry to such a place: "When you enter (as you never will) the Vernon Hotel."[50] The club's exclusivity is its guiding value, and the most notable privilege membership in The Twelve True Fishermen confers is admittance to the annual dinner.

The dinner itself is the pinnacle of exclusivity and superfluity. The *hors d'œuvres*, Chesterton explains, "were taken seriously because they were avowedly useless extras, like the whole dinner and the whole club."[51] This uselessness seems to convey the notion of a kind of late Victorian *ars gratia artes* ("art for the sake of art") aesthetic, but Chesterton would not have set much store by such a metaphysically bereft philosophy. If the highest point of the club is the annual dinner, the pinnacle of the dinner is the fish course, which the club regards as "sacred."[52] During this course, members use an ornate set of silver cutlery cast in the shape of fish, and it is this set of cutlery that attracts Flambeau's attention. The narrator explains that during the fish course diners use a "celebrated set of fish knives and forks which were, as it were, the insignia of the society, each being exquisitely wrought in silver in the form of a fish, and each loaded at the hilt with one large pearl."[53] The upper-class excess we see in the club is utterly disconnected from any *telos*, any "end," that could have virtue and goodness as its aim. Indeed, Chesterton says the club has "no history and no object."[54]

Because there were twenty-four seats at the table and only twelve "True Fishermen," the members could "occupy the terrace in the most luxurious style of all, being ranged along the inner side of the table, with no one opposite."⁵⁵ Members sit with no companion across the table. There is no diner they encounter when they look out from their seats at the table. Instead of confronting an "other," an object whose needs they may have to attend or whose reality they would be faced with acknowledging, they encounter only empty space. Indeed, the entire premise of the mystery in "The Queer Feet" is predicated upon the separation between the club members and the waiters. When the waiters realize the fish course cutlery has disappeared, there is an awkward lull in the otherwise smooth dinner service that makes the diners markedly uncomfortable. Chesterton uses this moment to emphasize the diners' separation from the reality of the others in their presence: "[A]ll those vague and kindly gentlemen were so used to the utter smoothness of the unseen machinery which surrounded and supported their lives, that a waiter doing anything unexpected was a start and a jar. They felt as you and I would feel if the inanimate world disobeyed—if a chair ran away from us."⁵⁶ The machinery around these men may be "unseen," but there is nothing wrong with their senses. They are in full possession of their faculty of sight, and they are also blind. The club members have neglected the authority of their senses to give them encounters with the real. It is not their sight that is impaired but their reason, and, as a result, they have cut themselves off from encounters with others.

The theme of exclusion resolves as Father Brown explains to the diners that it was precisely their indifference to the wait staff which enabled the crime. It is Father Brown who, shut away in a dark cloakroom, is attuned enough to his senses to unravel the mystery. He hears the cadence of Flambeau's footfalls on the floor and understands that someone is impersonating a waiter. Flambeau uses not the cover of darkness but the diners' inability to enlarge themselves to accomplish his theft. Father Brown explains this to them, and, as he does, he attracts another fish. Colonel Pound lingers to hear as much of the story as Father Brown is willing to tell. The priest explains the psychology on which Flambeau's crime depends as he notes, "Why should the gentlemen look at a chance waiter?"⁵⁷ Colonel Pound wants to hear the details of Flambeau's confession, but this the priest will not tell. The Colonel's questions reveal an interest in repentance, this time his own. And his repentance, like Flambeau's, will require him to understand others aright. Father Brown's final remark to the Colonel works to enlarge his mind by considering the external reality of another: "It must be very hard work to be a gentleman," says Father Brown, "but, do you know, I have sometimes thought that it may be almost as laborious to be a waiter."⁵⁸ This parting comment summons precisely the faculty that the Colonel fails to use during the dinner: his reason—his ability to permit into his mind an object other than himself.

"The Blue Cross" and "The Queer Feet" set Flambeau's eventual repentance in motion, and the moment of that repentance is complete in

"The Flying Stars." The thread that draws Flambeau back to his senses runs through the previous two stories. In the end, we see that Flambeau's change of heart is connected to his restored reason, which he decries in "The Blue Cross" and the failure of which he cynically uses in "The Queer Feet." Briefly, the story follows a Christmas gathering hosted by city magnate Sir Leopold Fischer and including, among others, his goddaughter, Ruby Adams, the journalist, Mr. Crook, and, of course, Father Brown. Sir Leopold has recently returned from travel, bringing with him three large and priceless African diamonds called "The Flying Stars." They are given this name in part for their glittering appearance and in part for their history of having been stolen numerous times.[59] The amusingly named Mr. Crook is a notable character in that he is a staunch socialist, which contrasts and creates tension with Sir Leopold's explicit capitalism. The ostensible plot, prior to the theft, advances when the guests decide to put on a British harlequinade, which is a comedic pantomime adapted from its Italian counterpart.[60] Flambeau, disguised as one of the characters featured in the pantomime, picks the pockets of Sir Leopold, hides the Flying Stars in his costume's stage jewelry, and escapes with them into Sir Leopold's garden. For the purposes of the present essay, what transpires in this garden is the crucial scene of the story.

When Father Brown catches up to Flambeau, the night is very much like the night of their first encounter in "The Blue Cross." In this moment, Flambeau is using his superior acrobatic skill to scale a "monkey tree" and complete his escape.[61] Chesterton describes the scene in this way: "The green gaiety of the waving laurels, the rich purple indigo of the night, the moon like a monstrous crystal, make an almost irresponsibly romantic picture; and among the top branches of the garden trees a strange figure is climbing, who looks not so much romantic as impossible. He sparkles from head to heel, as if clad in ten million moons."[62] This scene recalls that first discussion on the park bench between Father Brown and Flambeau, down to the numerous heavenly bodies that prompt Flambeau to assert his attack on reason. Indeed, Father Brown makes this connection when he first speaks to Flambeau: "[Y]ou really look like a Flying Star; but that always means a Falling Star at last."[63] Where once Flambeau looked up at the stars in the night sky and saw millions of reasons to doubt rationality and, therefore, morality, now he himself has become millions of stars on the night he will reclaim his moral dignity. Notably, whereas in "The Blue Cross," Flambeau's rejection of reason separates him from the external world and external objects, here Flambeau represents precisely what Chesterton believed happens in a moment of right perception. Flambeau has rightly subjected himself to the real; he has become the stars he could not previously comprehend. This represents a dynamic shift for Flambeau. In "The Blue Cross," Flambeau requests the treasure from Father Brown: "Just hand over that sapphire cross of yours, will you?"[64] In "The Flying Stars," Father Brown is the one to make the request, "And now, by the way, you might give me back those diamonds."[65] Father

Brown goes on to appeal to Flambeau in terms that recall Chesterton's self-believer. If Flambeau continues down this path of crime, his future will be isolated and confining. Flambeau will go on to cross moral line after moral line only to end up alone in his "free forest cold at heart and close to death, and the tree-tops will be very bare."[66] Flambeau then simultaneously casts away the diamonds and his life of crime. Chesterton's narrator frames the recovery of the diamonds as a "restoration," and, indeed, they are not the only things to be restored. As I have shown, Flambeau becomes the Flying Stars, and he is himself restored not only to the law-abiding society but to the external world from which he was formerly separated.

Conclusion: Repentance and Awakening the Moral Imagination

Flambeau's turn shows that, in the stories of Father Brown, repentance and restoration are one and the same. A right relationship to society arises from a right relationship to the world. Such a relationship is essentially a posture of humility. Far from Chesterton's self-believer, whose reality begins and ends within the self, the penitent demonstrates humility through a willing subjection to external reality. As Chesterton phrases it, in the proper application of reason "the mind actually becomes the object."[67] This process is not solely for criminals who need restoration. Indeed, as the club members in "The Queer Feet" show, it is for all those who hope to have genuine encounters with the real.

There remains one nagging question when considering the nature of Flambeau's repentance. Is there a contradiction between the notion of becoming the object, which seems to abolish separation, and recognizing the object as something not merely within the self, which seems to insist upon separation? In the chapter "The Romance of Orthodoxy," Chesterton offers a striking coda to his analysis of the self-believer that enables us to resolve this apparent contradiction. Here Chesterton shows that the goal of reason is not to become all things in a way that rejects difference and individuality. On the contrary, the mind can only be enlarged by the object if the object is a separate and distinct entity, wholly different from the subject. In this way, our reason can lead us not just to understand the other but to love the other. In this chapter of *Orthodoxy*, Chesterton refers to Anne V. Besant, a member of the Theosophical society which rejected all religions in favor of what she termed "the universal self."[68] This philosophy espouses the absence of individuality. It is possible to misunderstand Chesterton's reading of Aquinas as endorsing a similar view—a rejection of difference. But this is incorrect. Such a view, Chesterton claims, is as solipsistic as the self-believer because adherents to it do not become the object but rather subsume all objects into themselves. Chesterton goes on to explain why maintaining difference from the objects we contemplate and, in a sense, "become," is essential to Thomistic epistemology:

> I want to love my neighbour, not because he is I, but precisely because he is not I. I want to adore the world, not as one likes a looking glass, because it is one's self, but as one loves a woman, because she is entirely different. If souls are separate, love is possible.[69]

Chesterton's self-believer exists within the prison walls of his own mind precisely because he cannot permit anything into it that is not already there. He cannot in any sense become the external world because, being so full of the self, there is no room for the other. Within the idea that the mind rightly subjects itself to the other is the incontrovertible reality of the other. Both Flambeau and the members of The Twelve True Fisherman act to assert their wills on the world through acts of appropriation or exclusion. Father Brown's vision of restoration does not lose the object in the self but expands the self by admitting the object. This is why the mind that reasons by becoming the other can be said to be enlarged. As a detective, then, part of what the priest discerns as he pursues the criminal are such defects in reason. Such flaws affect the first principles that Chesterton believed were so essential for proper reasoning and proper evaluation of the surrounding world. In the end, Father Brown is proven right. Flambeau's argument is not merely a thinly veiled deception to enable a crime. As the little Essex priest says of Flambeau's rejection of reason, "it's bad theology."[70]

Notes

1. G.K. Chesterton, "The Queer Feet," in *The Annotated Innocence of Father Brown*, ed. Martin Gardner (Mineola, NY: Dover, 1998), 78.
2. The phrase "a twitch upon the thread" was adopted by Evelyn Waugh in *Brideshead Revisited* for the title of book II in which a wayward protagonist's longing for beauty draws him out of a life of moral profligacy.
3. G.K. Chesterton, *Orthodoxy* (1908; San Francisco: Ignatius Press, 1995), ch. 2, 32.
4. Ibid.
5. Ibid.
6. Ibid.
7. Ibid.
8. Sheridan Gilley, "Chesterton's Politics," *The Chesterton Review* 21, no. 1/2 (1995): 32.

9   For more on defamiliarization, see Viktor Shklovsky's "Art as Technique" (1917).
10 Alison Milbank, *Chesterton and Tolkien as Theologians: The Fantasy of the Real* (2007; New York: T&T Clark, 2009), 37.
11 Ibid., 37.
12 Peter Kreeft, *Summa of the Summa: The Essential Philosophical Passages of St. Thomas Aquinas'* Summa Theologica *Edited and Explained for Beginners* (San Francisco: Ignatius Press, 1990), 24.
13 G.K. Chesterton, *St. Thomas Aquinas* (1933; New York: Image, 2014), 81.
14 Ibid., 11.
15 Ibid., 12.
16 Ibid., 13.
17 Ibid., 122–3.
18 Ibid., 92–3.
19 Ibid., 155.
20 Chesterton himself figures into this book when alluding to Aquinas. In the first instance, Maritain references André Chevrillon's *Nouvelles études anglaises*, Librairie Hachette et Cie., Paris, 1910 (*Theonas* 7). In the referenced passage, Chevrillon characterizes the desire to "save the world" as the desire "to understand it in its reality and its beauty" (*le comprendre en sa réalité et sa beauté*) (Chevrillon 214). This reference is not cited in the 1969 reprinted edition of the text's English translation by F. J. Sheed and, I hope, is profitably identified here. The second mention of Chesterton comes in an explanation of temporal simultaneity (*Theonas* 94). In this passage, Maritain makes reference to Chesterton's comment on the miraculous nature of the daily sunrise—apparently a reference to "The Ethics of Elfland" in *Orthodoxy* (65–6).
21 Chesterton, *St. Thomas Aquinas*, 155.
22 Ibid., 155.
23 It is worth noting that this passage is framed within a fictional conversation. *Theonas* is composed of eleven such conversations, and the participating characters do not always speak in the role of teacher. This passage is taken from the first conversation "The Freedom of the Intellect" and given to Philonous, who seems to speak authoritatively here. In subsequent conversations, however, Philonous fills the role of interlocutor rather than teacher and articulates positions only to be refuted by someone like Theonas in conversation two or Pseudo-Hylas in conversation seven. The reader may accept Philonous's remarks here as aligned with Maritain's own views because here he argues the Thomistic position—as Chesterton recognized in his biography.
24 Jacques Maritain, *Theonas: Conversations of a Sage*, translated by F.J. Sheed (1933; Freeport, NY: Books for Libraries Press, 1969), 9. Milbank quotes this passage from *Theonas* at similar length to illustrate how Chesterton and Tolkien eschew the trap of Kantian subjectivity in favor of Aquinas's

belief that through the senses our minds are indeed suited to know "things in themselves," which Kant does not allow (19).

25 Chesterton, *St. Thomas Aquinas*, 154.
26 Ibid., 154.
27 Thomas Aquinas, *The Summa Theologiæ of St. Thomas Aquinas*, translated by Fathers of the English Dominican Province (Second and revised edition, 1920. Online edition by Kevin Knight, 2017), I, q. 79, a. 2, c.
28 Ibid., I, q. 79, a. 3, c.
29 G.K. Chesterton, "The Blue Cross," in *The Annotated Innocence of Father Brown*, ed. Martin Gardner (Mineola, NY: Dover, 1998), 17.
30 G.K. Chesterton, "The Flying Stars," in *The Annotated Innocence of Father Brown*, ed. Martin Gardner (Mineola, NY: Dover, 1998), 84.
31 Ibid., 99.
32 Ibid.
33 Chesterton, "The Blue Cross," 18.
34 Ibid., 24.
35 Ibid., 37, 38.
36 Ibid., 20, 15.
37 Ibid., 33.
38 Maritain, *Theonas*, 9.
39 Chesterton, "The Blue Cross," 33.
40 Ibid., 34.
41 Aquinas, *Summa Theologiæ*, I, q. 2, a. 3, c.
42 Chesterton, "The Blue Cross," 34.
43 Ibid., 34.
44 Ibid.
45 Ibid., 35.
46 Mark 1:17 (KJV).
47 Chesterton, *St. Thomas Aquinas*, 154.
48 Chesterton, "The Queer Feet," 65.
49 Ibid., 65.
50 Ibid., 67.
51 Ibid., 72.
52 Ibid., 74.
53 Ibid., 66.
54 Ibid.
55 Ibid., 73.
56 Ibid., 74.
57 Ibid., 81.

58 Ibid., 83.
59 Chesterton, "The Flying Stars," 89.
60 Chesterton, "The Flying Stars," fn. 9, 91.
61 Chesterton, "The Flying Stars," 86.
62 Ibid., 98.
63 Ibid.
64 Chesterton, "The Blue Cross," 35.
65 Chesterton, "The Flying Stars," 99.
66 Ibid., 100.
67 Chesterton, *St. Thomas Aquinas*, 154.
68 Chesterton, *Orthodoxy*, 138.
69 Ibid., 138–9.
70 Chesterton, "The Blue Cross," 39.

Bibliography

Aquinas, Thomas. *The Summa Theologiæ of St. Thomas Aquinas*. Translated by Fathers of the English Dominican Province. Second and revised edition. London: Burns Oates & Washbourne, 1920. Online edition by Kevin Knight, 2017.

Chesterton, G.K. "The Blue Cross." In *The Annotated Innocence of Father Brown*, edited by Martin Gardner, 15–40. Mineola, NY: Dover, 1998.

Chesterton, G.K. "The Flying Stars." In *The Annotated Innocence of Father Brown*, edited by Martin Gardner, 84–101. Mineola, NY: Dover, 1998.

Chesterton, G. K. *Orthodoxy*. 1908. San Francisco: Ignatius Press, 1995.

Chesterton, G.K. "The Queer Feet." In *The Annotated Innocence of Father Brown*, edited by Martin Gardner, 64–83. Mineola, NY: Dover, 1998.

Chesterton, G.K. *St. Thomas Aquinas*. 1933. New York: Image, 2014.

Chevrillon, André. *Nouvelles études anglaises*. Paris: Librairie Hachette et Cie, 1910.

Gilley, Sheridan. "Chesterton's Politics." *The Chesterton Review* 21, no. 1/2 (1995): 27–47.

Kreeft, Peter. *Summa of the Summa: The Essential Philosophical Passages of St. Thomas Aquinas' Summa Theologica Edited and Explained for Beginners*. San Francisco: Ignatius Press, 1990.

Maritain, Jacques. *Theonas: Conversations of a Sage*. Translated by F.J. Sheed. 1933; Freeport, NY: Books for Libraries Press, 1969.

Milbank, Alison. *Chesterton and Tolkien as Theologians: The Fantasy of the Real*. 2007; New York: T&T Clark, 2009.

ABOUT THE CONTRIBUTORS

Matthew Bardowell is Associate Professor of English at Missouri Baptist University, where he teaches British literature, world literature, and composition. His research centers on Old Norse and Old English poetry, as well as the works of J. R. R. Tolkien, C. S. Lewis, and their literary circle known as the Inklings. His work appears in *Renascence, Journal of the Fantastic in the Arts, Mythlore, The Ashgate Encyclopedia of Literary and Cinematic Monsters*, and *Worlds Gone Awry: Essays on Dystopian Fiction*. Bardowell holds a Ph.D. in English from Saint Louis University.

Jane Beal (Ph.D., University of California, Davis) is a tenured, full professor of English Literature at the University of La Verne. She has written the book *John Trevisa and the English Polychronicon* (2012) and co-edited the volume *Translating the Past: Essays on Medieval Literature* (2012). She also has written *The Signifying Power of Pearl* (2017), co-authored and co-edited *Approaches to Teaching the Middle English Pearl* (2018), and edited and translated *Pearl: A Middle English Edition and Modern English Translation* (2020). She is currently writing *Truth and Transformation in the Mythology of J.R.R. Tolkien*.

Alissa Burger (Ph.D., Bowling Green State University) is Associate Professor of English, Chair of the English Department, and Director of Student Success at Culver-Stockton College. She teaches courses in research, writing, and literature, including a single-author seminar on Stephen King. She is the author of *The Wizard of Oz as American Myth* (2012), editor of the collection *The Television World of Pushing Daisies* (2011), and editor of *Teaching Graphic Novels in the English Classroom: Pedagogical Possibilities of Multimodal Literacy Engagement* (2017).

Deirdre Flynn, Ph.D., is Lecturer in Twenty-First-Century Literature at Mary Immaculate College, University of Limerick. She has published widely on contemporary literature, Irish studies, Haruki Murakami, and literary urban studies. She recently co-edited two collections on Irish Literature with Palgrave Macmillan: *Irish Urban Fictions* (2018) and *Representations* *of Loss in Irish Literature* (2018). She is a member of the COST action Network Writing Urban Spaces and the Association for Literary Urban Studies.

Michael Hallam is Senior Lecturer at the University of Brighton, England, where he teaches nineteenth- and twentieth-century British and American literature. He gained his D.Phil., on British fiction during the 1940s, from the University of Sussex, where he has also worked as an associate tutor. His research focuses mainly on British modernism, especially the literature and cultural context of the First and Second World Wars and the interwar period. He has published book chapters and articles on a range of writers, including Wyndham Lewis, Naomi Mitchison, Rebecca West, Patrick Hamilton, and Graham Greene.

John J. Han is Professor of English and Creative Writing and Associate Dean of the School of Humanities and Theology at Missouri Baptist University. He is the author, editor, co-editor, or translator of thirty-three books, including *Wise Blood: A Re-Consideration* (2011), *The Final Crossing: Death and Dying in Literature* (with C. Clark Triplett, 2015), and *Worlds Gone Awry: Essays on Dystopian Fiction* (with C. Clark Triplett and Ashley G. Anthony, 2018). Han has also published more than fifty peer-reviewed articles and more than 2,300 poems. He earned his M.A. from Kansas State University and his Ph.D. from the University of Nebraska-Lincoln.

Aya Kubota teaches American literature in the Department of Intercultural Studies, the Faculty of Liberal Arts and Sciences, Bunka Gakuen University, Tokyo. She is the editor-in-chief of *Steinbeck Studies*, the peer-reviewed English-language journal of the Steinbeck Society of Japan. She has more than a dozen academic publications on John Steinbeck, Thornton Wilder, Ernest Hemingway, Nathaniel Hawthorne, Truman Capote, William Inge, and other American writers. She has also delivered numerous papers at conferences in and outside Japan. She holds a B.A. in English and an M.A. in English from Tokyo Woman's Christian University.

Beth McFarland-Wilson has presented papers on family systems theory as a critical interpretive tool at the MLA Annual Convention, West Point Academy, and the American Conference for Irish Studies. Her publications include an article on Richard Powers's *Prisoner's Dilemma* and a chapter on Ibsen's *A Doll's House*. She serves as Assistant Director of Undergraduate Studies in English and Coordinator of Teacher Licensure at Northern Illinois University. She holds a Ph.D. in English from Northern Illinois University.

Debaditya Mukhopadhyay is Assistant Professor of English at Manikchak College, affiliated with the University of Gourbanga, India. He has done his doctoral research on Anglo-American spy fiction. His research articles on various Indian and Hollywood film adaptations have been published in peer-reviewed and UGC-listed journals published from India. He has contributed chapters to edited collections published by Salem Press, McFarland, Edward Elgar Publishing, Routledge, Peter Lang, and Lexington Books. He has previously written research articles on *The Hound of the Baskervilles* and the film adaptation of the Bengali detective series featuring detective Shabor.

Nikita Gloria Pinto holds an M. Phil. in English from Stella Maris College, University of Madras, and an M.A. in English from the University of Delhi, India. An enthusiast of crime writing, she has published essays primarily on narratives of female criminality and monstrosity in historical crime fiction and true crime narratives. Apart from crime fiction, her research interests include science-fiction, posthumanism, freak studies, disability studies, graphic novels, diaspora writing, and South Asian literature.

Timothy Ruppert is Assistant Professor of English at Slippery Rock University. He received his Ph.D. in nineteenth-century British literature from Duquesne University in 2008. Since then, he has published on authors such as Mary Shelley, Lord Byron, Louisa Stuart Costello, and Anne Bannerman. He has also authored ten book reviews for various periodicals. Ruppert writes plays as well; titles within the last five years include *Savage Lands: A Colonial Comedy*, *Vivienne*, and *The Consorts*, which received a nomination for the Pulitzer Prize in Drama in 2017.

Andrew J. Spencer (Ph.D., Southeastern Baptist Theological Seminary) lives in Monroe, Michigan, with his wife and three children. He is a Senior Research Fellow for the Institute for Faith, Work, and Economics and writes regularly at EthicsAndCulture.com. His publications include *The Christian Mind of C. S. Lewis: Essays in Honor of Michael Traver* (2019), *Doctrine in Shades of Green: Theological Perspective for Environmental Ethics* (2022), and *Hope for God's Creation: Stewardship in an Age of Futility* (2023).

Andrea Tinnemeyer teaches courses in magical realism, detective fiction, Latinx literature and the Harlem Renaissance at The College Preparatory School in Oakland, California, and was previously an assistant professor at Utah State University. Among her publications are "'What a Man!': Black Masculinity in the Golden Age of Detective Fiction" (*Mean Streets* Vol. 3, Fall 2022), *A Students' Encyclopedia of Great American Literature* (Volume 1), and *Identity Politics and the Captivity Narrative after 1848* (2008). She dedicates this article in memory of her beloved aunt, Jimmie Kanning.

C. Clark Triplett is Emeritus Dean of Graduate Studies and Professor of Psychology at Missouri Baptist University. He served as co-editor (with John

J. Han) of *The Final Crossing: Death and Dying in Literature* (2015) and as co-editor (with John J. Han and Ashley G. Anthony) of *Worlds Gone Awry: Essays on Dystopian Fiction* (2018). Triplett is the author of many articles and book reviews published in *Intégrité*, *Cantos*, and *Fireflies' Light*. A native of St. Louis, he earned a B.A. from Southwest Baptist University, an M.Div. from Covenant Theological Seminary, an M.S.Ed. from Southern Illinois University at Edwardsville, and a Ph.D. from Saint Louis University.

Annette Wren is Assistant Professor of English at McMurry University, Abilene, Texas. Her areas of focus include Victorian literature, adaptation studies, detective fiction, and queer theory. In addition to previous publications and presentations on Sherlock Holmes and adaptation, she is working on her first monograph, which explores post-2010 adaptations and appropriations of the Sherlock Holmes canon through the lenses of gender and sexuality. Wren earned a B.A. in history and a B.A. in English from the University of Texas at Austin, an M.A. in English literature from Auburn University, and a Ph.D. in English literature from Texas Christian University.

INDEX

Alienation 7, 121
Amateur sleuth 9, 99, 213, 217, 230, 253
Androcentric society 122
Anger 34, 39, 122, 123, 140, 141
Antihero 83, 87, 89
Aquinas, St. Thomas 253, 256–60, 262, 266
Aristotle 19, 256, 257, 258
Artistic unity 100, 102
Auden, W. H. 138
  "Spain" (poem) 240

Bakshi, Byomkesh 162
Bandyopadhyay, Saradindu 8, 161–64, 167, 169–73
  The Quills of the Porcupine (novel) 8, 161–62, 164, 166–73
Batacan, F. H. 7–8, 137, 139–45
  Smaller and Smaller Circle (novel) 8, 137, 139–45
Benedict, Saint 197
Bengal 8, 162–66, 168
Benison, Jim 196–97
Bhadraloks 164–66, 170–71
Bible, the 186, 205 (*see also* Scripture)
Blasphemy 234
Boardman, Gwenn R. 181
Bogus penicillin 180, 183
Bosnian War, the 187
Branagh, Kenneth 6, 29–32, 36–40
British Empire Medal, the 196
Brown, Father 9, 137, 198, 253–56, 259–67
Browning, Robert 239
  "Porphyria's Lover" (poem) 239

Cadfael, Brother 9, 137, 195–207
Cambodian genocide, the 187

Camus, Albert 18
Capitalism 265
Caste 8, 152, 161–62, 164–66, 168–73
Catholic Church, the 8, 140–41, 145, 181, 183–86, 202, 205, 242
Celtic Tiger 84–86
Chandler, Raymond 139, 183
  The Simple Act of Murder (essay) 139
Chesterton, G. K. 9, 47, 138, 181, 198, 211, 253–67
  The Blue Cross (short story) 260–62, 264–66, 267
  The Flying Stars (short story) 259, 264–66
  The Innocence of Father Brown (anthology) 253–54
  Orthodoxy (apologetics) 254–55, 266–67
  The Queer Feet (short story) 254, 262–67
  St. Thomas Aquinas (biography) 256–58, 262–63, 266
Christie, Agatha 6, 15–24, 29–40, 138, 198, 211, 218, 228, 230
  And Then There Were None (novel) 16
  The Clocks (novel) 22–3
  Curtain (novel) 16
  Endless Night (novel) 16
  Lord Edgware Dies (novel) 21
  The Murder of Roger Ackroyd (novel) 6, 15–24
  Murder on the Orient Express (novel) 6, 16, 17, 29–40
  The Mysterious Affair at Styles (novel) 17
  The Witness for the Prosecution (short story) 16

INDEX

Class 8, 71, 87–89, 101, 110, 123, 125, 127, 161–62, 164–66, 168–73, 228–31, 237, 239, 242, 243, 262–63
Cleft chin murder, the 235
Clinical depression 121, 126
Coming of age 6, 53, 56–7
Consumerism 84
Corruption 6, 7, 8, 84, 140, 148, 149, 154, 156, 181, 241
Courage, courageous 19, 48, 83, 100, 106, 112, 150, 154, 236
Crime Writers Association (CWA) 198
Cult of female virginity 69, 75, 78
Curtis, James 230
    The Gilt Kid (novel) 230
    They Drive by Night (novel) 230
Czechoslovakia 197

Damnation 186, 240, 243
De Quincey, Thomas 15, 235
    "On Murder Considered as One of the Fine Arts" (essay) 235
Deontology 2–3
Depravity 127, 180, 202
Desai, Kishwar 8, 147–57
    Simran Singh trilogy (novels) 147–57
Detective Narrative 32, 111
Devil 24, 70, 138, 184, 185, 186
Dickens, Charles 5, 20
    Great Expectations (novel) 5, 20
Disillusion, disillusionment 127, 233, 234, 236
Dismemberment 124, 129
Disorder (*see also* Order) 60, 183, 220, 228, 231, 262
Disparity society (in Japan) 121
Dostoyevsky, Fyodor 130, 181, 232
    Crime and Punishment (novel) 130, 181, 232

Eliot, T. S. 228
    "Sherlock Holmes and His Times" (essay) 228
Entertainment (Graham Greene's term) 179, 181, 182, 185, 187, 231, 241
Epistemology 254–59, 260–62, 267

Euthanasia 18
Evil 8, 9, 18, 33, 34, 40, 50, 56, 89, 92, 101, 108, 137, 138, 140, 142, 143, 147, 149, 156, 161, 181, 185, 187, 195, 227, 239, 243, 259

Family breakdown 121
Family systems theory 100, 102–13
Fascism, Fascist 228, 230, 239–40
Fate 23, 54, 55, 68, 71, 73, 76, 78, 88, 143, 172, 215, 255
Female crime 121–3
Female crime novel 121–31
Female detective 15, 101
Feminism, feminist 7, 48–50, 52, 107–13, 122–9, 148, 157
Femme fatale 48, 237
Femme fiable 48–50
Flambeau 253–54, 255, 256, 259–67
Ford, Ford Madox 16
French, Tana 7, 83–93
    The Wych Elm (novel) 7, 83–93

García Márquez, Gabriel 6–7, 67–69, 72–78
    Chronicle of a Death Foretold (novella) 6–7, 67–78
Gardner, John 187
Gender 7, 49, 50, 78, 83, 101, 112, 121, 126, 148, 166, 168, 171
Gender inequality 7, 121, 129, 130
Genre 1, 2, 4, 5, 6, 7, 8, 9, 10, 16, 31, 32, 40, 45–7, 50–5, 56, 57, 58, 59, 60, 67, 68, 84, 85, 86, 100, 101, 113, 137, 147, 161, 163, 182, 183, 198, 206, 228, 229, 231, 232, 234, 240, 241, 244
Genre hybridity 6, 45–60
Ghosts 47, 50–1, 55, 57, 103, 105, 236, 243, 255
Gide, André 16, 23
    Les Faux-monnayeurs (novel) 23
Golden Age of Detective Fiction, the 6, 183, 228–32, 235–36, 253
Graves, Robert 230, 233
    Good-Bye to All That (memoir) 230

Greene, Graham 8–9, 138, 179–88, 227–28, 231–32, 236, 238, 240–44
  Brighton Rock (novel) 9, 227, 232, 237, 240–44
  The Power and the Glory (novel) 187
  The Third Man (novel) 8–9, 179–88
  Ways of Escape (autobiography) 179, 236, 240
Greeneland 180, 181, 240
Grief 36, 39, 53, 180, 231
Grotesque 229

Haliburton, Rachel 3–4, 30–31, 36, 39, 40, 47–8, 137, 150
Hamilton, Patrick 9, 227–8, 231–40
  Hangover Square (novel) 9, 227, 232, 236–40, 241, 244
  Rope (play) 9, 227, 231, 233–6, 239
  The West Pier (novel) 240
Hammett, Dashiell 183, 235–6
Hard-boiled crime fiction 47, 183, 235–6
Hastings, Arthur 21–2, 29
haunting 47, 51, 57, 86, 186, 230
"Herd" morality 233
Historical mystery 181, 183, 206
Homosexuality 233, 243
Honor, honorable 15, 68, 69, 71, 74, 75, 76, 83, 104, 169, 196, 201, 206, 214, 215
Honor killing 7, 67, 68, 69, 71–7, 78
Horror 6, 38, 45, 46, 47, 50, 51, 55–60, 233, 234, 244

Iles, Francis 15
  Malice Aforethought (novel) 15
Illness in fiction 48, 151, 201, 204, 206, 220
India 8, 147–57, 161–73, 197
Interwar 9, 227–32, 234, 236, 240, 244
Intrigue 1, 99, 101, 163, 182
Irish crime fiction 84–85, 89
Isherwood, Christopher 236, 243

James, Henry 4
  The Golden Bowl (novel) 4
James, M.R. 57
  "Oh, Whistle, and I'll Come to You, My Lad" (short story) 57–8
James, P.D. 155, 183
Japan, Japanese 7, 121–31, 163
Justice 1–2, 6–10, 15, 17, 18, 29–40, 47–51, 60, 67–9, 74, 92, 93, 137–9, 141–5, 147–57, 179, 180, 187, 195–207, 213, 222, 234, 240, 242, 243, 253–67

King, Stephen 6, 45–60
  Big Driver (novella) 49
  Bill Hodges (trilogy) 45, 46
  The Colorado Kid (novel) 6, 45–7, 51–5, 58, 59–60
  The Dark Half (novel) 45, 46
  The Dark Tower (series) 54–5
  The Gingerbread Girl (novella) 49
  Hard Case Crime (series) 6, 45, 46–7, 59–60
  IT (novel) 57
  Joyland (novel) 6, 45, 46–51, 55, 56, 59–60
  Later (novel) 6, 45, 46–7, 55–60
  Salem's Lot (novel) 45, 46
  The Shining (novel) 57
  The Talisman (novel) 54
Kirino, Natsuo 7, 121–31
  Out: A Thriller (novel) 7, 121–31
Kitada, Sachie 122
Korean War, the 187
Kunkel, Francis L. 181

Lawrence, D. H. 237
  "England, My England" (short story) 237
Le Carré, John 138
Leopold and Loeb murder case 233
Loneliness 129, 184
Luck 7, 83–4, 85, 87, 88, 89, 93, 217
Lust murder 121, 125, 127–8
Luther, Martin 182

Mafia 241
Magical realism 69

Male hymen 78
Maritain, Jacques 253, 256, 258, 259, 260, 261
Melville, Herman 181
Metafiction 16, 18, 21–4
Middlebrow 228–9, 231
Monster 15, 46, 99, 100, 187
Moral absolutism 36–7, 40, 144, 153
Moral ambiguity 2, 3, 4, 6, 7–9, 59–60, 67, 85, 90, 92, 127–29, 137, 139, 147, 148, 154, 157, 162, 172, 211–12, 213, 214, 218, 219, 222, 223
Moral authority 6, 68, 70, 75, 138
Moral certainty 2, 3, 4, 6, 7–9, 36, 54, 59, 137, 211–23, 231
Moral confusion 9, 102, 127–31
Moral judgment 2, 3, 6, 16, 20, 30, 32, 36, 40, 127, 212, 232, 239, 244
Moral standard 29, 30, 31, 71, 77, 161, 162, 165
Morality 1, 2, 5–7, 8, 9, 17, 29, 30, 31–2, 39, 40, 48, 50, 52, 68–9, 71, 76, 78, 83, 84, 89, 93, 123, 148, 152, 156, 181, 182, 183–6, 187, 195, 212–3, 233, 236, 242, 262, 265
Morphogenesis 7, 100, 102, 107–12

Narrative construction 36, 47, 59
Natural law 212
Naturalistic fiction 122
Nietzsche, Friedrich 185, 233
Nihilism, nihilist 9, 179, 181, 182, 183–6, 187, 233, 234, 236
1980s, the 206
1940s, the 272
1970s, the 100
1960s, the 100
1930s, the 163, 183, 196, 227, 228, 229, 230, 231, 232, 236, 237, 240, 241, 243
1920s, the 23, 183, 228, 229, 230, 231, 232, 233, 236
Noir novel 9, 46, 48, 84, 179, 235

Ontology 257
Oppression 83, 123, 153, 198

Order (*see also* Disorder) 5, 6, 10, 17, 29, 32, 36, 39, 47, 51, 53, 54, 59, 60, 84, 86, 87, 89, 101, 106, 108, 122, 147, 148, 149, 155, 161, 183, 213, 219, 222, 223, 228, 231, 256, 258
Orwell, George 235, 236
    "Decline of the English Murder" (essay) 235

Panopticon 72
Pargeter, Edith 9, 195–207
    She Goes to War (novel) 196
    (As Carr, Jolyon)
    Murder in the Dispensary (novel) 196
    (As Peters, Ellis)
    The Leper of St. Giles (novel) 9, 195–6, 201–4, 206–7
    The Leper of St. Giles (movie) 204–6
Patriarchy 8, 67, 71, 123, 125, 129, 148, 149, 151, 162, 164, 166, 169, 170
Peters, Ellis: *See* Pargeter, Edith
Philippines, the 7–8, 139–45
Physician-assisted suicide: *See* Euthanasia
Pirandello, Luigi 16
Plato 257
Poe, Edgar Allan 17, 198
    "The Tell-Tale Heart" (short story) 17
Poirot, Hercule 6, 16, 17–18, 21–3, 29–40, 47, 161, 162, 218, 230
Poverty 8, 88, 89, 124, 126–7, 129, 130, 140, 141, 144, 151, 155, 165, 203, 204, 206, 221
Prejudice 37, 75, 83, 108, 173, 204
Private eye, private detective 15, 31, 32, 99, 122, 137–45, 179, 182, 184, 217, 218
Privilege 7, 30, 49, 77, 83–5, 87–9, 92, 93, 110, 124, 145, 162, 166, 256, 263
Procedural knowledge (*techné*) 19
Psychological thriller 122
Puzzle 48, 99, 101, 102–3, 112

Race 67, 75, 83, 173
Reade, Charles 19
Realistic fiction 139, 196, 198, 240–1
Reality 5, 17, 23, 54, 57, 59, 60, 70, 74, 83, 84, 87, 89, 92, 127, 155, 156, 183, 206, 212, 242, 253, 254–67
Repentance 9, 253, 254, 259, 260, 262, 264, 266–7
Resolution 4, 6, 8, 10, 17, 32, 34, 45, 51–5, 58, 59–60, 69, 85, 86, 92, 101, 106, 107, 139, 143, 155, 156, 162, 212, 220, 222, 231, 235, 240, 264, 266
Restorative Justice 9, 155, 253–67
Retribution 244, 253
Revenge 38, 106, 122, 123–4, 129, 152, 153
Right and wrong 3, 16, 37, 69, 84, 92, 139, 171, 173, 181, 231, 243
Rinehart, Mary Roberts 15
Locked Doors (novella) 15

Saxon, Catherine 196
Sayers, Dorothy L. 7, 99–113, 138, 211–23, 228, 230, 231
Gaudy Night (novel) 99–113, 221
Scripture 141–2 (*see also* the Bible)
Secrets 7, 93, 100, 101, 102, 106–7, 141, 183, 196, 213, 214, 215, 222, 239, 241
Sex 8, 49, 69, 75, 77, 88, 90, 91, 108, 121, 122, 123, 125, 126, 127, 128, 130, 148, 149, 151, 153, 154, 186, 197, 202, 206, 213, 233, 235, 236, 237, 239, 241, 242, 243
Sexual needs of women 125, 127–8
Sexual pleasure 121, 125, 127–8
Sexualization of schoolgirls in Japan 121
Shelley, Mary 19
Sheppard, James 6, 16–18, 20–4
Sherlock Holmes 21, 31–2, 46, 47, 163–4, 198, 218, 228, 253
Shrewsbury Abbey 197, 198, 200, 201, 205
Shropshire 196, 197

Sin, sinful, sinner 69, 101, 182, 186, 187, 195, 211–13, 234, 240, 260
Sisterhood power 124–5
Six hundred sixty-six (666) 243
Social alienation 7, 121
Social hierarchies, critique of social hierarchies 8, 104, 140–5, 164–73
Social justice 47, 68, 139, 144, 151, 195, 198, 201–7
Status quo 141, 162
Steinbeck, John 180
Of Mice and Men (novella) 180
Stevenson, Robert Louis 19
Supernatural, the 45–7, 50, 55–9
Surveillance 72
Suspense 90, 101, 103, 105, 106–7, 121, 130, 168, 179
Suzumura, Kazunari 129

Thrill 121, 124, 179, 214
Todd, Marilyn 15
"Beyond the Tree Line" (short story) 15–16
Transgenerational influences 7, 100, 102, 103–5
Triangulations 7, 100, 102, 105–7
Truth 9, 10, 18, 23, 31, 34, 39, 46, 47, 48, 52, 54, 59, 60, 87, 91, 100, 101, 102, 105, 106, 107, 109, 110, 112, 113, 149, 150, 153, 167, 180, 184, 185, 196, 199, 200, 205–6, 211–23, 254, 255, 261

Ultraviolence 8, 46, 144
Uncanny 45
Uncertainty 50, 59, 60, 85, 86, 148, 214
Underworld 127
Universal themes 100–1
Unreliable narrator 17, 21, 83, 85
Urban 87, 121–2, 128, 162, 168, 235

Vampire 45
Vice 40, 232, 261
Victimhood 91–2, 153

Victorian medical writing 19–20
Vienna, Austria 180, 183, 184
Vietnam War, the 187
Vigilantism, vigilante justice 30, 38, 40, 147–57
Vindication 84, 151
Violence, violent 8, 9, 34, 46, 49, 55, 58, 73, 74, 76, 83, 107, 125, 129–30, 140, 144, 148, 152, 155, 156, 182, 183, 199, 203, 220, 227–8, 229–31, 234, 235, 236–40, 243, 244
Violence, gender-based 122–7, 147, 156, 157, 168
Virtue, virtuous 2, 10, 15, 40, 48, 49, 100, 102, 104, 105, 109, 112, 127, 129, 149, 150, 213, 220, 223, 232, 261, 263
Virtue ethics 2
Vocation, vocational 18, 74, 200, 211–23

Wales 196, 197, 200
Wallace, Edgar 181
Walston, Catherine 182, 185–6
Wealth, wealthy 71, 83, 84, 86, 89, 152, 171, 201, 202, 203, 217, 218, 220, 242
Whodunit 85, 92, 183, 229
Wimsey, Peter 99, 214–23, 230–1
Winspear, Jacqueline 19–20
    Maisie Dobbs (novel) 19–20
Wolfe, Peter 182, 185, 186
Women's rights 122–7, 151, 169
Woolf, Virginia 17, 23, 228–29, 231
    Orlando: A Biography 23
World War I 187, 220, 223, 227, 228, 229, 230, 231, 234, 236, 237, 243
World War II 129, 183, 187, 196, 197, 223, 227, 235, 241, 242

Yakuza 129, 132